THE BEST TEST PREPARATION FOR THE
ADVANCED PLACEMENT EXAMINATIONS

For Both U.S. & Comparative
GOVERNMENT & POLITICS

Written by political science educators and experts...to prepare you to do your best.

 Research & Education Association

THE BEST TEST PREPARATION FOR THE

ADVANCED PLACEMENT EXAMINATIONS

For Both U.S. & Comparative

GOVERNMENT & POLITICS

Anita C. Danker, M.A., M.Ed.
Social Studies Instructor
Hopkinton Jr/Sr High School, Hopkinton, MA

Scott J. Hammond, Ph.D.
Assistant Professor of Political Science
James Madison University, Harrisonburg, VA

Robert F. Gorman, Ph.D.
Associate Professor of Political Science
Southwest Texas State University, San Marcos, TX

Elliot Kalner, M.A.
Social Studies Instructor
Greenwich High School, Greenwich, CT

Jack Hamilton, Ph.D.
Professor of Political Science
University of Montevallo, Montevallo, AL

Wesley G. Phelan, Ph.D.
Assistant Professor of Political Science
Eureka College, Eureka, IL

Gerald G. Watson, Ph.D., J.D.
former Associate Professor and Director,
Political Science and Legal Studies Program
University of Portland, Portland, OR

Research & Education Association
61 Ethel Road West • Piscataway, New Jersey 08854

The Best Test Preparation for the
ADVANCED PLACEMENT EXAMINATIONS
IN BOTH U.S. AND COMPARATIVE
GOVERNMENT & POLITICS

Printed in the United States of America

Library of Congress Catalog Card Number 97-68614

International Standard Book Number 0-87891-884-1

Research & Education Association
61 Ethel Road West
Piscataway, New Jersey 08854

REA supports the effort to conserve and
protect environmental resources by
printing on recycled papers.

CONTENTS

ABOUT RESEARCH & EDUCATION ASSOCIATION

Research and Education Association (REA) is an organization of educators, scientists, and engineers specializing in various academic fields. Founded in 1959 with the purpose of disseminating the most recently developed scientific information to groups in industry, government, and universities, REA has since become a successful and highly respected publisher of study aids, test preps, handbooks, and reference works.

REA's Test Preparation series includes study guides for all academic levels in almost all disciplines. Research and Education Association publishes test preps for students who have not yet completed high school, as well as high school students preparing to enter college. Students from countries around the world seeking to attend college in the United States will find the assistance they need in REA's publications. For college students seeking advanced degrees, REA publishes test preps for many major graduate school admission examinations in a wide variety of disciplines, including engineering, law, and medicine. Students at every level, in every field, with every ambition can find what they are looking for among REA's publications.

Unlike most Test Preparation books that present only a few practice tests which bear little resemblance to the actual exams, REA's series presents tests which accurately depict the official exams in both degree of difficulty and types of questions. REA's practice tests are always based upon the most recently administered exams, and include every type of question that can be expected on the actual exams.

REA's publications and educational materials are highly regarded and continually receive an unprecedented amount of praise from professionals, instructors, librarians, parents, and students. Our authors are as diverse as the subjects and fields represented in the books we publish. They are well-known in their respective fields and serve on the faculties of prestigious universities throughout the United States.

ACKNOWLEDGMENTS

In addition to our authors, we would like to thank Dr. Max Fogiel, President, for his overall guidance which has brought this publication to its completion; Stacey A. Sporer-Daly, Managing Editor, for directing the editorial staff throughout each phase of the project; and Larry B. Kling, Revisions Editor, and William P. Murray for their editorial contributions.

STUDY
SCHEDULES

STUDY SCHEDULE FOR THE AP EXAM IN U.S. GOVERNMENT AND POLITICS

The following study schedule will help you become thoroughly prepared for the U.S. Government and Politics exam. Although the schedule is designed as a six-week study program, it can be condensed into three weeks if less time is available by combining two weeks into one. Be sure to set aside enough time each day for studying purposes. If you choose the six-week program, you should plan to study for at least one hour per day. If you choose the three-week program, you should plan to study for at least two hours per day. Keep in mind that the more time you devote to studying for the U.S. Government and Politics exam, the more prepared and confident you will be on the day of the exam.

Week	Activity
1	Read and study the introduction on the following pages. Then, take and score the practice AP Examination in U.S. Government and Politics Test 1 to determine your strengths and weaknesses. You should have someone with knowledge of U.S. Government and Politics score your essay. When you grade your exam, you should determine what types of questions cause you the most difficulty, as this will help you determine what review areas to study most thoroughly. For example, if you answer incorrectly a number of questions dealing with the Constitution, you should carefully study the section on Constitutional Framework. Begin studying the U.S. Government and Politics Review starting with the first section on Constitutional Framework.
2	Continue studying the section on Constitutional Framework, and also study The Federal Government section of the review. Make sure to answer all of the drill questions.
3	Study the Political Institutions and Special Interests section of the review and answer the drill questions.
4	Study the Public Opinion and Voter Behavior section, and the Civil Rights and the Supreme Court section of the review and answer the drill questions.
5	Study the glossary of U.S. Government and Politics terms.
6	Take and score the practice AP Examination in U.S. Government and Politics Test 2. Make sure to review all of the detailed explanations of answers. Restudy the section(s) of the review for any area(s) in which you are still weak.

STUDY SCHEDULE FOR THE AP EXAM IN COMPARATIVE GOVERNMENT AND POLITICS

The following study schedule will help you become thoroughly prepared for the Comparative Government and Politics exam. Although the schedule is designed as a six-week study program, it can be condensed into three weeks if less time is available by combining two weeks into one. Be sure to set aside enough time each day for studying purposes. If you choose the six-week program, you should plan to study for at least one hour per day. If you choose the three-week program, you should plan to study for at least two hours per day. Keep in mind that the more time you devote to studying for the Comparative Government and Politics exam, the more prepared and confident you will be on the day of the exam.

Week	Activity
1	Read and study the introduction on the following pages. Then, take and score the practice AP Examination in Comparative Government and Politics Test 3 to determine your strengths and weaknesses. You should have someone with knowledge of Comparative Government and Politics score your essay. When you grade your exam, you should determine what types of questions cause you the most difficulty, as this will help you determine what review areas to study most thoroughly. For example, if you answer incorrectly a number of questions dealing with the government of China, you should carefully study the section on The People's Republic of China.
2	Begin studying the Comparative Government and Politics Review starting with the first section on Britain. Make sure to answer all of the drill questions.
3	Study the section of the review on France and answer the drill questions.
4	Study the section of the review on the former Soviet Union and answer the drill questions.
5	Study the section of the review on The People's Republic of China and answer the drill questions.
6	Study the glossary of Comparative Government and Politics terms. Then, retake and score the practice AP Examination in Comparative Government and Politics Test 3. Make sure to review all of the detailed explanations of answers. Restudy the section(s) of the review for any area(s) in which you are still weak.

CHAPTER 1
Succeeding in the AP Government & Politics Courses

Chapter 1

Succeeding in the AP Government & Politics Courses

The objective of this book is to prepare you for the Advanced Placement Examination in Government and Politics by providing you with an accurate and complete representation of the test. To help prepare you for this, we give you reviews, glossaries, and practice tests for both the United States and Comparative exams.

If you are taking the United States Government and Politics exam, you should study the first part of this book, which has been designed to thoroughly prepare you for this test. Presented is a complete review of United States Government and Politics, which is complemented by a glossary of terms to help you get the most out of your study time. Two full-length practice United States Government and Politics exams are provided.

The second part of the book is devoted to the Comparative Government and Politics exam. If you are taking the Comparative exam, our Comparative Government and Politics review and glossary will cover what you need to know to score well on the test. One full-length practice exam is also included.

Following each practice exam is an answer key and detailed explanations to every question. The explanations not only provide the correct response, but also explain why the remaining answers are not the best choice.

By studying the appropriate review section(s), taking the corresponding exam(s), and studying the answer explanations, you can discover your strengths and weaknesses, and prepare yourself to score well on the AP in Government and Politics exam(s).

About the Advanced Placement Program

The Advanced Placement program is designed to provide high school students with the opportunity to pursue college-level studies while still attending high school. The program consists of two components: an AP course and an AP exam. In addition, the AP in Government and Politics curriculum is divided into two courses: United States Government and Politics, and Comparative Government and Politics.

If you wish to pursue an Advanced Placement in Government and Politics course you may enroll in the United States course, the Comparative course, or both. You will be expected to leave the course(s) with college-level writing skills and knowledge of government and politics. Upon completion of the course(s), you may then take the corresponding AP exam(s). Test results are then used to grant course credit and/or determine placement level in the subject when you enter college.

AP exams are administered every May. The exam schedule has been designed to allow you the opportunity to take both exams, if you are enrolled in both courses. If the United States exam is given during the morning administration, the Comparative exam will be given during the afternoon administration.

The AP United States Government & Politics Exam

The United States exam is 145 minutes in length and is divided into two sections:

I. **Multiple-Choice (approx. 50% of your grade):** This 45-minute section is composed of 60 questions designed to measure your understanding of facts, concepts, and theories pertinent to United States government and politics. Your ability to analyze and understand data, and the patterns and consequences involved with political processes and behaviors will also be tested. In addition you must have knowledge of the various institutions, groups, beliefs, and ideas relevant to United States government and politics.

II. **Free-Response (approx. 50% of your grade):** This 100-minute section consists of four mandatory questions, each of which accounts for one-fourth of your total free-response score. You should allot roughly 25 minutes—or one-quarter of the total time in the free-response segment—for each essay. Each question normally asks you to interrelate ideas from different content areas from among the topics listed below. In addition, you may also be asked to evaluate and define fundamental concepts in the study of United States politics, and possibly to analyze case studies that bear on political relationships and events in the United States. You will be required to demonstrate mastery of political interpretation, and analytic and organizational skills through writing. In addition, you may be presented with graphs, charts and tables from whose data you would be asked to draw logical conclusions.

Topics tested in the United States exam are:

Topics	% of Exam
I. Constitutional Underpinnings of United States Government	5-15%
II. Political Beliefs and Behaviors	10-20%
III. Political Parties, Interest Groups, and Mass Media	10-20%
IV. Institutions of National Government: The Congress, the Presidency, the Bureaucracy, and the Federal Courts	35-45%
V. Public Policy	5-15%
VI. Civil Rights and Civil Liberties	5-15%

The AP Comparative Government & Politics Exam

The Comparative exam is 120 minutes in length and divided into two sections:

I. **Multiple-Choice (approximately 50% of your grade):** This 45-minute section is composed of 60 questions designed to measure your understanding of facts, concepts, and theories pertinent to Comparative government and politics. Your ability to analyze and understand data, and the patterns and consequences involved with political processes and behaviors will also be tested. The countries normally tested in the multiple-choice questions include Great Britain, France, the former Soviet Union (Commonwealth of Independent States), and China; these are referred to as the core countries tested on the exam. For certain questions, basic knowledge of the United States will be assumed.

II. **Free-Response (approximately a combined 50% of your grade):** This section is divided into two parts.

Part 1 (30% of your grade) is 45 minutes in length and is composed of two essay questions, from which you will choose one on which to write. Each question normally asks you to interrelate different content areas from the topics listed below.

Part 2 (20% of your grade) is composed of four possible essays; students are asked to choose and write on one topic. Thirty minutes will be allowed for this. Comparative Free-Response questions *may* require you to compare one or two of the core countries (Great Britain, France, China, and the former Soviet Union) with the developing nation of either India, Mexico, or Nigeria. To do this, you must be able to demonstrate knowledge of the politics of one of these developing nations. In your essay, you may be asked to analyze case studies, and to evaluate and define fundamental concepts regarding Comparative politics. You will be required to demonstrate mastery of political interpretation and analytic and organizational skills through writing.

Topics tested in the Comparative exam are:

Topics	% of Exam
I. The Sources of Public Authority and Political Power	5-15%
II. Society and Politics	5-15%
III. The Relationship Between Citizen and State	5-15%
IV. Political and Institutional Frameworks	35-45%
V. Political Change	15-25%
VI. The Comparative Method	5-10%

About the Review Sections

As mentioned earlier, this book includes two reviews: a United States Government and Politics review and a Comparative Government and Politics review.

The United States Government and Politics Review covers all of the key information needed to score well on the United States exam. These topics include:

- Constitutional Framework
- The Federal Government
- Political Institutions and Special Interests
- Public Opinion and Voter Behavior
- Civil Rights and the Supreme Court

In addition, the review is followed by a glossary of United States government and politics definitions. Included are key political terms, people, court cases, programs, laws, etc., that often appear on this AP exam.

The Comparative Review provides a thorough discussion of the material tested on the Comparative exam. Reviewed are the government and politics of:

- Britain
- France
- The former Soviet Union
- The People's Republic of China

A glossary of Comparative government and politics terms that are likely to be encountered on the exam is also included.

By studying the appropriate review and glossary, and by taking the practice test(s), you can best prepare yourself to score high on the AP Exam in Government and Politics.

Scoring the Exam

After the AP administrations, more than 1,700 college and secondary school teachers are brought together, in June, to grade the exams. These readers are chosen from around the country for their familiarity with the AP program.

The Multiple-Choice sections of the Comparative Government and Politics and U.S. Government and Politics exams are scored by granting one point for each correct answer and deducting one-fourth of a point for each incorrect answer. Unanswered questions receive neither credit nor deduction.

The Free-Response essays on both exams are graded by readers chosen from around the country for their familiarity with the AP program. Each essay booklet is read and scored, with the reader for the Comparative exam providing the score of between 0 and 9 (with 0 being the lowest and 9 the highest) on Part I, and a score of between 0 and 5 (with 0 being the lowest and 5 the highest) on Part II. All four Free-Response essays on the U.S. exam are all scored on the 0-to-9 scale. When the essays have been graded by all of the readers, the scores are then converted.

The AP Government and Politics exam is based on a 120-point scale. The breakdown of the percentages and points is as follows:

U.S. Exam

	# of Questions	% of Exam	Scoring Range	Total Points
Multiple-Choice:	60 multiple-choice	50% (approx.)	1 point each	60 pts
Free-Response:	Answer all 4	50% (approx.)	0-9 scale (ea.)	60 pts

Comparative

	# of Questions	% of Exam	Scoring Range	Total Points
Multiple-Choice:	60 multiple-choice	50%(approx.)	1 point each	60 pts
Free-Response:	Answer 1 of 2	30%(approx.)	0-9 scale (ea.)	36 pts
Free-Response:	Answer 1 of 4	20%(approx.)	0-5 scale (ea.)	24 pts

Once raw scores have been obtained for each section, they are weighted to produce a composite score. Then the composite scores for each section are added together to form a total composite score for the exam. The range for the composite score is from 0 to 120.

Finally, the composite score is translated into a range of from 1 to 5, with 1 being the lowest and 5 the highest.

Scoring the Multiple-Choice Section

Use this formula to calculate your raw score for the multiple-choice section:

$$\underline{\hspace{3cm}} - (\underline{\hspace{3cm}} \times {}^1\!/_4) = \underline{\hspace{3cm}}$$

| # right | # wrong | raw score (round off to nearest whole number; if the number is less than zero, enter zero) |

Scoring the Free-Response Section

The following scoring criteria will be used in grading each essay:

Score	Explanation of Score
8-9	The thesis is extremely well developed and is supported with concrete evidence; all aspects of the question have been addressed thoroughly; discussions presented are balanced
6-7	The thesis is defined and supported; the evidence provided is very organized; the essay may be slightly imbalanced with one strong argument and one weak argument and/or discuss one topic more thoroughly than the next; sporadic factual errors may appear
5	A basic argument or thesis is provided; evidence given supports the argument or thesis, but does not clearly connect with the argument or thesis; only the formal facets of the question are dealt with, and informal facets are not adequately covered; not all aspects of the question are discussed
4	The thesis is not organized and is not referred to in the essay; the essay is little more than a recounting of facts and events; the essay may be overloaded with data; only one facet of the questions may be discussed; numerous factual errors may appear
3	The thesis is weak; evidence provided in support does not apply to the thesis; factual errors are apparent
2	The thesis is very weak; little or no factual evidence is provided to support the thesis; irrelevant and inaccurate information appears
1	An attempt is made to answer the question, but the support given is insignificant and the coverage topics is incomplete
0	The question is not answered with any significance

Free-Response Part II (Comparative only)

Score	Explanation of Score
5	The thesis is extremely well developed and is supported with concrete evidence; all aspects of the question have been addressed thoroughly; discussions are presented in a balanced way
4	The thesis is defined and supported; the evidence provided is very organized; the essay may be slightly imbalanced, with one strong argument and one weak argument; likewise, one topic may be more thoroughly explored than another; may be marred by sporadic factual errors
3	A basic argument or thesis is presented; evidence given supports the argument or thesis, but does not clearly connect with the argument or thesis; only the formal facets of the question are dealt with, and informal facets are not adequately covered; not all aspects of the question are discussed
2	The thesis is weak; evidence provided in support does not apply to the thesis; factual errors are apparent
1	An attempt is made to answer the question, but the support given is insignificant and the coverage of topics is incomplete
0	The question is not answered with any significance

It would be extremely helpful to find someone who is willing to score your essay—your teachers or anyone who is familiar with the test material. If you do, ask the person to assign each of your U.S. and Comparative (Part I) essays a score of 0 to 9. For your Comparative (Part II) essays, use the 0-to-5 scale.

If you must grade your own essays, try to be objective! In addition, you may want to give your essays three different grades. For instance, if you feel you did well, try giving the essay a score of 5, 6, or 7 to represent the various scores you may receive. By underestimating what your score may be, you are more likely to receive a better score on the actual exam.

Use the following formulae to determine your raw score for the Free-Response section:

United States Exam (Free-Response)

$$\underline{\hspace{3cm}} \times 1.66 = \underline{\hspace{3cm}}$$
Essay (1) score $\qquad$ raw score

$$\underline{\hspace{3cm}} \times 1.66 = \underline{\hspace{3cm}}$$
Essay (2) score $\qquad$ raw score

$$\underline{\hspace{3cm}} \times 1.66 = \underline{\hspace{3cm}}$$
Essay (3) score $\qquad$ raw score

$$\underline{\hspace{3cm}} \times 1.66 = \underline{\hspace{3cm}}$$
Essay (4) score $\qquad$ raw score

Comparative Exam

Part 1

_____ × 4 = _____
essay score · · · · · · raw score

Part 2

_____ × 4.8 = _____
essay score · · · · · · raw score

The Composite Score

Once you have obtained your raw scores for both the Multiple-Choice and the Free-Response sections, add the scores together to get your composite score:

United States Exam

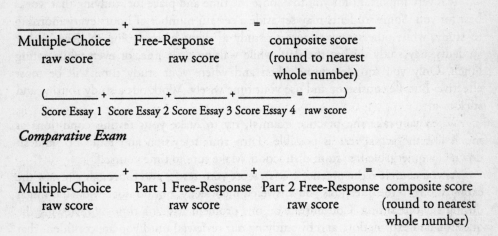

_____ + _____ = _____
Multiple-Choice · · Free-Response · · composite score
raw score · · · · · raw score · · · · (round to nearest
· whole number)

(_____ + _____ + _____ + _____ = _____)
Score Essay 1 · Score Essay 2 · Score Essay 3 · Score Essay 4 · raw score

Comparative Exam

_____ + _____ + _____ = _____
Multiple-Choice · · Part 1 Free-Response · · Part 2 Free-Response · · composite score
raw score · · · · · · raw score · · · · · · · · raw score · · · · · · · (round to nearest
· whole number)

Now compare your composite score with the scale below:

Composite Score	AP Grade
88 - 120	5
74 - 87	4
54 - 73	3
35 - 53	2
0 - 34	1

AP grades are interpreted as follows: 5-extremely well qualified, 4-well qualified, 3-qualified, 2-possibly qualified, and 1-no recommendation.

Scores that Receive College Credit and/or Advanced Placement

Most colleges grant students who earn a 3 or above college credit and/or advanced placement. You should check with your school guidance office about specific college requirements.

Studying for Your AP Examination

It is never too early to start studying. The earlier you begin, the more time you will have to sharpen your skills. Do not procrastinate! Last-minute studying and cramming is not an effective way to study, since it does *not* allow you the time needed to learn the test material.

It is very important for you to choose the time and place for studying that works best for you. Some students may set aside a certain number of hours every morning to study, while others may choose to study at night before going to sleep. Other students may study during the day, while waiting on a line, or even while eating lunch. Only you can determine when and where your study time will be most effective. But, be consistent and use your time wisely. Work out a study routine and stick to it!

When you take the practice exam(s), try to make your testing conditions as much like the actual test as possible. Turn your television and radio off, and sit down at a quiet table free from distraction. Make sure to time yourself.

As you complete the practice test(s), score your test(s) and thoroughly review the explanations to the questions you answered incorrectly, but do not review too much during any one sitting. Concentrate on one problem area at a time by reviewing the question and explanation, and by studying our review(s) until you are confident that you completely understand the material.

Since you will be allowed to write in your test booklet during the actual exam, you may want to write in the margins and spaces of this book when practicing. However, do not make miscellaneous notes on your answer sheet. Mark your answers clearly and make sure the answer you have chosen corresponds to the question you are answering.

Keep track of your scores! By doing so, you will be able to gauge your progress and discover general weaknesses in particular sections. You should carefully study the reviews that cover the topics causing you difficulty, as this will build your skills in those areas.

To get the most out of your studying time, we recommend that you follow the Study Schedule which corresponds to the exam you are taking. It details how you can best budget your time. If you are taking both exams, do not try to study for each at the same time. Try alternating days by studying for the United States exam one day and the Comparative exam the next.

Test-Taking Tips

Although you may be unfamiliar with tests such as the Advanced Placement exams, there are many ways to acquaint yourself with this type of examination and help alleviate your test-taking anxieties. Listed below are ways to help yourself become accustomed to the AP exam, some of which may also be applied to other standardized tests.

Become comfortable with the format of the AP Examination in Government and Politics that you are taking. When you are practicing to take the exam(s), simulate the conditions under which you will be taking the actual test(s). You should practice under the same time constraints as well. Stay calm and pace yourself. After simulating the test only a couple of times, you will boost your chances of doing well, and you will be able to sit down for the actual test much more confidently.

Know the directions and format for each section of the exam. Familiarizing yourself with the directions and format of the different test sections will not only save you time, but will also ensure that you are familiar enough with the AP exam to avoid nervousness (and the mistakes caused by being nervous).

Work on the easier questions first. If you find yourself working too long on one question, make a mark next to it in your test booklet and continue. After you have answered all of the questions that you can, go back to the ones you have skipped.

Use the process of elimination when you are unsure of an answer. If you can eliminate three of the answer choices, you have given yourself a fifty-fifty chance of getting the item correct since there will only be two choices left from which to make a guess. If you cannot eliminate at least three of the answer choices, you may choose not to guess, as you will be penalized one-quarter of a point for every incorrect answer. Questions not answered will not be counted.

Be sure that you are marking your answer in the circle that corresponds to the number of the question in the test booklet. Since the multiple-choice section is graded by machine, marking the wrong answer will throw off your score.

CHAPTER 2
United States Government & Politics Review

Chapter 2

Constitutional Framework

Historical Background

The United States Constitution was the result of a conscious effort on the part of several distinguished American political leaders to remedy the obvious defects of the Articles of Confederation. The Articles served as the national government from 1781 to 1787. Power was vested in a unicameral legislature which was clearly subordinate to the states. Representatives to the national Congress were appointed and paid by their state legislatures, and their mission was to protect the interests of their respective home states. Each state had one vote in the Congress, which could request but could not order states to provide financial and military support. Key weaknesses of the government included:

1) its inability to regulate interstate and foreign trade,

2) its lack of a chief executive and a national court system, and

3) its requirement that laws be passed by a majority of nine of the thirteen states and amendments be ratified by unanimous consent.

Sometimes referred to as the "critical period," the 1780s was a decade marked by internal conflict. With little power to impose control, the Congress presided over a deteriorating economic and political crisis which saw individual states print their own currency, tax the products of their neighbors, and ignore trade agreements with foreign nations. Inflation soared, many small farmers lost their property, and wealthy commercial interests were targeted as the villains. The most serious manifestation of the discontent of the agrarian population occurred in 1786 in rural western Massachusetts when Revolutionary War veteran Daniel Shays led a rebellion against foreclosures by seizing the courts and attacking the tax collectors. Shays' Rebellion symbolized the inability of the national government to promote order and to control unrest.

A series of meetings to consider reform of the Articles led to the calling of the Constitutional Convention in Philadelphia in 1787. Fifty-five delegates participated with every state represented except Rhode Island. Among the most prominent of the Founding Fathers were James Madison, who recorded the debate proceedings, George Washington, who was named president of the body, Gouverneur Morris, who wrote the final version of the Constitution, and elder statesman Benjamin Franklin.

Several issues divided the delegates including:

1) representation in the Congress,

2) regulation of interstate and foreign trade,

3) regulation of slavery, and

4) the method of choosing a chief executive.

Edmund Randolph offered the Virginia Plan which called for a strong national government with representation favoring the larger states. William Paterson of New Jersey countered with a plan that retained some of the state control of the national legislature featured in the Articles and that appealed to the smaller states because it called for equal representation in Congress. The dispute was resolved when the Connecticut delegation offered a compromise that included:

1) a bicameral legislature,

2) equal representation in the Senate, and

3) representation in the House of Representatives based on population. The Connecticut Compromise is sometimes called the "Great Compromise."

Other controversial questions were similarly resolved by compromises. The Commerce and Slave Trade Compromise gave Congress the power to regulate interstate and foreign trade but denied it the right to tax exports or to interfere with the slave trade for twenty years. The Three-Fifths Compromise allowed three out of every five slaves to be counted for the purpose of determining both representation and taxation. The Electoral College, which provides for an indirect method of choosing a president, was established to pacify those who desired an independent executive branch.

According to Article VII of the Constitution, nine of the thirteen states had to approve of the new government in order for it to become the law of the land. A battle ensued between those favoring the new plan, the Federalists, and those opposed to it, the Anti-Federalists. The disputed issues involved the increased power of the central government at the expense of the states and the lack of a bill of rights guaranteeing individual protections to the citizens. Pro-Constitution leaders James Madison, John Jay, and Alexander Hamilton published a series of articles known collectively as *The Federalist* to explain the Constitution and to persuade its opponents that their fears about a tyrannical central government were unfounded. One of the most quoted of the essays is James Madison's *Federalist 10* that expresses the

Founding Fathers' fear of factions and their belief that the Constitution would control the effects of such factions. The Constitution was ratified in 1788, and the new government convened in the spring of 1789.

☞ Drill: Historical Background

DIRECTIONS: Carefully read and answer each of the following questions which are based on the information which you have just read.

---

1. The national government under the Articles of Confederation

    (A)   consisted of three branches.

    (B)   promoted unity among the states.

    (C)   had a bicameral legislature.

    (D)   consisted of a unicameral legislature.

    (E)   required unanimous passage of all legislation.

2. Shays' Rebellion was significant because it

    (A)   allowed commercial interests to express their disenchantment with the status quo.

    (B)   symbolized the weakness of the central government under the Articles.

    (C)   was the first organized protest against the system of slavery in the South.

    (D)   expressed the discontent of the upper class.

    (E)   was a great victory for the agrarian interests.

3. The following leaders were all prominent among the leaders at the Constitutional Convention of 1787 EXCEPT

    (A)   Thomas Jefferson.   (D)   Gouverneur Morris.

    (B)   Benjamin Franklin.   (E)   George Washington.

    (C)   James Madison.

4. The Connecticut Compromise resolved the controversy at the Constitutional Convention involving

    (A) the method of choosing a president.

    (B) the regulation of interstate and foreign trade.

    (C) representation in Congress.

    (D) the protection of the institution of slavery.

    (E) ratification of the Constitution.

5. One purpose of the Electoral College was to

    (A) ensure that only qualified candidates would run for the presidency.

    (B) ensure an independent executive branch.

    (C) promote democracy.

    (D) provide for a direct method of choosing the chief executive.

    (E) give the small states an equal voice in choosing the president.

6. The stated purpose of the delegates to the Constitutional Convention of 1787 was to

    (A) write a new plan of government.

    (B) eliminate the growth of the institution of slavery.

    (C) raise more money by taxing exports.

    (D) construct a more democratic form of government.

    (E) reform the Articles of Confederation.

7. Congress under the Articles of Confederation

    (A) could require the states to provide financial support.

    (B) represented the interests of the individual states.

    (C) could conscript individuals for military service.

    (D) was dominated by a strong chief executive.

    (E) forcefully dealt with Shays' Rebellion.

8. James Madison's *Federalist 10* articulated the belief of the Founding Fathers that the Constitution would

    (A) lead to a tyranny of the majority.

    (B) promote the growth of political parties.

(C)   control the effects of factions.

(D)   allow the states to maintain their preeminence.

(E)   lead to a tyranny of the minority.

9.   A major concern of the Anti-Federalists involved

(A)   their desire to strengthen the central government.

(B)   their fear that the states would maintain their dominance under the new government.

(C)   their fear that foreign governments would try to overpower the new nation.

(D)   their belief that a strong chief executive was necessary.

(E)   their desire to see a bill of rights guaranteeing individual protections added to the Constitution.

Fundamental Principles Embodied in the Constitution

The Founding Fathers drew upon a variety of sources to shape the government that was outlined in the Constitution. British documents such as the Magna Carta (1215), the Petition of Right (1628), and the Bill of Rights (1689), all of which promoted the concept of limited government, were influential in shaping the fundamental principles embodied in the Constitution. British philosopher John Locke, who wrote about the social contract concept of government and the right of people to alter or abolish a government that did not protect their interests, was a guiding force.

One of the most significant of the basic principles embodied in the Constitution is the concept of a federal system which divides the powers of government between the states and the national government. Local matters are handled on a local level, and those issues that affect all citizens are the responsibility of the federal government. Such a system was a natural outgrowth of the colonial relationship between the Americans and the mother country of England. It is clearly stated in the Tenth Amendment which declares: "Those powers not delegated to the United States by the Constitution, nor prohibited by it to the States, are reserved to the States respectively, or to the people." The federal government and those of the separate states have powers that may in practice overlap, but in cases where they conflict, the federal government is supreme.

Another key principle is separation of powers. The national government is divided into three branches which have separate functions (legislative, executive, and judicial), but they are not entirely independent. These functions are outlined in Articles I, II, and III of the main body of the Constitution. Closely related to the concept of separation of powers is the system of checks and balances in which each of the branches has the ability to limit the actions of the other branches. The legislative branch can check the executive by refusing to confirm his appointments or by passing laws over his veto (by a two-thirds majority in both houses). The executive can check the legislative by use of the veto and on the judicial by appointing his choices to the federal bench. The judicial can check the other two branches by declaring laws to be unconstitutional.

Additional fundamental principles include:

1) the establishment of a representative government (a republic),

2) the belief in popular sovereignty or a government that derives its power from the people (the Preamble opens with the words, "We the People"), and

3) the enforcement of a government with limits, sometimes referred to as the "rule of law."

☞ Drill: Fundamental Principles Embodied in the Constitution

> **DIRECTIONS:** Carefully read and answer each of the following questions which are based on the information which you have just read.

10. British documents such as the Magna Carta, the Petition of Right, and the Bill of Rights

   (A) stressed the supremacy of the monarch.

   (B) advanced the concept of limited government.

   (C) were written by John Locke.

   (D) were rejected by the Founding Fathers.

   (E) were rejected by the British Parliament.

11. Under a federal system of government, all of the following are true EXCEPT

   (A) local matters are largely handled on a local level.

   (B) national matters are the responsibility of the federal government.

   (C) federal and state governments have powers that sometimes overlap.

   (D) in cases where powers are in conflict, the state government is supreme.

   (E) in cases where powers are in conflict, the national government is supreme.

12. The system under which each branch can limit the actions of the other branches is called

    (A) separation of powers.   (D) limited government.

    (B) checks and balances.   (E) representative government.

    (C) federalism.

13. The opening words of the Constitution, "We the People," express the fundamental principle of

    (A) popular sovereignty.   (D) federalism.

    (B) rule of law.   (E) republicanism.

    (C) constitutionalism.

14. The section of the Constitution that clearly states the concept of federalism is

    (A) Article I.   (D) the Tenth Amendment.

    (B) Article II.   (E) the Preamble.

    (C) Article III.

15. Under the system of checks and balances all of the following are allowed EXCEPT

    (A) the Senate's refusal to approve the president's appointment of a justice to the Supreme Court.

    (B) the Senate's refusal to ratify a treaty negotiated by the president and his foreign policy advisors.

    (C) the Senate's dismissal of a Cabinet member accused of accepting bribes.

    (D) the president's lobbying for a new crime bill to be passed in Congress.

    (E) the Supreme Court's ruling that an executive order is unconstitutional.

The Federal Government

The Legislative Branch

Legislative power is vested in a bicameral Congress which is the subject of Article I of the Constitution. The expressed or delegated powers are set forth in Section 8 and can be divided into several broad categories. Economic powers include:

1) to lay and collect taxes,

2) to borrow money,

3) to regulate foreign and interstate commerce,

4) to coin money and regulate its value, and

5) to establish rules concerning bankruptcy.

Judicial powers are comprised of the following:

1) to establish courts inferior to the Supreme Court,

2) to provide punishment for counterfeiting, and

3) to define and punish piracies and felonies committed on the high seas.

War powers of Congress are enumerated as follows:

1) to declare war,

2) to raise and support armies,

3) to provide and maintain a navy, and

4) to provide for organizing, arming, and calling forth the militia.

Other general peace powers include:

1) to establish uniform rules on naturalization,

2) to establish post offices and post roads,

3) to promote science and the arts by issuing patents and copyrights, and

4) to exercise jurisdiction over the seat of the federal government (District of Columbia).

In addition, the Constitution includes the so-called "elastic clause," which grants Congress implied powers to implement the delegated powers.

The Constitution also grants Congress the power to discipline federal officials through impeachment and removal from office. The House of Representatives has the power to charge officials (impeach), and the Senate is empowered to conduct the trials. These powers have been invoked infrequently. More significant is the Senate's power to confirm presidential appointments (to the Cabinet, federal judiciary, and major bureaucracies) and to ratify treaties. Both houses are involved in choosing a president and vice-president if no majority is achieved in the Electoral College. The House of Representatives votes for the president from among the top three electoral candidates with each state delegation casting one vote. The Senate votes for vice-president. This power has been exercised only twice, in the disputed elections of 1800 and 1824.

In Article V, the Constitution empowers Congress to propose amendments. A two-thirds majority in both houses is necessary for passage. In addition, amendments may be proposed by the legislatures of two-thirds of the states. In order to be ratified, three-fourths of the states must approve (through their legislatures or by way of special conventions, as in the case of the repeal of Prohibition).

Article I, Section 9, specifically denies certain powers to the national legislature. Congress is prohibited from suspending the privilege of habeas corpus unless the nation is in a state of rebellion or has been invaded. Other prohibitions include: 1) the passage of export taxes, 2) the passage of ex post facto laws, 3) the withdrawal of money from the national treasury without an appropriations law, and 4) the favored treatment of one port or state over another with respect to commerce.

The work of Congress is organized around a committee system. The standing committees are permanent and deal with such matters as agriculture, the armed services, the budget, energy, finance, and foreign policy. Special or select committees are established to deal with specific issues and usually have a limited duration. An example from recent history of a powerful select committee was the Senate Select Committee on Presidential Campaign Activities which investigated the Watergate scandal. Joint committees are comprised of members from both the House and the Senate, and they often deal with routine matters. The most short-lived yet often the most significant committees are the conference committees which must iron out differences between House and Senate versions of a bill.

One committee unique to the House of Representatives is the powerful Rules Committee. Thousands of bills are introduced on the floor of the House each term, and the Rules Committee acts as a clearinghouse to weed out those which are deemed unworthy of consideration before the full House. Constitutionally, all revenue-raising bills must originate in the House of Representatives. Consequently, all tax measures are sent to the powerful House Ways and Means Committee.

Committee membership is organized on party lines with seniority being a key factor, although in recent years length of service in the Congress has diminished in importance in the determination of chairmanships. The Democrats and the Republicans have special committees (e.g., the Senate Democratic Steering Committee) to consider assignments. The composition of each committee is largely based on the ratio of each party in the Congress as a whole. The party with the majority has a larger number of members on each committee. The chairmen of the standing committees are selected by the leaders of the majority party. Since the 1970s, committees have been required by law to adhere to written rules of procedure. This reform has diminished somewhat the power of committee chairmen, some of whom had previously behaved like virtual dictators in the control they exercised over their members.

The legislative process is at once cumbersome and time-consuming. A bill can be introduced in either house (with the exception of revenue bills, which must originate in the House), where it is referred to the appropriate committee. Next, the bill travels to a subcommittee which will schedule a hearing if the members deem that it has merit. The bill is reported back to the full committee, which must then decide whether or not to send it to the full chamber to be debated. A bill originating in the House must pass through the Rules Committee before going on to the full House. If the bill passes in the full chamber, it is then sent on to the other chamber to begin the process all over again. Any differences in the House and Senate versions of a bill must be resolved in a conference committee before being passed along to the president for consideration. Most of the thousands of bills introduced in Congress die in committee, with less than five percent becoming law.

Debate on major bills is a key step in the legislative process because of the tradition of attaching amendments at this stage. In the House, the rules of debate are designed to enforce limits necessitated by the size of the body (435 members). On the other hand, in the substantially smaller Senate (100 members), unlimited debate is allowed. Here, the filibuster, a tactic to block legislation, can delay action indefinitely. It was used on several occasions in the 1950s and 1960s by southern Senators seeking to kill civil rights legislation. Cloture is a parliamentary procedure that can be invoked by three-fifths of the membership to limit debate and bring a filibuster to conclusion.

Constitutional qualifications for the House of Representatives state that members must be at least twenty-five years of age, must have been U.S. citizens for at least seven years, and must be residents of the state that sends them to Congress. Tradition but not law dictates that members of the House live in the districts they represent. According to the Reapportionment Act of 1929, the size of the House is fixed at 435 members who serve terms of two years in length. The presiding officer in the House and generally the most powerful member is the Speaker, who is the leader of the political party of the majority. In recent history, the post has been dominated by Democrats. Sam Rayburn of Texas dominated the position throughout most of the 1940s and 1950s. Congressman Thomas "Tip" O'Neill, a colorful Democrat from Massachusetts, presided over the House during the Carter and Reagan administrations. Another Democrat, Texas's Jim Wright succeeded O'Neill, serving from 1987 to 1989, when he was forced into retirement by charges that stemmed from an ethics complaint that had been lodged against him by Minority Whip Newt Gingrich. The Democratic majority then voted in Thomas S. Foley of Washington, who held the Speakership through 1995. The mid-term election in 1994 saw the House shift to a Republican majority for the first time since the Eisenhower administration in 1954—a feat credited largely to a campaign strategy (known as the Contract With America) devised by Gingrich—and, as a result, his colleagues elected him Speaker. Like Wright, Gingrich too would be charged, in 1996, with House ethics violations. He was reprimanded and fined. Though he continued to serve as Speaker in 1997, the Georgian was weakened politically.

Members of the Senate are elected to terms of six years in length on a staggered basis so that one-third of the body is up for re-election in each national election year. The president of the Senate is the vice-president of the U.S., and as such he has a largely symbolic role, voting only in case of a tie. The presiding officer is the president *pro tempore*, an honor customarily conferred on the senior member of the party of the majority. More visible and generally recognized as the leaders of the Senate are the majority and minority leaders.

☞ Drill: The Legislative Branch

> **DIRECTIONS:** Carefully read and answer each of the following questions which are based on the information which you have just read.

16.   The chairmen of the standing committees of Congress are chosen

    (A)   by the voters.

    (B)   according to a strict seniority system.

    (C)   by the president.

    (D)   by the leaders of both political parties.

    (E)   by the leaders of the majority party.

17.   Bills may be introduced in either house of Congress with the exception of _____ bills, which must originate in the House of Representatives.

    (A)   agricultural   (D)   military

    (B)   revenue   (E)   education

    (C)   foreign aid

18.   Article I grants Congress the power to do all of the following EXCEPT

    (A)   declare war.   (D)   regulate interstate trade.

    (B)   collect taxes.   (E)   establish federal courts.

    (C)   appoint federal judges.

19. The "elastic clause" grants Congress

    (A) delegated powers.   (D) expressed powers.

    (B) inherent powers.   (E) war powers.

    (C) implied powers.

20. Permanent committees dealing with such matters as agriculture, finance, and foreign policy are known as

    (A) select committees.   (D) standing committees.

    (B) conference committees.   (E) ad hoc committees.

    (C) joint committees.

21. The House Committee that acts as a "clearing house" for the thousands of bills introduced each term is called the

    (A) Rules Committee.   (D) Legislative Committee.

    (B) Ways and Means Committee. (E) Clearing Committee.

    (C) Steering Committee.

22. Constitutional Amendments must pass in both houses of Congress by

    (A) a simple majority.   (D) a three-fourths majority.

    (B) a three-fifths majority.   (E) unanimous consent.

    (C) a two-thirds majority.

23. Article I, Section 9 prohibits Congress from exercising all of the following powers EXCEPT

    (A) the passage of import taxes.

    (B) the passage of export taxes.

    (C) the passage of ex post facto laws.

    (D) the withdrawal of money from the Treasury without an appropriations law.

    (E) the favored treatment of one port or state over another in matters of commerce.

24. The use of the filibuster, a tactic to block the passage of legislation,

    (A) has been declared unconstitutional by the Supreme Court.

    (B) is allowed in the both the House and the Senate.

    (C)   can be ended by a majority vote.

    (D)   was used in the 1950s and 1960s to stall civil rights legislation.

    (E)   can be ended by executive order.

25.   The number of members in the House of Representatives

    (A)   changes after each national census.

    (B)   was fixed at 435 by the Constitution.

    (C)   is based on an equal number from each house.

    (D)   was fixed at 435 by the Reapportionment Act of 1929.

    (E)   was fixed at 435 by a constitutional amendment.

The Executive Branch

Article II of the Constitution deals with the powers and duties of the president. The chief executive's constitutional responsibilities include the following:

1)   to serve as Commander-in-Chief,

2)   to negotiate treaties (with the approval of two-thirds of the Senate),

3)   to appoint ambassadors, judges, and other high officials (with the consent of the Senate),

4)   to grant pardons and reprieves for those convicted of federal crimes (except in impeachment cases),

5)   to seek counsel of department heads (Cabinet secretaries),

6)   to recommend legislation,

7)   to meet with representatives of foreign states, and

8)   to see that federal laws are "faithfully executed."

The president's powers with respect to foreign policy are paramount. Civilian control of the military is a fundamental concept embodied in the naming of the president as Commander-in-Chief: in essence, the nation's leading general. As such he can make battlefield decisions as well as shape military policy. This role has expanded in the twentieth century particularly with respect to such recent conflicts as Korea and Vietnam, where Presidents Truman, Eisenhower, Kennedy, Johnson, and Nixon, respectively, made war without formal declarations from Congress. Although the War Powers Act of 1973 was designed to limit the president's ability to commit American troops to foreign soil without informing Congress within forty-eight hours and prohibits him from leaving them engaged in conflict for more than sixty days without authorization from Congress, contemporary Presidents Reagan and Bush have still exercised broad military powers as in Grenada and Panama.

The president, in essence, shapes American foreign policy with his treaty-making and diplomatic powers. Treaties are usually negotiated with representatives of foreign states through the efforts of the Secretary of State, and they must be ratified by a majority of two-thirds in the Senate. An example of a controversial treaty which was rejected by the Senate despite the president's extraordinary efforts to garner support was that ending World War I. Despite Wilson's unprecedented involvement in the negotiations that produced the Versailles Treaty, an isolationist circle within the Senate refused to pass it due to the inclusion of a clause calling for American membership in the League of Nations. Presidents can circumvent the Senate by executive agreements with other nations. These must relate to treaties which have been previously negotiated. President Johnson used this power extensively to conduct the Vietnam War with minimum congressional involvement.

As a world diplomat, the president of the United States receives foreign heads of state and their representatives and formally acknowledges the existence of a government through the power of recognition. In recent years, U.S. presidents have attended a series of highly publicized summit conferences with foreign heads of state, particularly those of the former Soviet Union. These meetings have produced mixed results, although some, as in the case of the Nixon and Brezhnev summit in 1972 which led to SALT I, have been historically significant.

Attaining the presidency has evolved into an arduous, costly, and at times painful process despite the relatively simple constitutional requirements for qualifying for the office. Candidates must be at least thirty-five years of age, must be natural-born citizens, and must have resided in the United States for a minimum of fourteen years. Article II provides for an Electoral College in which each state has as many votes as it has members of Congress to formally select the president. Over time the Electoral College has become a ceremonial body due to the control the major political parties have over the election process. After the political parties have selected their nominees via caucuses, primaries, and conventions, the general election is held in November every four years. The electors are chosen by popular vote on a winner-take-all basis (with the exception of Maine which has a district plan), so that the candidate who receives a majority of the popular votes in each state receives all of the state's electoral votes. Electors meet in their respective state capitals in December and cast their ballots for president and vice-president. A majority of 270 electoral votes is needed to be elected. If no majority is achieved, the House of Representatives is empowered to choose a president from among the top three candidates. In this case, each state casts one ballot with a majority of 26 needed to win.

Presidential succession has become a key issue in recent years. The Constitution states that if the president dies or cannot perform his duties, the "powers and duties" of the office shall "devolve" on the vice-president. Until recently, when the vice-president assumed the office of president, his former position was left vacant. Since the passage of the Twenty-Fifth Amendment in 1967, the president has the power to appoint a new vice-president (with the approval of a majority of both houses of

Congress). In 1973, President Nixon invoked this power when Vice-President Spiro Agnew resigned due to criminal allegations and appointed Congressman Gerald Ford as his replacement. Ford in turn assumed the office of president when Nixon resigned under threat of impeachment. Ford then appointed Governor Nelson Rockefeller of New York as his own replacement. The Twenty-Fifth Amendment also provides for the vice-president to serve as acting president if the president is disabled or otherwise unable to carry out the duties of his office.

Although the Constitution makes no mention of a formal Cabinet as such, since the days of George Washington, chief executives have relied on department heads to aid in the decision-making process. Washington's Cabinet was comprised of a Secretary of State, a Secretary of the Treasury, a Secretary of War, and an Attorney-General. Today there are fourteen Cabinet departments, with Veterans Affairs being the most recently created post. Traditionally, the heads of the State and Defense Departments are highly visible and indispensable in helping the president to formulate foreign policy.

☞ Drill: The Executive Branch

> **DIRECTIONS:** Carefully read and answer each of the following questions which are based on the information which you have just read.

26. Characteristics of executive agreements include all of the following EXCEPT that

   (A) they are similar to treaties.

   (B) they must be ratified by the Senate.

   (C) they must be related to treaties previously negotiated.

   (D) presidents use them to circumvent the Senate.

   (E) they were used extensively to conduct the war in Vietnam.

27. The War Powers Act of 1973

   (A) enlarges the president's power to commit troops to foreign soil.

   (B) calls for the president to notify Congress within twenty-four hours of ordering military forces into operation.

   (C) prohibits the president from leaving troops engaged in combat for more than thirty days without authorization from Congress.

(D)   has crippled the president's power to exercise his constitutional military powers.

(E)   prohibits the president from leaving troops engaged in conflict for more than sixty days without authorization from Congress.

28.   All of the following are true of the Twenty-Fifth Amendment EXCEPT that

(A)   it allows the president to appoint a vice-president if a vacancy occurs.

(B)   it allows the president to name a successor of his own choice if he leaves office prematurely.

(C)   it provides for the vice-president to serve as acting president if the president is temporarily unable to perform his duties.

(D)   it was invoked by President Nixon when Vice-President Agnew resigned from office.

(E)   under its terms Gerald Ford became the first appointed president.

29.   The president's constitutional duties include all of the following EXCEPT

(A)   negotiating treaties.

(B)   granting pardons and reprieves in federal cases.

(C)   passing legislation.

(D)   appointing high-ranking federal officials.

(E)   executing the laws.

30.   Candidates for the offices of president and vice-president

(A)   must be at least 30 years of age.

(B)   must run in all of the presidential primaries.

(C)   must be lifelong residents of the United States.

(D)   must be native-born citizens.

(E)   must be members of an established political party.

31.   The Electoral College

(A)   functions largely independently of the major political parties.

(B)   provides for a winner-take-all system of election in all fifty states.

(C)   requires that the candidate who receives a plurality of the votes will be elected to the office of president.

(D)   meets continuously until a president is chosen.

(E)   requires that a candidate receive a majority of 270 electoral votes in order to be elected.

The Judicial Branch

Article III of the Constitution states that "the judicial power of the United States shall be vested in one Supreme Court, and in such inferior courts as the Congress may from time to time ordain and establish." Hence the Supreme Court is the only court mentioned specifically in document. Yet our contemporary judicial branch consists of thousands of courts and is in essence a dual system with each state having its own judicial structure functioning simultaneously with a complete set of federal courts. The most significant piece of legislation with reference to establishing a federal court network was the Judiciary Act of 1789. This law organized the Supreme Court and set up the federal district courts (13) and the circuit (appeal) courts (3). In 1891, the U.S. Court of Appeals was created to relieve the Supreme Court of some of its heavy case load. The district courts have original jurisdiction to hear federal cases involving both civil and criminal law. Each state has at least one federal district court while the larger states are divided into two or more jurisdictions. These courts handle thousands of cases annually and are plagued by long delays. Federal cases on appeal are heard in one of the Courts of Appeals. The decisions of these courts are final, except for those cases that are accepted for review by the Supreme Court.

The Supreme Court today is made up of a Chief Justice and eight Associate Justices. They are appointed for life by the president with the approval of the Senate, and they are routinely, but not exclusively, drawn from the ranks of the federal judiciary. In recent years, the appointment of Supreme Court Justices has been the focus of intense scrutiny and in the cases of Robert Bork and Clarence Thomas, the center of heated political controversy.

Each year, thousands of cases are appealed to the Supreme Court, but relatively few are accepted for consideration. The Court chooses its cases based on whether or not they address substantial federal issues. If four of the nine justices vote to consider a case, then it will be added to the agenda. In such cases, writs of certiorari are issued calling up the records from a lower court. The justices are given detailed briefs and hear oral arguments. Reaching a decision is a complicated process. The justices may scrutinize the details of the case with reference to the provisions of the Constitution. Precedence (stare decisis) is a key concept borrowed from the British legal tradition. If two cases are generally similar, then the decision in the earlier controversy usually stands. Breaks with the concept of precedence have sometimes had historic ramifications as when the 1954 Warren Court reversed *Plessy vs. Ferguson* (1896) and declared "separate but equal" accommodations to be unconstitutional. This decision (*Brown vs. Board of Education*) led to the school desegregation crises of the civil rights era.

The authority of courts to declare laws and executive actions to be unconstitutional is known as judicial review. This procedure was established in 1803 with the case of *Marbury vs. Madison*. In the last days of his term, Federalist President John Adams hastily appointed several justices of the peace for Washington D.C., the so-called "midnight judges." The incoming Democratic-Republican President Thomas Jefferson instructed his Secretary of State James Madison not to deliver the appointments. One of the disappointed justices, William Marbury, petitioned the Supreme Court to issue a writ of mandamus (a court order instructing a public official to perform his duties) to compel Jefferson to deliver the commissions. Chief Justice John Marshall, himself a Federalist, wrote the unanimous opinion refusing Marbury's request on the grounds that the section of the Judiciary Act of 1789 empowering the Supreme Court to issue writs of mandamus was unconstitutional. Hence, the power of judicial review was established. The Supreme Court is not alone in this power, as most state and federal courts may also exercise judicial review.

When all of the justices on the Supreme Court agree, the opinion issued is unanimous. In the case of split decisions, a majority opinion is written by one of the justices in agreement. Sometimes a justice will agree with the majority but for a different principle, in which case he/she can write a concurring opinion explaining the different point of view. Justices who do not vote with the majority may choose to write dissenting opinions to air their conflicting arguments.

According to Article III of the Constitution, the Supreme Court may exercise both original and appellate jurisdiction. Original jurisdiction relates to cases in which a state is a party to cases involving consuls, ambassadors, and other public ministers. By and large, the vast majority of cases that reach the Supreme Court do so on appeal from both lower federal courts and state supreme courts. It is the "court of last resort" in the appeals process, and its decisions stand.

Article III also outlines those conditions under which federal (as opposed to state) courts have original jurisdiction. These include:

1) cases in which the Constitution is involved,

2) cases involving federal laws,

3) cases dealing with treaties with foreign states and with Native American tribes,

4) cases arising out of crimes committed on the high seas or disputes over maritime transactions,

5) cases in which the U.S. government is a party,

6) cases stemming from disputes between two or more states,

7) controversies between citizens of different states,

8) conflicts between a state and citizens of another state,

9) disputes involving U.S. citizens and foreign nations, and

10) cases affecting public ministers and consuls.

In addition to the Supreme Court, the federal district courts, and the courts of appeals, several special courts at the federal level have been created by Congress. These courts are not addressed in Article III, for they deal with matters within the realm of congressional responsibility. The U.S. Tax Court handles conflicts between citizens and the Internal Revenue Service. The Court of Claims was designed to hear cases in which citizens bring suit against the U.S. government. Other special courts include the Court of International Trade, the Court of Customs and Patent Appeals, and the Court of Military Appeals.

☞ Drill: The Judicial Branch

DIRECTIONS: Carefully read and answer each of the following questions which are based on the information which you have just read.

32. Article III of the Constitution

    (A) set up the federal district court system.

    (B) organized the U.S. Supreme Court.

    (C) established the legislative courts.

    (D) set forth the instances in which federal courts have jurisdiction.

    (E) organized the courts of appeal.

33. The dual court system refers to

    (A) the district courts and the federal appeals courts.

    (B) the constitutional and the legislative courts.

    (C) civil and criminal courts.

    (D) the Supreme Court and the U.S. Courts of Appeals.

    (E) separate federal and state court systems.

34. The term *stare decisis* means

    (A) "separate but equal."   (D) "a concurring opinion."

    (B) "let the decision stand."   (E) "original jurisdiction."

    (C) "judicial review."

35. The Supreme Court decides to hear cases on appeal

    (A) whenever a state supreme court requests an opinion.

    (B) in all capital cases.

    (C) if they address substantial federal issues.

    (D) if a writ of mandamus is issued.

    (E) if a writ of certiorari is submitted for consideration.

36. The Supreme Court's jurisdiction encompasses all of the following situations EXCEPT

    (A) a case involving an ambassador.

    (B) review of a federal executive order.

    (C) review of a piece of federal legislation.

    (D) a Secret Service agent suspected of internal espionage.

    (E) a case in which a state is a party.

37. The procedure of judicial review was clearly established in

    (A) Article III of the Constitution.

    (B) *Plessy vs. Ferguson.*

    (C) *Marbury vs. Madison.*

    (D) the Preamble to the Constitution.

    (E) *Brown vs. Board of Education.*

38. The case of a U.S. citizen bringing suit against the federal government would be heard first in the

    (A) Court of Claims.   (D) District Court.

    (B) Supreme Court.   (E) Court of Appeals.

    (C) Tax Court.

The Federal Bureaucracy

In addition to the president's Cabinet, a series of independent agencies as well as the Executive Office of the president make up the so-called federal bureaucracy. The term itself, often used derisively, refers to a large body of government administrators.

The federal bureaucracy has grown from less than one thousand employees in the 1790s to an unwieldy body of close to three million in the mid 1980s.

Among the most important of the independent agencies are the regulatory commissions. The administrators of these powerful agencies are appointed by the president with the approval of the Senate. But unlike the Cabinet secretaries and other high appointees, they cannot be dismissed by the chief executive. These agencies were established to police big business, the first one being the Interstate Commerce Commission which was created in 1887 in response to popular protest against the abuses of the powerful railway industry. Today it also regulates surface and water transportation as well as some pipelines. Other major regulatory agencies of the federal government include:

1) the Federal Trade Commission, which is the main consumer protection agency of the federal government,

2) the Consumer Product Safety Commission, which sets standards of safety for manufactured products,

3) the Securities and Exchange Commission, which monitors the sale of stocks and bonds,

4) the Commodity Futures Trading Commission, which oversees practices in the sale of agricultural and mining resources,

5) the Board of Governors, Federal Reserve System, which is responsible for the nation's banking industry,

6) the Federal Communications Commission, which regulates the airwaves,

7) the National Labor Relations Board, which supervises labor-management practices, and

8) the Nuclear Regulatory Commission, which licenses and inspects nuclear power plants.

These independent agencies wield so much power that they have been referred to as the "fourth branch of the federal government." In recent years, under the administrations of Carter, Reagan, and Bush, however, the trend has been toward deregulation.

Another category of bureaucratic agencies includes the independent executive agencies and the government corporations. Some of the key executive agencies include the Central Intelligence Agency, the National Aeronautics and Space Administration, the Civil Rights Commission, and the Environmental Protection Agency. These agencies do not enjoy Cabinet status, but nonetheless are powerful entities with large employment forces and impressive budgets. The president appoints their top level executives with the approval of the Senate.

Government corporations are commercial enterprises established by Congress to perform certain necessary services. They trace their historical roots back to the First Bank of the United States, which was established under Secretary of the Treasury Alexander Hamilton in 1791. A more recent example of the government corporation is the Federal Deposit Insurance Corporation (FDIC), which insures bank deposits and which has been unusually active during the recent recession due to a rash of bank failures. The Tennessee Valley Authority was established under the New Deal of Franklin Roosevelt. Originally, it was conceived as a project to revive a depressed region, and today it oversees the generation of electric power in the states of the Tennessee Valley. The largest of the government corporations and the most familiar to the general public is the U.S. Postal Service, which was originally a Cabinet department.

The Executive Office of the president is comprised of several critical agencies and departments which oversee important administrative functions. Among the most powerful are the Office of Management and Budget, the Council of Economic Advisors, the Council on Environmental Quality, and the National Security Council, which advises the president on matters both domestic and foreign that threaten the safety of the nation.

The large and powerful federal bureaucracy shapes and administers government policy. It is inherently political despite sporadic efforts throughout the years to maintain the integrity of the bureaucratic staff. Dating back to the administrations of Andrew Jackson in the late 1820s, the practice of handing out government jobs in return for political favors (the spoils system) has been the rule. In response to a drive for reform in the 1870s, Congress passed the Civil Service Act (the Pendleton Act) in 1883 which established the framework for the modern day civil service. Under this law, the government is required to recruit federal workers on the basis of merit related to a competitive exam and to provide job security. A "veterans preference" policy does exist which boosts the scores of those who were honorably discharged from the military. The Hatch Act of 1939 placed restrictions on the political activities of civil service employees in an attempt to ensure the neutrality of government workers.

In recent years, as with the regulatory agencies, there has been a drive to streamline the bureaucracy. Presidents Carter and Reagan both made efforts to downsize the amount of paperwork stemming from bureaucratic agencies and to reduce the size of the federal work force. Recently, Vice-President Gore has dedicated himself to monitoring the number of rules emanating from federal agencies in a continuing effort to "streamline" government.

Meanwhile, President Clinton, the first Democrat to be returned to the White House since Franklin Delano Roosevelt, told the nation that the days of a large, all-encompassing federal government—in so many aspects the legacy of FDR's New Deal—were over.

☞ Drill: The Federal Bureaucracy

DIRECTIONS: Carefully read and answer each of the following questions which are based on the information which you have just read.

39.   The largest of the government corporations is the

(A)   Tennessee Valley Authority.

(B)   Bank of the United States.

(C)   U.S. Postal Service.

(D)   Federal Deposit Insurance Corporation.

(E)   Environmental Protection Agency.

40.   The civil service system was originally established to

(A)   provide jobs for veterans.

(B)   eliminate the abuses of the spoils system.

(C)   provide equal opportunities for women and minorities.

(D)   restrict the political activities of government employees.

(E)   investigate civil rights abuses.

41.   In recent years presidential policy with respect to the federal bureaucracy has been to

(A)   favor an increase in the number of workers to cope with the complexity of federal programs.

(B)   favor significant budget increases to fund new programs.

(C)   favor a downsizing of the work force.

(D)   request the creation of new agencies to regulate the transportation industry.

(E)   request the elimination of the Central Intelligence Agency.

42.   All of the following are true of the administrators of the regulatory commissions EXCEPT that

(A)   they are appointed by the president.

(B)   they must be approved by the Senate.

(C)   they are expected to be non-political in their recommendations.

(D)   they can be dismissed by the president.

(E)   they serve for a fixed number of years.

43.   The first regulatory agency to be created (1887) was the

(A)   Interstate Commerce Commission.

(B)   Federal Trade Commission.

(C)   National Labor Relations Board.

(D)   Federal Reserve Board of Governors.

(E)   Securities and Exchange Commission.

44.   All of the following are categorized as independent executive agencies EXCEPT the

(A)   Central Intelligence Agency.

(B)   National Aeronautics and Space Administration.

(C)   Civil Rights Commission.

(D)   Environmental Protection Agency.

(E)   Federal Deposit Insurance Corporation.

Political Institutions and Special Interests

Political Parties

A political party is an organization that seeks to influence the government and to determine public policy by electing officials from within its ranks. The Constitution does not mention political parties, and the Founding Fathers in general were opposed to them. Yet they developed simultaneously with the organization of the new government. In fact, it was the initial conflict over the interpretation of the powers assigned to the federal government by the Constitution that gave rise to the first organized American political parties.

The Federalist Party evolved around the policies of President Washington's Secretary of the Treasury, Alexander Hamilton. Hamilton and his supporters favored a "loose construction" approach to the interpretation of the Constitution, meaning that they advocated a strong federal government with the power to assume any duties and responsibilities not prohibited to it in the text of the doctrine. They generally supported programs designed to benefit the banking and commercial interests, and in foreign policy the Federalists were pro-British.

In opposition to the Federalists were the Democratic or Jeffersonian Republicans, who rallied around the Secretary of State. The modern Democratic Party traces its roots to the Jeffersonians. They were backed by those who believed in a "strict constructionist" approach, interpreting the Constitution in a narrow, limited sense. The Democratic-Republicans were mistrustful of a powerful central government, and sympathized with the needs of the "common man." They believed the small agrarian interests were the backbone of the nation along with shopkeepers and laborers. In the realm of foreign affairs, the Democratic-Republicans were pro-French. They wrested power from the Federalists in the election of 1800 when Jefferson narrowly defeated incumbent John Adams.

By the 1820s, the Democrats had divided into factions led by Andrew Jackson (Democrats) and John Quincy Adams (National Republicans). The Jacksonians continued the Jeffersonian tradition of supporting policies designed to enhance the power of the common man. Their support was largely rural with both small farmers and some large planters in their camp. The National Republicans, on the other hand, like their Federalist predecessors, represented the interests of eastern bankers, merchants, and some planters. Eventually, a new party was formed from the remnants of the old Federalists and the National Republicans. They called themselves the Whigs after a British party of the same name and were dedicated to opposing the policies of the Jacksonians. The Whigs wielded power throughout the decade of the 1840s, but like their Democratic rivals, they split apart in the 1850s over the divisive slavery issue. The modern Republican Party was born in 1854 as Whigs and anti-slavery Democrats sought to halt the spread of slavery. The Republicans built their constituency around the interests of businesses, farmers, laborers, and the newly emancipated slaves in the post-Civil War era.

According to Robert Weissberg in *Understanding American Government,* the history of the evolution of political parties in the United States illustrates three consistent patterns. First, there is the fact that there is an almost rhythmic "ebb and flow" to their power and effectiveness. One party rises, the other regroups only to increase in vitality as the other declines. A second characteristic of our modern political parties is their ability to resist the challenges of third party threats and, indeed, to co-opt their themes and appeal. Lastly, Weissberg observes that American political parties are resilient and powerful, because historically they have been able to adapt to ever-changing economic and social forces such as urbanization, industrialization, immigration, and reform movements.

Over the years, political parties have exerted a variety of functions essential to our democratic tradition. The most obvious function is the nomination of suitable candidates for local, state, and national office. This function, particularly at the national level, has been diluted to some extent by the popularity of primary elections to allow voters to express their preference for candidates. Gone are the days of raucous conventions and "smoke filled rooms" from which such "dark horse" candidates as Warren G. Harding emerged from obscurity to capture national elections. Political parties stimulate interest by focusing on their own strengths and on the weaknesses of their opposition. They also provide a framework for keeping the machinery of government functioning as seen in the way Congress is organized strictly on party lines. They raise money to support candidates and provide a forum for airing public issues.

American political parties appear in theory to be highly organized, but due to our geographic size and the federal system of government, they are in practice largely decentralized. At the local level, the fundamental unit of organization is the precinct. At the precinct level, there is usually a captain, leader, or committee to handle routine tasks such as registering voters, distributing party literature, organizing "grass-roots" meetings, and getting out the vote on election day.

The next unit of party organization is the county. States vary considerably with respect to the selection of party officials at this level. Some are elected by their precincts, others elected at the county level, and in some states, they are selected by party conventions. County committees/county party leaders are often in positions to hand out patronage jobs to those who work for the election of party candidates.

State central committees are critical to fund raising activities, and they are responsible for the organization of state party conventions. As with the counties, there is great variation from state to state concerning selection and composition of committees at this level. Like the county party leaders, these officials distribute party patronage jobs. State committees often formulate policies and traditions independently of the national committee.

In presidential election years, the national party committees are most visible. They plan the national nominating convention, write the party platform (a summary of positions on major issues), raise money to finance political activities, and carry out the election campaign. Representatives from each state serve on the national committees, and the presidential nominee chooses one individual to serve as party chairperson. Since the 1970s, the national committees have been more active in activities other than those strictly associated with the presidential campaign. Both the Democrats and Republicans have utilized the national committees to train would-be candidates and to recruit potential office holders.

The popularity of primary elections to screen and select the final party candidates has blunted the effect of party bosses and indeed the organizations themselves in controlling the political process. Closed primaries allow voters who are registered in a particular party to express their preferences for the party's candidates in the final election. Open primaries, on the other hand, allow voters to decide at the polls which party they will support. A few states allow "crossover" voting which permits voters registered in one party to vote for the candidates in the other party. This practice can lead to such devious practices as voting for the weakest choice in the opposition party to give an advantage in the final election to the candidate and the party a voter in actuality supports. By the time the long presidential primary season is over (from the New Hampshire primary in February to the California primary in June), the final nominees of the respective parties are well-known to voters, hence the national party conventions are anti-climactic.

The national nominating conventions were introduced in the 1830s by the Anti-Masonic Party and quickly adopted by the Democrats and the newly organized Whig Party. Other "third parties" leaving their marks on the American political scene include: 1) the American or Know Nothing Party which opposed Catholic immigration in the 1850s, 2) the Prohibition Party which opposed the use of alcohol and worked for the adoption of the Eighteenth Amendment, 3) the Populist Party of the 1890s which championed the cause of the farmers and workers and advocated the free coinage of silver, public ownership of major utilities, and electoral reforms such as the initiative and the referendum, 4) the Progressive or Bull Moose Party of Theodore Roosevelt (a splinter party which broke away from the Republican Party in 1912), which was built around the personality of the former president, and 5) the Socialist Party which was founded in the 1890s and which advocates economic planning and government ownership of major industries and resources. These parties have wielded considerable influence over the years, and although they have not captured the White House, they have highlighted important issues and have often influenced the programs and platforms of the major parties.

☞ Drill: Political Parties

DIRECTIONS: Carefully read and answer each of the following questions which are based on the information which you have just read.

45. An important characteristic of American political parties is the fact that they

    (A) are highly organized.

    (B) function independently of the federal system.

    (C) largely bypass local politics.

    (D) are highly decentralized.

    (E) enforce strict policies concerning membership and participation.

46. America's first political party was the

    (A) Democratic Party.   (D) Whig Party.

    (B) Democratic-Republican Party.   (E) Federalist Party.

    (C) National-Republican Party.

47. With reference to political parties, the U.S. Constitution

    (A) provided a general framework for their development.

    (B) made no mention of them.

    (C) provided a detailed plan for their organization.

    (D) specified that Congress be organized along party lines.

    (E) had to be amended to allow for their development.

48. All of the following are true of the Whig Party EXCEPT

    (A) it was popular during the 1840s.

    (B) it fragmented over the slavery issue.

    (C) it was created from the remnants of the Federalists and the National Republicans.

    (D) it traced its roots to the Jeffersonians.

    (E) it was dedicated to opposing the policies of the Jacksonians.

49. One characteristic *not* associated with the major American political parties is

    (A) a clear division between liberals and conservatives as seen in their affiliation with different parties.

    (B) their ability to resist third party threats.

    (C) their ability to cope with changing economic and social forces.

    (D) the cyclical nature of their popularity and effectiveness.

    (E) their evolution from the division within Washington's first Cabinet.

50. A type of election that encourages voters to support weak candidates is the

    (A) open primary.

    (B) closed primary.

    (C) crossover primary.

    (D) "off-year" election.

    (E) party caucus.

51. National nominating conventions to choose final presidential candidates were first introduced by which of the following third parties?

    (A) Bull Moose Party

    (B) Know Nothing Party

    (C) Anti-Masonic Party

    (D) Prohibition Party

    (E) Populist Party

Interest Groups

American officials and political leaders are continually subjected to pressure from a variety of interest groups to enact or quash policies friendly or hostile to their respective causes. These groups may be loosely organized (informal) with no real structure or regulations. A group of neighbors united in opposition to the building of a shopping mall on a wooded lot is an example of this type of interest group. They may hold meetings, distribute literature, circulate petitions, collect funds for legal fees, pack zoning board meetings, and command the attention of the local media. Using these techniques, such an informal interest group may effectively influence appropriate town politicians and accomplish the limited goal of halting the development of the woodland acreage.

Other interest groups are much more formal and permanent in nature. This type of interest group may have a large staff, suites of offices, and a broad agenda with clearly defined political objectives. Usually such a group has an economic interest which may range from agricultural to financial to industrial. Some formal interest groups are more altruistic with a reform agenda such as Common Cause and

Massachusetts Fair Share. This type of pressure group may be classified as a public-interest group.

Some formal interest groups are dedicated to the advancement or protection of a single issue. The National Rifle Association, which fights gun control legislation and the National Right to Life Committee, which seeks to roll back *Roe vs. Wade* and end legalized abortion are examples of powerful single issue pressure groups.

Interest groups use a variety of tactics to accomplish their goals. The most obvious strategy utilized by such groups is to lobby elected officials, particularly members of Congress, to advocate or to oppose policies favorable or unfriendly to their agendas. The majority of America's organized interest groups employ lobbyists in Washington. Business, labor, professionals, religious groups, environmentalists, consumer groups, and a host of others employ representatives to work for their benefit. They provide reports, statistics, and other forms of data to members of Congress to persuade them of the legitimacy of their respective positions. They may present expert testimony at public hearings, and they commonly manipulate the media to disseminate information favorable to their employers. They are not allowed to resort to such illegal tactics as presenting false and misleading information or bribing public officials. Since 1946, when Congress passed legislation regulating the activities of professional lobbyists, they have been required to register in Washington and to make their positions public. Such legislation cannot, of course, curb all abuses and underhanded practices inherent to a system of organized persuasion.

In recent years, in an attempt to circumvent legislation limiting contributions to political campaigns, a new type of pressure group, the political action committee (PAC), has evolved. Under current election laws, individuals may legally contribute $1,000 to candidates for national office. Interest groups such as PACs, on the other hand, can contribute $5,000 to candidates, and individuals may donate up to $5,000 a year to a political action committee. PACs have become increasingly popular and powerful in recent years. By the mid-1980s, there were over three thousand recognized political action committees. Despite their power and proliferation on the American political scene, political action committees have engendered a measure of controversy. Critics see these interest groups as just another means of diluting the influence the individual voter may realistically have on his/her elected representatives. Hence, some politicians refuse to accept PAC money.

In the mid-1990s, campaign finance reform edged ever closer to center stage until 1997, when charges of questionable fund-raising practices by both parties led to a call for congressional hearings into the matter.

☞ Drill: Interest Groups

> **DIRECTIONS:** Carefully read and answer each of the following questions which are based on the information which you have just read.

52.   Which of the following is an example of a single interest group?

(A)   National Right to Life Committee

(B)   Greenpeace

(C)   National Education Association

(D)   American Medical Association

(E)   National Organization for Women

53.   All of the following are legitimate functions of registered lobbyists EXCEPT

(A)   testifying at public hearings.

(B)   providing members of Congress with statistical data.

(C)   preparing reports.

(D)   presenting media spots.

(E)   nominating candidates for political office.

54.   Common Cause and the League of Women Voters are examples of

(A)   informal interest groups.   (D)   ideological groups.

(B)   single issue groups.   (E)   professional groups.

(C)   public interest groups.

55.   Political action committees (PACs)

(A)   have roots that originated in the nineteenth century.

(B)   have declined in popularity in recent years.

(C)   may contribute up to $1,000 a year to a political candidate.

(D)   may accept contributions of up to $5,000 from individuals.

(E)   may make unlimited contributions to political candidates.

56.   The principal function of a pressure group is to

(A)   provide campaign money to candidates for public office who favor its programs.

(B)   draw media attention to its cause.

(C)   obtain favorable policies from government for the cause it supports.

(D)   win congressional seats for its members.

(E)   accomplish all of the above.

Public Opinion and Voter Behavior

The Nature of Public Opinion

Public opinion is a misleading term, but generally it refers to the attitudes and preferences expressed by a significant number of individuals about an issue that involves the government or society at large. It does not necessarily represent the sentiments of all or even most of the citizenry. Public opinion, nonetheless, is an important component of any society, particularly a democratic republic such as the United States where the government in both theory and practice is based on the concept of popular sovereignty.

In general, Americans are less apt to base their opinions on a set ideology than they are to respond to a public issue or concern by considering what will work and supporting the most expedient solution. Still, there are labels applied to politically active individuals based on tradition and loosely related to party affiliation. Those who consider themselves to be conservatives usually are hesitant to espouse change and seek to preserve time-honored values and political traditions. They are sometimes labeled as "right-wing." Leftists or liberals are more receptive to change, and they are willing to use government to reform society. Moderates, or those in the political center, are somewhere in between these two. In reality, both the Republican and Democratic Parties are moderate political institutions, but the former tends to support a conservative approach to governing while the latter is somewhat more liberal in philosophy.

An individual's public opinions are rooted in his/her family, ethnicity, religious heritage, and socio-economic group. Although the family is not generally regarded as a political institution, young people see the outside world first through the eyes of their parents and care-givers. Youngsters who participate in mock elections and straw polls generally support the candidates that their parents favor. This rule may change as the young person enters the sometimes rebellious years of adolescence and young adulthood. In the tumultuous 1960s, when the term "generation gap" was coined, many anti-establishment radicals were indeed the children of traditional, patriotic, middle-class conservatives or moderates.

Schools are also important agents in molding politically conscious young people, particularly those from homes where public issues may be downplayed or ignored. Schools foster patriotism by opening the day with a salute to the flag, studying civic holidays, and requiring curriculum treatment of American history and government as an integral component of public education. Young people are encouraged to learn about the heroes of the republic and, at the secondary level, to express their informed opinions about contemporary issues.

In today's technological society, the influence of the mass media in molding public opinion cannot be over-emphasized. Radio, television, newspapers, and news magazines all play a critical part in informing the public about major issues, and the biases of those who make decisions about how to present information quite naturally affect the nature of the final product. The electronic media in particular have been criticized for over-simplification of complicated issues and for reducing major speeches to sound bites lasting for less than a minute. On a positive note, the media can be credited with heightening general interest about public affairs.

Political candidates often exploit the media to transmit their respective messages to the public and in so doing utilize a number of common propaganda techniques most often employed by corporate advertising campaigns. These techniques include:

1) the testimonial in which a well-known celebrity lends credibility to a candidate by endorsing his/her campaign,

2) the plain-folks approach in which the candidate mingles with working-class voters in an attempt to convince voters that he/she is one of them,

3) the band-wagon approach where the candidate tries to create the impression that individuals who do not support him/her will be left out because everyone else is doing so,

4) name-calling which consists of labeling the opponent with terms which carry negative connotations such as "extremist" or, in the election of 1988, "liberal," and

5) employing glittering generalities such as "life, liberty, and the pursuit of happiness" and "peace and prosperity" to sway voters.

Measuring the effects of the media on public opinion is indeed difficult and pinpointing where the public stands on a given issue is a difficult assignment, but certainly polls such as those administered by the Gallup and Harris organizations are fairly accurate in predicting voter behavior. Pollsters usually address a random sample of the population reflecting a cross-section of society with carefully constructed questions designed to elicit responses that do not mirror the biases of the interviewer. Results are tabulated and generalizations presented to the media.

Public opinion polls have been criticized on a variety of fronts. Some suggest that despite the sophistication of professional pollsters, many polls are poorly designed and/or the answers of the subjects are improperly interpreted. Another criticism is that they oversimplify complicated issues and encourage pat answers to complex problems. One type of election poll that has been severely criticized is the so-called exit poll in which an interviewer questions voters about their preferences as they leave polling places. These polls may be accurate, although with reference to sensitive issues voters may avoid being candid and respond only as they think is proper. Another problem with exit polls arises if the media present the results while voting is still in progress and predict the outcome before all potential voters have had the opportunity to express their choices. In the election of 1980, Ronald Reagan was declared the victor over Jimmy Carter by some of the major news outlets before the polls closed on the West Coast, thereby robbing a large segment of the electorate of the sense that its participation mattered.

In the 1990s, exit polling continued to engender controversy, with critics urging the media to exercise self-restraint by keeping their projections to themselves until all ballots are cast.

☞ Drill: The Nature of Public Opinion

> **DIRECTIONS:** Carefully read and answer each of the following questions which are based on the information which you have just read.

57. The *least* important agent in molding public opinion among the young would probably be

    (A)   older family members.   (D)   socio-economic groups.

    (B)   school curriculum.   (E)   religious role models.

    (C)   peer group members.

58. Media influence on the formation of public opinion has been criticized for all of the following reasons EXCEPT

    (A)   oversimplification of complicated issues.

    (B)   reducing major speeches to brief sound bites.

    (C)   biased presentations.

    (D)   heightening general interest in public issues.

    (E)   focusing on the trivial and the sensational.

59. All of the following are characterizations of public opinion EXCEPT

    (A)   it reflects the attitudes of a majority of the population.

    (B)   it involves attitudes about public issues.

    (C)   it influences the decisions of public officials.

    (D)   it is measured by pollsters.

    (E)   it is an important component of any society.

60.   Both the Republican and Democratic Parties

    (A)   appeal mainly to conservative voters.

    (B)   appeal principally to liberals.

    (C)   are based on clearly defined ideologies.

    (D)   usually embrace a moderate approach to solving society's problems.

    (E)   eschew a pragmatic approach to problem-solving.

61.   A propaganda device in which a candidate advertises an endorsement from a celebrity figure is called

    (A)   "the band-wagon approach."   (D)   "the plain-folks technique."

    (B)   "the testimonial."   (E)   "name-calling."

    (C)   "a glittering generality."

Voter Behavior

Suffrage (the right to vote) qualifications in the United States have historically been determined by the individual states, but in response to a variety of reform efforts, amendments have been added to the Constitution to broaden the size of the electorate. In 1870 following the Civil War, the Fifteenth Amendment was ratified making it illegal to deny a citizen the right to vote due to "race, color, or previous condition of servitude." Despite the intent to enfranchise the former slaves, a number of legal devices were utilized to deny blacks the right to vote. Among these were the poll tax, literacy test, and the infamous "grandfather clause," which denied suffrage to those whose grandfathers had not been legally entitled to vote. In the spirit of the modern civil rights movement, in 1964 the Twenty-Fourth Amendment was passed outlawing the poll tax as a voting qualification in federal elections. Women had gained the vote in 1920 with the ratification of the Nineteenth Amendment which barred the federal government as well as the separate states from denying women access to the polls. During the Vietnam War, when eighteen-year-olds were subject to the draft, the Twenty-Sixth Amendment was added to the Constitution, granting them the vote in both federal and state elections.

In recent years much attention has been focused on the topic of voter apathy, for despite historic efforts to extend suffrage to all segments of the adult population, participation in the electoral process has been on the decline. Several theories have been advanced to explain this trend. There is a widespread belief that Americans are dissatisfied with their elected officials and mistrust all politicians; therefore, they have been "turned off" to the system and refuse to participate. Of course, some Americans do not vote because they are ill, handicapped, incarcerated, or homeless and do not have access to the ballot. Others such as college students who do not live at home find it cumbersome and inconvenient to register and use absentee ballots. While most of the attempts to explain voter apathy in the United States focus on it as a negative aspect of our civic culture, some analysts disagree and see disinterest in the ballot as a sign that the majority of the citizenry are satisfied with the system and with life in America in general; hence, they feel no sense of urgency about participating in the political process.

Attempts to explain how people vote as they do in American elections have produced few consistent generalizations because each election has its own unique character. However, a few suggestions can be offered to explain some of the factors that determine how Americans vote. One obvious consideration is party identification. For those who harbor a strong sense of loyalty to the Democratic or Republican Party, the choice of whom to support particularly in presidential elections is fairly predictable. Still, only one-termer Jimmy Carter, in 1976, broke the Republicans' lock on the White House between 1968 and 1992, despite the fact that there are more registered Democrats. (It is well to note, too, that Bill Clinton's successful Democratic campaigns in 1992 and 1996 at times co-opted traditional GOP issues.) In addition, the number of voters who register with no party affiliation is on the rise. Another factor that may explain the vote in a particular election is related to a candidate's stand on a controversial issue such as abortion rights. Many pro-choice and right-to-life voters use this issue as a so-called "litmus test" to determine which candidates they will support. Factors such as age, sex, education, socio-economic group, religion, occupation, and geography also play a part in shaping voter behavior.

☞ Drill: Voter Behavior

> **DIRECTIONS:** Carefully read and answer each of the following questions which are based on the information which you have just read.

62. Which of the following generalizations is true of the American electorate?

   (A) Voter indifference is always an indication of dissatisfaction with public officials.

   (B) Participation in the political process is on the rise.

(C)   Party identification is insignificant in explaining why Americans vote as they do.

(D)   Some voters use a "litmus test" with reference to a single critical issue to determine whom they will support.

(E)   Young people vote in large numbers because they have a comparatively greater amount of free time than middle-aged voters.

63.   Which of the following amendments to the Constitution outlawed the poll tax in federal elections?

(A)   The Twenty-Sixth   (D)   The Fourteenth

(B)   The Twenty-Fourth   (E)   The Fifteenth

(C)   The Nineteenth

64.   Which of the following factors is probably most significant in determining how an individual will vote in a presidential election?

(A)   Occupation   (D)   Geography

(B)   Income level   (E)   Religion

(C)   Party loyalty

65.   The principal reason why eighteen-year-olds were enfranchised in 1971 was

(A)   universal education.

(B)   the Vietnam War.

(C)   higher income levels.

(D)   availability of information via the electronic media.

(E)   the civil rights movement.

Civil Rights and the Supreme Court

Historical Background and the Bill of Rights

As with other traditional aspects of the American civic culture, the origins of the concept of fundamental freedoms and unalienable rights can be traced to the British heritage and to the thinkers of the Enlightenment. In crafting the Declaration of Independence in 1776, Thomas Jefferson and his comrades coined the phrases "all men are created equal" and "life, liberty and the pursuit of happiness" to indicate why governments exist—to insure the protection of these basic rights. The list of grievances which makes up the body of the Declaration contains several references to King George III's failure to uphold the civic rights that subjects of the British crown considered their birthright. The signers of the document complained that the King refused to accept laws that were passed for their common good, that he deprived many of them of trial by jury, that he obstructed justice, that he kept standing armies among them in times of peace, that he taxed them without their consent, and that in general, he behaved like a tyrant.

When constructing the Constitution, the Founding Fathers attempted to include passages to insure the protection of civil liberties such as in Article I, Section 9 where specific provisions are set down for maintaining the right of *habeas corpus*. Similarly, in Article III, Section 2 trial by jury for all federal crimes with the exception of cases involving impeachment is affirmed. However, one criticism of the document voiced by some of the Anti-Federalists who opposed its ratification was its lack of a bill of rights protecting the civil liberties of individual citizens.

During the first session of Congress in 1789, the first ten amendments were adopted and sent to the states for ratification. They were formally added to the Constitution as a package in 1791. These amendments are known collectively as the Bill of Rights, and they contain protections of those individual freedoms which in many ways define what it is to be an American. However, most of the rights enumerated in the Bill of Rights are extended to "all persons" living in the United States, including aliens.

The amendment that Americans in general hold most dear is undoubtedly the First Amendment, which protects our freedom of expression and which specifically guarantees the following rights: freedom of religion, freedom of speech, freedom of the press, freedom of assembly, and freedom to petition the government. In the case of religion, Congress is barred from establishing a state religion and from preventing individuals from worshipping freely. The right to assemble must be carried out "peaceably."

Another category of fundamental freedoms protected by the Bill of Rights involves due process or the rights of the accused. The Fourth Amendment outlaws "unreasonable searches and seizures" and mandates that warrants be granted only "upon probable cause." The section of the amendment that affirms the "right of the people to be secure in their persons" has been cited by abortion rights activists as a source of constitutional protection for women to make private decisions concerning reproduction. The broad provisions of the Fifth Amendment call for grand juries, bar double jeopardy, insist that defendants not be compelled to testify against themselves, protect due process in general, and require the government to compensate anyone whose private property is taken for public use (eminent domain). The Sixth Amendment guarantees to those accused of criminal offenses a speedy trial by a jury of peers, to be informed of the charges, and to be represented by an attorney. The Eighth Amendment prohibits "excessive bail and fines" and restrains the state from imposing "cruel and unusual punishments." The "cruel and unusual" clause has been invoked by opponents of capital punishment to justify their position.

As originally formulated, the provisions of the Bill of Rights were geared to the federal government. For the most part, the separate states have constitutions which include lists of protections similar to the Bill of Rights. Following the Civil War, the Fourteenth Amendment was added to the Constitution to extend the rights of citizenship to the former slave. In so doing, the framers of this amendment specified that no state could abridge the rights of citizenship nor "deprive any person of life, liberty, or property, without due process of law, nor deny to any person within its jurisdiction the equal protection of the laws." States now must conform to the federal concept of civil liberties.

☞ Drill: Historical Background and the Bill of Rights

DIRECTIONS: Carefully read and answer each of the following questions which are based on the information which you have just read.

66. The First Amendment protects all of the following freedoms EXCEPT

   (A) freedom of religion.

   (B) freedom of choice.

   (C) freedom of the press.

   (D) freedom of speech.

   (E) freedom of assembly.

67. Jefferson's reference to "unalienable rights" in the Declaration of Independence relates to

   (A) laws passed by Parliament.

   (B) laws passed by the colonial legislatures.

   (C) laws that did not protect aliens.

   (D) traditions of the Enlightenment.

   (E) rights that cannot legally be taken away.

68. When creating the Constitution, the Founding Fathers did not include a bill of rights because

   (A) the Anti-Federalists opposed such a bill.

   (B) they had too many other issues to consider.

   (C) they were unsure of what to include.

   (D) they believed such a bill was unnecessary because the states already had such protections.

   (E) James Madison lobbied against such a bill.

69. The Fifth Amendment guarantees all of the following legal protections EXCEPT

   (A) freedom from double jeopardy.

   (B) freedom from being compelled to testify against oneself.

   (C) freedom from cruel and unusual punishments.

    (D)   indictment by a grand jury.

    (E)   compensation for land taken by eminent domain.

70.   States are now prohibited from infringing upon the rights protected by the federal Bill of Rights because of

    (A)   an executive order issued by President Washington.

    (B)   a provision in the Fourteenth Amendment.

    (C)   legislative action by the first Congress.

    (D)   an introduction to the document which mandates it.

    (E)   their state constitutions which require it.

The Supreme Court and Individual Rights

Over the years the American judicial system, particularly the U.S. Supreme Court, has been responsible for enforcing the protections originally listed in the Constitution, those guaranteed in the Bill of Rights, and those specified in other legislation and amendments. Numerous landmark decisions have been rendered by the Supreme Court in its mission to protect the rights of the people of the United States. Among the most significant are the following:

Gitlow vs. New York (1925) in which a Socialist lost his free speech case but in which the Court affirmed the contention that the states could be required to adhere to the Bill of Rights.

Brown vs. Board of Education (1954) an equal protection case which overturned *Plessy vs. Ferguson* (1896) and which declared school segregation to be unconstitutional.

Engel vs. Vitale (1962) which outlawed prayer in public schools.

Abington Township vs. Schempp (1963) which abolished Bible reading in public schools.

West Virginia Board of Education vs. Barnette (1943) which overturned *Minersville School District vs. Gobitis* and which ruled that a law that mandated compulsory saluting of the flag was unconstitutional.

Near vs. Minnesota (1931) a freedom of the press case which forbade states to use the concept of prior restraint (outlawing something before it has taken place) to limit publication of objectionable material except during wartime or in cases of obscenity or incitement to violence.

New York Times vs. United States (1971) another freedom of the press case, this ruling allowed the publication of the controversial Pentagon Papers during the Vietnam War.

Tinker vs. Des Moines School District (1969) in which the Court ruled that wearing black armbands in protest against the Vietnam War was protected by the First Amendment. More recently, the Court has expanded the concept of "symbolic speech" and has protected such activities as burning the flag and cross burning by the KKK.

Mapp vs. Ohio (1961), a case which upheld and extended to states the Court's exclusionary rule which bars at trial the introduction of evidence which has not been obtained legally. Recently, particularly with reference to drug cases, the Court has modified this ruling so that evidence that might not have been initially obtained legally but which would eventually have turned up through lawful procedures can be introduced.

Gideon vs. Wainwright (1963) ruled that courts must provide legal counsel to poor defendants in all felony cases. A later ruling extended this right to all defendants facing possible prison sentences.

Escobedo vs. Illinois (1964) extended the right to counsel to include consultation prior to questioning by authorities.

Miranda vs. Arizona (1966) in which the Court mandated that all suspects be informed of their due process rights before police interrogate them.

Korematsu vs. United States (1944) upheld the constitutionality of a 1942 order that all persons of Japanese ancestry including American citizens be relocated and detained. This measure was viewed as a wartime necessity. The Court also ruled (in the *Endo* case) that it *was* unconstitutional for any individual whose loyalty to the nation had been established to be restricted in his/her freedom of movement.

Bakke vs. The Regents of the University of California (1978), a reverse discrimination case in which the Court declared the University's quota system for minority students to be unconstitutional while it at the same time upheld the legitimacy of affirmative action policies in which institutions consider race as a factor when determining admissions.

Roe vs. Wade (1973) in which the Court legalized abortion so long as the fetus is not viable (able to survive outside the womb).

Webster vs. Reproductive Health Services (1989), an abortion rights case which allowed states more discretion and upheld their right to limit the use of public funds, buildings, or personnel in administering abortions. Recently, a Pennsylvania law calling for a twenty-four-hour waiting period for abortions, for unmarried women under eighteen years of age to receive the consent of one parent or from a judge in order to obtain an abortion, and for women to be informed by medical personnel of the specifics of the procedure and of alternatives was upheld. However, a provision of the law requiring that married women inform their spouses of their decision to have an abortion was struck down.

☞ Drill: The Supreme Court and Individual Rights

DIRECTIONS: Carefully read and answer each of the following questions which are based on the information which you have just read.

71. The *Gideon, Escobedo,* and *Miranda* cases all concerned which of the following issues?

    (A) School prayer

    (B) Saluting the flag

    (C) The rights of the accused

    (D) Eminent domain

    (E) Freedom of speech

72. A case which expanded the concept of symbolic speech to include wearing armbands in protest was

    (A) *Tinker vs. Des Moines.*

    (B) *Engel vs. Vitale.*

    (C) *Abington Township vs. Schempp.*

    (D) *Mapp vs. Ohio.*

    (E) *Bakke vs. Regents.*

73. The significance of the *Gitlow* case was that it

    (A) affirmed the right of a Socialist to make inflammatory speeches.

    (B) mandated that state governments uphold the provisions of the federal Bill of Rights.

    (C) interpreted the death penalty as a cruel and unusual punishment.

    (D) upheld the constitutionality of the exclusionary rule.

    (E) outlawed reverse discrimination.

74. In a recent ruling concerning a Pennsylvania law restricting abortion rights, the Court upheld all of the following EXCEPT

    (A) the legality of abortions if the fetus is not viable.

    (B) parental notification in the case of an unmarried minor.

    (C) spousal notification in the case of a married woman.

    (D) a twenty-four-hour waiting period before obtaining an abortion.

    (E) requiring that medical personnel provide information about alternatives.

75. In the *Korematsu* case (1944) the Supreme Court

   (A)   declared the Japanese relocation to be unlawful.

   (B)   declared that U.S. citizens of Japanese origin be exempted from the relocation order.

   (C)   upheld the measure as reasonable in wartime.

   (D)   ruled that Japanese residents of the West Coast were entitled to equal protection.

   (E)   ruled that reverse discrimination was a major factor in the decision.

United States Government and Politics Review

ANSWER KEY

1.	(D)	20.	(D)	39.	(C)	58.	(D)
2.	(B)	21.	(A)	40.	(B)	59.	(A)
3.	(A)	22.	(C)	41.	(C)	60.	(D)
4.	(C)	23.	(A)	42.	(D)	61.	(B)
5.	(B)	24.	(D)	43.	(A)	62.	(D)
6.	(E)	25.	(D)	44.	(E)	63.	(B)
7.	(B)	26.	(B)	45.	(D)	64.	(C)
8.	(C)	27.	(E)	46.	(E)	65.	(B)
9.	(E)	28.	(B)	47.	(B)	66.	(B)
10.	(B)	29.	(C)	48.	(D)	67.	(E)
11.	(D)	30.	(D)	49.	(A)	68.	(D)
12.	(B)	31.	(E)	50.	(C)	69.	(C)
13.	(A)	32.	(D)	51.	(C)	70.	(B)
14.	(D)	33.	(E)	52.	(A)	71.	(C)
15.	(C)	34.	(B)	53.	(E)	72.	(A)
16.	(E)	35.	(C)	54.	(C)	73.	(B)
17.	(B)	36.	(D)	55.	(D)	74.	(C)
18.	(C)	37.	(C)	56.	(C)	75.	(C)
19.	(C)	38.	(A)	57.	(C)		

CHAPTER 3
Comparative Government & Politics Review

Chapter 3

Britain

Structural Comparison between the American and British Constitutions

A constitution is a basic plan for organizing and operating a government. It is an instrument that formally establishes political institutions and structures, allocates and distributes power, and places restraints and limits to prevent the use, misuse, or abuse of power. A constitution often represents an ideological expression of the ruling elites, as well as being a rationalization and legitimation of their right to exercise and wield power.

Constitutions originate in a number of ways—for example, by 1) fiat, 2) constituent assembly, and 3) evolution. Constitutions that are imposed from above, as in the case of dictatorial regimes, exemplify constitutions by fiat (e.g., the Soviet Constitution of 1936 has been referred to as the Stalin Constitution). The American Constitution of 1787, however, originated and developed through a constituent assembly of delegates (i.e., the Philadelphia Convention). The British Constitution, on the other hand, is unique. It is not represented by one single document, it has no specific date of origin; it is an amalgam of different sources. As an example of constitutional evolution, the British Constitution evolved historically over a long period of time, gradually taking shape and gaining acceptance.

The American Constitution, in contrast, consists of one written document, comprising 7 articles and 27 amendments. It is generally regarded as the oldest, wholly written constitution still in effect as an official governing document. The British Constitution is not made up of one document, but includes a combination of written and unwritten components. In fact, the British Constitution emanates from four distinct sources:

1) historical documents (the Magna Carta of 1215, the Bill of Rights of 1689, etc.);

2) statutes and acts of Parliament (e.g., the Electoral Reform Act of 1832, Parliament Acts of 1911 and 1949);

3) principles of English common law based on judicial decisions and precedents defining civil liberties and property rights; and

4) unwritten custom and tradition, such as annual meetings of Parliament, the collective responsibility of the prime minister and cabinet to the House of Commons, the Royal Assent, selection of the prime minister from the House of Commons. This fourth component, called "conventions" in Britain, has played a vital role in the constitutional development of the British political system.

The flexibility of the American and British constitutions allows them both to adapt to the currents of societal change. The American Constitution can be changed to respond to new values through:

1) acts of Congress,

2) the formal amendment procedure, or, more importantly,

3) the Supreme Court's power of judicial review.

By contrast, in Britain, with parliamentary supremacy and no formal power of judicial review, there are two major ways to enact changes in the constitution:

1) parliamentary statutes and

2) common law precedents.

If Parliament passes an act, it automatically amends the constitution. Conversely, if Parliament repeals a law, it is automatically deleted from the constitution. Similarly, new legal precedents deriving from court litigation expand the scope of the British Constitution.

The constitutional structures of the American and British political systems are considerably different. The American Constitution provides for a *federal system* in which power is constitutionally divided between the national government and its sub-national components (states) by virtue of the allocation and dispersion of various types of powers. These types include powers exclusively delegated to the national government, concurrent powers shared by both national government and the states, and powers reserved for the states. By contrast, Britain has a *unitary system* where power is centralized and the governing authority is not constitutionally shared between the national government and its regional components.

The constitutional structures of the American and British political systems also vary in another way. The American Constitution provides for a *republic* in which the head of state is elected. In Britain, on the other hand, the British Constitution provides for a *monarchy* in which the head of state (the monarch) is determined by heredity.

Perhaps the most significant difference between the American and British political systems involves the distinctions between presidential and parliamentary systems. The American Constitution provides for a *presidential system with a separation of powers*. The president, as head of government, is not formally accountable to the Congress for his actions and tenure. He is independent of the Congress electorally—it is incompatible to be a member of Congress while serving as president—and is assured a four-year term with or without maintaining majority congressional support short of death, resignation, impeachment, or conviction of a crime. Moreover, the president in such a system combines the roles and functions of both head of government and head of state. The British Constitution, in contrast, provides for a *parliamentary system with a fusion of powers*. Unlike his executive counterpart in the United States, the prime minister concurrently holds a legislative seat in the House of Commons as a member of Parliament and—with his Cabinet—is formally responsible and accountable to the House of Commons for his actions and tenure. In addition, the prime minister's term cannot exceed a five-year limit without new elections. The prime minister's tenure, moreover, is predicated on maintaining majority parliamentary support as a necessary mandate for his continued incumbency. While the prime minister's role as a member of Parliament overlaps and intertwines in a parliamentary system, the roles of head of government and head of state are divided and are performed by two separate individuals in Britain (i.e., the prime minister and the monarch, respectively).

☞ Drill: Structural Comparison between the American and British Constitutions

> **DIRECTIONS:** Carefully read and answer each of the following questions which are based on the information which you have just read.

1.   The British Constitution is similar to the American Constitution because it

   (A)   is completely written.

   (B)   incorporates the principle of judicial review.

   (C)   has a specific date of origin.

(D)   has flexibility that takes changing values into account.

(E)   has a formal and elaborate amendment procedure.

2.   The British Constitution was originated by

(A)   a constitutional assembly.

(B)   a revolutionary document.

(C)   an evolutionary process.

(D)   an act of Parliament.

(E)   a national referendum.

3.   All of the following are elements of the British Constitution EXCEPT

(A)   the monarch's emergency decree powers.

(B)   historical documents.

(C)   unwritten customs and traditions.

(D)   common law principles.

(E)   statutes of Parliament.

4.   If the British Constitution contained an analogue to the American Constitution's Tenth Amendment—which provides for reserved powers to the states—Britain would have a

(A)   republican system.   (D)   unitary system.

(B)   confederal system.   (E)   federal system.

(C)   presidential system.

5.   Which of the following terms most accurately describes Britain's Constitutional structure?

(A)   Unitary parliamentary monarchy

(B)   Federal presidential monarchy

(C)   Unitary presidential monarchy

(D)   Federal parliamentary monarchy

(E)   Republican parliamentary monarchy

6. Which statement most accurately describes why Britain is a monarchy?

   (A) The head of state is elected.

   (B) The head of state is hereditary.

   (C) The head of government is hereditary.

   (D) The head of government is appointed.

   (E) Both the head of government and the head of state are elected.

7. The British Constitution's fusion of powers is characterized by all of the following statements EXCEPT

   (A) the prime minister exclusively serves in the legislative branch as a member of Parliament.

   (B) if the prime minister loses majority parliamentary support, the prime minister must tender his resignation.

   (C) the legislative and executive branches overlap by virtue of the dual roles played by the prime minister.

   (D) the prime minister cannot effectively govern if he/she can no longer command majority support in the House of Commons.

   (E) the prime minister and the Cabinet demonstrate collective responsibility and accountability to the House of Commons.

8. In Britain's parliamentary system

   (A) there is a separation of powers.

   (B) the prime minister has a statutory four-year term.

   (C) the head of government is formally accountable to the judicial branch.

   (D) the head of government and head of state roles are performed by the same person.

   (E) None of the above.

Political Structures and Features

The Executive (Monarch and Prime Minister)

In Britain, the executive consists of two separate individuals—the monarch, who is the hereditary head of state and the prime minister, who is the elected *de facto* head of government.

The monarch has been limited to performing ceremonial, symbolic, and nominal *pro forma* functions. The monarch opens sessions of Parliament, accepts the resignations of incumbent prime ministers and cabinets that no longer have a parliamentary mandate, and "invites" the designated majority party leader from the House of Commons (the dominant house of the British Parliament) to form a new government. Reconciled to its present-day limited and decorative role, the British monarch presides rather than rules, acquiesces to the sovereign will of Parliament, affixes the Royal Assent to every parliamentary act (since 1707), provides a symbol of national unity, and perpetuates the continuity of the state.

Since 1902, the prime minister has traditionally been selected by the monarch from the majority party in the House of Commons. The prime minister and Cabinet collectively exercise the head of government functions. They formulate and attempt to enact a party program that generally receives parliamentary approval due to majority party cohesiveness and discipline. Both prime minister and Cabinet must maintain a parliamentary majority in the House of Commons as a mandate for continued rule. Parliamentary elections for the House of Commons must be held within a five-year period—therefore, prime ministers have a statutory limit of up to five years before their tenure must be renewed by legislative mandate (elections). More frequently than not, future prime ministers have obtained some earlier experience in other "inner Cabinet" positions, such as Home Secretary, Foreign Secretary, Defense Minister, or Secretary of the Exchequer. Opposition parties have their own parallel "Shadow Cabinets" from which to draw future prime ministers and other cabinet members.

The Legislature (House of Commons and House of Lords)

Britain has a bicameral legislature consisting of the House of Commons (the lower house) and the House of Lords (the upper house).

In the 1987 elections, the House of Commons consisted of 650 members who were elected from 650 single-member districts, known as parliamentary boroughs. The majority that controls the House of Commons generally guarantees that government bills will be given top legislative priority, thus virtually assuring their passage. Over the years, the House of Commons has become the dominant chamber of the British Parliament, exercising the sovereign will of the British people. In fact, the House of Lords is virtually powerless to prevent the House of Commons from enacting a bill into law and can only suggest amendments. Because of its electoral roots and the statutory restrictions placed upon the House of Lords, through the Parliament Acts of 1911 and 1949, the House of Commons has truly become the centerpiece of the British political system.

The House of Lords is today relegated to a secondary role in the legislative process. By far the weaker chamber, the House of Lords essentially fulfills an advisory and consultative function. Consisting of over 1,000 peers, the House of Lords includes both *hereditary peers,* who hold their seats by hereditary right and who can transmit their peerages to their offspring, and *life peers,* who by virtue of achievement or merit hold their non transferable peerages just for their own lifetime. Other than examining and revising bills from the House of Commons, or urging fuller discussion before acting too hastily on controversial legislation, the House of Lords' most prestigious role is that of representing the highest appellate court in Britain, under the tutelage of specially appointed "Law Lords" and the Lord Chancellor.

Political Parties and Voting

Britain has traditionally had a competitive two-party system—currently, the Conservative (or Tory) Party and the Labour Party. Yet trends indicate that the hold of the two parties has been eroded somewhat by the recent growth of the Social and Liberal Democratic Party (SLDP), or the Alliance, as it is sometimes known, and by the existence of various regional parties in Northern Ireland, Scotland, and Wales. Multi-party competition at the parliamentary borough level suggests that the traditional two-party model is in the process of evolution.

The electoral system has exerted a powerful and continuing influence in shaping the traditional two-party model. Britain's single member district (SMD) electoral system, based on the "winner takes all" principle, has greatly advantaged the Conservative and Labour Parties in the allocation of seats in the House of Commons, while disadvantaging newer, less well-established or regional parties. The way this principle works is that a single party candidate for each parliamentary borough must be chosen by either a majority or a plurality vote. Seats in the House of Commons, in other words, are not distributed by proportional representation in accordance with the percentage of the national vote each party wins. Given the entrenched positions of the two major parties, the SMD system has thus tended to perpetuate the viability of the two major parties, much to the chagrin and distress of their challengers.

Recent Events (1992–1996)

In April 1992, some sixteen months after taking over the government from Margaret Thatcher in November 1990, John Major was given a narrow mandate in his own right to continue as the next prime minister. Winning the fourth consecutive election since 1979, the Conservatives (Tories) defied the political pundits by winning 336 seats out of the 651-seat House of Commons. However, with a reduced parliamentary majority needed to govern, the Conservatives seemingly had just enough of a cushion in the short term to ensure passage of the government's program, if party discipline and attendance on crucial roll call votes were enforced by the party whips. Whether the slim Conservative majority would prove viable for the next five years, however, was open to conjecture.

By 1995, the opposition Labour Party, now headed by Tony Blair (who replaced twice-defeated PM candidate Neil Kinnock), was enjoying a double-digit lead over the Conservatives in the public opinion polls. Capitalizing on voters' fears of unemployment (despite low inflation and a recovering economy), and Conservative Party vacillation on closer links to European union, the Labour Party proposed a radical series of constitutional reforms. Included in this program was the need to have a specific written bill of rights, elected assemblies for Scotland and Wales, decentralization (devolution) of power to England's regions, more freedom for local government, reform of the House of Lords, and a referendum to revise the current SMD electoral system of parliamentary representation. With a shrinking majority between 1992 and 1995, due to over a half-dozen Conservative MP deaths and growing Conservative defections, by November 1996 the Conservatives had only a razor-thin majority of one seat. While special elections for the vacant seats were and are possible, the Conservatives had not won a special election in seven years. While the Conservatives could still govern in conjunction with smaller parties to enact legislation, John Major's political future was becoming increasingly tenuous. Beset by a serious challenge to his personal and party leadership, the British electorate would have the final say regarding the next House of Commons elections before the mandatory May 22, 1997, deadline.

Another recurrent issue that refuses to go away is the issue of Scottish nationalism. While the Scottish Nationalist Party's membership in the House of Commons dropped from five seats to three after the 1992 elections, Scotland's desire for an independently elected parliament in Edinburgh went unabated. Eschewing violence to revise the union of England and Scotland (and the merging of their parliaments in 1707), Scotland has insistently called for increasing autonomy and home rule from the highly centralized government in London. No doubt Scotland's North Sea oil and gas resources, coal, water, and a well-developed finance and insurance sector have given the Scots a renewed sense of self-confidence. Nevertheless, despite an increasing formula to disburse more government expenditures to service the needs of Scotland in 1993, many Scots were intrigued and supportive of the Labour Party's proposal of "devolution."

This pledge would provide for a referendum within a year after the general election in which the Scots would be able to decide whether they wanted a parliament of their own and whether it would have taxation powers. While falling short of the full independence desired by some, it would be a meaningful first step toward autonomous self-rule. Obviously, the outcome of the next general election, regarding a Conservative or Labour victory, would have a direct bearing upon the Scottish issue.

On March 13, 1996, the conscience of Britain was rudely shocked when a deranged killer entered a primary school in Dunblane, Scotland, with four licensed handguns and slaughtered sixteen children, a teacher, and then himself. The impact of this heinous crime reverberated with numerous outcries for Draconian restrictions on ownership of handguns in Britain. Without a written constitution or a specific bill of rights elevating the ownership of a handgun to the level of a civil right, the British had ended unlicensed gun ownership in 1920. Nonetheless, as a result of this brutal massacre, the government of John Major initiated legislative proposals that would severely infringe upon the owners of Britain's 200,000 legally licensed handguns, as well as its 2,118 gun clubs.

Calling for the destruction of some 80 percent of these weapons (with the exception of .22 caliber pistols), the pending legislation would give Britain some of the toughest gun control laws in the world. With a relatively small gun lobby led by the British Shooting Sports Council (unlike the potent and financially formidable National Rifle Association in the United States), and given the increasing number of people who were killed in handgun-related deaths (e.g., 33 in 1992 to 77 in 1994), the British response to the Dunblane tragedy reflected quite a different gun subculture than that evinced by their American counterparts. Undoubtedly, with national indignation against gun violence cresting, the passage of some type of restrictive legislation is all but assured.

Probably the issue that has been most resistant to solution has been the unending and sporadic violence in Northern Ireland. Established by the Government of Ireland Act in 1920, the six Protestant-dominated Northern Counties, commonly referred to as Ulster, have posed a difficult and insoluble problem for Britain. Having the only regional parliament and home rule in the United Kingdom (in addition to its formal inclusion in the British Parliament in London), Northern Ireland has remained in turmoil. Periodic violence, for example, broke a cease-fire accord established in 1994 when a series of bombings in Britain and at a British Army base in Northern Ireland occurred in 1996. Holding the Irish Republican Army (IRA) responsible for a variety of terrorist acts, the government of John Major refused to permit Sinn Fein (the political wing of the predominantly Catholic IRA) to participate in the ongoing peace talks in Belfast unless the IRA resumed the cease-fire. Conversely, the IRA indicated there would be no cease-fire until it was allowed to send representatives to the June 10, 1996, all-party peace talks. Seemingly at an impasse, peace talks began with the British and Irish governments and all major political parties from Ulster with the notable exception of Sinn Fein. By excluding Sinn Fein, which had long fought to end British rule in Northern Ireland, and despite mediation efforts by former U.S. Senator George Mitchell, the long-term prospects for creating a comprehensive and effective peace in Northern Ireland were not bright.

Economy and Economic Union

The British economy has experienced a significant recovery under the Tory government of John Major since 1992. Yet, in spite of reducing the number of unemployed from 2.7 million in 1992 to about 2 million by the end of 1996, British workers still expressed a disturbing degree of job insecurity. Downsizing of corporate operations, eliminating job redundancy, increasing the number of part-time jobs, and reducing out-of-work benefits, no doubt, contributed to this insecure state of mind. The policies of the chancellor of the exchequer (Kenneth Clarke), however, have helped to keep Britain's rate of inflation in the 3 percent range during the 1995–1996 period. In the final analysis, John Major's government could take a large measure of credit for the improved performance of Britain's rebounding economy.

One of the greatest difficulties encountered by John Major's government, however, is Britain's somewhat less than convincing commitment to join the Economic and Monetary Union (EMU). Such a commitment would necessarily involve accepting a single European currency called the "euro." Major's Tory Party, in fact, has been split by a faction called "Euroskeptics" who are vehemently opposed to efforts to control British fiscal policy, even if Britain's pound sterling remains outside the single currency. Major has not yet forcefully asserted whether the Tories would make those necessary economic changes in the next five years to conform to the "Euro" if the Tories were to win the next House of Commons election in 1997. Thus, because of formidable internal dissension within his own party, the intentions of John Major (or any PM successor) remain somewhat shrouded with ambiguity.

☞ Drill: Political Structures and Features

> **DIRECTIONS:** Carefully read and answer each of the following questions which are based on the information which you have just read.

9.   The British monarch

    (A)   is the head of government.

    (B)   is elected.

    (C)   initiates legislation by introducing bills.

    (D)   performs ceremonial, symbolic, and nominal functions.

    (E)   can exercise emergency decree powers.

10. The British monarch performs all of the following functions EXCEPT

    (A) presides over Cabinet meetings.

    (B) affixes the Royal Assent to parliamentary legislation.

    (C) opens sessions of Parliament.

    (D) formally selects the prime minister from the majority party.

    (E) accepts resignations of prime ministers and cabinets.

11. Since the turn of the twentieth century, prime ministers have generally been selected from

    (A) Whitehall.   (D) the House of Commons.

    (B) the House of Lords.   (E) the Privy Council.

    (C) the Law Lords.

12. The concept of *collective responsibility* is best defined by the relationship between

    (A) the monarch and the prime minister.

    (B) the Law Lords and the prime minister.

    (C) the prime minister and the Cabinet.

    (D) the Lord Chancellor and the monarch.

    (E) None of the above.

13. The tenure of a prime minister and Cabinet cannot exceed what period of time before parliamentary elections must be held for the House of Commons?

    (A) Three years   (D) Six years

    (B) Four years   (E) Seven years

    (C) Five years

14. Incumbent prime ministers generally succeed in having their legislative programs and agendas enacted because of

    (A) majority party cohesiveness and discipline.

    (B) the use of mass media.

(C)   their personal popularity and charisma.

(D)   minority party cooperation.

(E)   appeals by the monarch for parliamentary unity.

15.   The "Shadow Cabinet" refers to

(A)   the prime minister's most important advisors.

(B)   members of the prime minister's Cabinet who hold less powerful or less prestigious portfolios.

(C)   alternate members or stand-ins representing the majority party's "inner Cabinet."

(D)   sub-ministerial positions in the Cabinet.

(E)   the Honorable Opposition's alternate Cabinet.

16.   All of the following statements about the British Parliament are true EXCEPT

(A)   it is bicameral.

(B)   the House of Lords is the less democratic and weaker of the two chambers in Parliament.

(C)   the House of Commons is larger in size than the House of Lords.

(D)   the House of Lords is basically a consultative and advisory body.

(E)   members in the House of Commons are elected from single member districts.

17.   Top legislative priority is generally given to

(A)   Private Bills.   (D)   Government Bills.

(B)   Money Bills.   (E)   Bills of Particulars.

(C)   Bills of Attainder.

18.   The effects of the Parliament Acts of 1911 and 1949 have been to

(A)   enhance the role of the monarch.

(B)   weaken the role of the monarch.

(C)   enhance the power of the House of Lords.

    (D)   weaken the power of the House of Lords.

    (E)   weaken the power of the prime minister.

19.   The most substantive role played by the House of Lords involves

    (A)   the ability to veto legislative bills.

    (B)   appointing the prime minister and Cabinet.

    (C)   granting life peerages.

    (D)   exercising the power of judicial review.

    (E)   acting as Britain's highest appellate court.

20.   Membership in the House of Lords

    (A)   is fixed in number.

    (B)   involves both hereditary and life peerages.

    (C)   is limited to renewable five-year terms.

    (D)   only includes titled nobility.

    (E)   is permanent and cannot be renounced.

21.   Britain's *traditional* political party system generally corresponds to a

    (A)   competitive two-party system.

    (B)   dominant one-party system.

    (C)   totalitarian elitist one-party system.

    (D)   multi-party system.

    (E)   noncompetitive two-party system.

22.   The newest and most important national party that has emerged in Britain is the

    (A)   Labour Party.   (D)   Social and Liberal Democratic Party.

    (B)   Environmental Party.   (E)   Conservative Party.

    (C)   Socialist Party.

23. The SMD system used to elect members to the House of Commons by a majority or plurality vote in each electoral district

    (A) tends to favor regional parties.

    (B) tends to encourage the growth of multiple parties.

    (C) proportionally allocates the distribution of legislative seats in the House of Commons.

    (D) aids and abets the development of totalitarian parties.

    (E) promotes and strengthens the two-party model.

France

The Origins of the Fifth Republic: The Imprint of Charles de Gaulle

The Fifth Republic was created on the discredited ruins of the Fourth Republic (1946-1958). France under the Fourth Republic was characterized by enormous parliamentary instability and governmental crisis. The twenty-one premiers and cabinets, averaging a life span of six to seven months saw the National Assembly all too often paralyzed and ineffectual. These "revolving door" governments were perpetuated, in part, by a multi-party system based upon proportional representation. Unable to rule with a clear consensus and direction, France muddled through one domestic crisis after another until the Fourth Republic ultimately foundered on two foreign policy issues: the humiliating defeat and withdrawal from the French-Indo-China War in 1954, and the divisive War for Algerian Independence (1954-1962).

Coming to the rescue of an ailing and politically dysfunctional France was Le Grand Charles (Charles de Gaulle), a man whose legendary reputation and exploits as the irrepressible leader of the Free French during World War II had preceded him. Draping himself in the French tricolor (the national flag) and committing himself to restoring *la gloire* of France, General de Gaulle promised to recapture the lost greatness of the French nation. While de Gaulle appealed to the ethnic pride of the French people, he also demanded that they accept his peculiar brand of leadership on his own terms—a new constitution and form of government. The "de Gaulle Constitution" of 1958 was submitted to a national referendum in September 1958 and was overwhelmingly approved. The Fifth Republic was born!

☞ Drill: The Origins of the Fifth Republic: The Imprint of Charles de Gaulle

> **DIRECTIONS:** Carefully read and answer each of the following questions which are based on the information which you have just read.

24. The Fourth Republic exhibited all of the following features EXCEPT

    (A) It was often afflicted by political paralysis and indecision.

    (B) It had frequent "revolving door" governments.

    (C) It was generally more successful in resolving domestic rather than foreign issues.

    (D) It had a multi-party system based on single member district representation.

    (E) The French-Indo-China War and the War for Algerian Independence were two of its most bitter failures.

25. The Fifth Republic was the product of

    (A) the inspiration and leadership of Charles de Gaulle.

    (B) an attempt to restore France's greatness.

    (C) a nationalistic appeal to the French people.

    (D) a weary electorate disillusioned with the inadequacies of the Fourth Republic.

    (E) All of the above.

26. The Fifth Republic became a reality when

    (A) riots and popular discontent forced the involuntary expiration of the Fourth Republic.

    (B) a de Gaulle-inspired constitution was submitted to a national referendum and approved.

    (C) de Gaulle imposed a new constitution by fiat.

    (D) a *coup d'état* overthrew the Fourth Republic.

    (E) the Communists abandoned their opposition and formed a National Front Government.

Political Structures and Features

The Executive (President and Prime Minister)

The Fifth Republic's Constitution of 1958 created a mixed, or hybrid, presidential-parliamentary form of government. Completely eliminating the Fourth Republic's parliamentary dominance of a weak president, the Fifth Republic invested formidable power and authority in the hands of the president. Accordingly, the power upon the president, with the subsequent diminution of the role of the prime minister, marked one of the most significant changes between the Fourth and Fifth Republics.

The "dual executive" was theoretically maintained with the head of state role played by the president. A figurehead in most parliamentary systems, the president emerged by constitutional design as the dominant political force in the Fifth Republic. Popularly elected to unlimited, renewable seven-year terms, the president was endowed with an impressive array of powers that most heads of state could only envy. In addition, the president was constitutionally empowered to be the guarantor and protector of the Constitution, national independence, and the territorial integrity of France (Article 5), to appoint the prime minister (Article 8), to reside over the Cabinet and the Council of Ministers (Article 9), to call for national referendum (Article 11), and to dissolve the National Assembly and arrange for new elections after "consulting" with the prime minister and the presiding officers of the National Assembly and Senate (Article 12). Moreover, the president was also the commander-in-chief (Article 15), could assume emergency decree authority to deal with national crises or emergencies (Article 16), and could exercise the right to pardon (Article 17). Finally, the president was also provided with a wide range of appointment powers and authority over foreign affairs and defense, including the ability to negotiate and ratify treaties. In sum, the French president was to assume extraordinary constitutional power that was to dwarf the role played by his constitutional "junior partner," the prime minister.

While the president of France (head of state) reflects a separation of powers due to his electorally independent position, the prime minister (head of government) mirrors the more conventional parliamentary model of fusion of powers and legislative accountability. The prime minister, who is appointed by the president from the majority party or coalition, nominates his Council of Ministers (Cabinet), which in turn is appointed by the president. Clearly playing a subordinate role in this dual executive, the prime minister's main function is to direct and manage the operation of the government, which must sustain a working majority in the National Assembly to be effective. Subject to legislative accountability and censure, the prime minister and his Council of Ministers can only be overturned by an absolute majority of the National Assembly, or be outmaneuvered by the powerful president. Thus, the prime minister and Cabinet are politically vulnerable in two ways. Finally, the fusion of powers, a characteristic of most parliamentary models, is strictly forbidden by the "incompatibility rule" (Article 23); this rule prohibits cabinet ministers from holding concurrent seats in Parliament. This last feature closely corresponds to the separation of powers principle found in presidential systems; consequently, the combination of both presidential and parliamentary elements is reflected by the duality of the French executive.

The Legislature (National Assembly and Senate)

The French Parliament is a bicameral legislature composed of the National Assembly (the lower house) and the Senate (the upper house). The parliament is dominated by the executive branch in a number of ways. The prime minister and Council of Ministers (henceforth collectively referred to as the government) initiate the legislative process and provide the conduit between the president and the parliament. Moreover, the Legislature is restricted from either increasing or decreasing the government's budget and is also confined to legislating matters that are specifically delegated to it. If the National Assembly becomes too independent or obstructionist, it faces the ultimate sanction of presidential dissolution—or possibly even emergency decree legislation. The government also sets the legislative agenda in the National Assembly, where government bills (known as Law Projects) have priority over private bills (known as Law Proposals). While the National Assembly has the ultimate right to censure and overturn the government by an absolute majority, it is often reluctant to do so for fear of incurring the wrath of the president. This subservience of the parliament to the executive clearly represents another distinct feature that delineates the Fifth Republic from its predecessor.

As of the 1988 elections, the National Assembly consisted of 577 members—555 members from France and 22 from overseas departments and territories. Originally, the members of the National Assembly were elected from single member districts with a two-ballot system. Deputies could be elected by a simple majority on the first ballot. Failing a majority, a plurality sufficed on the second ballot. This method of selection was temporarily suspended in 1985—for the 1986 National Assembly elections—with the proviso that no party could enter a candidate on the second ballot unless it had won at least 12.5% of the vote on the first ballot. This change was significant because it disadvantaged some minor or fringe parties, such as the xenophobic National Front.

Barring a dissolution, the National Assembly deputies serve a term not to exceed five years. While not allowed to establish its own legislative agenda, the Constitution does allow the National Assembly to enact legislation on its own accord in such areas as civil rights and liberties, declarations of war, the penal code, amnesty, issuance of currency, nationalization and privatization of property, and electoral procedures. Thus, while the National Assembly is circumscribed and limited in many ways, it is the more powerful of the two chambers in the French Parliament.

The Senate, much like its British counterpart, the House of Lords, is a much weaker chamber. The Senate consists of 319 members, with 296 seats allocated to France, 13 seats to the overseas departments and territories, and 10 seats to French nationals abroad. Senators serve nine-year terms, with one-third of the Senate indirectly elected by an electoral college at three-year intervals. Since the government, which is not formally accountable to the Senate, can easily bypass the Senate in the legislative process merely by asking the National Assembly to pass a bill by a simple majority vote, the Senate has been perceived by many as nothing more than a redundant or vestigial body. In fact, the Senate has little substantive power other than delaying legislation being considered by the National Assembly.

The Constitutional Council

Another distinctive feature of the Fifth Republic is the creation of the Constitutional Council. This quasi-judicial body is designed to be a constitutional arbiter—that is, to establish the appropriate parameters of executive and legislative competence. Where conflict or overlap might occur, the Constitutional Council's purpose was to clarify jurisdiction and exercise a form of judicial review regarding the constitutionality of laws passed by Parliament. The Constitutional Council consists of nine regular members or judges, three chosen by the president, three by the President of the National Assembly, and three by the President of the Senate. The judges serve nine-year terms. In addition, all former presidents of the Republic are *ex-officio* members for life. Among the functions the Constitutional Council fulfills, beyond its power to determine whether laws and treaties are in conformity with the Constitution, are validating presidential and legislative elections, monitoring the referendum procedure, and being "consulted" before the president can invoke emergency decree legislation. In sum, the Constitutional Council plays a valuable conciliatory role in resolving government-president-parliament conflict.

Political Parties

France today has a multi-party political system; consequently, it has been difficult for any one single party to clearly dominate the Parliament. Initially adopting the single member district with two-ballot system, the political party system has stabilized into a left-of-center bloc (Socialist Party and Communist Party) and a bourgeois or right-of-center bloc (Rally for the Republic, Union for French Democracy, and National Front). After flirting with proportional representation for the 1986 National Assembly elections because it gave the Socialists a short-lived tactical advantage, the Fifth Republic soon re-adopted its original SMD with a two-ballot format for the 1988 National Assembly elections.

The French political scene currently encompasses the following five major political groups:

1) The Socialist Party (PS) advocates nationalization of key industries, promotes social welfare programs, and draws most of its support from labor and trade unions;

2) The Rally for the Republic (RPR) is the neo-Gaullist party, moderately committed to the ideals and nationalism of the late President Charles de Gaulle, is generally right-of-center, and draws most of its support from the middle and upper classes and the rural areas;

3) The Union for French Democracy (UDF), a loose confederation of centrist parties formed in 1978, is conservative in outlook, and receives most of its electoral support from the urban middle classes;

4) The Communist Party (PCF), drawing its support from labor, the trade union movement, and local governments, has traditionally espoused a nationalistic brand of democratic Euro-Communism (despite its support of the Soviet CPSU), opposes French membership in NATO and European integration, and promotes closer relations with the Communist-bloc countries (N.B. With the rapid demise of the Soviet Union and its Communist-bloc satellites, the PCF has undergone major ideological and programmatic revision); and

5) The National Front (FN), an ultra-conservative, rabidly nationalistic political movement, drawing its strength from the urban working class, that seeks to expel immigrants (particularly North African Arabs), rejects all forms of socialism, and supports popular capitalism.

Recent Events (1992–1996)

On March 21, 1993, some 26 million French voters cast ballots for the 577 seats of the lower house of the French Parliament, the National Assembly. In a somewhat complicated SMD + two-ballot election, involving a majority and/or plurality process, candidates who won their district by more than 50 percent of the registered vote won the seat outright, but if they fell short of a majority only those candidates who received more than 12.5 percent on the first round were eligible to run on the second round. As a result of this winnowing process that eliminated narrow, ephemeral, or frivolous parties, generally only the larger traditional parties benefited. A week later on the second round, with a reduced playing field, either a majority or plurality vote (i.e., usually a unified or jointly endorsed candidate) sufficed to decide the outcome for the remaining electoral districts.

The final returns of the National Assembly elections resulted in a calamitous defeat for the Socialists. The Socialist Party, which controlled the presidency and the National Assembly between 1981 and 1986, had suffered a setback in the 1986–1988 period of "cohabitation" (where the Socialist president had to work with a conservative-controlled National Assembly) but had regained a temporary dominance between 1988 and 1993. The 1993 elections, however, renewed the possibility of a lame-duck cohabitation period between the ailing 76-year-old Socialist President François Mitterrand (who indicated his intention to retire at the end of his term in 1995 and died in 1996) and the opposition-controlled National Assembly. Undoubtedly, the electoral defeat of the Socialists would significantly presage the views of the French electorate for the 1995 presidential elections.

The 1993 winning conservative coalition, called the Union for France, consisted of the Rally for the Republic (RPR), the Union for French Democracy (UDF), and several other conservative allies. While winning approximately 40 percent of the vote in the first round, the conservative coalition ended up winning 84 percent of the seats in the National Assembly (487 out of 577), the largest parliamentary majority enjoyed by any political group since 1815.

In retrospect, the disastrous showing of the Socialists in the 1993 elections reflected the growing dissatisfaction of the French electorate with rising unemployment (over 12 percent), embarrassing corruption scandals, and a relatively stagnant economy. Furthermore, a low voter turnout of 69 percent of the 37.5 million eligible voters who cast ballots provided yet another indication of growing political alienation. Besides the Socialist Party's debacle, Jean-Marie Le Pen's extreme rightist National Front disappeared into political oblivion, while the environmental alliance between the Greens and the Ecology Generation yielded no tangible results. Additionally, several prominent presidential hopefuls, such as former Socialist Prime Minister Michel Rocard, had their presidential ambitions dashed when they failed to win or hold on to their electoral districts. Understandably, the peculiarities of the SMD + two-ballot system, which inherently enhanced the electoral chances of the dominant parties, resurrected complaints from the Socialist, Communist, and National Front leaders to reintroduce proportionality in the voting system in order to make the National Assembly more reflective of the national mandate. Nonetheless, when all was said and done, the indisputable fact was that the Socialist honeymoon was over.

In 1995, two years after the sweeping conservative victory in the National Assembly elections, the French electorate returned to the polls to find a successor to replace President Mitterrand for the ensuing seven years. In the first round on April 23, 1995, various candidates, representing the whole political spectrum, contested the presidency. Needing to win a majority on the first round to be elected outright, none of the candidates was able to do so. The fragmented vote meant that only the top two presidential contenders in the first round would be eligible to run in the runoff round two weeks later. The results of the first round reflected the following breakdown:

1995 PRESIDENTIAL ELECTIONS

Candidate	Party	Percent
Lionel Jospin	Socialist	23.2
Jacques Chirac	RPR	20.6
Edouard Balladur	RPR	18.5
Jean-Marie Le Pen	National Front	15.1
Others		22.6
Total		100.0

The second-round runoff on May 7, 1995, involved a major realignment of the political forces and *ad hoc* alliances. In the interval between the two rounds, much like the parliamentary elections for the National Assembly, the fractured right-of-center bloc for Chirac and Balladur coalesced around Jacques Chirac, the mayor of Paris and former two-time prime minister. Meanwhile, the left-of-center bloc of Socialists, Communists, and Environmentalists rallied around the candidacy of the former Socialist education minister, Lionel Jospin.

On Jacques Chirac's third try for the presidency, the proved victorious, winning 52 percent of the vote to Jospin's 48 percent. Promising to reduce France's 12.2 percent unemployment rate, Chirac indicated his intention to introduce a package of measures to encourage the private sector to hire additional workers, as well as to implement cuts in heavy business taxes as a means to accomplish this. Moreover, he suggested that he would continue the privatization policies of former Prime Minister Balladur and sell off state-owned enterprises, a position consistent with the Conservative stance on the centrality of the free enterprise principle.

After the election, and within a short period of time, Chirac's well-paved intentions led to increasing ambiguities about his economic policies. His new prime minister (the former foreign minister), Alain Juppé, was placed in the unenviable position of trying to reconcile reducing the budget, creating jobs, and strengthening the franc all at the same time, a seemingly impossible task. Contradicting President Chirac's earlier campaign promise to reduce France's tax burden with a big but "temporary" tax rise, and attempting to cut government spending on social welfare from 5 percent of the GDP (1995) to 3 percent in 1997, in conformity with the conditions set by the Economic and Monetary Union, Juppé's policies created a maelstrom. As a result of the foregoing and faced with the prospect of reduced public spending, the French public sector unions (which were threatened with increasing layoffs, a loss of job prerequisites, and expanded workweeks) responded by staging their largest 24-hour strike in a decade on October 10, 1995. In short, the tugs and pulls of the domestic economy and the commitment of France to join the Economic and Monetary Union as part of an integrated Europe seemed to be at odds and incompatible in the near term. Nonetheless, President Chirac, for the moment, appeared adamant about France's intention to join the EMU by January 1, 1999. That goal for some remained a moot, if not an undesirable, option.

In the area of foreign affairs, some of Chirac's enigmatic policies have also caused controversy. In an era when the Cold War has been eclipsed, and in which the former Soviet Union no longer posed a direct threat to the security of Western Europe, Chirac announced his intention to resume nuclear testing in the Pacific to a chorus of protests by anti-nuclear coalitions and environmentalist groups, and particularly the Nordic bloc of Sweden, Finland, and Norway. In other areas, however, France demonstrated a more conventional role in foreign affairs as a leading power in Europe by assuming a responsibility to assist in the Bosnian Peacekeeping Force. And on June 8, 1996, thirty years after President de Gaulle unilaterally had pulled France out of NATO, Chirac announced that France would resume participation in that organization. Somewhat similar to France's inconsistent domestic policies involving the pragmatism of short-term national interest versus the long-term goal of European integration, Chirac's foreign policies also reflected a perplexing dichotomy. Zigzagging between France's need to assert its independence of action in foreign affairs and the compelling need to become an integral part of a united Europe has left Chirac, like his predecessors, to walk a find line in foreign affairs. Notwithstanding this ambivalence, it remains to be seen if Chirac can extricate France from this persistent and intractable identity quandary of sorting out and establishing which course will best serve the future of France's national self-interest.

☞ Drill: Political Structures and Features

> **DIRECTIONS:** Carefully read and answer each of the following questions which are based on the information which you have just read.

27. The Fifth Republic's Constitution of 1958 provided France with a

    (A) parliamentary system.

    (B) federal system.

    (C) confederal system.

    (D) mixed presidential-parliamentary system.

    (E) presidential system.

28. Unlike the Fourth Republic, the Fifth Republic conferred formidable powers on the

    (A) president.
    (B) National Assembly.
    (C) prime minister.
    (D) Council of Ministers.
    (E) Senate.

29. All of the following features characterize the French head of state EXCEPT

    (A) he is elected to serve a renewable seven-year term.

    (B) he insures the territorial integrity of the nation.

    (C) he nominates the Council of Ministers.

    (D) he is the guarantor and protector of national independence.

    (E) he is the Commander-in-Chief.

30. The president's formally assigned constitutional powers exclude the power to

    (A) call for a national referendum.

    (B) make important governmental and diplomatic appointments.

    (C) grant pardons.

    (D) negotiate and ratify treaties.

    (E) initiate, direct, and manage the legislative agenda of the government.

PEAK OF POWER

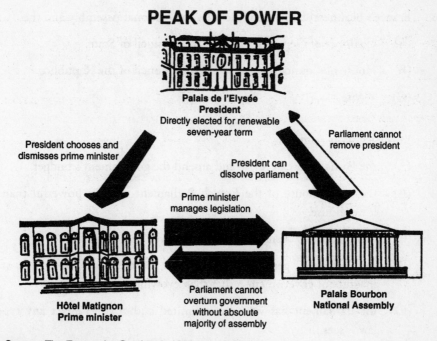

Source: *The Economist*, October 1, 1988, pp. 19-20, 22.

31. Which one of the following statements is inconsistent with the chart on the previous page?

(A) It is apparent that the president is formally accountable to the Parliament.

(B) The president seems to be a more powerful and secure figure than the prime minister.

(C) The prime minister and his Cabinet can be overturned by an absolute vote of the National Assembly.

(D) The president can probably exert influence over the National Assembly by threatening dissolution.

(E) The prime minister is selected and dismissed by the president.

32. One of the most controversial aspects of the president's power is his

(A) use of the item veto.

(B) power to declare laws unconstitutional.

(C) right to reject constitutional amendments.

(D) ability to invoke emergency decree authority.

(E) constitutional authority to outlaw totalitarian parties.

33. France's bicameral Parliament includes the National Assembly and the

(A) Chamber of Deputies.   (D) Council of State.

(B) House of Councillors.   (E) Council of the Republic.

(C) Senate.

34. In the legislative process

(A) the Parliament can revise and amend the government's budget.

(B) the upper house of the French Parliament is more powerful than the lower house.

(C) "law proposals" usually have priority over "law projects."

(D) the Parliament generally acquiesces to the initiative and agenda of the incumbent government rather than evolving its own.

(E) the Parliament has virtually unlimited authority to enact any type of law it sees fit.

35. Which of the following electoral systems has been used most often in the Fifth Republic to elect deputies to the National Assembly?

(A) Multiple member districts with one ballot

(B) Single member districts with two ballots

(C) Proportional representation using party lists

(D) Territorial representation based on departmental lists

(E) Indirectly through an electoral college

FIFTH REPUBLIC OF FRANCE
Recent National Assembly Elections

POLITICAL PARTY	1973	1978	1981	1986	1988
Rally for the Republic (RPR) Gaullists	183	154	85	150	128
Union for French Democracy (UDF) Centrists*	119	124	65	127	130
Socialist Party (PS) Leftist Radical Movement (MRG)	90	113	285	215	276
Communist Party (PCF)	73	86	44	35	27
Others**	26	14	12	50**	16
	(491)	(491)	(491)	(577)	(577)

*The UDF was formed in 1978 as a federation of the following centrist parties: Republican Party (Giscardiens), Center for Social Democrats, Movement of French Social Democrats, and the Radical Party.

**In the 1986 election this number included 33 seats won by the ostracized National Front (led by Jean-Marie Le Pen), an ultra-conservative right-wing party and 17 others from the Independents and "Diverse Right" (most of which supported the RPR/UDF coalition). In 1988 the RPR/UDF coalition lost its majority control to the Socialists who fell 13 seats short of an absolute majority. The National Front lost all but one of its seats in the National Assembly. The Socialist plurality attempted to govern through the formation of flexible coalitions—led by Michel Rocard, the Socialist prime minister.

36. Based on the above chart of recent National Assembly elections, how did the electoral system used in the 1988 National Assembly elections affect the outcome?

(A) It resulted in a Communist Party victory.

(B) The RPR/UDF formed a new majority party coalition.

(C) The National Front was all but eliminated as an effective political force.

(D) The Socialists won an absolute majority of the seats.

(E) The three smallest parties were able to form a viable coalition to govern.

37. France's upper house in Parliament

    (A) is a weak chamber with little substantive power.

    (B) is larger in size than the National Assembly.

    (C) is directly elected by the French people.

    (D) has renewable five-year terms for its members.

    (E) can effectively block bills approved by the National Assembly.

38. The Constitutional Council's main purpose is to

    (A) determine the appropriate grounds for presidential impeachment and removal.

    (B) act as the highest appellate court for criminal and civil cases.

    (C) formulate constitutional amendments.

    (D) protect and preserve fundamental civil liberties.

    (E) ascertain if the laws and treaties enacted by the Parliament and president are in conformity with the Constitution.

39. All of the following statements regarding the Constitutional Council are true EXCEPT

    (A) It can invoke emergency decree powers during times of national crisis.

    (B) All former presidents are lifetime members of the Constitutional Council.

    (C) There are nine regular members on the Constitutional Council who each serve nine-year terms.

    (D) It validates presidential and legislative elections.

    (E) It oversees national referenda.

40. France's political party system can best be described as a

    (A) competitive two-party system.

    (B) dominant one-party system.

    (C) system where the Church plays a major role.

    (D) multi-party system.

    (E) party system dominated by extremist parties on both the Right and Left.

41. Standing for the privatization of state enterprise and fearful of competing for jobs with foreigners in an economic downturn, which political party's platform does not conform to or represent French mainstream politics?

(A)   Socialist Party

(D)   Union for French Democracy

(B)   Rally for the Republic

(E)   Republican Party

(C)   National Front

The Former Soviet Union
(Commonwealth of Independent States)

The Ideological Origins and Foundations of the Soviet System

The official ideology of the Soviet Union for most of its legal existence (1917-1991) was the doctrine of Marxism-Leninism. The major tenets of Marxist thought and analysis formed the ideological foundation of the Soviet system, especially the concept of historical and dialectical materialism involving an antagonistic but inevitable class struggle in various stages of historical development. This theory postulated that society evolved through distinct historical stages: primitive communism, slavery, feudalism, capitalism, a transitional stage of socialism, and finally communism. The pre-communist stages of historical development were characterized by a dialectical struggle between adversarial classes, pitted against each other in bitter class warfare. But it was Lenin's theoretical and revisionist contributions that provided the quintessential nature of the Soviet regime. While Karl Marx laid the ideological foundation it remained for Vladimir Lenin, as the practitioner, to apply and revise Marxist ideology after the Bolsheviks seized power in 1917. Adapting to the political realities entailed in maintaining and consolidating power, Lenin made meaningful and pragmatic ideological revisions to cope with the practical problems and exigencies faced by the emergent Soviet state. As a result, the Leninist variant, refined and amended by Lenin's successors, in may ways distorted and contravened the true democratic and populist ideals of Marxism.

Lenin's significant ideological revisions of Marxism were:

1) The idea of a highly dedicated, disciplined, and organized cadre of professional revolutionaries. The pre-eminent role of a single, elitist political party, to act as the vanguard of the proletariat and to exercise an effective political monopoly over the course and direction of the

entire Soviet system, was to become a major element of Lenin's political creed. Thus was born an undemocratic, if not totalitarian, element in the political genesis of the Soviet state—the establishment of a single, elitist political party (later to be named the Communist Party of the Soviet Union or CPSU).

2) The principle of democratic centralism, which was to become a corner-stone of the hierarchical and organizational decision making of the Bolshevik Party/CPSU. Specifically designed to avoid factionalism and dissension, democratic centralism provided for a system of vertical decision making within the CPSU pyramid. For example, once decisions were made by higher bodies of the CPSU (the Politburo or Secretariat), these decisions were binding, authoritative, and obligatory upon all lower bodies of the party without reservation or evasion.

3) His theory of imperialism, regarding what happened to "overripe" capitalist states that were in the highest, or monopoly, stage of capitalism. According to Lenin, during the imperialistic stage of capitalism the bourgeoisie (the owners of the means of production) strives to maximize profits and seeks new markets, raw materials, and economic opportunities abroad to help subsidize the increasing oppression of the proletariat (the exploited and impoverished workers) at home. To accomplish this, the mother country exports imperialism and exploitation abroad by acquiring formal or informal empires (colonies, protectorates, spheres of influence, etc.). The headlong competition by the more developed capitalist states to acquire colonies, according to Lenin, would inevitably lead to increasing friction, economic rivalries, and ultimately to imperialist wars. Imperialism represented capitalism's last gasp to stave off the final day of reckoning, proletarian revolution.

4) His willingness to accept tactical flexibility as a method of achieving his final goals. Justifying the use of capitalist means to attain his ends, Lenin promoted the concept that short-term ideological contradictions were tolerable, and even permissible, if the long-term communist goals could be better served. Thus, Lenin's implementation of the New Economic Policy (1921-1924), a program that entailed a temporary retreat from the socialization of private property, allowed peasants to keep title to their land and to produce foodstuffs for a free market and for profit. This apparent contradiction of Marxist beliefs was justified by Lenin as a realistic means to avert famine and to enable the Bolsheviks to consolidate power. Lenin's tactical flexibility to preserve, protect, and defend Bolshevik power was clearly manifested as a fundamental feature of communist ideology.

Lenin's Theory of Uneven Development, otherwise known as the Theory of the Weakest Link, provided an additional theoretical contribution to the dogma of Marxism-Leninism. Revising Marx's notion that the class struggle in capitalism would culminate in a violent class upheaval and revolution first in the more advanced capitalist states (such as England or Germany), where the contradictions of the class struggle were more pronounced, Lenin offered a theoretical explanation why this upheaval occurred first in Russia, an agrarian nation in the early throes of industrialization. Lenin claimed that Russia's small industrial economic base (with its commensurately small, unorganized proletariat) was overburdened by famine, depression, and World War I. These factors exacerbated class divisions and led to an elevated class consciousness. This combination of events resulted in Russia becoming the "weakest link" in a long chain of capitalist nations. Thus, in spite of Marx's predictions, Lenin explained why Russia became the first, albeit most unlikely, capitalist nation to undergo a Marxist revolution.

Lenin was to become a revered revolutionary ideologue who adapted theory to practice. Faced with the practical circumstances of seizing power and rationalizing its use, Lenin redefined Marx's beliefs with his own unique analyses. In his effort to consolidate power and legitimize the existence of the Soviet state and the Bolshevik Party, Lenin revised Marxist ideology to conform to the idiosyncratic elements of the Russian experience.

☞ Drill: The Ideological Origins and Foundations of the Soviet System

DIRECTIONS: Carefully read and answer each of the following questions which are based on the information which you have just read.

42. The officially recognized ideology of the Soviet Union from 1917 until the Gorbachev era was

(A) Marxism.

(D) Marxism-Leninism.

(B) Evolutionary Socialism.

(E) Leninism-Stalinism.

(C) Leninism.

43. Marx

    (A) implemented his ideas in the Russian Revolution.

    (B) generally adhered to more undemocratic ideas than Lenin.

    (C) was the theoretician who provided an ideological foundation for Lenin's ideas.

    (D) was influenced by Lenin's concepts of the class struggle.

    (E) rejected the concept of historical materialism.

44. Lenin sought to

    (A) create a highly disciplined, organized, and elitist one-party system.

    (B) abolish all political parties.

    (C) develop a democratic multi-party system.

    (D) eliminate the pre-Revolution, pro-Tsarist parties.

    (E) emulate the traditional competitive two-party model of England.

45. Democratic centralism

    (A) inadvertently created factionalism and dissension within the Bolshevik Party/CPSU.

    (B) opened up the decision-making process to the grassroots level by increasing the role of primary party organizations.

    (C) was a Marxist concept rejected by Lenin.

    (D) promoted a more pluralistic decision-making process.

    (E) was a vertically-structured hierarchical decision-making process within the Bolshevik Party/CPSU.

46. According to Lenin, imperialism

    (A) occurred in the earliest stages of capitalist development.

    (B) inevitably led to international conflict and war.

    (C) resulted from the reduction of the class struggle at home.

    (D) was an outgrowth of "underripe" capitalism.

    (E) was the humane response of capitalism to the needs of the lesser developed countries.

47. The New Economic Policy (1921-1924)

    (A) was a pragmatic response reflecting Lenin's tactical flexibility.

    (B) demonstrated Lenin's ideological purity and devotion to Marxist principles.

    (C) accelerated the socialization of property.

    (D) was based upon Lenin's conviction that collectivization of private property should be totally abandoned.

    (E) reflected Lenin's adherence to the use of socialist means to achieve socialist ends.

48. Lenin's Theory of Uneven Development

    (A) supported Marx's prediction that proletarian revolution would occur first in a more developed and industrialized capitalist state.

    (B) suggested that England or Germany was more likely to have a proletarian revolution than Russia.

    (C) stated that with respect to its revolutionary potential, Russia was the weakest and most vulnerable of the capitalist nations undergoing industrialization.

    (D) justified why Russia's large industrial base and well-organized proletariat led to the outbreak of the Russian Revolution.

    (E) explained that class consciousness and proletarian discontent actually diminished during wartime because of increasing nationalism.

49. In the final analysis, Lenin

    (A) was a dogmatic theoretician adhering to Marxist orthodoxy.

    (B) was an impractical political reformer.

    (C) put ideological matters before practical concerns.

    (D) rejected Marx's ideas about dialectical materialism.

    (E) demonstrated a flexible approach to assure political self-preservation.

Political Structures and Features

During most of the Soviet Union's life span, its political system exhibited an intricate paralleling and interlocking relationship that reflected a dualism with the government, a virtual captive of the CPSU. In other words, the government was not an independent entity, but merely a vertical and horizontal extension of CPSU influence and control. Recognized by Article 6 of the Soviet Constitution of 1977 as the pre-eminent political institution of the Soviet system, the CPSU became the "leading and guiding force of Soviet society and the nucleus of its political system." The government, clearly the subordinate partner of this dichotomous relationship, was not directly operated or run by the CPSU per se, but was guided and led by the decisions emanating from the Politburo and Secretariat. Following the Leninist principle of democratic centralism, CPSU members at various levels in the government hierarchy took their cues and policy positions from the "party line." Also, since the CPSU effectively exercised a political monopoly to the exclusion of all other political parties, there was no formally organized political opposition to offer viable alternatives that could challenge the CPSU's hegemonic control. (The chart on p. 94 of CPSU/government structure not only illustrates the vertical hierarchy of power, but also indicates the collateral and horizontal penetration of the CPSU at every level of governmental authority.)

The Structure of Soviet Government (1977-1985)

From the foregoing, it could be construed that the governmental structures of the state were nothing more than cooperative instruments of the CPSU. Nonetheless, the government presented a separate structural hierarchy that reflected a conventional parliamentary model exemplified by many Western European systems. The special nature of the totalitarian elitist one-party system in the Soviet Union, however, reduced the traditional model to a sham. Without the existence of a formal or legal opposition, competitiveness within the parliamentary system was nonexistent. Hence, the constant need of a political party to cultivate and maintain majority support to govern effectively in parliamentary systems became a nonissue.

The center of the national government and the highest organ of the state was the bicameral Soviet parliament, the Supreme Soviet of the USSR. Composed of a 750-member lower chamber, the Soviet of the Union, and a 750-member upper chamber, the Soviet of Nationalities, the Supreme Soviet was elected for a five-year term. Among its other powers, the Supreme Soviet theoretically exercised exclusive legislative power, chose its executive branch of government (the Presidium of the Council of Ministers headed by the prime minister), selected judges to the Supreme Court of the Soviet Union, elected its own steering committee (the Presidium of the Supreme Soviet), and was empowered to amend the Soviet Constitution by a two-thirds vote.

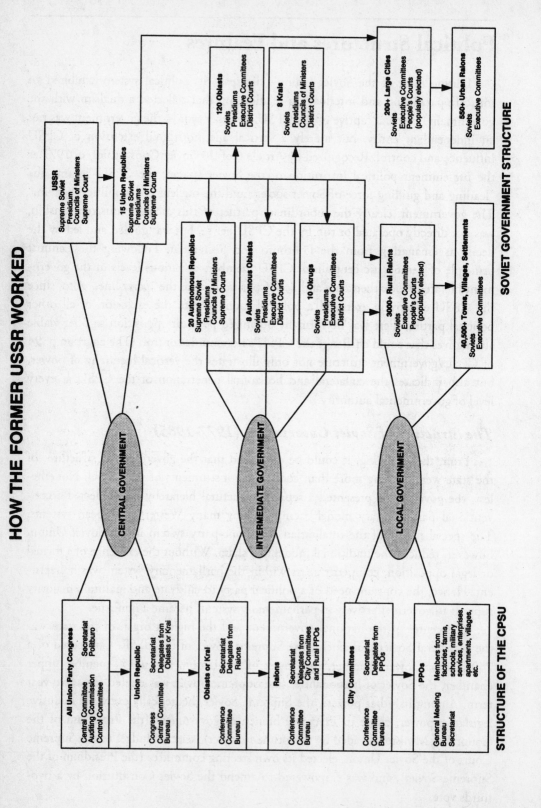

HOW THE FORMER USSR WORKED

SOVIET GOVERNMENT STRUCTURE

STRUCTURE OF THE CPSU

THE GOVERNMENT

The President

Elected by secret ballot of the Congress. There is a limit of two 5-year terms. President accountable to Congress and has broad powers.

Council of Ministers

Headed by the Prime Minister, the Council runs the government. Ministers must be approved by the Supreme Soviet.

Presidium

Headed by the President, the Presidium is a coordinating body including various vice-presidents and the chairman of the Supreme Soviet's committees and commissions.

Supreme Soviet

Formerly the nominal supreme legislative body, its 542 members are elected by Congress. The Supreme Soviet meets twice a year for 3 or 4 months at a time and considers all legislative and administrative issues.

Congress of People's Deputies

The new representative legislative body. It convenes annually for several days to rule on major issues. Of its 2,250 members, 1,500 were elected from territorial and national districts, 750 from "public organizations" such as the party and unions. The Supreme Soviet voted in October 1989 to abolish the seats reserved for such organizations in response to popular criticism of the practice as nondemocratic.

THE PARTY

The Politburo

Formerly the country's chief policymaking body, many of its decisions on policy (economic and nationalities, for example) and personnel (election or appointment of officials) have now been taken over by government institutions. Currently has 11 voting members, 8 nonvoting.

The Secretariat

Headed by the General Secretary assisted by a large permanent staff. The Secretariat used to run the day-to-day affairs of the former Soviet Union; its role was reduced by the reforms.

The Central Committee

Consists of about 230 members since Gorbachev's housecleaning in April 1989, in which 74 members "resigned." Meets twice a year to discuss and approve policies, and no longer serves to rubber-stamp Politburo decisions. It elects the Politburo and the Secretariat; Gorbachev used a special plenum in October 1989 to remove several opponents from the Politburo and to promote allies.

The Communist Party Congress

Theoretically the party's supreme policymaking body, consisting of delegates elected by party organizations around the former USSR. It meets once every 5 years. The Congress elects the Central Committee. In practice, the Congress has been another rubber-stamp body for the party leadership.

The Dismantling of the Soviet State: The Rise and Fall of Mikhail Gorbachev (1985-1991)

In 1985, when Mikhail Gorbachev became General Secretary of the CPSU, traditionally the most powerful political position in the Soviet Union, he set in motion a series of irreversible events that were to shake the Soviet system to its very foundations. With reformist zeal, Gorbachev attempted to resuscitate the Soviet Union's corrupt and ailing political and economic system, inherited from the long but stagnant Brezhnev tenure (1964-1982). Introducing such concepts and initiatives as *glasnost* (openness), *perestroika* (economic restructuring), and *demokratizatsia* (democratization), Gorbachev hoped to jump-start the economy and end the stultifying political cronyism typifying the moribund rule of Brezhnev.

In 1988, Gorbachev suggested a total revamping of the Soviet political system. Hoping to disconnect the CPSU apparatus from the higher levels of the government, Gorbachev proposed the creation of a new, more powerful government, with a new and more independent Soviet presidency. Accountable to a new "super" representative legislative body called the Congress of People's Deputies, the Soviet president would no longer play just a nominal or ceremonial role. He would be elected by a secret ballot of the Congress of People's Deputies for up to two five-year terms and would hold broad powers. (See chart, p. 95.) When the Congress of People's Deputies was not in session (it would meet only once per year), it would be represented by a smaller Supreme Soviet of 542 members (271 from each chamber) which would act as the Congress's steering body for up to eight months per year.

Between 1989 and 1991, Gorbachev dissolved the old Supreme Soviet altogether, replacing it with the Congress of People's Deputies and a new, but smaller, Supreme Soviet. Nevertheless, forces beyond Gorbachev's immediate control were causing the rapid disintegration of the Soviet Union and its political system. Despite the assertions of independence from Moscow made by the Baltic states of Estonia, Latvia, and Lithuania; ethnic violence and bloodshed in Azerbaijan and Armenia, and the reluctance of the CPSU to abrogate its constitutionally recognized monopoly on power and its "leading role" (Article 6), Gorbachev steadfastly attempted to salvage the beleaguered remnants of the Soviet Union and forge them into a loose federation of associated states, with a common currency and military. By mid-1991, Gorbachev had obtained the agreement of nine Soviet republics for a draft of a new union treaty, excluding the Baltic states, Moldavia, Georgia, and Armenia. This new political configuration proved to be stillborn, however, when events outstripped Gorbachev's ability to exercise control and direction over the accelerating disintegration of the Soviet Union. In a last-gasp effort, Communist hard-liners, who sought to prevent the realization of the new union treaty, placed Gorbachev under house arrest at his Crimean retreat and endeavored to impose Draconian means to restore the old order. The unsuccessful coup ironically led to Gorbachev's final demise as he became marginalized. Turning authority over to an emergency State Council until a new union government could be formed, Gorbachev's position became even more tenuous. With the Soviet economy in shambles and the Soviet government insolvent, Gorbachev appeared to be increasingly isolated. Gorbachev's chief political rival, Boris Yeltsin, who as President of the Russian Republic had become the recognized leader of the anti-coup forces, superseded Gorbachev as the nation's most prominent political figure. Assuming the role of *de jure* leader of Russia, he orchestrated the formation of a new confederal union led by Russia, the Ukraine, Byelorus, and eight other republics. This new Commonwealth of Independent States (CIS)—which symbolized the final unravelling of the Soviet Union—was a confederal arrangement with many unresolved problems. The CIS, in fact, did not bode well for a stable political future. As the death knell of the Soviet Union sounded, Gorbachev's political world ended with a whimper rather than a bang. A president without a country, Gorbachev submitted his resignation in December 1991 and went into political retirement.

The Political Labyrinth (1992-1996)

Since Gorbachev's resignation, the former Soviet system has been in a state of continual turmoil and crisis. Undoubtedly, the Russian Federation (now Russia) with a population of approximately 152 million (and to a lesser extent Ukraine, with a population of approximately 52 million) became the main focal point and linchpin of the Commonwealth of Independent States. Russia, in particular, during the 1992-1993 period experienced severe intra-governmental conflicts between the highest constitutional organ of state power in Russia: the Congress of People's Deputies and the presidency (under Boris Yeltsin). At the core of the their jurisdictional dispute was the critical question over power and power-sharing: "Who was going to decide the country's future?"

In January 1992, President Yeltsin and his chief economist (and later prime minister from June-December 1992) Yegor Gaidar launched a number of radical economic reforms removing government price supports, privatizing various key industries, and encouraging free-market principles. However, the ensuing months of intense political wrangling and in-fighting between the 1,068-member Congress of People's Deputies (which was elected in March 1990 and was an anachronistic throwback to the former Communist regime) and President Yeltsin led to political gridlock that paralyzed the entire political system.

Opposing many of Yeltsin's economic initiatives and fearing his propensity for political self-aggrandizement and desire to concentrate more power in the presidency, Yeltsin's parliamentary opposition led by Alexander Rutskoi (Vice President) and Ruslan Khasbulatov (Speaker of the Congress of People's Deputies) attempted to derail his program and regain control over the government. Frustrating Yeltsin's initiatives (e.g., it needed only a simple majority of 535 votes to block his reforms), and proposing its own program and political agenda, the Congress of People's Deputies put itself on a collision course with the Russian president. Gaidar's removal as the reformist prime minister in December 1992 as a last-minute compromise only temporarily papered over the growing political crisis. In fact, shortly thereafter when the largely conservative (and former Communist holdover) Congress of People's Deputies sought to renege on a legislative-executive power-sharing agreement hammered out at the end of 1992 and to severely curtail Yeltsin's powers, Yeltsin's riposte was to call for a national referendum on April 25, 1993, to decide, once and for all, who should rule Russia. Condemning Yeltsin's actions as unconstitutional, but stopping short of voting for his impeachment, his political opponents chose to challenge the legality of the referendum and to ignore its results.

The outcome of the April 25 referendum gave President Yeltsin an increased foundation of legitimacy to continue his political reforms and initiatives. Of the 69 million people who voted, 57.4 percent expressed confidence in President Yeltsin's leadership and 53.7 percent approved of his economic policies. While over two-thirds (70.6 percent) of those who voted desired early elections for the Congress of People's Deputies (due in 1995), the results fell short because the Constitutional Court ruled that Yeltsin had to get at least half of the total electorate (53.5 million people) and only 44.3 million did so.

While the results of the national referendum were heart-warming for President Yeltsin, the political stalemate still remained. Four days after the referendum, in an effort to overcome his parliamentary opposition while he still had the political momentum, Yeltsin presented the broad outlines of a draft constitution (consisting of 130 articles) that would abolish the Congress of People's Deputies and the post of vice president. Additionally, and somewhat similar to the formidable powers accorded the French president, Yeltsin's draft provided for a strong presidential system where the president could appoint the prime minister, chairman of the Central Bank, and the three most senior judges. A two-chamber federal parliament would confirm these appointments, but the president would have the power of dissolution if the Parliament refused to confirm his nominee for prime minister. Furthermore, only the three senior judges could initiate impeachment proceedings against the president.

On July 12, 1993, after hand-picking most of its 585 members, the constitutional assembly adopted Yeltsin's draft—only somewhat modified and diluted—by the required two-thirds vote necessary (433). The problem, however, was that the Congress of People's Deputies had to approve the new draft constitution by a two-thirds vote, *not* the constitutional assembly Yeltsin had convened. Complicating matters even more was the fact that even before the constitution could be submitted to the Congress for its approval or rejection, Russia's 88 republics and regions (i.e., 20 "republics" and 68 "ordinary regions") first had to agree on the allocation of federal, republic, and regional powers over such matters as language, citizenship, military control, property rights, customs collections, tax revenues, etc. These divisive and contentious issues made Yeltsin's task seem almost insurmountable. Yet, even conceding a successful resolution of these sensitive issues, Yeltsin still faced the almost guaranteed rejection of the draft constitution by the Congress of People's Deputies. The gridlock thus continues.

Breaking the deadlock and circumventing the recalcitrant Congress of People's Deputies, President Yeltsin brought the issue directly before the Russian people. By submitting the draft constitution to a referendum, Yeltsin provided an aura of legitimacy for the proposed constitutional change. While only 28 percent of the eligible electorate voted, 52 percent of the voters approved the proposed constitution that was promulgated in December 1993.

The Russian Constitution of 1993 embraced a strong presidential regime (similar to the French and American models), a bicameral parliamentary system (similar to the German model), a separation of powers (similar to the American model), and a federal and republican form of government. How "democratic" the new constitution would become in practice was and is a matter for conjecture. The only true test would be the test of time. Without a well-established democratic tradition or ethos ingrained in the Russian political experience, the prospects for a Western-style constitutional democracy were not overly bright.

In the 1990s another serious challenge to Yeltsin's leadership arose in the form of ethnic nationalism, specifically the separatist independence movement in Chechnya. In the summer of 1991 the All-National Congress of Chechen People (ANCC) announced that Moslem-dominated Chechnya in the North Caucusus region would secede from the Soviet Union and the Russian Federation. When General Dzhokhar Dudayev become the first popularly elected president of Chechnya in October 1991, he announced his intention to carry out the earlier proclamation of independence.

Between 1994 and 1996 the Chechen leadership arranged the withdrawal of Russian troops from the republic, but the Russians steadfastly refused to recognize the legitimacy of the Chechen separatist movement for independence or to negotiate directly with Dudayev (who dogmatically endorsed independence as the only acceptable option).

When negotiations proved fruitless, Moscow resorted to a full-scale military operation in December 1994 and invaded Grozny, the Chechen capital. The unpopular and destructive war dragged on intermittently, with the Russians sustaining serious losses and the Chechen cities, towns, and villages reduced to rubble.

After the death of Dudayev in 1996, a tenuous cease-fire agreement was put in place pending the outcome of the Russian presidential elections in June. However, negotiations faltered and eventually broke down, leading to a resumption of violence in August 1996. Soon after, Yeltsin designated his newly appointed national security adviser, General Aleksandr Lebed, to broker an agreement that would finally resolve the outstanding differences between the two sides.

Facing an intractable situation, Lebed had less than enthusiastic support for his peace initiatives from other Kremlin government officials and rivals, who viewed him as a loose cannon and his peace initiatives as a capitulation to separatist demands. Nevertheless, on August 28, 1996, Lebed was able to secure a demilitarization of Russian and Chechen troops from southern Chechnya. The long-term consequences, however, are still unsettled and inconclusive regarding total and absolute independence from Moscow, especially after Yeltsin summarily dismissed Lebed in October 1996.

On December 17, 1995, legislative elections were held in the lower house of the Russian Parliament, the State Duma. Patterned after the German model of the Bundestag (the lower house of the German Parliament), half (225) of the 450 members of the State Duma were elected in SMD (Single-Member District) constituencies, while the other half (225) were elected according to party lists.

Similar to the German Bundestag as well was the requirement that no political party would be accorded formal representation in the State Duma if that party did not win an SMD outright, or win at least 5 percent of the national vote in order to win a party list seat. As a result of these electoral features, the State Duma hoped to escape the political pitfalls of fragmentation and proliferation of party representation in the legislature that plagued such ill-fated parliamentary regimes as the German Weimar Republic (1919–1933) and the French Fourth Republic (1946–1958).

The voting patterns of the Russian electorate in 1995, on one hand, showed a recentering of political gravity as the pro-Communist parties—including the Communist Party of the Russian Federation (CPRF), the Agrarian Party, and the Russian Communist Workers Party—made an impressive resurgence from 1993 (98 seats) to 1995 (188 seats). On the other hand, the main losers in the 1995 elections were the reformist/pro-government parties that supported the policies of President Yeltsin. The reformist and pro-government parties (including Our Home is Russia, Yabloko, and Democratic Choice of Russia, among others) dropped 50 seats between 1993 (171 seats) and 1995 (121 seats).

The principal nationalist party opposition, the Liberal Democratic Party, under the unpredictable and quixotic leadership of Vladimir Zhirinovsky, lost 12 seats between 1993 (63 seats) and 1995 (51 seats). In effect, the results of the election reflected the growing disenchantment of the electorate with the absence of tangible improvements in the standard of living, the growing criminal violence, and the gnawing and residual doubts about the impact of privatization.

After five years of President Yeltsin's rule, the Russian people had an opportunity to renew or repudiate a mandate for his continuing leadership. On June 16, 1996, Russian presidential elections were held. Under the new Constitution of 1993, the elections for Russia's president clearly reflected the influence of the French Fifth Republic's two-ballot model. On the first-round ballot, Russians could select their choice from among the ten candidates who entered the race. For the election to be valid, at least 50 percent of the eligible electorate were required to vote. If fewer than 50 percent voted, the election would be declared invalid. If no contender received a majority of the votes cast on the first-round ballot, a runoff election would be held for the top two vote-getting candidates several weeks later. Unlike the 1991 election prior to the adoption of the Constitution of 1993, the president would serve a four-year term (rather than the five-year term provided earlier).

As a result of growing disillusionment, Yeltsin's popularity had declined precipitately since 1991. The burgeoning crime rate, rampant corruption, a stagnant standard of living, the demoralization of the Russian military, and the divisive and costly war in Chechnya all plagued Yeltsin's re-election hopes. Yet, Yeltsin showed great resiliency and resourcefulness in using the powers of the state to mobilize a massive propaganda machine to outmaneuver his political rivals. In the end, his domination of the mass media, combined with numerous electoral irregularities leading to "adjusted" results, guaranteed Yeltsin's ultimate victory.

Failing to win a majority of the vote on the first-round ballot of the presidential elections, despite impressive results in Moscow and St. Petersburg, Yeltsin won only about 35 percent of the overall vote. Gennadi Zyuganov, the head of the Communist Party of the Russian Federation (CPRF), and Yeltsin's chief adversary, won 32 percent of the vote. Lagging far behind, but nonetheless politically significant for the second-round ballot, was retired General Aleksandr Lebed running as an independent nationalist. Lebed won 14.7 percent of the vote. Other also-rans included Grigori Yavlinsky (head of the liberal Yabloko Party), who won 7.4 percent, and Vladimir Zhirinovsky (head of the ultra-nationalist Liberal Democratic Party), whose steady political decline resulted in only 5.8 percent of the vote.

The results of the first-round ballot led to an intense flurry of political activity by Yeltsin strategists to secure his victory in the July 3 runoff. Pragmatic and astute, Yeltsin exhibited his political savvy by co-opting General Lebed as his national security adviser on June 18, jettisoning Defense Minister Pavel Grachev (a long-time Lebed foe), and dismissing several other key personnel that would appease the Yavlinsky faction. The net results of these politically expedient measures proved electorally productive on July 3, as Yeltsin won 55 percent of the vote, Zyuganov 40 percent, while 5 percent cast a protest vote against both candidates. In the final analysis, Yeltsin's knack for political survival and his effective use of the mass media yielded a remarkable comeback and electoral victory. It now remained to be seen whether the poor health of the ailing 65-year-old leader would allow him to complete his full term, which would end in 2000.

Yeltsin's re-election, however, did not go untarnished. The Lebed "factor" offered interesting insights and glimpses into the Byzantine intrigue of Kremlin politics, as well as revealing some of the unbridled ambitions of those who would opportunistically seek to exploit a potential power vacuum. Riding the crest of personal popularity after winning almost 15 percent of the vote in the first round of the presidential elections on June 16, 1996, Lebed played a pivotal role in Yeltsin's subsequent victory. Inducing the former general and independent nationalist candidate to support him on the second round, Lebed's co-optation proved crucial to the final outcome. Yeltsin named Lebed to be secretary of the Security Council and an aide to the president in national security affairs.

Upon striking a deal with Yeltsin, Lebed immediately made a *volte-face* and announced his unwavering support of President Yeltsin to fight crime and corruption and to work unstintingly to end the war in Chechnya. Lebed's prestige and

THE RUSSIAN ECONOMY

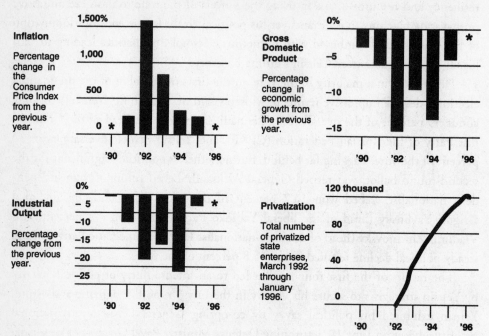

All indexes and percentage changes are "real," or adjusted for inflation.
*Data not available for year.

Sources: "Russian Economic Trends." Russian European Center for Economic Performance; Russian State Committee for Statistics; PlanEcon

tough no-nonsense image immeasurably enhanced Yeltsin's prospects on the second round of presidential elections on July 3, 1996. Nevertheless, after Yeltsin's victory was assured—and despite Lebed's brokered peace accord with Chechnya in August 1996—Lebed's undisciplined ways and outspoken criticism enmeshed him in increasing controversy. Lebed's bitter rivalry with General Anatoly Kulikov (the new defense minister), his claim that Moscow's failure to pay soldiers' salaries would lead to an armed revolt, and charges that Yeltsin's serious health problems involving his pending heart bypass surgery would leave the country in a political vacuum and without effective presidential leadership, sealed his fate.

These and other inflammatory actions and statements persuaded Yeltsin that Lebed was a dangerous political liability. Having overstepped his authority and publicly challenging Yeltsin's ability to govern proved to be an intolerable situation. On October 17, 1996, Yeltsin angrily dismissed his national security chief and relieved him of all his responsibilities. Lebed's immediate removal, however, did not necessarily eliminate him as a future presidential contender. Not less than three hours after his ignominious demise, Lebed announced his intention to run for the presidency. The Lebed "factor" is a specter still lurking on the political horizon.

Whether Yeltsin has the physical durability and stamina to survive to the end of his term is subject to great speculation. His assorted ailments led to long stretches of time where he simply disappeared from public view, adding even more fodder to the rumor mill. Having sustained a minor heart attack in June-July 1996, Yeltsin finally owned up to his serious health problems and submitted to a heart bypass operation in November 1996. Because of his disability and poor health and with no vice president provided for in the Constitution of 1993, Yeltsin's tenure seemed uncertain at best.

There surely was no dearth of potential successors, many of whom had expressed their undisguised ambition to replace Yeltsin. When Yeltsin underwent heart surgery, he temporarily transferred his presidential powers (e.g., the commander-in-chief's responsibility regarding Russia's nuclear arsenal) to Prime Minister Viktor Chernomyrdin. After his recovery from surgery, he immediately reclaimed them. Among the members of the presidential inner circle were the rather bland head of government, Chernomyrdin, the unpopular Anatoly Chubais, Yeltsin's chief-of-staff (head of presidential administration) and architect of Yeltsin's privatization policies, and Yeltsin's daughter, Tatyana Dyachenko.

If Yeltsin does not fully recover and his health deteriorates further, Chernomyrdin would rule the country on an interim basis for three months and then have to call for new elections. In such an eventuality various presidential contenders/pretenders could declare themselves as candidates. Included in this group would be the popular cashiered national security chief, Lebed; the popular mayor of Moscow, Yuri Luzhkov; CPRF leader, Zyuganov, and the Yabloko Party leader Yavlinsky, among others. In the final analysis, institutionalizing the lines of political succession has never been an entrenched feature or a strong suit of the Soviet or post-Soviet experience. With an embryonic constitution barely four years old, a lack of legitimizing tradition or practice to use as a guide, and a strong penchant in Russian politics for an authoritarian leader, it would be foolhardy to predict the eventual outcome. What can be said with a greater degree of assurance is that the post-Soviet period has not resolved this earlier institutional defect of succession by defining the issue with greater clarity.

Other Unresolved and Sundry Problems of the Former Soviet Union

To compound the legislative-executive political crisis in Russia is a compendium of other related political, economic, social, and demographic issues. With over 100 ethnic groups, languages, and dialects existing among Russia's 152 million people, the fact remains that more than 40 million are non-ethnic Russians. This cultural, linguistic, and religious mosaic includes Armenians, Tatars, Mongolians, Moslems, Jews, Bashkirs, Uzbeks, Kazakhs, Turkmen, among others. Conversely, more than 30 million ethnic Russians live in the former 14 non-Russian Soviet republics (e.g., Russians represent about one-third of Latvia's population and over 40 percent of Kazakhstan's). Protection of Russian minorities in the former Soviet republics and preventing ethnic discrimination of Russia's non-Russian minorities have become thorny issues in the Commonwealth of Independent States. This powder keg has the potential of rivaling, if not replicating, the "ethnic cleansing" and feudal bloodletting that has afflicted the former Yugoslavia.

In addition to the various ethnic and religious conflicts affecting large portions of the former Soviet Union, another major concern involves the stability and relationship between Russia and Ukraine, the two largest Slavic republics in the former Soviet Union. Political tensions have become exacerbated because of conflicting claims regarding the Crimea (and Sevastapol), the ownership and control over the Black Sea Fleet, and the dismantling and disposition of Ukraine's strategic nuclear weapons arsenal, which includes 176 ICBMs and 1,240 warheads. Yet, despite the growing tensions between Russia and Ukraine, they are inextricably tied to each other economically with respect to their agricultural, industrial, and energy needs. A peaceful resolution of their outstanding differences is regarded by both Russia and Ukraine as being absolutely essential for the future political and economic stability of the area.

Most importantly, the economic crisis in Russia has yet to be resolved. The economic collapse of the former Soviet Union has made Russia a beggar in world capital markets. Promising to undertake harsh and austere economic measures to stem hyperinflation, to curb military spending, to slash government budgets, and to stop subsidies to inefficient state-owned enterprises, Russia was able to secure a $24 billion loan guarantee from the International Monetary Fund over a two-year period to assist Russia in its economic restructuring. Nonetheless, structural difficulties, involving the transition from a state-run command economy to a free-market economy, continue to plague and bedevil the Russian economy. Bottlenecks, scarcities/shortages, managerial inefficiency, corruption, black-market profiteering, and the decline of oil and natural gas production have all combined to bring Russia to the brink of bankruptcy. The emergence of a "bandocracy" (bandit bureaucracy) and organized crime (Russian mafias) have distorted the distribution of economic benefits even more and have created a "new class" of Russian millionaires. With increasing economic polarization between the rich and the poor and the subsequent discontent it has generated, Yeltsin is under even greater pressure to demonstrate to the masses the universal benefits of a free-market capitalistic system.

Finally, with the demise of the single elitist totalitarian one-party system (CPSU) in 1990 and the outlawing of the CPSU in 1991 and the Russian Communist Party in 1992, there emerged a rapid and unparalleled growth of political activity throughout the former Soviet Union. Within a short period of time more than 500 different parties, movements, political clubs, civic organizations, and fronts appeared in what was the former Soviet Union. More than 20 political parties formed in Russia alone, representing a whole and varied spectrum of ideologies and viewpoints. While voluntary citizenship participation and a "civic culture" are still in an embryonic stage, Russia's diversity and pluralistic fabric have found expression through a proliferation of political organizations ranging from the reactionary Pamyat, to the moderate Democratic Party of Russia and People's Party of Free Russia, to the new and legal Communist Party of the Russian Federation. These parties and organizations, in fact, may be a mixed blessing for Russia because while more Russians may be more directly involved in the democratic process of participating in rallies, publishing their own newspapers, and engaging in other types of political activities, the increasing political fragmentation and atomization of Russian society is, ironically, contributing to its continuing political instability. In other words, too much democracy could be deleterious to Russia's political health. Whether Russia can successfully withstand its experiment with democracy in an increasingly crisis-ridden society and be able to sustain it, or revert to its more restrictive authoritarian tradition, remains an open question.

Epilogue: Prognosis for the Future

The pace of events is so fast that it is impossible to predict with any degree of confidence how permanent or transient the dismantling of the Soviet system will be. The political system is in a state of flux. While the Soviet system and its Marxist-Leninist foundations have been largely discredited, the lack of a democratic foundation or experience in Russian/Soviet history complicates the future political direction of the former Soviet Union. Moreover, the authoritarian tradition is still strong, particularly in Russia, and historically, confederal systems have not demonstrated much stability. At best, the short-term agenda will probably reflect pragmatic and expedient measures to deal with the monumental problems besetting Russia and its confederal allies. Whether the new configuration will be able to use and practice democratic methods, combine free enterprise with some degree of state ownership, and materially resolve the overwhelming difficulties faced by ordinary citizens, remain to be seen. A political backlash from those who have become increasingly disenchanted could result in a conservative or reactionary renaissance and a restoration of the authoritarian tradition and dictatorship. At this point, the CIS is truly at a crossroads.

☞ Drill: Political Structures and Features

> **DIRECTIONS:** Carefully read and answer each of the following questions which are based on the information which you have just read.

50. The reference to the existence of political dualism in the Soviet Union refers to the relationship between the

    (A) government and the military.

    (B) CPSU and its formal opposition.

    (C) CPSU and the government.

    (D) Union Republics and the National Government.

    (E) military and the CPSU.

51. According to Article 6 of the Soviet Constitution of 1977, the "leading and directing force of Soviet society" is the

    (A) CPSU.   (D) All-Union Congress.

    (B) Supreme Soviet.   (E) KGB.

    (C) Presidium of the Council of Ministers.

52. The method by which the CPSU exercises its influence over the government is best described as

    (A) using the apparatus of the KGB.

    (B) using the Soviet military.

    (C) running the government directly.

    (D) applying the Weakest Link Theory.

    (E) using the principle of democratic centralism.

53. The Supreme Soviet

    (A) is the judicial branch of the Soviet government.

    (B) represents the highest organ of the State.

    (C) is more powerful than the CPSU.

    (D) is an independent legislative body.

    (E) provides a unicameral forum for political discourse and debate.

54. The Soviet Parliament does all of the following EXCEPT

    (A) Elects judges to the Supreme Court of the USSR.

    (B) Selects the General-Secretary of the CPSU.

    (C) Amends the Soviet Constitution by a two-thirds vote.

    (D) Forms the executive branch consisting of the prime minister and the Presidium of the Council of Ministers.

    (E) Elects the Presidium of the Supreme Soviet to act as its steering committee.

55. The Soviet parliamentary model dramatically differs from most Western European parliamentary systems because

(A)   the prime minister is directly accountable to the Supreme Soviet.

(B)   a minority government can be overturned by a vote of no-confidence.

(C)   there is no fusion of powers between the legislative and executive branches of government.

(D)   an elitist one-party system negates the possibility of competitiveness or political opposition.

(E)   it has a unicameral Parliament.

56.   When Mikhail Gorbachev became General Secretary of the CPSU in 1985, he attempted to reform the Soviet system through all of the following EXCEPT

(A)   increasing the role of the KGB and military.

(B)   supporting a more tolerant policy towards intellectual inquiry and dissent.

(C)   encouraging an economic restructuring.

(D)   calling for democratic reforms and more popular participation.

(E)   revamping the relationship between the CPSU and the government.

57.   Gorbachev sought to

(A)   increase the role and power of the CPSU in Soviet society.

(B)   decrease the role and powers of the Council of Ministers.

(C)   increase the role and powers of the Soviet prime minister.

(D)   increase the role of the Russian Orthodox Church.

(E)   increase the powers of the Soviet president and disconnect the CPSU from governmental structures.

58.   Gorbachev's proposed "super-legislative" body to supersede the Soviet Parliament was called the

(A)   All-Union Congress.

(B)   Congress of People's Deputies.

(C)   Supreme Soviet.

(D)   People's Chamber.

(E)   Presidium of the Supreme Soviet.

59. The forces unleashed by Gorbachev's policies

    (A) strengthened the claims for independence by the Baltic States.

    (B) led to greater ethnic tension between Soviet republics.

    (C) subjected the CPSU to greater criticism and censure.

    (D) resulted in increasing disillusionment with the corruption and inefficiency of the Soviet system.

    (E) All of the above.

60. Following the attempted coup to isolate and remove Gorbachev from power in August 1991,

    (A) Gorbachev's position and powers eroded rapidly.

    (B) the plotters were executed at summary trials.

    (C) the economy rebounded as a sign of new confidence in Gorbachev's leadership.

    (D) a nationalistic resurgence occurred in an impressive demonstration of national unity.

    (E) Gorbachev's chief rival, Boris Yeltsin, was ousted from power.

61. The Commonwealth of Independent States

    (A) provided for a unitary political arrangement in which the role of the central government was strengthened.

    (B) was designed by Mikhail Gorbachev's hard-line opponents.

    (C) replaced Gorbachev's new union treaty.

    (D) settled most of the disagreements among the former Soviet republics.

    (E) was supported by all of the former Soviet republics.

62. The prognosis for the Commonwealth of Independent States suggests that

    (A) the former Soviet Union is in for a period of increasing stability.

    (B) democratic forces are clearly ascendant and secure.

    (C) authoritarianism is discredited and is unlikely to reappear.

    (D) economic problems will quickly be resolved.

    (E) it will be short-lived.

63. Since Gorbachev's resignation, Russia has

    (A) declined in importance.

    (B) exhibited political stability.

    (C) been afflicted by a power-sharing crisis between the legislative and executive branches.

    (D) reinstated the CPSU.

    (E) seen the Congress of People's Deputies become the dominant political institution.

64. Yeltsin's major parliamentary opponents

    (A) favored the restoration of the CPSU.

    (B) sought to strengthen presidential power.

    (C) chose to ignore the results of the national referendum.

    (D) wanted to increase the pace of economic reforms.

    (E) urged a military *coup d'état* to overthrow him.

65. The April 25, 1993 referendum demonstrated

    (A) disapproval of Yeltsin's leadership.

    (B) a desire to have earlier parliamentary elections.

    (C) disapproval of Yeltsin's socioeconomic policies and programs.

    (D) approval of early elections for the Russian presidency.

    (E) greater support for the position of the Congress of People's Deputies.

66. The results of the April 25 national referendum

    (A) were accepted without reservation by the Congress of People's Deputies.

    (B) precipitated widespread military unrest.

    (C) definitively broke the political deadlock between the legislative and executive branches.

    (D) encouraged the Congress of People's Deputies to draft a new constitution.

    (E) gave Yeltsin greater legitimacy to call for a new constitution with enhanced presidential powers.

67. The constitutional assembly that adopted a draft of a new constitution on July 12, 1993,

    (A) most likely would have that decision overturned by the Congress of People's Deputies.

    (B) was acting at the behest of the Congress of People's Deputies.

    (C) announced that ratification of the draft constitution would require a simple majority approval of the 20 republics.

    (D) was invalidated by a ruling of the Constitutional Court.

    (E) satisfied the demands of all of Russia's 20 republics and 68 ordinary regions.

68. Russia is currently experiencing

    (A) cultural harmony.

    (B) discrimination against non-Russian ethnic minorities.

    (C) linguistic homogeneity.

    (D) a major resurgence of Stalinist ideas about national minorities.

    (E) a growing sense of national cohesiveness and unity among Russia's minorities since the collapse of Communism.

69. All of the following issues are creating serious conflict between Russia and Ukraine EXCEPT

    (A) control over the Black Sea Fleet.

    (B) claims over the port of Vladivostok.

    (C) claims over the Crimea and Sevastapol.

    (D) control and ownership of strategic nuclear weapons.

    (E) None of the above.

70. Under Yeltsin's policies and guidance, Russia's economy was characterized by

    (A) a reduction of subsidies to state-run enterprises.

    (B) the ability to generate sufficient domestic investment capital on its own.

    (C) an increase in military budgets.

    (D) encouragement for the printing of more money.

    (E) a more equitable distribution of national income.

71. Russia's current political party structure is

    (A) characterized by a single, elitist totalitarian one-party system.

    (B) dominated by the reactionary Pamyat movement.

    (C) becoming increasingly influenced by the doctrines of the Russian Orthodox Church.

    (D) one that reflects the development of a multi-party system searching for a consensus.

    (E) basically a two-party system involving Yeltsin's Democratic Party of Russia and his parliamentary opposition's coalition front.

The People's Republic of China

The Revolutionary Setting

The formation of the Chinese *Weltanschauung* (world view) can be explained, in part, by the historical and political evolution of China as it emerged from semi-colonial subservience. At the beginning of the twentieth century, China was a weak and divided country under the corrupt rule of the Manchu dynasty. Exploited by the so-called "open door," China had been subjected to the degradation of imperialism and the spheres of influence imposed by the major Western powers, including Japan. As a consequence of foreign economic penetration and intervention, one of the main currents of Chinese political thought that emerged was a distinct xenophobia that resented any foreign involvement in Chinese affairs. Not only were foreign values and culture rejected, but this was paralleled by a reaffirmation of Chinese nationalism. The various strains of political thought that combined to form the ideological fabric of the PRC cannot be fully understood without first examining the historical background that led to the Chinese communist state in 1949.

The modern Chinese state evolved through a number of distinct historical and ideological stages from 1911 to the present. The overthrow of the Manchu dynasty and imperial rule in 1911 marked the first stage in creating a new China under the idealistic efforts of Dr. Sun Yat-sen. China then experienced a period of political fragmentation that disunited the Chinese nation, as provincial warlords maintained their own personal fiefdoms with private armies for almost two decades (1916-1936). It was during this unstable period that the KMT (Guomindang or Nationalists), under the leadership of Generalissimo Chiang Kai-shek, mended its internal ideological differences and purged the Chinese Communist Party (CCP) from the ranks of the revolutionary movement. Between 1927 and 1937, the KMT was able to establish a modicum of political hegemony over China by mitigating the effects of warlordism and by promoting national unification and modernization. Expediency led the KMT to enter into a pragmatic united front with the CCP, with which it had been engaged in a bloody guerrilla civil war, to fight their common enemy, the Japanese militarists and imperialists. With the surrender of Japan in 1945, open warfare between the KMT and the CCP erupted again as the fragile alliance disintegrated. Between 1945 and 1949, China engaged in a fratricidal civil war.

The KMT's ultimate failure and demise provides a revealing lesson in revolutionary ineptitude. Unresponsive to the real needs of the Chinese people, the KMT had not undertaken any meaningful political or economic reforms. The absence of land reform, the repression of intellectual dissent, the rampant graft and corruption, the ineffective KMT military strategy to eliminate the Communists as rivals, and destabilizing hyperinflation in the late 1940s all contributed to the growing alienation of the Chinese people from KMT rule. Outmaneuvered by the People's Liberation Army (PLA), the KMT and its tattered forces fled to the island of Formosa (Taiwan), surrendering mainland China to the victorious Communists. On October 1, 1949, the People's Republic of China (PRC) was established.

☞ Drill: The Revolutionary Setting

DIRECTIONS: Carefully read and answer each of the following questions which are based on the information which you have just read.

72. At the turn of the twentieth century, China

   (A)   was virtually a colonial dependent of the Western powers.

   (B)   welcomed the presence of Western powers to help uplift China's backward economy.

   (C)   had a government enjoying wide popular support.

   (D)   had a well-developed Communist Party.

   (E)   had enthusiastically embraced many of the cultural values of the Western powers.

73. Between 1916 and 1936

   (A)   China was under the rule of the Manchu dynasty.

   (B)   China experienced an unparalleled period of political stability.

   (C)   China was politically subdivided by provincial warlords.

(D) the CCP emerged as the dominant political force in China.

(E) China adopted a Western-style parliamentary democracy.

74. The KMT's rule in China was characterized by

(A) impressive land reform measures.

(B) an efficient and honest governmental bureaucracy.

(C) a wide tolerance for political criticism.

(D) a KMT alliance with Communist forces to resist Japanese aggression.

(E) a determination to break the will and the resistance of the CCP.

The Ideological Foundations of the People's Republic of China

The official ideology of the PRC embraces the tenets of Marxism-Leninism-Maoism (Mao Zedong's doctrine). As was the case in the Soviet model, the PRC adopted Marx's concept of historical materialism. This theory postulated that society evolved through distinct historical stages: primitive communism, slavery, feudalism, capitalism, a transitional stage of socialism, and finally, communism. The pre-communist stages of historical development were characterized by a dialectical struggle between adversarial classes, pitted against each other in bitter class warfare. The end result of the internal conflicts and contradictions in capitalism, involving the *bourgeoisie* and the *proletariat,* was a "dialectical leap" into the transitional stage of socialism (a sort of half-way house between capitalism and communism). According to Marx, when the dialectic became exacerbated in capitalism, violent bloody class warfare would lead to the overthrow of the existing bourgeois-dominated social order (the capitalist economic mode of production) and its derivative trappings (what Marx called the super-structure), the laws, courts, bureaucracies, military, police, etc. Lenin's contributions, cited earlier in the section on the Soviet Union, modified and revised many of Marx's ideas. Specifically, Lenin's Theory of Imperialism and his Theory of Uneven Development (Weakest Link Theory) seemed particularly appropriate for the Chinese model. His explanation of capitalist nations in the monopoly stage of capitalism seeking to exploit the underdeveloped Third World conformed with China's experience as a less developed country. Lenin's treatise was borne out by China's historical legacy, a fact which helped to rationalize China's backwardness and underdevelopment. Lenin's Theory of Uneven Development was similarly used to juxtapose Chinese nationalism with imperialistic exploitation to establish the legitimacy of China's communist revolution. Lenin's Theory of Democratic Centralism, involving the creation of a professional cadre of dedicated and disciplined revolutionaries to serve as the vanguard of the proletariat, became the final Leninist linchpin in the PRC ideological foundation.

The doctrine of Mao Zedong, the last part of the Chinese ideological trilogy, dominated the PRC from its inception in 1949 until Mao's death in 1976. A practical theoretician who freely interacted with and organized workers and peasants, Mao was to engender a reverence bordering on unbridled adulation. Preferring to be called a "great teacher," Chairman Mao made vital and idiosyncratic contributions to Chinese communist ideology. Among his most important Marxist-Leninist revisions include:

1) Peasantry as the primary revolutionary force, rather than the Eurocentric idea of the urban proletariat as the primary revolutionary group;

2) Mass line was the policy recognizing the need to establish populist roots with the peasants and workers whose virtue and wisdom would help direct CCP policy in positive directions;

3) Theory and practice entailed the idea that empirical experiences must be pragmatically and continually incorporated into theoretical doctrine so that theory doesn't become sterile or divorced from changing realities;

4) Contradiction was a continuation of the dialectical conflicts elaborated by Hegel and Marx, but refined the concept of the class struggle to include the numerous contradictions in Chinese society (e.g., Mao differentiated between "antagonistic contradictions," involving interclass conflicts between proletariat and bourgeois elements, which were to be ruthlessly rooted out and "non-antagonistic contradictions," involving intra-party and class disputes capable of being resolved through education, consciousness-raising, rectification campaigns, self-criticism, and use of the mass line to break ideological or factional deadlock); and

5) Permanent revolution involved Mao's notion that society is in a constant state of flux which generates a continuous class struggle with its attendant contradictions, some of which could lead to bourgeois retrogression, a state that should be prevented at all costs.

☞ Drill: The Ideological Foundations of the PRC

DIRECTIONS: Carefully read and answer each of the following questions, which are based on the information which you have just read.

---

75. The Marxist contribution to the official ideology of the PRC did not include the notion that

    (A) society evolved in distinct stages of historical development.

    (B) interclass harmony was the dialectical lever of societal change.

    (C) the base or mode of production created its own super-structure.

    (D) socialism was a transitional stage which preceded the full development of a communist society.

    (E) qualitative changes between historical stages resulted in "dialectical leaps."

76. Lenin explained China's backwardness and underdevelopment

    (A) as outgrowths of political fragmentation and warlordism.

    (B) through his Theory of Democratic Centralism.

    (C) by virtue of the Confucian tradition of passivity and male chauvinist values.

    (D) as by-products of the ineptitude of the Manchu dynasty.

    (E) was caused by imperial powers seeking to acquire raw materials, exploit the use of cheap labor, and find new markets in Third World countries such as China.

77. Maoism diverged from Marxism-Leninism by placing special emphasis upon the revolutionary role and potential of the

    (A) intellectuals.   (D) military.

    (B) urban proletariat.   (E) government bureaucracy.

    (C) peasants.

78. To prevent the leadership of the CCP from becoming too isolated from the needs of the people, Mao

(A) called for popular referenda.

(B) suggested periodic renewal of CCP leaders by popular election.

(C) advocated the emergence of a competitive multi-party system.

(D) sought to co-opt and mobilize the masses in forming the party line.

(E) promoted the idea that "antagonistic contradictions" were desirable.

79. According to Mao, permanent revolution was necessary to

(A) prevent the resurgence of reactionary forces and bourgeois backsliding.

(B) reform the command structure of the PLA.

(C) internationalize the class struggle beyond China's frontiers.

(D) justify the existence of the CCP.

(E) deter the possibility of capitalist encirclement.

Political Change and Modernization

From its creation in 1949 to the present day, the PRC has undergone a continuous search for an appropriate developmental model. In fact, Mao and his successors have relied upon eclectic approaches that have vacillated between emulating and repudiating the Soviet model, between centralization and decentralization, between adoption and rejection of capitalist incentives, and between the pursuit of isolationism and the search for international economic cooperation and involvement with capitalist countries.

The period from 1949 to 1957 marked a preoccupation with securing the goals of the revolution, attaining security, and promoting a program of rapid industrialization patterned after the Soviet (Stalinist) model of long-term centralized planning. A massive land reform occurred between 1949 and 1952, resulting in the distribution of 113 million acres to 300 million landless peasants. The effect was to break the back of the large landholders' political and economic power by distributing land to small landholders, tenants, and agricultural laborers. The leveling of the rural economy and society was but a precursor to collectivizing agriculture and establishing a more communal form of land tenure, called agricultural producers' cooperatives (APCs). The period from 1949 to 1957 also stressed securing the goals of the revolution by ruthlessly eradicating any residual vestiges of KMT influence. Achieving a semblance of internal security provided the stability to initiate the First Five-Year Plan (1953-1957), a Stalin-inspired economic program to channel investment into heavy industry, largely through forced savings squeezed from the agricultural sector, but also with considerable Soviet aid and technical assistance.

The second major experiment in modernization, between 1958 and 1976, involved a distinctly Maoist model of development. This was an effort to establish a socialist economic model more compatible with China's indigenous conditions and needs. Using the creative forces of the masses, Mao sought to utilize China's vast human resources to overcome capital shortages by undertaking a program called the *Great Leap Forward* (1958-1960). This initiative was closer to the CCP's revolutionary tradition than to the Soviet model as China attempted a policy of mass mobilization and decentralization to harness the energies of labor-intensive, small-scale enterprise. Rural communities were to build "backyard furnaces" and exercise greater local initiative. Paralleling these changes, Mao pursued an intensified effort to spread the Great Leap Forward to the countryside by consolidating the APCs into a larger and more collectivized unit, the commune. The communization program in agriculture created new local political and economic units of production. In 1959, there were 26,000 communes (averaging about 10,000 peasants), 75,000 in the early 1960s, and about 50,000 in 1970. They were to become the mainstay of agricultural production and the rural economy. Despite these earlier programs, however, the most controversial and disruptive Maoist initiative during this period was the unleashing of the *Cultural Revolution* (1966-1969). This was Mao's crusade to refurbish the revolutionary spirit that was increasingly corrupted by the influences of "capitalist roaders" and other bourgeois elements, who were attempting to install a revisionist system. This attempt to rid society of these corrupting influences, and reliance on the masses to enforce egalitarian principles and the mass line, led to widespread criticism, a discrediting and decimation of the CCP, the emergence of the idealistic and overly zealous Red Guards searching for ideological heretics, and uncontrolled violence and near-anarchy. While large numbers of the political elite were purged, bureaucratism attacked, and the masses mobilized for political action, events soon took on a force and logic of their own, leading to excesses far beyond Mao's intentions. With public order rapidly disintegrating, the Maoists, fearful of losing control over the situation, called in the PLA to restore order and stability.

Following the deaths of Mao Zedong and Zhou Enlai in 1976, China began its third major effort to find an appropriate development and modernization model. The post-Mao succession struggle was characterized by bitter factional disputes within the CCP and the government, between ardent Maoist radicals led by Jiang Qing, Mao's wife (who led a group known as the Gang of Four), and former Premier Zhou Enlai's moderate supporters led by Deng Xiaoping. Eventually the moderates prevailed as the radical leaders and their allies were outmaneuvered, arrested, brought to trial, and disgraced. With the moderates securely in charge, China has embarked upon a socialist modernization program reflecting a less dogmatic and more flexible approach incorporating a blend of both Maoist and foreign techniques. Mao's immediate successor, Hua Guofeng, was removed in 1981. He was succeeded by Hu

Yaobang, a protegé of Deng Xiaoping, who at the age of 87, was recognized in 1992 as China's paramount leader. With Hu as the pragmatic CCP boss from 1982 to 1987 and the innovative and reformist Zhao Ziyang as the premier from 1980 to 1987, the PRC's moderate course seemed well charted. Deng's position as the leader behind the scenes continued as he allowed the decollectivization of agriculture, permitted tens of thousands of Chinese students to go abroad for higher education, and encouraged private businesses to form. In 1987, however, he removed Hu Yaobang as CCP general secretary, and in 1989, Zhao Ziyang was similarly removed. Deng indicated that his successors would be Li Peng, who as acting premier gained the permanent premiership in 1987, and Jiang Zemin, who became the new general secretary of the CCP in 1989. After whetting the appetite of China's university students for democracy and reform, the 1989 Democracy Movement in Beijing's Tiananmen Square was brutally suppressed by the PLA, with the support, or at least acquiescence, of Deng. The gerontocracy that ruled the PRC seemed increasingly mired in uncertainty and conflict over the nature, scope, and extent of reform. China is still wending its way through its own unique modernization maze in its continuing effort to raise the standard of living for more than one billion people.

Recent Events (1992-1996)

During the 1992-1993 period the PRC continued on its somewhat enigmatic, if not ambivalent, course of combining its pragmatic approach of implementing free-market capitalist experimentation to build a "socialist market economy" with a Leninist political orthodoxy preserving the preeminent role of the CCP and one-party rule. The 14th CCP Congress in October 1992 reaffirmed this dualistic policy as evidenced by CCP chief Jiang Zemin's keynote address where he called for a "fundamental restructuring of the economy" without engaging in ideological dog-matism or debates while, at the same time, exhorting the delegates to "strengthen the people's democratic dictatorship" and to "crack down on the activities of hostile forces." This unusual dichotomy, but with the apparent *de facto* endorsement and approval of Deng Xiaoping (the undisputed senior leader who, ironically, had been without an official government or party portfolio since 1990), led to some sardonic and insightful political humor—"Under the leadership of the Communist Party, we're advancing from socialism to capitalism."

Before the 14th CCP Congress concluded its sessions, it selected its Central Committee (189 full members, 130 alternates), replacing nearly half of its member-ship. The Central Committee, in turn, chose a new Politburo (13 members), and shortly thereafter the party leaders (and most importantly, Deng Xiaoping) deter-mined the membership of the Politburo Standing Committee (7 members), the CCPs all powerful decision-making body. The composition of this 7-member body will undoubtedly play a critical role in the power struggle and political succession expected after Deng's death.

While seeking to avert a divisive power struggle that could precipitate a military coup, cause political fragmentation, or create a political stalemate (leading to rule by committee), in March 1993 Deng (and other party elders) bolstered Jiang Zemin's position as the heir apparent by expanding his roles to include not only the head of the CCP, but head of state (replacing General Yang Shangkun as President) and head of the military (Chairman of the Central Military Commission). Nonetheless, other contenders also existed. For example, Zhu Rongji, a former mayor of Shanghai, deputy prime minister, and a member of the Politburo Standing Committee, who has been referred to as "China's Gorbachev" for his fervor in economic restructuring, was also one of the leading contenders for the top spot. On the other hand, Qiao Shi, chairman of the National People's Congress (NPC), director of internal security services, and a member of the Politburo Standing Committee, shouldn't be overlooked either as a legitimate possibility for paramount leader. In the final analysis, the lack of a clear institutionalized mechanism to provide for political succession clouds the political horizon of the PRC and has become a recurrent source of instability.

In 1996, while the 92-year-old Deng's aging presence was still felt—though decreasingly—as China's paramount leader, President Jiang Zemin began to position himself for the anticipated succession struggle that has, in fact, ensued since Deng's death in February 1997. Despite being a consensus builder and an accommodationist regarding the collective leadership of the CCP elders, the military, the regional groupings and factions, Jiang continued to face many formidable obstacles to his unchallenged leadership.

Establishing the People's Armed Police (PAP) as a potential counterweight to the formidable 3 million-member People's Liberation Army (PLA), Jiang could now use the PLA as an instrument of last resort. Moreover, Jiang made a concerted effort to weaken the influence of the PLA as a dominant political force in the pending succession struggle by using promotion, mandatory retirement of senior officers over age 65, and rotational transfers of top military personnel at two- to three-year intervals to reduce the possibility of military entrenchment and Caesarism.

Urging continuing military submission and compliance to the CCP, Jiang emphasized the authoritative role of the party's leadership and the need for the military to follow and enforce the directives of the CCP's Central Committee. Nonetheless, the debate still raged on as to the exact extend of the PLA's enigmatic role as initiator or agent in shaping and/or directing policy, especially on such thorny issues as China's claims to the Spratly Islands, the absorption of Taiwan, and the appropriate response to U.S. pressure regarding human rights.

No doubt the 15th CCP Congress, scheduled for the fall of 1997, should clarify the future leadership directions of China when it is slated to make important personnel changes at the highest level (e.g., the Politburo Standing Committee). Most decidedly, the fate of Jiang's continuing leadership hangs in the balance.

Many unresolved bilateral issues still separate the United States and the People's Republic of China. Such issues as trade, the selling of nuclear and missile technology, and U.S. arms sales to Taiwan have served to complicate the relations between the two nations. Yet probably the most contentious question is China's dismal record of human rights abuses and the resulting obstacles it has placed on the road to a closer and more cordial bilateral relationship.

Regarding U.S. support of the UN resolution condemning China for human rights abuses as unwarranted and intrusive meddling into China's internal affairs, Beijing's leaders have asserted its independence of action by sending leading Chinese dissidents to jail, labor camps, or exile. In 1996, to punctuate its crackdown on dissidents, Wang Dan, one of the most prominent dissidents of the 1989 Tienanmen Square democracy movement, was sentenced to prison for eleven years for his critical writings that, according to authorities, plotted "to subvert the government." This insistent Chinese defiance of international protests suggested that Jiang and hardline Prime Minister Li Peng had the acquiescence, if not the active support, of the broader CCP leadership and military in this unstable era of transition. In the short term, it would seem that a meaningful democratization or liberalization of the political regime in such a period of leadership uncertainty was not an immediately achievable prospect.

Hong Kong

Finally, an ancillary issue regarding the People's Republic of China that has aroused great interest and speculation is the future of Hong Kong, the PRC's "Window to the West." On July 1, 1997, Hong Kong will revert to Chinese sovereignty after 155 years of British rule. The transfer from British to Chinese sovereignty, agreed to in 1984 by the bilateral Sino-British Joint Declaration, will allow China to establish a Hong Kong Special Administrative Region (SAR).

This agreement would permit Hong Kong to keep its democratic system (replete with a mini-constitution entitled the Basic Law, a document which was promulgated by China's National People's Congress in April 1990) and free market economy (i.e., it would remain a free port using the Hong Kong dollar and a separate customs territory, as well as maintaining itself as an international financial center) for the next 50 years.

The future governor of Hong Kong, known as the "chief executive," would be from Hong Kong and be chosen by the Provisional Legislature (which would be reconstituted and renamed the Legislative Council after the July 1 transfer). In fact, on December 11, 1996, the PRC announced that Tung Chee-hwa (C. H. Tung), a shipping magnate and businessman who's supported by the British as well, would be appointed chief executive when Chinese control starts on July 1. While Tung's selection is reassuring to Hong Kong's capitalists, as well as to the United States and other Western nations, there are many unresolved misgivings and anxieties held by those who are concerned about China's long-term commitment to democracy and protection of human rights in Hong Kong, especially after the brutal suppression of the Tiananmen Square pro-democracy movement in 1989. At this point, Hong Kong's "window" is somewhat translucent rather than transparent. No doubt the future will demonstrate more clearly whether such anxieties were justly warranted.

☞ Drill: Political Change and Modernization

DIRECTIONS: Carefully read and answer each of the following questions which are based on the information which you have just read.

---

80. The PRC's earliest effort to establish a model of development reflected

    (A) a flexible and pragmatic approach.

    (B) the incorporation of capitalist incentives for industry.

    (C) an emphasis on the Soviet model of centralized planning.

    (D) the priority of the agricultural sector.

    (E) a rejection of a collectivized form of agriculture.

81. China's Great Leap Forward (1958-1960) was conceived by Mao as an effort to accelerate economic development by

    (A) substituting human resources for the scarcity of investment capital.

    (B) using the PLA to build up the economic infrastructure of the country.

    (C) attracting foreign capital from international lending institutions.

    (D) establishing greater bureaucratic and centralized control over the economy.

    (E) decollectivizing the agricultural producers' cooperatives.

82. The Cultural Revolution (1966-1969) represented

    (A) an artistic and literary renaissance.

    (B) a strengthening of the role and influence of the CCP.

    (C) a repudiation of the mass line.

(D)   an effort to encourage greater intellectual freedom.

(E)   an effort to purge the CCP and government of revisionists and reactionaries ("capitalist roaders").

83.   In the decade following the deaths of Mao Zedong and Zhou Enlai in 1976,

(A)   there was a strong sense of unity and cohesiveness within CCP ranks.

(B)   a new younger generation of top leaders emerged.

(C)   moderate elements of the CCP eventually took charge.

(D)   Maoist dogmatism became the dominant ideological strain of the new leadership.

(E)   the Gang of Four supported Deng Xiaoping as the paramount leader and heir-apparent to Mao.

84.   Deng Xiaoping's revealing statement, "It makes no difference if a cat is black or white—so long as it catches mice," implied

(A)   politics (ideology) should take precedence over economics.

(B)   economics should not be governed by politics.

(C)   rodent infestation could be eliminated by using capitalist incentives.

(D)   modernization should be based upon an unswerving commitment to a specific set of ideological principles.

(E)   the PLA should use any means necessary to root out bourgeois elements and bureaucratism.

85.   The 1992-1993 policies of the PRC reflected

(A)   an increasing reliance upon free-market principles.

(B)   a political liberalization allowing for an intra-party primary in the CCP.

(C)   the growing role of the PLA to inject itself into the civilian political sector.

(D)   the willingness of the CCP to accept the formation of opposition political parties.

(E)   the decreasing role of the PRC's gerontocracy led by Deng Xiaoping.

86. Deng's preferred successor whose institutional position was strengthened in 1993, and who held party, state, and military posts, was

    (A) Li Peng.

    (B) Zhu Rongji.

    (C) Qiao Shi.

    (D) Jiang Zemin.

    (E) Yang Shangkun.

Political Structures and Features

The Government

Similar to the pre-Gorbachev Soviet model, the Chinese political system also exhibits a parallelism of government and party. The government, the administrative structure of the state, is really subject to the interlocking structure and control of the CCP. The Constitution of 1982, in fact, recognizes the pre-eminence and leading role of the CCP, a feature excluded from the three previous PRC constitutions. As outlined by the constitution, the basic task of the government is to achieve socialist modernization by using public ownership in tandem with the "individual economy"— that is, to provide a combination of economic planning with the supplementary role of regulation by the market (Article 15). In short, the government is the subordinate partner in this unequal relationship. (See the following chart for the vertical and horizontal government and CCP structures, as well as their overlapping and inter-locking relationships.)

The head of state is chosen by the National People's Congress (NPC) and it is largely a ceremonial post. The constitution grants the NPC Standing Committee the authority to send and receive ambassadors and to ratify or abrogate treaties. The head of government roles, however, are exercised by the State Council (Cabinet) and its chairperson (premier) who are collectively and formally responsible for their actions to the NPC. Nonetheless, the CCP holds effective political power, and even though Deng Xiaoping had no longer held a formal position, he was generally recognized as the country's de facto leader until his death in 1997.

According to the Constitution of 1982, the NPC "is the highest organ of state power" (Article 57). Its membership is selected through a series of elections in the 22 provinces, 5 autonomous regions, 3 major municipalities, and by the PLA. This nominal unicameral legislative body does not act independently of the party, but compliantly initiates legislation and enacts laws consistent with the wishes of the

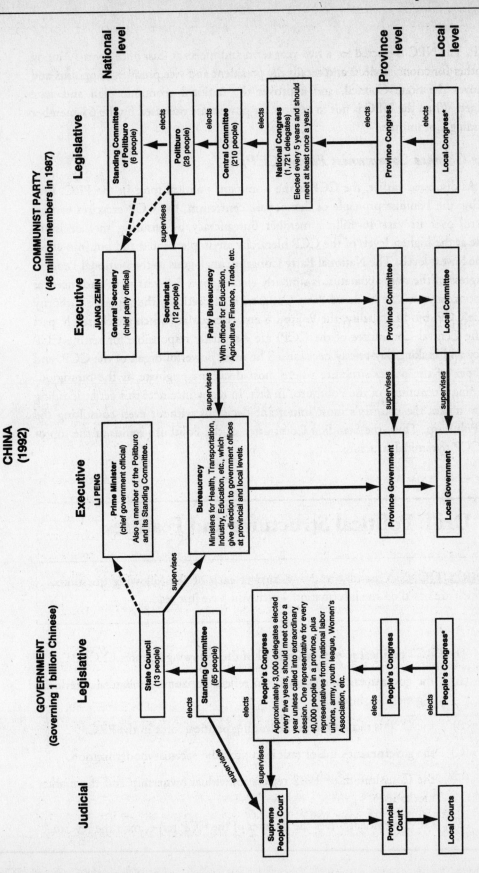

CCP. The NPC is elected for a five-year term and meets at least once a year. Among its other functions, it elects and recalls the president and vice president, appoints and removes the State Council, and approves the national economic plan and state budget. When the NPC is not in session, its powers are exercised by the 65-member Standing Committee.

The Chinese Communist Party (CCP)

As discussed earlier, the CCP is the dominant political force in the PRC. Embracing the Leninist principle of democratic centralism, the CCP exercises vertical control over its vast 46-million member bureaucracy by ensuring that decisions made at the highest levels of the CCP hierarchy are implemented and put into effect at the lowest levels. The National Party Congress, analogous to the National People's Congress of the state apparatus, is similarly elected for a five-year term and meets at least once a year. The National Party Congress is theoretically the supreme authority of the CCP, but in actuality, the Politburo and Secretariat (which are chosen in part by the Central Committee of the CCP) are essentially responsible for setting CCP policy and making day-to-day decisions. The most powerful organ of the CCP, and the apex of the power structure where most decisions originate, is the prestigious Standing Committee of the Politburo. In fact, in many instances this geriatric ruling clique makes the country's most important decisions without even consulting the full Politburo. Thus, the Standing Committee of the Politburo stands at the top of the CCP pyramidal structure.

☞ Drill: Political Structures and Features

> **DIRECTIONS:** Carefully read and answer each of the following questions, which are based on the information which you have just read.

87. The PRC's political system exhibits all of the following features EXCEPT

    (A) the government and party often reflect horizontal, collateral interlocking memberships.

    (B) the CCP is recognized as the leading political force in the PRC.

    (C) the government's major task is to promote socialist modernization.

    (D) the Constitution of 1982 rejects individual ownership and the market mechanism.

    (E) the government serves the dictates of the CCP rather than the reverse.

88. The PRC's legislative body that selects the head of government (premier) and the Cabinet is called the

    (A) State Council.   (D) People's National Assembly.

    (B) Central Committee.   (E) National People's Congress.

    (C) Standing Committee.

89. The very top of the decision-making hierarchy of the CCP, a small coterie of senior leaders who exercise enormous power, is called the

    (A) Central Committee.

    (B) Standing Committee of the Politburo.

    (C) National Party Congress.

    (D) Central Advisory Commission.

    (E) Secretariat.

Comparative Government and Politics Review

ANSWER KEY

1.	(D)	24.	(D)	47.	(A)	70.	(A)
2.	(C)	25.	(E)	48.	(C)	71.	(D)
3.	(A)	26.	(B)	49.	(E)	72.	(A)
4.	(E)	27.	(D)	50.	(C)	73.	(C)
5.	(A)	28.	(A)	51.	(A)	74.	(D)
6.	(B)	29.	(C)	52.	(E)	75.	(B)
7.	(A)	30.	(E)	53.	(B)	76.	(E)
8.	(E)	31.	(A)	54.	(B)	77.	(C)
9.	(D)	32.	(D)	55.	(D)	78.	(D)
10.	(A)	33.	(C)	56.	(A)	79.	(A)
11.	(D)	34.	(D)	57.	(E)	80.	(C)
12.	(C)	35.	(B)	58.	(B)	81.	(A)
13.	(C)	36.	(C)	59.	(E)	82.	(E)
14.	(A)	37.	(A)	60.	(A)	83.	(C)
15.	(E)	38.	(E)	61.	(C)	84.	(B)
16.	(C)	39.	(A)	62.	(E)	85.	(A)
17.	(D)	40.	(D)	63.	(C)	86.	(D)
18.	(D)	41.	(C)	64.	(C)	87.	(D)
19.	(E)	42.	(D)	65.	(B)	88.	(E)
20.	(B)	43.	(C)	66.	(E)	89.	(B)
21.	(A)	44.	(A)	67.	(A)		
22.	(D)	45.	(E)	68.	(B)		
23.	(E)	46.	(B)	69.	(B)		

AP EXAMINATION IN
United States Government & Politics

PRACTICE TEST 1

AP EXAMINATION IN
UNITED STATES GOVERNMENT AND POLITICS

Test 1

Section I

TIME: 45 Minutes
60 Multiple-Choice Questions
50% of Total Grade

(Answer sheets appear in the back of this book)

DIRECTIONS: Read the following questions and incomplete sentences. Each is followed by five answer choices. Choose the one answer choice that either answers the question or completes the sentence. Make sure to use the circles numbered 1 through 60 when marking your answers on your answer sheet.

---

1. Which of the following is used to effect the release of a person from improper imprisonment?

    (A)   A writ of mandamus

    (B)   A writ of habeas corpus

    (C)   The Fourth Amendment requirement that police have probable cause in order to obtain a search warrant

    (D)   The Supreme Court's decision in *Roe vs. Wade*

    (E)   The constitutional prohibition against ex post facto laws

2. When a member of the House of Representatives helps a citizen from his or her district receive some federal aid to which that citizen is entitled, the Representative's action is referred to as

    (A)   casework.   (B)   pork barrel legislation.

(C)   lobbying.   (D)   logrolling.

(E)   filibustering.

3.   One advantage incumbent members of Congress have over challengers in election campaigns is the use of

(A)   unlimited campaign funds.

(B)   national party employees as campaign workers.

(C)   the franking privilege.

(D)   unlimited contributions from "fat cat" supporters.

(E)   government-financed air time for commercials.

4.   Major differences between procedures in the House of Representatives and the Senate would include:

I.   In the House, time for debate is limited, while in the Senate it is usually unlimited.

II.   In the House, the rules committee is very powerful, while in the Senate it is relatively weak.

III. In the House, debate must be germane, while in the Senate it need not be.

(A)   I only   (D)   I and II only

(B)   II only   (E)   I, II, and III

(C)   III only

5.   In the case *McCulloch vs. Maryland* (1819), the Supreme Court

(A)   gave a broad interpretation to the First Amendment right of freedom of speech.

(B)   claimed the power of judicial review.

(C)   struck down a law of Congress for the first time.

(D)   gave a broad interpretation to the "necessary and proper clause."

(E)   denied that the president has the right of executive privilege.

6.   Which of the following statements about the cabinet is FALSE?

(A)   It includes heads of the 14 executive departments.

(B)   It includes members of the House of Representatives.

(C)   Although not mentioned in the Constitution, the cabinet has been part of American government since the presidency of George Washington.

(D)   Presidents may appoint special advisors to the cabinet.

(E)   Senators may not serve in the cabinet.

7.   The major responsibility of the Federal Reserve Board is to

(A)   implement monetary policy.

(B)   control government spending.

(C)   regulate commodity prices.

(D)   help the president run the executive branch.

(E)   keep records of troop strength in army reserve units across the country.

8.   Which of the following statements most accurately compares political parties in the United States with those in other Western democracies?

(A)   Parties in the United States exert a greater influence over which candidates run for office.

(B)   Parties are much more centralized in the United States.

(C)   There are usually more political parties in other Western democracies.

(D)   Party members in the national legislature are much freer to vote against the party line in other Western democracies.

(E)   Party label is the principal criterion for voting for a candidate in the United States, whereas it is relatively unimportant in other Western democracies.

9.   Which of the following is among the differences between a parliamentary and a presidential system?

I.   In a parliamentary system, there is little or no separation of powers as in a presidential system.

II.   In a parliamentary system, the chief executive officer is not chosen by a nationwide vote as in a presidential system.

III.   In a presidential system, the chief executive officer may call elections for all members of the legislature at any time, unlike in a parliamentary system.

(A)   I only   (D)   I and II only

(B)   II only   (E)   I, II, and III

(C)   III only

10.   The statement "America has a pluralistic political system" means

 (A)   there are many subcultures within American society.

 (B)   political power is divided between national and state governments.

 (C)   many interest groups compete in the political arena to influence public policy.

 (D)   rural interests are overrepresented in the national legislature.

 (E)   candidates for national office are usually elected by plurality vote.

11.   Which of the following best describes the relationship between educational background and participation in politics?

 (A)   The more schooling one has, the more likely one is to vote.

 (B)   The less schooling one has, the more likely one is to run for public office.

 (C)   There is no relationship between educational background and participation in politics.

 (D)   People with a high school education are more likely to vote than either those who did not finish high school or those with a college degree.

 (E)   Those with no formal schooling have a greater personal interest in policy and tend to vote more often than those with high school diplomas.

12.   According to the information in the tables on the next page, which of the following statements is true?

 (A)   A black female in a service occupation is more likely to vote Democrat than a white male skilled worker.

 (B)   A white female earning under $10,000 is more likely to vote Republican than a white male earning over $50,000.

 (C)   A white male with no high school diploma is less likely to vote Democrat than a white male with some college education.

 (D)   A black male earning $10,000–$19,999 is more likely to vote Republican than a white male earning $20,000–$29,999.

 (E)   A white female with a high school diploma is more likely to vote Democrat than a black female with no high school diploma.

PARTY IDENTIFICATION BY SEX

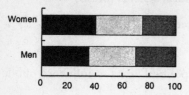

PARTY IDENTIFICATION BY OCCUPATION

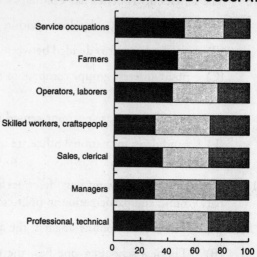

PARTY IDENTIFICATION BY RACE

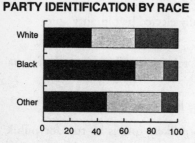

PARTY IDENTIFICATION BY EDUCATION

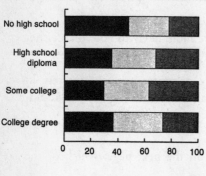

PARTY IDENTIFICATION BY INCOME

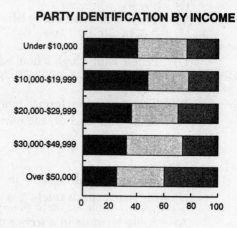

■ Republicans   ▨ Independents   ■ Democrats

From Janda, Berry, Goldman, *The Challenge of Democracy*, p. 286

13. Which of the following were LEAST likely to have voted for Franklin Roosevelt in 1940?

   (A)   Southerners   (D)   Racial minorities

   (B)   White northern business leaders   (E)   Union members

   (C)   Blue collar workers

14. The federal constitution guarantees which of the following rights to persons arrested and charged with a serious crime?

    I.   To have an attorney appointed for them if they cannot afford to hire one

II.   To remain silent

III.   To compel witnesses in their favor to appear to testify if the case goes to court

(A)   I only   (D)   I and II only

(B)   II only   (E)   I, II, and III

(C)   III only

15.   The purpose of grandfather clauses and literacy tests, used in the southern states in the late 1800s and early 1900s, was to

(A)   prevent illiterate whites from voting.

(B)   prevent recent immigrants from voting.

(C)   prevent Hispanics from running for public office.

(D)   prevent blacks from voting.

(E)   prevent "carpetbaggers" from running for public office.

Question 16 refers to the following excerpt from a Supreme Court decision.

It is emphatically the province and duty of the courts to say what the law is... If two laws conflict with each other, the courts must decide on the operation of each... If, then, the courts are to regard the Constitution, and the Constitution is superior to any ordinary act of the legislature, the Constitution and not such ordinary act, must govern the case to which they both apply.

16.   This decision of the Supreme Court upheld the principle that

(A)   a law contrary to the Constitution cannot be enforced by the courts.

(B)   Congress has the power to pass laws to carry out its constitutional duties.

(C)   interpretation of laws is a legislative function.

(D)   a law passed by Congress overrides a constitutional provision with which it conflicts.

(E)   courts are not equipped to decide questions of constitutional law.

17.   "Mark-up sessions," where revisions and additions are made to proposed legislation in Congress, usually occur in which setting?

(A)   The majority leader's office

(B)   On the floor of the legislative chamber

(C)   In party caucuses

(D)   In joint conference committees

(E)   In committees or subcommittees

18.   Which of the following has chief responsibility for assembling and analyzing the figures in the presidential budget submitted to Congress each year?

(A)   Department of Commerce

(B)   Department of Treasury

(C)   Federal Reserve Board

(D)   Office of Management and Budget

(E)   Cabinet

19.   The term "executive privilege" refers to

(A)   the right of the president to veto legislation proposed by Congress.

(B)   the limited right of the president to withhold certain information from Congress and the public.

(C)   the right of the president to appoint and receive ambassadors.

(D)   the limited right of the president to pardon persons convicted of federal crimes.

(E)   the limited immunity of the president from prosecution for certain misdemeanors.

20.   Senator Pettifogger gets an item inserted into the federal budget which allocates $6,000,000 for building a ski lift at a resort in his home state. This is known as

(A)   a filibuster.   (D)   grease for the gears.

(B)   pork barrel legislation.   (E)   Senatorial courtesy.

(C)   logrolling.

21.   Which of the following statements reflects an elitist view of American politics?

(A)   American politics are dominated by the military-industrial complex.

(B)   Thousands of competing interest groups influence public policy-making.

(C)   Large states dominate public policy because of their overrepresentation in Congress.

(D)   American politics are dominated by rural areas at the expense of urban areas.

(E) Since only one registered voter in three votes in off-year congressional races, Congress represents only the politically active.

22. All of the following are formal or informal sources of presidential power EXCEPT

(A) the fact that the president is elected indirectly by the public, not by Congress.

(B) Supreme Court decisions which have expanded the president's emergency powers.

(C) high public approval ratings.

(D) the veto power.

(E) the ability to introduce legislation in either house of Congress.

23. Civil servants in the federal bureaucracy may sometimes successfully resist presidential initiatives because

(A) they can go directly to Congress with their budget requests.

(B) they have more opportunities to influence public opinion than the president does.

(C) they are directly responsible to Congress, but not to the president.

(D) they may not be removed from office for political reasons.

(E) they have influence over the president through campaign contributions.

24. The 1985 Gramm-Rudman Act

(A) outlawed the use of federal funds for abortions.

(B) established a mechanism for balancing the federal budget.

(C) prohibited the use of any federal funds for aiding the Contras in Nicaragua.

(D) changed the tax code to eliminate loopholes for the wealthy.

(E) provided for the destruction of intermediate range nuclear missiles in Europe.

25. In a single member district, plurality vote system

(A) a runoff election is usually necessary to determine the winner.

(B) parties are assigned seats based on the proportion of votes they receive in a district.

(C) the candidate with the most votes represents the district.

(D) some votes count more than others in determining which candidate wins the election.

(E) third parties are more likely to win seats than in proportional representation systems.

26. The top official in the Department of Justice is the

(A) Solicitor General.   (D) Attorney General.

(B) Secretary of Justice. (E) Chief Justice.

(C) Secretary of State.

27. Which of the following is a FALSE statement about the Democratic Party's national convention?

(A) It selects the state party chairmen.

(B) It determines the national party platform.

(C) It nominates the party's candidate for president.

(D) It has "super delegates" not chosen by state primaries and caucuses.

(E) It sets the time and place for the next national convention.

28. All of the following statements represent positions the Supreme Court has taken on the First Amendment right to freedom of religion EXCEPT that

(A) public school officials may write a non-denominational prayer for school children to recite at the beginning of each school day.

(B) public school teachers may not conduct devotional readings of the Bible in class.

(C) a copy of the Ten Commandments may not be posted on the walls of public school classrooms.

(D) Creation Science may not be taught in public schools.

(E) states may not outlaw the teaching of evolution in the public schools.

29. The Constitution, as ratified in 1788, provided for popular vote for

(A) election of the president.

(B) election of senators.

(C) ratification of treaties.

(D) ratification of constitutional amendments.

(E) None of the above.

30. The Great Compromise of 1787

   (A) resolved the controversy over the status of slaves under the Constitution.

   (B) provided for an electoral college for selection of the president.

   (C) provided for the direct election of senators.

   (D) provided for equal representation of states in the Senate and representation based on population in the House.

   (E) added a Bill of Rights to the Constitution.

31. Which of the following best defines the term "judicial restraint"?

   (A) A decision by judges to limit the number of cases they decide per year

   (B) Refusal by judges to lobby Congress for funds

   (C) A practice by which judges remove themselves from cases in which they have a personal interest

   (D) The tendency of judges to interpret the Constitution in light of the original intent of its framers

   (E) Willingness of judges to decline participation in partisan political campaigns

32. A bill introduced in the House or Senate will most likely

   (A) be passed by the first house but not the second.

   (B) be passed by both houses and become law.

   (C) be sent to the rules committee, then the full house.

   (D) die before it is referred to committee.

   (E) be referred to the appropriate committee, but never reach the floor of the house.

33. Which of the following is true of the president's veto power?

   I. A president may veto certain items in a bill but approve the rest.

   II. A president may pocket-veto a bill by refusing to sign it for 10 days while Congress is in session.

   III. A presidential veto may be overridden by a two-thirds vote of both houses of Congress.

   (A) I only   (B) II only

(C)   III only   (D)   II and III only

(E)   I, II, and III

34.   Which of the following is true of independent regulatory commissions?

   (A)   They exercise quasi-legislative, quasi-judicial, and executive functions.

   (B)   They each form part of one of the 14 cabinet-level executive departments.

   (C)   They regulate certain parts of the federal bureaucracy.

   (D)   They are directly responsible to the president.

   (E)   They were created by the executive branch to help execute federal law.

Source: *Guide to Congress,* 2nd ed. (Washington, D.C.: Congressional Quarterly Inc., 1976), p. 563.

35. The subject of the cartoon on the previous page is most likely

(A) the influence of environmental issues on Congressional behavior.

(B) a gerrymandered Congressional district.

(C) the role of money in influencing the outcome of an election.

(D) the beastly effect of politics on the character of a congressman.

(E) "dinosaur bills," which congressmen sponsor for the folks back home.

36. The War Powers Resolution of 1973 may be invoked by Congress to accomplish which of the following?

(A) Prevent the president from deploying troops abroad

(B) Declare war

(C) Force the extradition of foreign ambassadors caught spying in the United States

(D) Limit the period for which the president may deploy troops abroad in hostile situations

(E) Force reductions in the defense budget in times of peace and stability

37. Changes in the House of Representatives since the early 1970s have resulted in all of the following EXCEPT

(A) strengthening of the seniority system for determining committee chairmanships.

(B) an increase in the total number of subcommittees.

(C) an increase in the total number of congressional staff.

(D) an increase in the power of junior members of the House.

(E) very high reelection rates for incumbents during the 1980s.

Questions 38 and 39 are based on the following excerpt from a major Supreme Court decision.

The object of the [14th] amendment was undoubtedly to enforce the absolute equality of the [white and black] races before the law, but in the nature of things, it could not have been intended to abolish distinctions based upon color, or to enforce social, as distinguished from, political, equality, or a commingling of the two races upon terms unsatisfactory to either. Laws permitting, even requiring, their separation, in places where they are liable to be brought into contact, do not necessarily imply the inferiority of either race to the other, and have been generally, if not universally recognized as within the competency of the state legislatures in the exercise of their police power. The most common instance of this is connected with the establishment of separate schools for white and colored children, which have been held to be a valid exercise of the legislative power even by courts of states where the political rights of the colored race have been longest and most earnestly enforced.

38. The decision quoted above, which upheld the doctrine of "separate but equal," was from the case

   (A)   *Dred Scott vs. Sanford,* 1857.

   (B)   *West Virginia Board of Education vs. Barnette,* 1943.

   (C)   *Plessy vs. Ferguson,* 1896.

   (D)   *Columbus Board of Education vs. Penick,* 1979.

   (E)   *Mapp vs. Ohio,* 1961.

39. The case that overturned the above decision was

   (A)   *Brown vs. Board of Education,* 1954.

   (B)   *Swann vs. Charlotte-Mecklenburg County Board of Education,* 1971.

   (C)   *Engel vs. Vitale,* 1962.

   (D)   *Luther vs. Borden,* 1849.

   (E)   *Cantwell vs. Connecticut,* 1940.

40. The concept of "dual federalism" is best characterized by which of the following statements?

   (A)   The states may exercise only those powers delegated to them by Congress.

   (B)   The states have reserved powers which Congress may regulate as it sees fit.

   (C)   The powers of the states and the federal government overlap to such a degree that it is impossible to distinguish the two in practice.

   (D)   The state and federal governments are each sovereign and independent within their respective spheres of influence.

   (E)   The states created the federal government and have the right to nullify laws which, in their opinion, violate the federal Constitution.

41. Which of the following issues was left by the Constitutional Convention for the states to decide?

   (A)   The method of electing the president

   (B)   Qualifications of the electorate for voting in federal elections

   (C)   The method of ratifying amendments to the Constitution

(D) Qualifications for members of the House and Senate

(E) Whether or not to levy protective tariffs on imported goods

42. Given the current method of electing the president, which of the following is NOT possible?

(A) The presidential candidate with the most electoral votes fails to be elected president

(B) A presidential candidate with a majority of the popular votes fails to be elected president

(C) A presidential candidate with less than a majority of the popular vote is elected president

(D) A presidential candidate with less than a majority of the electoral votes is elected president

(E) A presidential candidate with a majority of the electoral vote fails to be elected president

43. A discharge petition is used in the House of Representatives to

(A) kill a bill that is under consideration on the House floor.

(B) force the rules committee to discharge a bill back to a standing committee that has reported the bill out with unacceptable amendments.

(C) force a discharge rule on a bill under consideration on the House floor so that amendments may be made to the bill.

(D) force a bill out of a committee which has held it for 30 days without reporting it out.

(E) send to the Senate a bill that has been approved by the House.

44. Which of the following Supreme Court decisions involved the Fourth Amendment prohibition against unlawful search and seizure?

(A) *Baker vs. Carr,* 1962   (D) *Korematsu vs. United States,* 1944

(B) *Roe vs. Wade,* 1973   (E) *Gideon vs. Wainwright,* 1963

(C) *Mapp vs. Ohio,* 1961

45. The Thirteenth, Fourteenth, and Fifteenth Amendments to the Constitution were intended primarily to

(A) protect the rights of blacks against infringement by southern state governments.

(B) expand the suffrage to women, blacks, and 18 year olds.

(C)   protect freedom of speech, religion, and assembly.

(D)   increase the power of the federal government in order to prevent the outbreak of another civil war.

(E)   apply the Bill of Rights to the state governments.

46.   Federal courts have responded to disputes between the president and Congress by

(A)   usually deciding in favor of Congress.

(B)   usually deciding in favor of the president.

(C)   terming the disputes "political questions" and generally refusing to hear or decide them.

(D)   deciding in favor of the president on domestic policy disputes and in favor of Congress on foreign policy disputes.

(E)   deciding against Congress only when it overrides a presidential veto and passes a law limiting the power of the president.

47.   When the House rules committee issues a closed rule

(A)   the House gallery is closed to the public during debate of a bill.

(B)   a particular bill may not be amended during floor debate.

(C)   vote on a bill is closed to those members who were not present during debate on the bill.

(D)   a particular bill may not be calendared without going first to the rules committee.

(E)   a bill passed in the House is closed to amendment in the Senate.

48.   One of the major problems with national government under the Articles of Confederation was that

(A)   the executive branch was too strong vis à vis the legislative branch.

(B)   the government had no power to levy direct taxes.

(C)   the national judiciary failed to exercise judicial review.

(D)   the Articles of Confederation were amended too frequently.

(E)   the bicameral legislature deadlocked frequently on controversial, but necessary, legislation.

49. Which of the following statements about the national media is/are TRUE?

    I.   Magazines and newspapers need no license to publish in the United States.

    II.   It is more difficult for a public figure or official to win a libel suit against the media in the United States than in any other country.

    III.   The U.S. government can exercise restraint over the media to prevent the publication of sensitive government information.

    (A)   I only   (D)   I and II only

    (B)   II only   (E)   I and III only

    (C)   III only

50. Which of the following statements is true about political action committees (PACs)?

    (A)   PACs have been an important part of American politics since the Great Depression.

    (B)   PACs gain influence over certain candidates by heavily subsidizing their campaigns.

    (C)   The number of PACs has grown dramatically between 1973 and the present.

    (D)   Formation of PACs is restricted to business and labor groups.

    (E)   The number of ideological PACs has increased much more slowly than the number of business or labor PACs.

51. Which of the following statements about the Equal Rights Amendment is false?

    (A)   It passed both houses of Congress, but was never ratified by three-fourths of the states.

    (B)   Congress extended the time limit for ratification of the amendment.

    (C)   Some states that ratified the amendment later tried to rescind their ratification.

    (D)   The amendment was intended to restore certain rights to blacks and Hispanics that had been restricted by a series of Supreme Court decisions.

    (E)   It was endorsed by every president from Harry Truman to Jimmy Carter.

52. The Federalist Papers

    I.   were written by Washington, Madison, and Adams.

    II. provided a theoretical justification for the Revolutionary War.

    III. are considered an authoritative commentary on the U.S. Constitution.

    (A) I only   (D) I and II only

    (B) II only   (E) I and III only

    (C) III only

53. Which of the following statements about interest groups are accurate?

    I.   Interest group activities, to influence public policy-making at the national level, are aimed almost entirely at Congress.

    II. The influence of labor unions on public policy-making has declined since 1945.

    III. Business organizations are the most numerous and powerful interest groups in America.

    (A) I only   (D) I and II only

    (B) II only   (E) II and III only

    (C) III only

54. During the past three decades, all of the following changes have occurred in political behavior and public opinion in the United States EXCEPT

    (A) the declining importance of political ideology as a factor influencing presidential nominations to the Supreme Court.

    (B) an increase in support for Republican presidential candidates in the South.

    (C) an increase in the influence of the conservative wing on the Republican Party.

    (D) a drop in voter turnout for congressional and presidential elections.

    (E) an increase in the number of voters who declare themselves to be Independents.

55. The first party competition for public offices in the United States occurred between which parties?

    (A) Federalists and Whigs

    (B) Whigs and Jeffersonian Republicans

(C) Federalists and Jeffersonian Republicans

(D) Democrats and Whigs

(E) Democrats and Republicans

56. The term "gender gap" refers to

(A) the fact that women turn out to vote in larger numbers than men.

(B) differences in political opinions between men and women.

(C) the fact that women live longer than men.

(D) the fact that men hold a much larger proportion of elective political offices than women do.

(E) a general apathy among women regarding electoral politics, which is not observable among men.

57. Of the following issues, which would be LEAST likely to be in the Republican national platforms of 1988 and 1992?

(A) Opposition to quotas to remedy past discrimination in housing, employment, and education

(B) Support for a reduction in the capital gains tax

(C) Support for a women's right to choice on abortion

(D) Support for a balanced budget amendment

(E) Opposition to increasing the minimum wage

58. Most vice presidential candidates are selected

I. by the party's nominee for president.

II. to balance the ticket.

III. based on their qualifications to succeed to the presidency in case of the death of the president.

(A) I only   (D) I and II only

(B) II only   (E) I, II, and III

(C) III only

59. All of the following are tenets of Keynesian economics EXCEPT

(A) an unregulated capitalist economy will inevitably go through boom and bust cycles.

(B) in order to stimulate production, government should cut tax rates to give producers incentives to produce.

(C) government should stimulate the economy by increased spending during times of high unemployment.

(D) government should reduce spending during times of high inflation.

(E) government should increase tax rates during times of high inflation.

60. Which of the following statements about public opinion polling is TRUE?

(A) Straw polls are scientific polls usually conducted by newspapers.

(B) The larger the population in question, the larger the sample size must be to maintain the same sampling error.

(C) Requirements for randomness may be satisfied quite easily by having respondents phone answers in to a television station.

(D) Overly technical questions may cause sampling error.

(E) Telephone surveys are generally unreliable because they target only those who can afford telephones.

STOP

This is the end of Section I.

If time still remains, you may check your work only in this section.
Do not begin Section II until instructed to do so.

Section II

TIME: 100 Minutes
4 Free-Response Questions
Approx. 50% of Total Grade

DIRECTIONS: Write an essay based on each of the following four questions. Be sure to pace yourself by allotting about one-fourth of your time, or 25 minutes, for each question. Where appropriate, use substantive examples in your answers. Your essays should be numbered to correspond with the questions to which you are responding.

---

1. **Arkansas Presidential Election Results**

<u>1992</u>
Clinton (D)   505,823 (53%)
Bush (R)   337,324 (35%)
Perot (I)   99,132 (10%)

<u>1988</u>
Dukakis (D)   349,237 (42%)
Bush (R)   466,578 (56%)

U.S. Presidential Election Results

<u>1992</u>
Clinton (D)   44,908,233 (43%)
Bush (R)   39,102,282 (37%)
Perot (I)   19,741,048 (19%)

<u>1988</u>
Dukakis (D)   41,809,074 (46%)
Bush (R)   48,886,097 (53%)

Recent election results illustrate the "favorite son" phenomenon still has an impact in American electoral politics.

a) What might you infer about American political behavior based on this data?

b) What impact does this kind of voting have for American politics?

2.   The development of primary elections has produced major changes in the nomination process in the United States. Discuss how BOTH direct primary elections and presidential primary elections have affected the traditional role of the two major political parties in the United States.

3.   What is the relationship between the executive and legislative branches of government in the making of foreign policy? In explaining this relationship, identify some of the specific issues that have arisen in recent years over the respective powers of the two branches.

4.   Identify what is meant by "interest group" and explain how such groups function in contemporary American political life.

END OF EXAM

UNITED STATES GOVERNMENT AND POLITICS

TEST 1

ANSWER KEY

1. (B)	16. (A)	31. (D)	46. (C)
2. (A)	17. (E)	32. (E)	47. (B)
3. (C)	18. (D)	33. (C)	48. (B)
4. (E)	19. (B)	34. (A)	49. (D)
5. (D)	20. (B)	35. (B)	50. (C)
6. (B)	21. (A)	36. (D)	51. (D)
7. (A)	22. (E)	37. (A)	52. (C)
8. (C)	23. (D)	38. (C)	53. (E)
9. (D)	24. (B)	39. (A)	54. (A)
10. (C)	25. (C)	40. (D)	55. (C)
11. (A)	26. (D)	41. (B)	56. (B)
12. (A)	27. (A)	42. (E)	57. (C)
13. (B)	28. (A)	43. (D)	58. (D)
14. (E)	29. (E)	44. (C)	59. (B)
15. (D)	30. (D)	45. (A)	60. (D)

DETAILED EXPLANATIONS
OF ANSWERS
TEST 1

Section I

1.   **(B)**   A writ of habeas corpus is a court order which directs an official who is detaining someone to produce the person before the court so that the legality of the detention may be determined. The primary function of the writ is to effect the release of someone who has been imprisoned without due process of law. For example, if the police detained a suspect for an unreasonable time without officially charging the person with a crime, the person could seek relief from a court in the form of a writ of habeas corpus. (A) is incorrect because a writ of mandamus is a court order commanding an official to perform a legal duty of his or her office. It is not used to prevent persons from being improperly imprisoned. The Fourth Amendment requirement that police have probable cause in order to obtain a search warrant regulates police procedure. It is not itself a mechanism for affecting release of a person for improper imprisonment, so (C) is incorrect. Answer (D) is incorrect since the decision in *Roe vs. Wade* dealt with a woman's right to have an abortion. It had nothing to do with improper imprisonment. Answer (E) is incorrect since the prohibition against ex post facto laws is not a mechanism for affecting the release of someone who is improperly imprisoned. Rather, it declares that changing the legal implications of an act, after the act has been committed, is improper.

2.   **(A)**   (A) is the best answer since the term "casework" is used by political scientists to describe the activities of congressmen on behalf of individual constituents. These activities might include helping an elderly person secure social security benefits, or helping a veteran obtain medical services. Most casework is actually done by congressional staff, and may take as much as a third of the staff's time. Congressmen supply this type of assistance for the good public relations it provides. Answer (B) fails because pork barrel legislation is rarely if ever intended to help individual citizens. Pork barrel legislation authorizes federal spending for special projects, such as airports, roads, or dams, in the home state or district of a congressman. It is meant to help the entire district or state. Also, there is no legal entitlement on the part of a citizen to a pork barrel project, such as there is with social security benefits. (C) is not the answer because lobbying is

an activity directed toward congressmen, not one done by congressmen. A lobbyist attempts to get congressmen to support legislation that will benefit the group which the lobbyist represents. Log rolling, (D), is incorrect because it does not refer to congressional service for constituents. It refers instead to the congressional practice of trading votes on different bills. Congressman A will vote for congressman B's pork barrel project and in return B will vote for A's pork barrel project. Filibustering, (E), is incorrect. It is a technique used in the Senate to postpone a vote on a piece of legislation. The Senate has a tradition of unlimited debate and nongermane debate. This means that a senator may hold the floor for as long as (s)he likes and need not confine his/her remarks to the bill under consideration. Senators opposing a bill might get control of the floor and talk until the supporters agree to withdraw the bill from consideration.

3. **(C)** The franking privilege is the right of congressmen to send mail to constituents at public expense. Challengers do not enjoy this privilege. Observers have noticed that the amount of free congressional mail increases during election years, as members try to keep their names before their constituents. Answer (A) is incorrect since incumbent congressmen certainly do not have access to unlimited campaign funds. Congressmen may spend as much of their own money as they wish, and they are free to raise money from contributors. But no candidate has unlimited personal funds, nor can incumbents raise unlimited funds from contributions. Answer (B) is incorrect because incumbents and challengers may both have access to national party employees as campaign workers. Both political parties have campaign committees for the House and Senate. All of the committees supply campaign managers, communications directors, and fund raising experts to challengers and incumbents during election campaigns. (D) is incorrect because the Federal Election Campaign Act of 1974 placed a limit of $1,000 per election on individual contributions to political candidates. This put an end to so called "fat cat" contributors who used to contribute vast sums to candidates. (E) is incorrect because the federal government does not finance any aspect of congressional campaigns.

4. **(E)** The correct response is (E), since major differences between procedures in the House and Senate include all three of the features mentioned. Because the size of the House is fairly large, with 435 members, time for debate must be limited. If each member was allowed to speak as long as (s)he wanted on every bill, the House could not complete all of its business. Also, debate in the House must be germane. That is, when a member rises to speak, his/her comments must be related to the subject under consideration. This is another time-saving mechanism. The Senate has only 100 members, and is not as rushed for time as the House. The Senate has traditionally allowed members to speak as long as they wish, and does not force them to confine their remarks to the subject at hand. In the House, the rules committee is very powerful. No bill may get to the House floor without a rule from the rules committee. The rule gives

the conditions for debate. The rule sets the time limit for debate and states whether and on what conditions the bill can be amended. The rules committee in the Senate has no such powers.

5.   **(D)**   In *McCulloch vs. Maryland* (1819), the Supreme Court struck down a Maryland law which levied a tax on the Baltimore branch of the bank of the United States. The Court's ruling was based on its interpretation of the "necessary and proper clause" of the Constitution. This clause may be found in Article I, section 8, of the Constitution. The Court ruled that the necessary and proper clause gives to Congress all powers which make it more convenient for Congress to carry out the enumerated powers of Article I, section 8. (Enumerated powers are those which are specifically mentioned.) The clause is also known as the "elastic clause" since the Court ruled that it gives unspecified powers to Congress. The Court's ruling gave the broadest possible interpretation to the clause, making it possible for Congress to do many things which are not specifically mentioned in the Constitution. By contrast, the Court could have ruled that the clause gave Congress only those powers which are absolutely indispensable to carrying out the enumerated powers. Such a narrow interpretation of the clause would have limited Congress to those activities without which it could not possibly carry out the enumerated powers. (A) is incorrect since *McCulloch vs. Maryland* did not deal with freedom of speech. Answer (B) fails because the power of judicial review (the right of the Court to strike down laws of Congress and to review the actions of the executive) was claimed by the Court in *Marbury vs. Madison*, 1803. (C) is incorrect since the Court had previously struck down a law of Congress in *Marbury vs. Madison*. Finally, (E) is incorrect because *McCulloch vs. Maryland* had nothing to do with the question of executive privilege.

6.   **(B)**   The question asks which statement about the Cabinet is false. Answer (B) is false, and, therefore, the correct answer. The Constitution states in Article I, section 6, that no person holding any office under the United States may be a member of Congress. Since Cabinet positions are offices under the United States, Cabinet officials may not be members of Congress. Answers (A) and (D) are true. The Cabinet includes the heads of each of the 14 executive departments (State, Treasury, Interior, etc.) as stated in (A). In addition, the president may appoint any other high ranking official whom he wishes to the Cabinet, as stated in (D). Answer (C) is true. President Washington was the first to hold Cabinet meetings. Every president since Washington has used the Cabinet as a tool for managing the federal bureaucracy. So answer (C) is not the correct choice. Answer (E) is not the correct choice. As we saw in the explanation for answer (B), the Constitution states that no one holding office under the United States may be a member of Congress. This means that senators may not be members of the Cabinet.

7. **(A)** The Federal Reserve Board is a government agency consisting of seven members appointed for 14-year terms by the president, with the consent of the Senate. This board is at the head of the Federal Reserve System, which is comprised of member banks across the country. The primary function of the Federal Reserve Board is to implement monetary policy. The Federal Reserve Board has three methods of implementing monetary policy. First, it can change the reserve requirement, which is the amount of cash that member banks must keep on deposit in a regional Federal Reserve Bank. An increase in the requirement reduces the amount of cash a bank has on hand to loan. Second, the board can change the discount rate, which is the interest rate that member banks must pay to borrow money from a Federal Reserve Bank. A higher rate discourages a member bank from borrowing and lending more money. Third, the board can buy and sell government securities. To increase the money supply the board sells securities. To decrease the money supply the board buys securities. Answer (B) is the most plausible alternative to (A), but fails because controlling government spending is a function of Congress and the president. Answer (C) is incorrect because the Federal Reserve Board has nothing to do with regulating commodity prices. Answer (D) is incorrect because the Board does not help the president run the executive branch. Answer (E) is incorrect because the Board does not keep records of troop strength in army reserve units.

8. **(C)** The three largest countries of Western Europe—the United Kingdom, France, and the Federal Republic of Germany—have either a multi-party system or a two-plus party system. A multi-party system is one in which three or more major parties compete for seats in the national legislature, while a two-plus party system has two large parties and one or more small parties. The United Kingdom has a two-plus party system. There are two large parties, the Conservatives and Labour. The Liberals are a smaller third party and there are even smaller regional parties in Scotland, Northern Ireland, and Wales. France has a multi-party system. The Socialists, Neo-Gaullists, and Republicans are major parties, while the Communists and the National Front are small parties with few seats in parliament. The Federal Republic of Germany has a two-plus party system. The major parties are the Christian Democratic Union and the Social Democratic Party. At the fringes of public life are the Greens and the Neo-Nazis. The United States, by contrast, has only two parties which successfully compete on a national basis from one election to the next. These are, of course, the Democrats and the Republicans. Answer (A) is incorrect. In Western European countries, party leaders determine which persons will run for office under the party banner. In the United States, on the other hand, candidates for office are selected by the voters in primary elections. Sometimes in the United States a candidate whom the party leadership detests wins the primary, and thus the right to run for office under the party banner. In most Western European countries, political parties are much more centralized than in the United States; therefore, (B) is false. Answer (D) is false. Because the parties are centralized in Western Europe, and because party leaders select candidates for national office, a party member in the national legislature seldom votes against the party. If one did, party leaders would remove his or her name from the ballot in future elections. Answer (E) is incorrect. Since party

members vote the party line almost all of the time in Western Europe, voters tend to not focus on the personalities of candidates, but rather on the party label. In the United States, where legislators vote their personal preference as often as the party line, party label is less important to voters. Voters in the United States tend to focus more on the personalities of candidates than European voters.

9. **(D)**   In a parliamentary system the chief executive, normally called the prime minister, is a member of parliament, the legislative body. The majority party in the lower house of the parliament selects its leader to be prime minister. The prime minister then selects a Cabinet from among the members of the lower house who are in his/her party. The prime minister and Cabinet are the highest executive officers of the country, and are usually referred to as the government. There is no strict separation of powers, since the executive branch is made up of members of the legislature. In a presidential system, by contrast, the president is not a member of the legislature and is selected by popular, not by legislative vote. Cabinet members may not sit in the legislature. There is, then, a strict separation of powers, and I is true. In a presidential system, the voters choose the president either by direct popular vote or through an electoral college. In a parliamentary system, the majority party in the lower house of parliament chooses one of its members as prime minister. The general public does not participate in choosing the prime minister. So choice II is also true. In a parliamentary system the prime minister may call special elections for the lower house of the legislature whenever (s)he wants. In a presidential system the president may not call a special election for members of the legislature, so III is false. The answer, then, is (D), I and II.

10. **(C)**   Political scientists use the term "pluralistic" to describe a political system in which innumerable groups of people share cultural, economic, religious, or ethnic interests. These groups organize and spend great amounts of time and money competing to influence government policy-making. The pluralistic concept of democracy is in contrast to the elitist model, which states that policy-making is dominated by elites such as wealthy industrialists, military leaders, or organizations such as the Trilateral Commission. Therefore, the answer is (C). Answer (A) fails because pluralism stresses not only cultural groups, but economic, religious, and other types of groups. Also important to pluralism is the idea that the different groups do not merely exist, but compete to influence public policy-making. Answer (B) fails because the term to describe a system in which political power is divided between national and state governments is "federalism." Answer (D) fails because to say that one group is overrepresented is more like an elitist view than a pluralistic view of politics. It is true that candidates for national office are elected by a plurality vote method, (E). "Plurality vote" means that the candidate who gets the most votes, even if less than a majority, wins the election. However, the term "pluralism" does not refer to this method of election, so answer (E) is wrong.

11. **(A)** As the graph on the next page shows, there is a direct correlation between voter turnout and educational level. Those with four years or more of college are more likely to vote than are those with one to three years of college. Those with one to three years of college are more likely to vote than are high school graduates. High school graduates are, in turn, more likely to vote than are those with less than a high school education. The answer is (A), the more schooling one has, the more likely one is to vote. Voting is only one form of political participation. Other forms are running for office, working in political campaigns, and contributing to campaigns. While it is difficult to find statistics which show the correlation between educational status and running for office, we do know that most people who are completely inactive (that is, do not participate in politics in any way) typically have little education and low incomes and are relatively young. Therefore, it is safe to conclude that the less education one has, (B), the LESS likely one is to run for office; so (B) is not the answer. Answer (C) is clearly wrong, since many studies have shown a direct correlation between advanced educational status and political participation by voting. Answer (D) is wrong, as is clear from the graph above. Those with a high school education are NOT more likely to vote than are those with a college degree. Answer (E) is wrong because, as the graph shows, the less education one has, the less likely one is to vote. It is logical to infer from this that those with no formal schooling are less likely to vote than are those with a high school education.

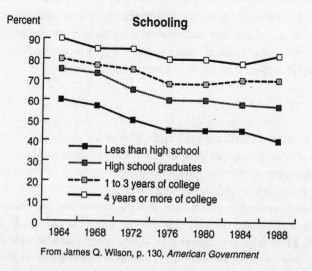

From James Q. Wilson, p. 130, *American Government*

12. **(A)** The table shows party identification by social groups. The term "party identification" refers to the psychological attachment of a voter to a political party. A voter with a Republican Party identification is, of course, likely to vote Republican in a given race, while a voter with a Democrat identification is likely to vote Democrat. (A) is the correct response. We can see from the chart that blacks are more likely to be Democrats, while whites are more likely to be Republicans. Females are more likely than males to be Democrats. About 50% of people in service occupations are Democrats, while less than 20% are Republicans. Skilled workers are slightly more likely to be Republicans than Democrats. Taking all of these factors into consideration, we may

infer that a black female in a service occupation is more likely to vote Democrat than a white male skilled worker, (A). Answer (B) is false. Females are more likely to be Democrats than are males. Those making under $10,000 are more likely to be Democrats than are those making $50,000 or more. Answer (C) is false. Those with no high school diploma are more likely to be Democrats than are those with some college. Answer (D) is false. Blacks are less likely to be Republicans than are whites, and people earning $10,000-$19,999 are less likely to be Republicans than are those earning $29,999. Answer (E) is false. Whites are less likely to be Democrats than are blacks. Those without high school diplomas are less likely to be Democrats than are those with high school diplomas.

13. **(B)** In 1932, Franklin Roosevelt was elected president in a landslide vote, ending a 12 year period of Republican domination of the presidency. This election is considered by political scientists a "realigning election." A realigning election is one in which a sharp, lasting change occurs in the coalition of voters which supports each of the parties. In the election of 1936, Roosevelt drew into the Democratic Party a coalition of urban workers, blacks, southern whites, and Jews. Most of the urban workers were also union members. The coalition did not include large numbers of business interests, which continued to vote for the Republican Party. This coalition continued to support the Democratic Party until approximately 1968, when white Southerners began to vote for the Republican candidate for president more often than for the Democratic candidate. The answer is (B), northern business leaders, since most of these voters supported the Republicans in each of the years Roosevelt ran for president (1932, 1936, 1940, and 1944). Answer (A) is wrong because most Southerners, white and black alike, voted for Roosevelt each time he ran for president. Answer (C) is wrong because blue collar workers heavily supported Roosevelt in each of his elections. Answer (D) is wrong because blacks and Jews, two prominent racial minorities, voted for Roosevelt. Answer (E) is false because union members, who were mostly blue collar workers, heavily supported Roosevelt.

14. **(E)** The Fifth Amendment to the U.S. Constitution states "No person shall… be compelled in any criminal case to be a witness against himself…." The Supreme Court held in *Miranda vs. Arizona,* 1966, that "In order to…permit a full opportunity to exercise the privilege against self-incrimination, the accused must be adequately and effectively apprised of his rights and the exercise of those rights must be fully honored." This means that when police apprehend a suspect in a criminal case they must immediately tell the person that (s)he has a right to remain silent. The Sixth Amendment to the U.S. Constitution states "In all criminal prosecutions, the accused shall enjoy the right…to have compulsory process for obtaining witnesses in his favor, and to have Assistance of Counsel for his defense. The compulsory process clause means that the accused can subpoena witnesses in his/her favor to appear in court to testify for the

defense. (A subpoena is a court order which commands a person to appear at a certain time and place to give testimony upon a certain matter.) The assistance of counsel clause of the Sixth Amendment was interpreted by the Supreme Court in *Argersinger vs. Hamlin,* 1972, to mean that if the accused cannot afford an attorney, (s)he is entitled to have one appointed at government expense, in any felony or misdemeanor criminal case in which, if the accused is found guilty, (s)he may be sentenced to jail. It is clear from the above that the rights mentioned in statements I, II, and III are all guaranteed by the Constitution. Therefore, answer (E) is correct.

15. **(D)** Before the Civil War most blacks in the South were slaves. They were not citizens and had no civil or political rights. After the war, the Fourteenth and Fifteenth Amendments were added to the Constitution. The Fourteenth Amendment extended citizenship to blacks. The Fifteenth Amendment stated that the "right of citizens of the United States to vote shall not be denied or abridged by the United States or by any state on account of race, color, or previous condition of servitude." Contrary to what one might assume, blacks did not immediately gain full voting rights. During the 1870s the Supreme Court held that the Fifteenth Amendment did not automatically confer the right to vote on anybody. States could not pass laws to prevent anyone from voting on the basis of race, but they could restrict persons from voting on other grounds. This interpretation of the Fifteenth Amendment allowed southern states to use several techniques to effectively exclude blacks from voting. Since most former slaves were illiterate, prospective voters were often required to pass literacy tests. Poll taxes were also levied, which kept blacks, who were mostly poor, from voting. Since many whites were also poor and illiterate, grandfather clauses were enacted to allow them to bypass the legal restrictions on voting. Grandfather clauses stated that if you or your ancestors had voted before 1867, you could vote without paying a poll tax or passing a literacy test. Answer (D) is correct because the purpose of grandfather clauses and literacy tests was to keep blacks from voting. Answer (A) is wrong because the purpose of the grandfather clause was to allow poor and illiterate whites to escape voting restrictions. Answer (B) is wrong because the intent of the restrictions was to prevent blacks, not immigrants, from voting. In addition, there was little immigration into the South during the time in question. Answers (C) and (E) are wrong because the measures were restrictions on the right to vote, not on the right to run for office.

16. **(A)** The passage is taken from the landmark case *Marbury vs. Madison,* 1803. What the passage means, in everyday language, is:

1. Interpreting laws is a judicial function. 2. When two laws conflict, the courts must decide which will be enforced. 3. The Constitution is superior to laws passed by Congress or state legislatures (called statutory law). 4. Therefore, if a statute conflicts with the Constitution, the statute cannot be enforced by the courts.

Answer (B) is incorrect because the passage says nothing about Congress's right to pass laws to carry out its duties. Rather, the passage deals with a conflict between statutory and Constitutional law. Answer (C) is incorrect because it contradicts the main thesis of the passage. The passage clearly says that it is the duty of COURTS, not legislatures, to "say what the law is," which means the same as "interpretation of laws." Answer (D) is incorrect because the passage says when an act of the legislature and the Constitution conflict, the Constitution governs the case. Answer (E) is incorrect because the passage states specifically that if two laws conflict, the courts must decide the operation of each. It then posits a case where the two laws in conflict are an act of the legislature and the Constitution. The clear implication is that, in such a case, the courts must decide on the operation of the Constitution, which means deciding questions of Constitutional law.

17. **(E)**   After a bill is introduced into either house of Congress, it is referred to the appropriate committee. The bill will then usually be referred by the committee to a subcommittee. After holding a hearing on the bill, the subcommittee will then have a mark-up session where revisions and additions are made to the bill. The bill is then referred back to the full committee, which may also hold a hearing and have a mark-up session. Answers (A), (B), and (C) are incorrect because mark-up sessions do not occur in the majority leader's office, on the floor of the legislative chambers, or in party caucuses. Answer (D) is the most plausible alternative to (E), because a joint conference committee is, after all, a committee. However, proposed legislation goes to a joint conference committee only after it has passed both houses of Congress. The Constitution requires that before a piece of legislation can become law, it must pass both houses in identical form. The purpose of the joint conference committee is to iron out differences in a bill that has passed one house in a different form than in the other. It is true that changes are made to such a bill in a joint conference committee, to satisfy members of both houses. However, the term "mark-up session" refers only to the activity of standing committees and subcommittees in Congress, not to joint conference committees.

18. **(D)**   The Office of Management and Budget is the chief presidential staff agency. Its primary responsibility is to put together the budget that the president submits to Congress. Each agency and office of the executive branch must have its budget requests cleared by OMB before it gets into the president's budget. The OMB also studies the organization and operations of the executive branch, to ensure that each office and agency is carrying out its appropriate duty, as assigned by law. Answer (A) is incorrect because the Department of Commerce does not help the president to draw up his annual budget. The Department of Commerce was created in 1903 to protect the interests of business people at home and abroad. Answer (B) is incorrect because the Department of Treasury is not involved in drawing up the president's budget. The functions of the Treasury Department include collecting taxes through the Internal

Revenue Service, an administrative unit of Treasury, administering the public debt, and coining money. Answer (C) is incorrect because the main responsibility of the Federal Reserve Board is the implementation of monetary policy (see explanation for question 7). It has nothing to do with drawing up the president's annual budget. Answer (E) is incorrect because the Cabinet does not help the president draw up his budget. It advises the president on the administration of the executive departments.

19. **(B)** In 1974, in the case *United States vs. Nixon*, the Supreme Court declared that the president has an executive privilege to protect military, diplomatic, and sensitive national security secrets from disclosure. However, the material may be successfully subpoenaed if needed by either the defense or the state in a criminal prosecution. (A) is incorrect since the right of the president to veto proposed legislation is called the veto power. It has nothing to do with the president's right to protect information from disclosure. (C) is incorrect because the right of the president to appoint and receive ambassadors is unrelated to the executive privilege of withholding certain information. (D) is incorrect because the president's power to pardon is unrelated to executive privilege. Also, the president has an unlimited, not a limited, right to pardon persons convicted of federal crimes. (E) is incorrect because the president enjoys no immunity from prosecution for misdemeanors or felonies.

20. **(B)** Special spending projects sponsored by members of Congress for their home states or districts are known as pork barrel legislation. (A) is incorrect because a filibuster is an attempt in the Senate to talk a bill to death by preventing it from coming up for a vote. (C) is incorrect because logrolling is the term used to designate vote-swapping by members of Congress for special projects. (D) is incorrect because "grease for the gears" is a fictitious term made up as a distractor for this question. (E) is incorrect because "Senatorial courtesy" refers to an informal practice whereby the president seeks to have a judicial nominee approved by the senior senator from the state in which the nominee will sit.

21. **(A)** An elitist view of American politics stresses that the policy-making process is dominated by a small, unrepresentative minority. In *The Power Elite*, published in 1956, the American sociologist C. Wright Mills argued that corporate leaders, top military officers, and key political leaders dominated American politics. (B) is incorrect because the view that thousands of competing interest groups influence policy-making is called a "pluralistic" view of politics. (C) is incorrect because the view that large states dominate public policy, if such a view is held by anyone, has no name. Such a view would be difficult to defend, since all states get two senators regardless of population. (D) is incorrect because such a view has no specific name. Again, such a view would be difficult

to defend, since rural areas have such a small population relative to urban areas, and state legislators and U.S. representatives are chosen on the basis of population. (E) is plausible but incorrect. It is true that only about one-third of eligible voters turn out in off-year Congressional races (the figure was 33% in 1986). However, this fact does not provide the basis for an elitist theory, since it is not clear that election outcomes would have been different if twice as many voters had voted. Also, low voter turnout does not necessarily mean that policy-making is insulated from public opinion and wishes, which is central to elitist theories.

22. **(E)** The president does not have the ability to personally introduce legislation in either house of Congress. To introduce legislation in either house, one must be a member of that house. (A) is incorrect because the fact that he is elected indirectly by the people, not by the legislature as in parliamentary systems, is a source of power and independence for the president. (B) is incorrect because the Supreme Court has expanded the president's emergency powers. See, for example, the Prize Cases, 1863; and *Korematsu vs. U.S.*, 1944. (C) is incorrect because when the president has high public approval ratings, as measured in opinion polls, he is in a much better position to push his legislative proposals through Congress. (D) is incorrect because the veto power can be wielded very effectively by presidents to prevent the passage of legislation they don't like. President Bush had vetoed more than 20 bills by January 1992, and none of the vetoes had been overridden by Congress.

23. **(D)** Nearly all civil servants have jobs that are, practically speaking, beyond reach of the president. The only reasons for which a federal civil servant can be fired are misconduct or poor performance, and then only if the person's supervisor is willing to invest a great deal of time and effort. Civil servants cannot be fired for political reasons. This gives civil servants the opportunity to thwart or delay presidential initiatives by halfhearted compliance or passive noncompliance with presidential directives. (A) is incorrect because all agency budget requests must be submitted to and approved by the Office of Management and Budget before they can be sent to Congress. (B) is incorrect because the president has many more opportunities to influence public opinion than do civil servants. The presidency is a much more high-profile office than any civil service position, and the president has access to television and newspaper coverage that civil servants generally do not. (C) is incorrect because, technically, the federal bureaucracy is part of the executive branch, and is directly responsible to the president. (E) is incorrect because the Hatch Act, passed in 1939, made it illegal for civil servants to solicit campaign contributions.

24. **(B)** In 1985, Congress passed the Gramm-Rudman Act with the intent to

balance the federal budget by 1992. The law created a plan whereby the budget deficit for each year from 1986 through 1991 could not exceed a specified, declining amount. Therefore, the correct response is (B). (A) is incorrect because the Hyde Amendment of 1976 outlawed the use of federal funds for abortions, except where the life of the mother is at stake. (C) is incorrect because the Boland Amendments outlawed the use of federal funds to aid the Nicaraguan Contras. (D) is incorrect because the Gramm-Rudman Act did not change the tax code. (E) is incorrect because the INF Treaty of 1987 provided for the destruction of intermediate range missiles in Europe.

25. **(C)** The "single member district" part of the term means that each district gets a single representative. The "plurality vote system" part means that the candidate with the most votes, even if less than a majority, wins the election. Therefore, (C) is the correct answer. (A) is incorrect because a runoff election is not necessary in a plurality voting system. If the candidate with the most votes wins, whether or not (s)he gets a majority, there is no need for a runoff. (B) is incorrect because each district gets only one representative in a single member district system. (D) is incorrect because there is no requirement that some votes count more than others in a single member district, plurality vote system. Members of the U.S. House of Representatives are chosen by the single member, plurality vote system. In elections for U.S. Representatives, each person's vote counts the same as any other person's vote. (E) is incorrect because third parties are more likely to win seats in a multi-member district, proportional representation system. In such systems, each district gets several representatives, and each party gets a number of seats proportionate to its total vote in the district election. Third parties are more likely to gain seats, since it is possible for them to get 10% or 20% of the vote, and thus 10% or 20% of the seats for the district. In single member district, plurality vote systems, by contrast, the party with the plurality gets the one seat, and all others get nothing.

26. **(D)** The Attorney General is the Cabinet official in charge of the Justice Department. (A) is incorrect because the Solicitor-General is the third-ranking official at the Justice Department. (B) is incorrect because there is no federal official designated Secretary of Justice. (C) is incorrect because the Secretary of State is in charge of the State Department. (E) is incorrect because the Chief Justice sits on the Supreme Court.

27. **(A)** The question asks which statement is false. (A) is the correct response because the state party conventions choose their respective state party chairmen. (B) is a true statement. The party platform is written at the national party convention. (C) is a true statement, since the convention does nominate the party's candidate for president. (D) is a true statement since the Democratic Party, unlike the Republican Party, has several hundred "super delegates" who are free to vote for the nominee of their choice

at the convention. The super delegates are Democratic governors, congressmen, and other distinguished party members. (E) is a true statement because one of the functions of the convention is to set the time and place of the next convention.

28. **(A)** The question requires you to identify the false statement. The correct response is (A), since the Court declared in *Engel vs. Vitale,* 1962, that a nondenominational prayer written by New York officials for recitation in public schools at the beginning of each school day, was unconstitutional. (B) is a true statement because the Court declared in *Abington School District vs. Schempp,* 1963, that a Pennsylvania law which required daily Bible reading in public schools was unconstitutional. (C) is a true statement because in *Stone vs. Graham,* 1980, the Court held unconstitutional a Kentucky statute which required the posting of a copy of the Ten Commandments, purchased with private funds, on the wall of every classroom in the state. (D) is a true statement because in *McLean vs. Arkansas Board of Education,* 1982, the Court held unconstitutional a law requiring that creation science be taught in public schools. (E) is a true statement because in *Epperson vs. Arkansas,* 1968, a law prohibiting the teaching of the theory of evolution in public schools was declared unconstitutional by the Court.

29. **(E)** The Constitution, as it came from the Constitutional Convention in 1788, provided for a direct popular vote for none of the items listed. Direct popular vote means that the general public votes on the item and that vote immediately determines the outcome of the election or issue. (A) is incorrect because the president is elected not by direct popular vote but by the electoral college. Originally, state legislatures chose the electors who made up the electoral college. (B) is incorrect because senators were originally chosen by the state legislatures. The Seventeenth Amendment, adopted in 1913, provides for popular election of senators. (C) is incorrect because treaties are ratified by a two-thirds vote of the Senate. (D) is incorrect because constitutional amendments are ratified in one of two ways. The first is by three-fourths of the state legislatures. The second is by three-fourths of state ratifying conventions. Congress determines which method will be used.

30. **(D)** The Great Compromise, also known as the Connecticut Compromise, occurred at the Constitutional Convention of 1787. It was a compromise between two plans known as the Virginia, or Large State Plan, and the New Jersey, or Small State Plan. It provided for a Senate in which each state would receive two senators, and a House of Representatives in which representation would be based on population. (A) is incorrect because the Great Compromise had nothing to do with the slavery question. (B) is incorrect because the Great Compromise had nothing to do with the electoral college. (C) is incorrect because senators were selected by state legislatures until the passage of

the Seventeenth Amendment. (E) is incorrect because the Great Compromise occurred during the Constitutional Convention, while the Bill of Rights was added to the Constitution after the Convention was over.

31. **(D)** There are two schools of thought on the proper method of constitutional interpretation by the judiciary. One is called "judicial activism." Advocates of this school believe that the intentions of those who wrote the Constitution should not be authoritative for the decision of controversial matters in the present. They say that judges should be free to adapt the Constitution to changing political and social circumstances. The other school is called "judicial restraint." Advocates of this school stress that the Constitution was a great contract by which the American people created a government. This contract laid the ground rules for the operation of the government, and it provided a formal process of amendment for changing those ground rules. In order to understand the ground rules, say advocates of restraint, one must determine the original intentions of those who wrote and ratified the Constitution. For unelected judges to assume to themselves the power to change the Constitution, according to this school, is for the judges to usurp a power that was not given them by the Constitution or the people. Therefore, the correct answer is (D). Answer (A) is incorrect because there is no general process by which judges limit the number of cases they hear in a year. Justices on the Supreme Court do have a lot of control over which cases they hear, through a process called "certiorari." When litigants appeal to the Court to have their cases heard, the justices vote on the merits of the cases. If four justices vote to hear a particular case, they issue a "writ of certiorari" to the lower court, ordering all documents relevant to the case to be sent up to the Supreme Court. Answer (B) is incorrect because judges do not lobby funds from Congress. Answer (C) is incorrect because when judges remove themselves from a case they are said to recuse themselves. Answer (E) is incorrect because judicial restraint refers to a method of interpreting the Constitution and has nothing to do with political campaigns.

32. **(E)** The vast majority of bills never make it out of committee to the floor of the chamber. Many are introduced by a member only to get publicity, or so the member can tell constituents that (s)he did something about the matter. (A) is incorrect since most bills die in committee. If a bill dies in committee, it cannot be considered, much less passed, by the whole house. There is a seldom-used procedure by which a bill can be forced out of committee in the house. First, 218 members must sign a discharge petition, then the petition must be approved by a majority vote of the full house. However, attempts to force a bill out of committee by discharge petition have succeeded only about 3% of the time in the twentieth century. (B) is incorrect because only a fraction of all bills introduced in either house ever become law. (C) is incorrect because bills are sent to the rules committee only after being reported out of a standing committee. Since most die in standing committee, they never make it to the rules committee. (D) is incorrect

because every bill introduced in either house is referred by the presiding officer to the appropriate committee.

33. **(C)** The correct response is (C) because I and II are false. A president may not veto particular items in a bill (I). Such a power is called a line-item veto, and is held by 43 governors in the U.S. A president may not pocket-veto a bill by holding it 10 days while Congress is in session (II). In such a case the bill becomes law without the president's signature. If Congress adjourns during the 10 day period, the bill is pocket-vetoed. The only true statement is III, the president's veto can be overridden if two-thirds of both houses vote to pass the bill despite the veto.

34. **(A)** When it created the independent regulatory commissions, Congress gave them the power to pass regulations (legislative), enforce the regulations (executive), and conduct hearings to determine the punishment for violators of the regulations (judicial). Answer (B) is incorrect because independent regulatory commissions, while nominally in the executive branch, are not included in any of the 14 executive departments. Answer (C) is incorrect because the regulatory commissions do not regulate the federal bureaucracy. Rather, some guard against unfair business practices, others police the side effects of business, such as pollution, and others protect consumers from unsafe products. Answer (D) is incorrect because the commissions were set up by Congress to be independent of the president. They are headed by commissioners who are appointed for fixed terms and are not removable by the president. The commissions must also be bipartisan in membership. Answer (E) is incorrect because the commissions were created by Congress.

35. **(B)** This is a famous political cartoon from 1812, when the Massachusetts state legislature created a misshapen district which would be a "safe district" for Congressman Elbridge Gerry. A safe district is one in which a particular political party, or in this case a particular person, is almost certain to win. When cartoonist John Gilbert saw the district he added a head, wings, and claws and called it a salamander. Newspaper editor Benjamin Russell replied that it should be called a "Gerrymander." The term has been used ever since to describe any congressional district of contorted boundaries which is created as a safe seat for a political party or candidate. Answer (A) is incorrect because the cartoon has nothing to do with environmental issues or congressional behavior. Answer (C) is incorrect because the cartoon has nothing to do with the influence of money on elections. Answer (D) is incorrect because the cartoon has nothing to do with the character of congressmen. Answer (E) is incorrect because the term "dinosaur bill" is a fictitious term concocted as a distractor for this question.

36. **(D)** The War Powers Resolution stipulates that the president can deploy troops abroad in situations where hostilities are imminent for only 60 days, unless Congress approves a longer deployment, declares war, or cannot meet because the nation is under attack. (A) is wrong because the War Powers Resolution does not authorize Congress to prevent the initial deployment of troops abroad by the president. Answer (B) is wrong because the Constitution gives Congress the power to declare war. The usual procedure begins with a request from the president for a declaration of war, which is then adopted by the Congress by joint resolution and signed by the president. The War Powers Resolution did nothing to change this procedure. Answer (C) is wrong because the War Powers Resolution has nothing to do with extradition of foreign ambassadors. Answer (E) is incorrect because the War Powers Resolution has no direct relation to the defense budget.

37. **(A)** The seniority system has been weakened in a number of ways since the early 1970s. In 1910, the House stripped the Speaker of some of his powers, including the important one of appointing committee members and chairmen. After the Speaker lost the power to appoint committee chairmen, the House began using the seniority system for determining committee chairmen. Whichever member of the majority party had the longest continuous service on the committee automatically became chairman. In addition, it was possible for a member to chair more than one subcommittee. In 1971, House Democrats made two important changes in the seniority system. First, they decided that no member could chair more than one subcommittee, which opened up several subcommittee chairmanships for mid-career members. Second, they decided to select committee chairmen by secret ballot in the Democratic caucus. While seniority no longer meant an automatic chairmanship, it was still honored in every case. In 1975, junior members of the House dealt the seniority system another blow by removing three senior committee members from chairmanships. In 1985, Les Aspin was selected chairman of the House Armed Services Committee despite the fact that he was not the most senior Democrat on the committee. Clearly, seniority has been weakened, not strengthened, since the early 1970s. (B) is incorrect because the "revolt" of 1975 resulted in an increase of the number of subcommittees. This allows members to gain information on proposed legislation from expert witnesses during subcommittee hearings, reducing members' need to rely on party leadership for information. (C) is incorrect because the "revolt" of 1975 resulted in an increase of congressional staff. Increased staff gives a member extra people to research issues, again freeing junior members from control by senior members, who formerly had larger staffs. (D) is not the correct response, since junior members have gained more power, more staff, and more access to information in subcommittees, through the weakening of the seniority system. In addition, the increase in the number of subcommittees resulted in the creation of more subcommittee chairmanships. This means more positions of authority are available to junior members. Now a large number of congressmen chair a committee or subcommittee. (E) is incorrect because reelection rates for incumbent representatives were very high during the 1980s. In 1986, the reelection rate was 97%, while in 1988 it was 98%. Two

things contribute to this. The first is the franking privilege, which allows incumbents to send mail free of charge. The second is the recent addition of television studios on Capital Hill in which congressmen can tape messages at public expense and send them home to local stations to be aired as "news from Washington." These privileges give incumbents an advantage over challengers and contribute to high reelection rates.

38. **(C)** The quotation is from *Plessy vs. Ferguson*, 1896. (A) is incorrect because in the Dred Scott case, which was before the Civil War, the Supreme Court held that blacks had no political rights under the Constitution. In the last sentence of the quotation, the Court mentions the political rights of blacks, and that these rights had been earnestly enforced in some states. Therefore, the case the quotation is an excerpt from must have been subsequent to the Dred Scott case. (B) is incorrect because in *West Virginia vs. Barnette*, the Court struck down a West Virginia law which required children in public schools to salute the flag and say the Pledge of Allegiance at the start of each school day. (D) is incorrect because in *Columbus Board of Education vs. Penick*, the Court declared that the public schools of Columbus, Ohio, were racially segregated in violation of the desegregation decision of *Brown vs. Board of Education*, 1954. (E) is incorrect because *Mapp vs. Ohio* dealt with a Fourth Amendment illegal search and seizure issue.

39. **(A)** In *Brown vs. Board of Education*, the Supreme Court declared racial segregation of public schools unconstitutional, even though the facilities of the white and black schools were equal. This effectively overturned the decision in Plessy, which had upheld the doctrine that racial segregation in public schools was constitutional so long as the facilities were of equal quality (separate but equal). (B) is incorrect because *Swann vs. Charlotte-Mecklenburg* did not itself establish the principle that state-sponsored segregation was unconstitutional. Rather, *Swann vs. Charlotte-Mecklenburg* dealt with the question of how to implement the *Brown vs. Board of Education* decision. (C) is incorrect because *Engel vs. Vitale* dealt with state-sponsored prayer in public schools. It had nothing to do with desegregation. (D) is incorrect because *Luther vs. Borden* was a "political question" case. It established the rule that certain political controversies would not be decided by the federal courts. The most common type of political question involves a dispute between the executive and legislative branches over the scope of their respective powers. (E) is incorrect because *Cantwell vs. Connecticut* dealt with the issues of freedom of speech and religion. It had nothing to do with desegregation of public facilities.

40. **(D)** The concept of dual federalism was predominant in American government from the post-Civil War period until approximately the 1930s. A typical description of this concept was given by the Supreme Court in the Tarbells case, 1872:

There are within the territorial limits of each state two governments (state and national), restricted in their spheres of action, but independent of each other, and supreme within their respective spheres. Each has its separate departments, each has its distinct laws, and each has its own tribunes for their enforcement. Neither government can intrude within the jurisdiction of the other or authorize any interference therein by its judicial officers with the action of the other.

(A) is incorrect because dual federalism held that the states had certain powers which were specifically reserved to them by the Tenth Amendment. These could be exercised regardless of congressional action. (B) is incorrect because it describes the current concept of federalism, which might be called one of national supremacy. In the case *Garcia vs. San Antonio,* 1985, the Supreme Court declared that henceforth Congress should decide for itself to what extent it ought to regulate those powers that were originally reserved to the states by the Tenth Amendment to the Constitution. This means, in effect, that there are no longer any reserved powers of the states upon which Congress may not encroach. This concept is radically different from that of dual federalism. (C) is incorrect because the term for this concept of federalism is cooperative federalism. (E) is incorrect because it expresses a view typically referred to as the theory of nullification. This theory was held by many in the South before the Civil War. Perhaps the most famous advocate of this theory was John C. Calhoun.

41. **(B)** The original Constitution said nothing about what qualifications would be required for voting in federal elections. Article I, section 4, states:

The times, places and manner of holding elections for Senators and Representatives, shall be prescribed in each state by the legislature thereof; but the Congress may at any time by law make or alter such regulations, except as to the places of choosing Senators.

The Fifteenth Amendment prevented the states from denying persons the right to vote on the basis of race; the Nineteenth Amendment extended the right to vote to women; the Twenty-Fourth Amendment outlawed the use of the poll tax by states; and the Twenty-Sixth Amendment extended the right to vote to persons eighteen years of age or older. (C) is incorrect because two methods of ratifying amendments are given in Article V. Congress is given the power to decide which method will be used for any proposed amendment. (D) is incorrect because the qualifications for members of the House and Senate are stipulated in Article I. (E) is incorrect because Article I, section 10, of the Constitution says that a state cannot, without the consent of Congress, levy duties on imports or exports "except what shall be absolutely necessary for executing its inspection laws."

42. **(E)** The Constitution states in the Twelfth Amendment that "The person having the greatest number of [electoral] votes for President, shall be President, if such number be a majority of the whole number of Electors appointed...." (A) is incorrect because to win in the electoral college a candidate must receive a majority of the electoral votes, not merely a plurality. If three or more candidates received electoral votes, it would be possible that none received the necessary majority. In that case the decision would be made in the House of Representatives. In 1824, Andrew Jackson received 99 electoral votes, John Quincy Adams 84, William Crawford 41, and Henry Clay 37. The House of Representatives chose John Quincy Adams as president, despite the fact that Jackson had the most electoral votes. (B) is incorrect because the president is not elected directly by popular vote, but rather by the electoral college. Whichever candidate wins a plurality of the popular vote in a state wins that state's electoral vote. It is possible for a candidate to win a majority of the popular vote nationwide, but not win a majority of the electoral votes. This happened in 1876, when Samuel J. Tilden won 51% of the popular vote, but lost the presidency to Rutherford B. Hayes by an electoral vote of 184 to 185. (C) is not correct because several presidents have won less than a majority of the popular vote, but a majority of the electoral vote. This happened in 1876, as explained above. It has also happened several times when three or more candidates split the popular vote, with the president-elect winning a majority of the electoral vote (1824, 1844, 1848, 1856, 1860, 1880, 1884, 1888, 1892, 1912, 1948, and 1968). (D) is incorrect because if no candidate wins a majority of the electoral vote, the House of Representatives selects the president from among the top three popular vote-getters.

43. **(D)** A discharge petition is used to force a bill out of a standing committee which has refused to report the bill out to the full House. In the House, a bill cannot reach the floor unless reported out of a committee. A bill that has not been reported out within 30 days after referral to committee may be subject to discharge. The discharge petition must be signed by an absolute majority of House members (218). The motion to discharge is then voted on, and carries with a majority vote of those present and voting. The rules committee may be discharged of a bill after 7 days, rather than the 30 required for other committees. (A) is incorrect because the only way for a bill on the floor to be killed is by a negative vote by a majority of those present and voting. (B) is incorrect because a discharge petition cannot be used to force the rules committee to send a bill back to the committee to which the bill was originally referred. (C) is incorrect because a discharge petition is not used to open a bill up to amendments on the floor of the House. In the House, bills reported out of a standing committee go to the rules committee. The rules committee gives each bill a rule which specifies the time limit for debate on the bill, and whether or not the bill may be amended during floor debate. When the bill comes to the floor for debate, the first thing voted on is the rule assigned by the rules committee. Most of the time the rule is routinely approved. If it is rejected, its opponents may substitute a rule more to their liking. This process does not involve a discharge petition. (E) is incorrect because a bill approved by the House is certified by the clerk, printed on blue paper, and automatically sent to the Senate for its consideration.

44. **(C)** Although the Fourth Amendment protects the public against unreasonable search and seizure, the precise way by which that protection is to be enforced is not stipulated in the Amendment. Before 1914, any person whose Fourth Amendment rights were violated by federal authorities had as their only recourse a civil suit for damages against the offending official. Any evidence gained through the illegal search was admissible in court. Persons whose Fourth Amendment rights were violated by state officials had no recourse whatsoever under the Fourth Amendment, since it did not originally apply to the states. In 1914, in *Weeks vs. U.S.,* the Supreme Court established the exclusionary rule, which allowed evidence obtained illegally by federal officials to be excluded from trial in federal courts. In *Wolf vs. Colorado,* 1949, the Court applied the Fourth Amendment to the states, but did not apply the exclusionary rule to the states. This meant that, while evidence seized illegally by a state official was still admissible in a state court, the person whose rights were violated could now sue the offending official for violation of the person's civil rights. In *Mapp vs. Ohio,* 1961, the Court finally applied the exclusionary rule to state officials and courts. (A) is incorrect because *Baker vs. Carr* dealt with the reapportionment of the Tennessee State Assembly. (B) is incorrect because *Roe vs. Wade,* 1973, dealt with a woman's right to an abortion. (D) is incorrect because *Korematsu vs. U.S.,* 1944, dealt with the president's power to exclude Japanese Americans from military districts during World War II. (E) is incorrect because *Gideon vs. Wainwright,* 1963, dealt with the right of indigents accused of felonies to have lawyers appointed at state expense to defend them.

45. **(A)** Amendments Thirteen (1865), Fourteen (1868), and Fifteen (1860) were adopted in order to protect the rights of former slaves after the Civil War. The Thirteenth Amendment forbids slavery or involuntary servitude anywhere in the United States or in any place subject to its jurisdiction. It therefore prevented the reimposition of slavery in the southern states. The Fourteenth Amendment restricts the powers of states; the most important provisions are those that forbid a state to deprive any person of life, liberty, or property without due process of law, or to deny any person equal protection of the law. The Fifteenth Amendment prohibits states from denying anyone the right to vote on the basis of race, color, or previous condition of servitude. This was clearly meant as a precaution against attempts by southern states to prevent blacks from voting. (B) is incorrect because the Nineteenth Amendment extended the suffrage to women, and the Twenty-Sixth Amendment extended it to 18 year olds. (C) is incorrect because the First Amendment provides protection for speech, religion, and assembly. (D) is incorrect because these amendments did not increase the power of the federal government in any way which could help prevent another civil war. The due process clause of the Fourteenth Amendment has been used by the Supreme Court to apply the Bill of Rights to the state governments. However, it is not at all clear from the debates which took place in Congress when the amendment was proposed that this use of the due process clause was intended by the authors of the amendment. In addition, it was not until *Gitlow vs. New York,* 1925, that the Court thought to use the due process clause of the Fourteenth Amendment for that purpose. Therefore, (E) is incorrect.

46. **(C)** The Supreme Court has generally been very reluctant to intervene in disputes between the executive and legislative branches over the extent of their respective powers. Such disputes have traditionally been termed "political questions," which the Court finds to be outside the scope of its jurisdiction. The settlement of political questions, according to the Court, is left to the voters through the electoral process. In *Goldwater vs. Carter,* 1979, the Court invoked the political questions doctrine to avoid ruling on whether or not President Jimmy Carter could unilaterally terminate the United States' mutual defense treaty with Taiwan, which Senator Barry Goldwater held that he could not do. In 1987, a federal district court dismissed as a political question a lawsuit brought by Democratic congressmen, charging President Reagan with violating the War Powers Resolution by deploying the American navy in the Persian Gulf without notifying Congress. (A), (B), and (D) are incorrect because the Court usually declines to decide disputes between the two branches. (E) is incorrect for the same reason; in addition, the War Powers suit discussed above adds an additional gloss on this point. The War Powers Resolution was passed in 1973, over the veto of President Richard Nixon. The federal district court threw out the 1987 case as a federal question, even though the resolution limited the powers of the presidency and was passed over Nixon's veto. The court did not decide against Congress, it simply refused to hear the case at all.

47. **(B)** A bill's route to the floor of the House lies through the House rules committee. First, a bill is introduced by a member. The presiding officer refers the bill to a standing committee, which often sends it to a subcommittee. After being referred out of committee, the bill goes on one of the calendars. Next, the bill goes to the rules committee. The bill's sponsor and the chairman of the committee which reported the bill will appear before the rules committee to request a rule on the bill. The rules committee will issue either a closed or open rule on the bill. A closed rule means that no amendments, or only those proposed by the committee that reported the bill, can be considered during floor debate. An open rule means that amendments may be proposed by any participant in the debate on the floor. Answer (A) is incorrect because the rules committee does not have the power to close the gallery to the public. Answer (C) is incorrect because there is no House procedure to prevent members from voting on a bill if they miss all or part of the debate on the bill. Answer (D) is incorrect because bills are calendared after being reported out of committee, before going to the rules committee. Answer (E) is incorrect since one house of Congress cannot prevent the other from amending any bill passed by the first house.

48. **(B)** The Continental Congress was not given the right to levy direct taxes on individual citizens. Instead, the Articles of Confederation only allowed the Congress to requisition money from the state governments. A requisition amounted to the same thing as a request. When the state governments fell behind in making their requisition

payments, Congress was unable to force payment of the money. For this reason, the continental treasury was constantly empty. (A) is incorrect because there was no separation of powers under the Articles of Confederation. The government consisted of a Congress alone, made up of delegates from each of the states. (C) is incorrect since there was no national judiciary under the Articles of Confederation. (D) is incorrect because the Articles of Confederation were very difficult to amend. Amendment required unanimous consent of the thirteen states, and Rhode Island always refused to go along with any proposed amendments (for which it came to be known as Rogue Island). (E) is incorrect because the Continental Congress was a unicameral body.

49. **(D)** Whereas television and radio stations must be licensed to operate in the United States, newspapers and magazines need not be. Therefore, statement I is true. It is more difficult for a public figure or official to win a libel suit against the media in the United States than in another country, so statement II is true. The Supreme Court has held that before the news media can be found guilty of libelling a public figure or official, the person must show not only that what was published was false and damaging to his/her reputation, but also that it was published with "actual malice," a rule not used in other countries. The legal definition of actual malice is reckless disregard for the truth or falsity of the story. Since reckless disregard is difficult to prove, winning libel suits is difficult for public officials and figures in the U.S.

50. **(C)** The Campaign Finance Reform law of 1973 made it legal for corporations and labor unions to form PACs. PACs quadrupled in number between 1975 and 1982, and are still forming. (A) is incorrect because PACs were unimportant in American politics before the campaign reform law of 1973. Indeed, one well-known dictionary of American politics, copyrighted in 1972, does not even have an entry for political action committee. (B) is incorrect for two reasons. First, by law a PAC can contribute no more than $5,000 to a candidate for a primary campaign, and no more than $5,000 during a general election campaign. A total contribution of $10,000 is not likely to buy a PAC a great deal of influence these days, when campaigns for Congress cost in the hundreds of thousands of dollars. Secondly, there are literally thousands of PACs, so there is PAC money available on every side of every issue. Candidates can accept PAC money and still decide for themselves how to vote on the issues. (D) is incorrect because PACs may be formed by a variety of groups, or even by an individual. When Representative Charles Rangel was running for Whip of the Democratic Party in the House, he set up a PAC that made campaign contributions to other representatives' campaigns, hoping they would then vote for him as Whip. (E) is incorrect because the number of ideological PACs has increased at a faster rate than business or labor PACs in recent years. In the 1988 election there were nearly 600 ideological PACs. Ideological PACs now raise more money than business or labor PACs, although they contribute less to candidates. This is due to the fact that they spend more than other PACs on advertising per dollar raised.

51. **(D)** The question asks which statement is false. The correct answer is (D) since the purpose of the equal rights amendment was to protect and enlarge the rights of women, not of blacks and Hispanics. The operative clause read "Equality of rights under the law shall not be denied or disparaged by the United States or any State on account of sex." (A) is not a false statement because both houses of Congress passed the amendment in 1972, and sent it to the states for ratification. The necessary three-fourths of the state legislatures never ratified the amendment, so it died in 1982. (B) is not a false statement because Congress did extend the time limit for ratification. The original time limit expired in 1979, but before that date arrived Congress extended the time limit to 1982. (C) is not a false statement because Nebraska and Tennessee, which had ratified the amendment, tried to rescind their ratification. (E) is not a false statement because every president from Truman to Carter, and both political parties, did endorse the amendment.

52. **(C)** Only statement III is correct. James Madison has long been considered the Father of the Constitution, since he wrote the Virginia Plan which was introduced at the Constitutional Convention, and which greatly influenced the content of the Constitution. His authorship of several of the Federalist Papers, which explain the Constitution in great detail, lends great weight to their analysis. Alexander Hamilton, author of several of the Federalist Papers, also attended the Constitutional Convention. Statement I is false since Washington and Adams were not contributors to the Federalist Papers. The three authors were Madison, Hamilton, and John Jay. Statement II is false since the Federalist Papers did not provide a theoretical justification for the Revolutionary War. That war ended in 1783, and the Federalist Papers were written in 1787-1788. The primary purpose of the Federalist Papers was to persuade the voters of the state of New York to elect delegates to their state ratifying convention who would vote to ratify the Constitution. They provided a detailed commentary on the Constitution to satisfy New Yorkers that it was a well-written document. Therefore (C), III only, is correct.

53. **(E)** Statements II and III are both accurate. Statement I is inaccurate because interest groups spend a lot of time and effort lobbying executive agencies and courts, as well as legislatures. Since Congress often merely sets general guidelines for the federal bureaucracy to follow, executive agencies must write specific regulations to guide the implementation of the laws. After a law is passed, then, lobbyists try to influence rule making by the bureaucrats who implement policy. Interest groups also spend a great deal of time trying to influence the courts. Some groups file civil suits on behalf of persons or causes they support. Others might write an amicus brief (a statement of how the case should be decided, offered by someone not a party to the suit) to influence the decision of a court case. Statement II is accurate because union membership in the United States peaked in 1945, when nearly 36% of all workers were unionized. Since then, union membership has fallen steadily. By 1984, only about 19% of workers were unionized.

Declining membership in unions reflects changes in the economy, with fewer jobs being created in the manufacturing sector and more in the service sector. Also contributing to loss of union clout was President Reagan's unfriendliness to union demands, as evidenced by the wholesale firing of the striking airline traffic controllers during his first term. Statement III is accurate because of the nearly 7,000 groups represented in Washington over half are corporations. Among the largest business organizations are the Chamber of Commerce, the National Association of Manufacturers, and the National Federation of Independent Businesses.

54. **(A)** Presidents Reagan and Bush emphasized political ideology as a factor in choosing their nominees to the Supreme Court. The single most important issue has been a potential candidate's stand on *Roe vs. Wade*, 1973. In that case, the Supreme Court held that the right to privacy included a woman's right to choose an abortion, at least in the first trimester of pregnancy. Roe is perhaps the most controversial decision of the Court in the last 30 years. Republican presidents have tried to nominate Justices who would vote to overturn Roe, while Democratic senators have done their best to thwart those nominations. (B) is incorrect because there has, in fact, been an increase in support for Republican presidential candidates in the South in the last 30 years. From the end of Reconstruction until the 1950s, the Democratic candidate for president could count on solid support from the states of the old Confederacy. However, that began to change in the 1960s. In the six elections since 1964, the Democratic candidate for president has won a majority of the southern states only once, in 1976. The Democratic candidate has not won Virginia and has won Mississippi, Alabama, Florida, South Carolina, and North Carolina only once each, since 1964. (C) is incorrect because the conservative wing of the Republican Party has increased in influence in the past 30 years. After a bitter battle at the 1964 Republican National Convention, conservative Republicans managed to nominate Barry Goldwater as the party's candidate for president. This was the beginning of the takeover of the party by its conservative wing. In 1968, the party nominated Richard Nixon, a strongly anticommunist conservative. In 1980 and 1984, the party nominated Ronald Reagan, long a conservative influence within the party. The conservative wing of the party has also managed to dominate the party's platform at most of the last seven party conventions. (D) is incorrect because voter turnout has decreased in the last 30 years. In 1960, about 62% of the voting age population voted in the presidential election. In 1988, less than 50% did. (E) is incorrect because the number of people declaring themselves to be Independents increased from about 21% in 1962 to 33% in 1986.

55. **(C)** The first political parties to compete for public office in the United States were the Federalists and Jeffersonian Republicans, sometimes called the Democratic Republicans. An earlier alignment of political sentiment took place between the Federalists and Antifederalists. Of these two groups, the former supported ratification

of the Constitution, while the latter opposed ratification. These two groups did not compete against each other for public office, because the Antifederalist organization ceased to exist after the Constitution was ratified. After the Constitution was ratified, the Federalists won most of the offices in the new government. Many former Antifederalists joined the Jeffersonian Republicans, who began to organize in the early 1790s in opposition to Federalist policies. The Jeffersonian Republicans won control of Congress and the presidency in the election of 1800. The Federalists soon faded from the scene, and were almost nonexistent by 1820. (A) is incorrect because the Whigs organized in the 1830s, after the Federalists had passed from the political scene. (B) is incorrect because the Whigs appeared after the Jeffersonian Republicans had lost power. (D) is incorrect because the Whigs and Democrats competed in the 1830s, after the initial competition between the Federalists and Jeffersonian Republicans had occurred. (E) is incorrect because the Democrats and Republicans began to compete in the 1850s, long after the initial competition between the Federalists and Jeffersonian Republicans had occurred.

56. **(B)** The term gender gap refers to the fact that women and men have noticeably different views on a variety of political questions. According to a poll taken in 1990, women support gun control by 85%, compared to men's 72%; they support more spending for social security by 60% to men's 50%; they support less military spending by 40% to men's 49%; and they support more spending for the homeless by 80% to mens' 68%. In addition, women tend to vote Democrat in larger numbers than men do. In the 1984 presidential election, 57% of women voted for Reagan, compared to 61% of men. (A) is incorrect because although women do turn out to vote in larger numbers than men, the term gender gap does not describe this fact. (C) is incorrect because although women do have a longer life expectancy than men, the term gender gap designates measurable differences in political views between men and women. (D) is incorrect because although men do hold a higher percentage of elective offices than women, the term gender gap refers to measurable differences in political views between men and women. (E) is incorrect because women are not more apathetic than men regarding electoral politics. They turn out to vote in higher numbers than men.

57. **(C)** The Republican national platform for all three presidential election years in the 1980s contained clauses supporting the antiabortion position. President Bush has taken a strong right to life position, and the Republican position in general is expressed in the Hyde Amendment, which forbids the use of federal funds to pay for abortions. (A) is incorrect because both the 1984 and 1988 Republican platforms contained clauses opposing quotas to remedy past discrimination. (B) is incorrect because the 1988 Republican platform contained a clause calling for a reduction of the capital gains tax to 15%. President Bush has long favored a reduction of the tax. (D) is incorrect because the 1988 Republican platform called for a balanced budget amendment. It is quite likely

that this support for a balanced budget amendment will be repeated in the 1992 platform. (E) is incorrect because the 1988 Republican platform opposed increasing the minimum wage. It is likely that this position will also be taken in the 1992 platform.

58. **(D)**   The correct answer is (D), I and II. Statement I is true because each of the major parties allows great discretion to its nominee for president in choosing his or her running mate. Statement II is correct because balancing the ticket is a major consideration for a presidential candidate in selecting a running mate. Geographical balance is very important. In 1988, George Bush, from Texas, chose Dan Quayle from Indiana. Michael Dukakis, from Massachusetts, chose Lloyd Bentsen from Texas. In 1980 and 1984, Ronald Reagan, from California, chose George Bush from Texas. In 1984, Walter Mondale, from Minnesota, chose Geraldine Ferraro from New York. Statement III is not necessarily true. Many presidential candidates apparently do not take the qualifications of their running mates into consideration. Many people believed that Quayle was not well-qualified to be president, and surely any number of Republicans would have brought more sheer experience and accomplishments to the ticket. Franklin Roosevelt thought so little of his vice president, Harry Truman, that he did not even bother to inform him that the United States was building an atomic bomb near the end of World War II.

59. **(B)**   Keynesian economics was based on the idea that an unregulated capitalist economy will inevitably go through a boom and bust cycle (A). As employment increases, more money will be available to consumers, and spending for consumer goods will then increase. This stimulates inflation, as more money purchases available goods. Producers will produce more and more goods, until overproduction occurs. This is the boom part of the cycle. As overproduction occurs, producers will cut back on production, laying off workers. As workers are laid off, less money will be available for consumers to spend on goods. Demand for consumer goods will decline. As demand declines, producers cut back on production even more. This is the bust side of the cycle. Keynes taught that government should step in to regulate the boom and bust cycle. During times of high unemployment, government should engage in deficit spending to create jobs, (C). This will put money in consumers' pockets, which will stimulate demand. Increased demand will cause producers to hire more workers in order to increase output to meet the increased demand. During times of high inflation, government should raise taxes, (D). It should also increase taxes, (E). These policies will take money out of circulation and prevent the economy from heating up too much and going into a boom period. Keynesian economic theory stresses the demand side, as opposed to the supply side of the economy. Keynesian policies attempt to either stimulate or reduce demand in order to regulate the business cycle. Supply side economics, on the other hand, stresses the supply side of the economy. Supply siders rejected much of the Keynesian analysis in the late 1970s, when the economy went into

a period of so-called stagflation. The economy was experiencing inflation and stagnation—two conditions which Keynesian economics said could not happen at the same time. Supply siders said that the stagflation could be explained by the fact that government had placed too many disincentives on producers in the form of high taxes. The way to get the economy going was to focus on the supply side instead of the demand side. By cutting tax rates (B), the government would remove disincentives from producers, who were currently disinclined to produce because government was taking too much of the profit in the form of taxes. If producers were allowed to keep more profit, they would increase production, pulling the economy out of recession. Since cutting tax rates was a feature of supply side economics, but not of Keynesian economics, the correct answer is (B).

60. **(D)** Overly technical questions ask about subjects that the general public has little or no knowledge of. This can cause sampling error, because when people answer questions they do not understand, their answers are unreliable. (A) is incorrect because straw polls are unscientific. They are usually conducted by newspapers and magazines. In the typical straw poll, reporters ask questions at shopping malls and other locations, and report the results back to the newspaper or magazine. The problem with straw polls is that there is no way to ensure that the sample of individuals giving answers is representative of the larger population. (B) is incorrect because one surprising feature of sampling error is that its magnitude depends on sample size and not on population size. Population size refers to the total number of people in the group in question. Sample size refers to the total number of people in the population who are sampled. A random sample of 1,500 residents of New York City will be as reliable an indicator of what New York City residents think on an issue as a random sample of 1,500 residents of the State of New York will be of what residents of the State of New York think on an issue. (C) is incorrect because having people phone in answers to a poll does not satisfy the requirements for randomness. The sample would be biased since only those who felt strongly about the issue in question would bother to phone in their response. This group would not be representative of the overall population. (E) is incorrect because almost everybody can afford a telephone. Since this is the case, a random telephone survey produces a relatively representative sample group.

Section II

Question 1–Sample Essay Scoring 0 to 3

The data proves that presidential candidates who win in their home states win the overall election. Voters in their home state know the candidate better than other voters in the country, and if they like the candidate from their home state, then he or she is the best candidate.

It is important that the best person be elected President, and the state they come from doesn't matter. People like it when the President is from their own state, because it gives them a sense of pride in where they come from. President Clinton always talks about being from Arkansas, so people from Arkansas like him.

People often elect a President for reasons other than political ones, such as how he or she looks on television and what kind of sound bites he makes. In the end, it seems that superficial reasons matter more than things like issue positions and ideology.

Analysis of Sample Essay Scoring 0 to 3 (Question 1)

This essay begins to answer the question and is not exactly incorrect, but it does not provide any useful analysis. While it is true that candidates who win the national election win their home state, it is also true that candidates often lose the national election and still win in their home state. While the second statement of the paragraph may be true in some cases, there is no evidence provided that it is a general rule. It seems like it might be a thesis statement, but the rest of the essay does not connect to this.

Again, the first sentence is true, but it is such an obvious truism that it does not need to be stated here. Also, the rest of the paragraph has nothing to do with the statement. In fact, the whole paragraph is not structured and contributes very little to the essay. At this point, the author has lost focus on the original question and is not developing any points around which he or she could structure an essay.

The final paragraph attempts to get back to the matter at hand, and tries to extract some greater relevance from the data, but all this paragraph really amounts to, ultimately, is a restatement of some fairly common criticisms of the campaign process which have little to do with the data presented. The author offers a conclusion, but again, it has little to do with the rest of the essay.

The problem with this essay is not so much based in the factual mistakes, but rather in the lack of focus and organization, as well as a lack of any in-depth analysis of the question.

Question 1–Sample Essay Scoring 4 to 6

The data here demonstrate the fact that presidential candidates tend to win their home states. Clinton did better in Arkansas than he did in the nation as a whole, even though he won the election, and did much better than Dukakis, the Democrat from 1988. Historically, presidential candidates tend to win their home states.

This gives an advantage to candidates from larger states, because they have more electoral votes, and the home candidate has a good chance of winning them. This is why most Presidents tend to be from large states. While Clinton was an exception, both Bush and Reagan were from two of the largest states, Texas and California.

People vote this way because often they know more about the candidate from their home state, and because people vote for candidates they know well. While a long national campaign might dissipate the advantage, people still know things about the candidate from their own state, and are more aware of the successes he or she has had. If the candidate hadn't been successful at one level, it is unlikely that they would have been nominated to be the Presidential candidate.

Analysis of Sample Essay Scoring 4 to 6 (Question 1)

Overall, there is nothing wrong with the essay; the information and analysis presented is generally solid and factually correct. It does a good job making a comparison between the election results of 1988 and 1992. However, the analysis does not go into depth or draw the more significant implications. The first paragraph, for instance, does little more than restate the question. There is no explicit thesis, other than the one suggested by the question itself.

The second paragraph correctly identifies the advantage this gives to candidates from larger states, but does not balance, by contrasting it with the disproportional greater representation of the smaller states in the electoral college. The problem is not accuracy, but depth, and a fuller analysis of context. The author does do a good job of providing some historical evidence that candidates from larger states do better, and this begins to look like the thesis statement that should have been in the first paragraph.

The final paragraph attempts some explanation of why this might be the case, but again the analysis is somewhat skimpy. It begins to answer the question of what this demonstrates about American voting behavior, but it does not draw the broader implications. The answer skims the surface of the question, but does not probe it at all. Finally, there is little in the way of a concluding statement that could tie the essay together.

Question 1–Sample Essay Scoring 7 to 9

While the table presents limited information, it does show that Clinton, a Democrat from Arkansas, did much better in Arkansas than the Democratic candidate in 1988. While it is true that Clinton on the whole did much better than Dukakis, in Arkansas the total vote increase was proportionally better than in the United States as a whole. This suggests that some of Clinton's advantage in Arkansas reflects the fact that he is an Arkansas native. Historically, even candidates who lose badly overall tend to win their home states. The home state advantage illustrates some important principles of the American Electoral System.

One of the implications of this phenomenon is that parties will tend to nominate candidates from large states, which have a high number of electoral votes. While there are, of course, exceptions, in general successful presidential candidates have been from larger states. To some extent, this offsets the proportional advantage that small states have in the electoral college, where the number of votes a state has is based on the number of members of Congress each state has.

A further implication of this phenomenon is that many people base their vote on criteria other than party identification and ideology. It is clear, for example, that Clinton's road to the White House was paved to a large extent by a single-minded focus on a particular issue—the economy—which the campaign's pollsters as well as independent opinion surveys had shown was the biggest concern of voters among the vast middle class. Too, Clinton, in stark contrast to Dukakis, ran an extremely efficient campaign that made it a point to hit back quickly at opponents on virtually every issue that they raised. This created a sense of momentum that served to place Clinton on the offensive, full of energy and vitality.

So while the "favorite son" phenomenon certainly fed into the ultimate triumph of Clinton over a strong Democratic field and an incumbent Republican (who, after all, had once benefited from historically high approval ratings), it is also important to acknowledge and figure in the fact that Clinton's was an especially well-oiled campaign. And Bill Clinton's challengers and backers alike agree that there are few politicians who are better campaigners. Clinton's one-on-one appeal is a celebrated fact and one that provided him deep-rooted support in the small state of Arkansas.

Dukakis, by contrast, was perceived as wooden, and was vulnerable to bad photo opportunities like the one in which he stuck his helmeted head out of a tank. Though intended by his handlers to make him look like a commander-in-chief, he came out looking merely silly. And, though it's unfair, there's no doubt this bad photo op took its toll, eroding even his natural base of support in the urban Northeast. Indeed, it would be interesting to see data on Dukasis's 1988 performance in Massachusetts to see to what extent this was the case.

But confined as we are to the tables presented, the 10-percentage point gap between Clinton's Arkansas performance (53%) and his national performance (43%) would seem to owe a good bit to the "favorite son" phenomenon. (Likewise, one might venture that George Bush's connections to neighboring Texas, manifest by his son's catapulting to the governorship of the Lone Star State, are part of the 3-point advantage he enjoyed in Arkansas as against the national level.)

In the rough and tumble of a presidential campaign, there's plenty of room for interplay among a host of different factors. And one should be careful not to misattribute correlation for causation. But we do know that a candidate's appeal is based on a cluster of assessments that voters use to determine how the candidate stacks up on leadership and empathy— a sense that the voter believes that the candidate "understands people like me" and can "represent my interests." A geographic proximity to the candidate gives the voter a sense of familiarity, and establishes an emotional link to the candidate. In the end, American voters are voting not just for an ideology or a party, but for a person to whom they are entrusting the country.

As for the general impact on American politics, one ought to tread carefully in extrapolating from such limited data. A more considered approach would require comparisons over time and among parties.

Analysis of Sample Essay Scoring 7 to 9 (Question 1)

After an introduction elaborating the "favorite son" phenomenon, the essay states a general hypothesis about the phenomenon having important implications. While it might be nice to have a more specific thesis, given the time constraints on the essay writer, this seems an adequate thesis statement. Importantly, the essay is organized around this thesis statement.

The second paragraph draws the more obvious conclusion about candidates tending to do well in their home states, and that candidates from states with a large number of electoral votes will necessarily have an advantage in the election. It also nicely contrasts this with the advantage that small states have, due to their proportional overrepresentation in the Congress and electoral college.

The essay goes on to draw further implications, not explicitly found in the data. The analysis could go in several directions here, and the one chosen by the author is both reasonable and interesting. The analysis is balanced, acknowledging that factors that determine a voter's choice are not always evidently political, but still reasonable. Finally, the conclusion ties the essay together, drawing out and expanding the thesis about the possible implications of the "favorite son" phenomenon while taking care not to overreach. The essay does lack certain compositional niceties such as transitions between paragraphs, but given the time constraint of 25 minutes, the emphasis should go to content over form, and in this case, the content is solid.

Question 2–Sample Essay Scoring 0 to 3

The development of direct primary elections has changed the nomination and election process in the United States. Today, the voters both nominate the candidates and elect public officials. Consequently, candidates for public office must get the support of the voters in order to be nominated and elected. In order to win elections, successful candidates must get support from their political party, from interest groups, and from the media.

The two major political parties are the oldest political organizations in the United States. Both major political parties have campaign organizations throughout the United States at the national, state, and local levels. They have been quite successful in getting most voters to think of themselves as "Democrats" or "Republicans." The voters' "party identification" often influences how they vote. Consequently, most candidates for public office associate with one of these two major parties, because this will almost automatically assure them of a certain number of guaranteed votes in any election. Those people who vote for all their party candidates are called "straight-ticket" voters.

These parties work hard to get their candidates elected. They raise money for their party candidates. They also provide many of the volunteer campaign workers who help in the candidate's election campaign. They usually work for all the party candidates, whether the candidates are liberal, moderate, or conservative. The political parties are more concerned with winning elections than they are with public policy. They are "party oriented," not issue oriented. This is how the word "partisan" originated.

The role of interest groups and the media have also become more important in modern times. The greater emphasis on elections has made campaigns become more expensive. Candidates for public office increasingly depend on individual and interest group contributions to finance their campaigns. In addition, candidates have come to rely more on the media to communicate their campaign themes and messages to the electorate.

In the 1990s, the candidates for Congress and most state executive and legislative offices are the winners of their state's direct party primary elections. Similarly, the presidential candidates are usually those candidates who have won most of the presidential primaries.

Analysis of Sample Essay Scoring 0 to 3 (Question 2)

This essay lacks a central thesis. The first paragraph recognizes that voters now nominate candidates, but fails to describe the nomination process before the development of direct and presidential primaries. Consequently, given the absence of any historical perspective, it does not address the theme of change.

The second paragraph of the answer contains a description of the traditional relationship between party identification and voting behavior. The answer includes a specific reference to "straight-ticket" voting as an example of this relationship. Although the information in this paragraph is generally accurate, it is largely irrelevant to the question. Party identification and straight-ticket voting may be influential in general elections, but are rarely a factor in primary elections since all the candidates are usually in the same political party.

The essay continues this problem in the third paragraph. The paragraph contains a brief discussion of the traditional campaign roles of the two major parties, and cites such examples as fundraising and volunteer campaign activity on behalf of the candidates. Once again the information provided is generally accurate, but it is largely irrelevant to the question. The party will be actively involved in fundraising and campaigning during general elections, but not in primary elections.

Also among the essay's problems is a weak conclusion. The fourth paragraph is a superficial reference to the increased campaign roles of interest groups and the media, but no mention is made about how this may be related to the development of primary elections. The fifth and final paragraph merely restates the opening statement that the candidates for public office are the winners of the primary elections.

Overall, the essay not only lacks a central thesis, it provides no historical perspective. The description of the changing role of political parties is vague, and the importance of that change is not developed. The answer is simplistic and incomplete. It ignores the differences between general elections and primary elections, and fails to distinguish between direct primaries and presidential primaries. The emphasis is upon campaign activities, not upon how primary elections have changed the role of political parties.

Question 2–Sample Essay Scoring 4 to 6

The development of direct primary elections has changed the nominating process. In the past, before the use of primary elections, political parties controlled the selection and nomination of virtually all candidates. In modern times, the voter controls the selection and nomination of candidates for nearly all elected public offices.

There are no national primary elections. Direct primary elections and presidential primary elections are held at the state level. Both involve voters in the nomination process. However, the two types of primaries operate differently, and each serves a somewhat different purpose.

"Direct" primary elections are used by both major parties to nominate candidates for public office. They are used to nominate candidates for Congress, most state offices, and many local offices. They are decisive and the winners of the various primaries are the party nominees.

"Presidential" primary elections do not nominate any candidates for any office. Instead, they are used to select delegates to the national nominating conventions. They provide a means by which the voters in the state presidential primary can indicate their preference for a particular presidential candidate, and even elect some convention delegates pledged to that candidate at the national convention, but they are not decisive.

The growing importance of voters in the nomination process has weakened the traditional influence of political party leaders. In addition the increasing campaign roles of interest groups and the media, along with the expanding use of television, public relations, and opinion polling, have combined to make all candidates less dependent upon the party leadership and organizations in their election campaigns. Contemporary candidates can run for party nomination and election to public office without the support of the party leadership and organization.

Analysis of Sample Essay Scoring 4 to 6 (Question 2)

This essay begins with the general thesis that the development of primary elections has replaced party control of the nomination process with voter control. The thesis, however, is not well developed because it lacks a historical perspective. No reasons are given, for example, to explain how or why this change occurred.

The essay does provide a good descriptive narrative. The information provided is tightly organized and factually accurate. The second paragraph aptly notes that all primaries are at the state level rather than the national level. In addition, direct primaries and presidential primaries are clearly contrasted in the third and fourth paragraphs.

The fifth and final paragraph affirms the thesis that the development of primary elections has weakened party leadership and organization. The essay also recognizes that contemporary candidates are less dependent on that leadership and organization than in the past. However, the essay does not explore the consequences of these changes.

Although the question is answered directly and succinctly, this essay does not substantially address all elements of the question. It does not seem to appreciate fully the importance of the neutral role of the party leadership and organization during nominating campaigns, nor the consequences of that role.

Question 2–Sample Essay Scoring 7 to 9

The development of primary elections was an outgrowth of the Populist Movement during the late 1800s. The Populists believed the dominant business interests had acquired too much influence over political parties and the nomination process. They believed that an unsavory alliance between the "plutocrats" (wealthy industrialists) and political party leaders had developed, producing a situation in which financial campaign support by the business interests was rewarded with favorable pro-business public policies.

The Populists supported policies of economic reform that were intended to improve the economic conditions of rural and urban working class Americans. However, they came to believe such economic reforms were not possible unless political reform was first accomplished. It was their view that the people's power to elect public officials had been compromised by the control over the nomination of candidates exercised by the business-party leadership alliance.

The Populists were among the first organized groups to call for "returning power to the people." In order to accomplish this objective, they championed numerous election reforms, including the right to vote for women, the direct election of United States senators, direct primary elections, and a national presidential primary. Although the Populists were unsuccessful in accomplishing these reforms in their third-party movement, most of their reforms were adopted and implemented into law by "progressive" leaders in the Democrat and Republican parties.

Two of those political reforms, direct primary and presidential primary elections, were intended to remove the party leadership's stranglehold over nominations. These reforms were intended to take the nomination out of the "smoke-filled room" and return it to the people through the ballot box. Since neither reform was enacted by Congress, each developed gradually and in a variety of forms through legislation enacted independently at the state and local level.

Direct primaries first appeared at the turn of the century in Wisconsin and Florida, and over the ensuing four decades slowly spread to the other states. In 1948, Connecticut, the last state to provide for direct primary elections, completed the process. Direct primary elections, sponsored by each party, replaced convention nominations by the party leaders with popular nominations by the voters. Thus, the term "direct" primary is meant quite literally—the winner of the party primary, nominated directly by the voters, is the party nominee.

Presidential primaries, in contrast, might be called "indirect primaries." The Populist proposal calling for each party to nominate their presidential candidate in a national presidential primary has never been implemented. Instead, individual states gradually and independently adopted legislation permitting political parties to use presidential primaries as a method for selecting delegates to attend their party's national nominating convention. The winner of a presidential primary has not won the party nomination. Instead, the presidential primary winner has won only a bloc of delegates who are more or less committed to his/her nomination at the national convention.

It should be noted that the development and expansion of the use of presidential primaries for delegate selection, which began in 1912, has not yet been completed. However, an important phase in that development was reached in 1968. Prior to that year, a majority of convention delegates were selected by the state party leaders. Since 1968, an increasing number of convention delegates have been selected in the state party presidential primaries. In 1912, Theodore Roosevelt won all 12 Republican presidential primaries held that year, but lost the nomination to William Howard Taft on the first ballot at the national convention. Although possible, it is highly unlikely that a candidate who wins more than one-half, if not all, of his party's 40-odd presidential primaries would be denied the convention nomination.

The development of primary elections and presidential primaries has neutralized the party leaders and party organizations in the nomination process. State party conventions have gone by the wayside: state leaders no longer select the party candidates for national, state, and local offices, nor do they select the vast majority of national convention delegates.

There can be no doubt that this weakened party role and influence has also affected the candidates and the nature of election campaigns. The route to elected office no longer requires individuals to work their way up within the party organization. Anyone can declare candidacy and seek the nomination in the party primaries. Each candidate for nomination, however, must build his/her own campaign organization, raise campaign contributions, and plan and execute the campaign. Consequently, since the party is neutral during the primaries, candidates must rely more on interest groups for campaign contributions and on the media for political communication (including newspaper accounts and advertising).

Analysis of Sample Essay Scoring 7 to 9 (Question 2)

This essay provides a strong and consistent thesis that integrates all parts of the question. The thesis recognizes that the development of direct primary and presidential primary elections began as a conscious effort to reform the political process. The demand for popular nominations was a rejection of the influence and control of the political party bosses under the convention system.

The thesis is logically and persuasively presented within a historical perspective in the first three paragraphs of the essay. This historical perspective is essential to answering the question. In order to discuss the change in the role of the political parties, it is first necessary to describe what the role was before the change.

The fourth paragraph recognizes that all primary elections are authorized and conducted at the state and local level. The fifth and sixth paragraphs clearly explain the differences between direct primaries and presidential primaries. Each paragraph provides factual information and examples which accurately describe the gradual development of direct primaries from the 1890s through 1948, and of presidential primaries from 1912 through 1968. The seventh paragraph shows an awareness that the process has not yet been completed for the presidential primaries.

The concluding paragraphs return to the central thesis. They accurately identify the most important consequence of that change, the neutralization of both the party leadership and the party organization during the nomination process.

Finally, the essay shows a clear understanding of the importance of the change from convention nominations to primary nominations, and understands the consequences of that change. The final paragraph alludes to what were perhaps unintended consequences of this change in the nomination process. The neutralization of the party, which forces candidates to build campaign organizations and finance their own campaigns, has also contributed to an increase in the influence of interest groups and the media. This, in turn, has contributed to increasing candidate independence from party leaders and organizations.

Question 3—Sample Essay Scoring 0 to 3

The President and Congress continually struggle over the control of the foreign policy of the United States. This occurs because the Constitution does not clearly spell out the relative roles of each, although it does specify that they share power on such matters as treaty making and diplomatic appointments.

The President has considerable power because he has access to information from his Cabinet, advisors, and the government bureaucracy. He therefore presumably knows more than anyone else and also controls to a considerable degree what the rest of us know. Congress, on the other hand, does not have as many resources. It can obtain information through "leaks," the press, and various contacts with the government bureaucracy. But hearings provide the major means by which Congress obtains information and expresses its opinion on foreign policy matters. Usually, however, these hearings take place in the wake of a crisis, reacting to , rather than shaping events.

These hearings often lead to the formulation of laws, a second means by which Congress influences foreign policy. Such laws include controls over the CIA and presidential use of American troops. During the past twenty years these two issues have been of considerable importance because of the Vietnam War and involvement in Central American revolutions. Congress also controls the budget, which has an indirect influence on foreign policy, particularly use of the military.

The power balance between the President and Congress on setting a course in foreign policy is ever in flux, with one or the other asserting dominance depending on the situation.

Analysis of Sample Essay Scoring 0 to 3 (Question 3)

The opening paragraph presents a thesis but in a highly generalized way. It refers to the Constitution but does not say specifically what the document contains about the powers of the President and Congress with regard to foreign policy.

The second paragraph makes a vague reference to the President having "considerable power" but does not describe in detail the sources of his information. Similarly, the description of Congress's sources of information is generalized. Although over the next two paragraphs the essay refers to hearings, laws, and budget as means by which Congress influences foreign policy, it does not place these things within any framework. Rather, it just goes from one item to the next without having introduced them with an organizing statement. Nothing is described in any detail. The essay makes only a brief reference to recent controversies.

The final paragraph refers to the theme of change and struggle over time, introduced in the first paragraph, but ends rather abruptly. There is no conclusion drawing the various elements of the essay together.

Question 3–Sample Essay Scoring 4 to 6

The Constitution is somewhat vague regarding the distribution of power in the making of foreign policy. Although the President has the power to make treaties and appoint diplomatic personnel, he shares that power with the Senate. Similarly, although he is commander-in-chief, he must rely on Congress to declare war and raise and maintain the military.

The President draws upon considerable resources in conducting foreign policy and shaping public opinion in support of his policies. The National Security Counsel provides information and advice. Each President determines the extent to which he depends on the NSC. A second resource is the State Department, which works with diplomatic officials around the world, sending and receiving communications. The Secretary of State is a political appointee, who may or may not have significant influence on the President. A third resource is the CIA, which has the responsibility to collect information regarding other nations. It also engages in covert action.

Congress obtains information regarding foreign policy through briefings provided by the executive branch and bureaucracy, unofficial contacts with government employees, and the press. Because it does not actually conduct the nation's foreign policy, it brings its influence to bear through other means. Since the Vietnam War, Congress has sought to curb the President's power to conduct foreign policy independently. It has limited his freedom to commit troops and has instituted new requirements for reporting by the CIA regarding covert activities. When concerned about the direction of certain foreign policy actions, Congress can hold hearings that provide opportunity for obtaining new information, expressing views, and molding public opinion. Also, Congress can influence foreign policy through its control of the budget. Nevertheless, it has not frequently used the budget as a means of shaping foreign policy.

The struggle between the President and Congress for control of foreign policy is ongoing. Generally the President holds the preponderance of power but at various times has had to share that power to a greater extent with Congress.

Analysis of Sample Essay Scoring 4 to 6 (Question 3)

The first paragraph describes the constitutional basis for the distribution of power between the President and Congress with regard to foreign policy. But it lacks details.

The second paragraph briefly outlines the various sources from which the President draws in developing foreign policy. Somewhat more detail would help the essay.

The following paragraph discusses the role of Congress. Although it describes Congress's sources of information, it does not present a framework for its discussion of Congress's influence on foreign policy, namely identifying law, hearings, and budget. Each of these is discussed, some with supporting detail, but there is no conceptual framework. The concluding paragraph is again quite general and does not advance understanding much beyond what was introduced in the first paragraph.

Question 3–Sample Essay Scoring 7 to 9

The Constitution does not specifically describe the distribution of power regarding the making of foreign policy. Article II states that the President has the power to make treaties, but to be ratified, they must obtain a two-thirds majority approval from the Senate. He also has the power to appoint ambassadors and other diplomatic personnel, but again with the "advice and consent" of the Senate. A different but related function is the President's role as commander-in-chief, a power also given by Article II of the Constitution. Congress, however, has the power to declare war and to raise and support the military, as outlined in Article I. This power sharing between the President and the Senate makes for a continual struggle between the two for primacy in the making of foreign policy.

The President draws upon a number of resources in conducting foreign policy and molding public opinion in support of his policies. The National Security Council, created in 1947, advises the President on issues related to national security. The State Department handles the day-to-day diplomatic affairs of the United States, communicating with embassies and monitoring crises, although the Secretary of State's influence on the President varies according to their relationship. The Central Intelligence Agency (CIA), established in 1947, collects information but also engages in covert action. By drawing upon the advice and information provided by these and other entities, the President develops policies that govern the relationship of the U.S. with other nations.

Congress also has its sources of information: briefings from the executive branch, documents in the Library of Congress, the Congressional Budget Office, unofficial contacts with government employees, and the press. But its primary influence over foreign policy lies in three areas: laws, hearings, and finances.

Since the Vietnam War, Congress has sought to establish legal curbs on presidential power. The War Powers Resolution (1973) limited the number of days troops could be committed without Congressional approval, but Congress has had difficulty enforcing this requirement. Congress has sought to control the covert activities of the CIA by requiring the President to notify it regarding secret operations.

Congress also uses hearings as a means of influencing foreign policy. Such hearings are held prior to approval of the Secretary of State, for instance, and enable Congressional members to indicate their concerns. And hearings are held with regard to particular crises, usually after the fact, as in the Iran-Contra scandals of the 1980s.

Finally, Congress influences foreign policy through its control of the budget. This is particularly apparent in the defense budget, which indirectly influences some of the President's foreign policy decisions. For the most part, however, Congress has not used its budget-making power as a tool to force foreign policy decisions. A good example is the Vietnam War, which never received Congressional approval but which Congress continued to fund. The struggle between the presidency and Congress for control of foreign policy is ongoing. From the close of World War II until the mid-1960s, the President dominated the making of foreign policy. As a result of the Vietnam War, Congress began to reassert its authority, but because of his access to information, and because many decisions are made in a crisis situation, the President continues to maintain the upper hand.

Analysis of Sample Essay Scoring 7 to 9 (Question 3)

The opening paragraph begins with a description of the constitutional basis of presidential and Congressional power in relationship to foreign policy, with specific references to Articles. It concludes with a thesis statement regarding the struggle for primacy.

The second paragraph describes the sources of information and advice that the President draws on and concludes with a statement of their significance. Detail like dates strengthen this paragraph.

The third paragraph describes the sources of Congressional information, but most importantly it clearly states the three primary areas by which Congress asserts influence: law, hearings, and finance. The next three paragraphs discuss each of these elements, giving specific examples for each which address the question's requirement that the essay identify issues that have arisen in recent years. The final paragraph refers back to the theme of struggle introduced in the first paragraph and then offers an historical perspective that leads directly to the closing statement, which asserts that the President will continue to maintain primacy in the making of foreign policy.

Question 4—Sample Essay Scoring 0 to 3

Interest groups are organizations, representing business, professional, labor, or other concerns, which actively promote the views of that group in an effort to influence public policy and action. These groups represent such interests as medicine, manufacturing, labor, the environment, and the elderly. Some groups also focus on a single issue such as abortion.

The people who advocate the positions of these groups are called lobbyists. They often try to become personally acquainted with legislators and public officials. By establishing a friendship they are then in a better position to argue their case and influence the individual's actions. Some lobbyists are also former government workers or office holders. But interest groups are also involved with money, lots of it. Through their political action committees (PACs) they raise money from their members, which is then used in election campaigns. Some of the money goes directly to the candidate's campaign while other money is used independently for such things as printed matter and advertizing in the media. Although there have been efforts at campaign finance reform, some of it directed at the roles of interest groups, not much has been accomplished.

Interest groups also become active when specific legislative proposals affect them. Those groups focusing on a single issue are especially active in this respect. When the Clinton administration proposed to change the health care system, for instance, various groups on all sides of the issue began sending mass mailings and obtaining advertizing spots on radio and television. The opposition to health care reform seems to have had some effect on Congress, which voted down the proposals.

Although there are frequent calls to limit the political actions of interest groups, little has actually been accomplished.

Analysis of Sample Essay Scoring 0 to 3 (Question 4)

The first paragraph provides a definition of interest groups but does not distinguish between those that pursue what are traditionally considered "private" concerns and those advocating what are called "public" issues.

Paragraph two briefly describes lobbyists but only in rather general terms. It does note that many effective lobbyists formerly worked for the government, but it fails to mention the limits placed on such former employees. Although the paragraph mentions PACs, it does not state what they are or the legal rules under which they work. It does not clearly distinguish between the $5,000 PACs can give to a candidate and their "independent" activities.

The third paragraph gives a specific example of how interest groups operate on a single issue, but in this case the discussion would be stronger with more generalization regarding single-issue activities before going into the example. As the paragraph is written, the reader does not know whether mass mailing and advertising spots are generally used or were used only on this issue. The concluding statement says little. It needs discussion of the implications of interest groups for American democracy that would bring the reader back to the definition offered in the first paragraph.

Question 4–Sample Essay Scoring 4 to 6

In the United States, people in business and the professions as well as those having common concerns, such as union members or environmentalists, regarding various issues have formed organizations to promote their views. These organizations are often called "interest groups" because they represent and promote particular goals regarding government policy and action. Among these groups are the American Medical Association, representing physicians, the American Association of Retired People, advocating the cause of the elderly, the Sierra Club, pushing environmental concerns, and the chambers of commerce representing small business owners.

These groups advocate their causes through a number of means. They make personal contact with legislators and other public officials, using these opportunities to discuss their concerns and attempt to bring the individual to their point of view. But money probably plays the most significant role. Lobbyists—the term used for those people who advocate the interest group's position—sometimes provide personal favors, such as restaurant meals, to legislators. But increasingly they have become involved in election campaigns. In the mid-1970s federal law began allowing businesses and unions to establish political action committees (PACs) that could donate $5,000 to a candidate and independently campaign for that candidate. Since that time, PACs have become an increasingly important part of American election campaigns, raising and spending money that is supposedly independent of the candidate. These PACs also provide workers for campaigns, engage in voter registration drives, and conduct other activities that help individual candiates.

In addition to working with candidates, many interest groups focus on a particular issue. When legislation favoring expansion of abortion rights appears, for instance, the

National Right to Life Committee might go to work mailing brochures, purchasing advertising on TV, radio, and the print media, and appearing at legislative hearings.

Despite an effort in 1946 to control the political activities of interest groups, not much has been achieved. Interest groups seem to be embedded in the American political landscape.

Analysis of Sample Essay Scoring 4 to 6 (Question 4)

The first paragraph gives a good definition of interest groups. It would be strengthened by distinguishing between those groups advocating "public" issues and those championing "private" issues. The names of groups at the end of the paragraph is good, but repeats to some degree the more general statement made at the beginning. The writer's The second paragraph describing lobbying activity is quite good. More specificity would strengthen it, however. Rather than simply saying "federal law," the writer could refer specifically to the Federal Election Campaign Act, passed in 1974. The third paragraph adequately describes single issue activities by interest groups.

The weakest part of the essay is the final paragraph. It does not discuss why there is interest in limiting the political activities of interest groups or the implications of these groups for American democracy. Both elements need discussion in some detail. For instance, discussion of efforts to limit activities should make reference to the First Amendment while discussion of implications for democracy should discuss a variety of viewpoints.

Question 4–Sample Essay Scoring 7 to 9

Although the term *interest groups* can include anyone with common concerns, such as farmers or parents, recent discussion has focused on formal organizations that seek, on behalf of their members, to influence government policies and actions. Although traditionally interest groups have primarily represented private concerns, such as business, labor or professional needs, in the 1960s public interest groups began emerging, focusing on such issues as the environment, health care, consumer protection, and the rights of various minorities. Also, some interest groups focus on a single issue like abortion or gun control.

A major means used by interest groups is lobbying, which includes personally visiting legislators and public officials, attending Congressional and other public hearings, and making friends with staff members and bureaucrats. Some of the most effective lobbyists are former legislators or other office holders who know both how the system works and many individuals within the system. Because of the potential for corruption, former government workers are prohibited from lobbying the agencies they served for a minimum of one year after leaving government employment.

The lobbyist's most powerful tool is money. Lobbyists frequently provide vacations, restaurant meals, and small gifts, and purchase tickets to fund-raising events; campaign contributions and fund-raising are their most important activities. The Federal Election Campaign Act (1974) allowed unions and corporations to establish political action committees (PACs) to contribute $5,000 to individual candidates. After the Supreme Court ruled unconstitutional one part of the law that had limited expenditures on behalf of but not under the control of a candidate, PACs began to play a major role in political campaigns. In addition to their direct $5,000 contributions to candidates, PACs could now conduct unlimited independent campaigning on behalf of a candidate. Their activities include voter-registration drives, advertising, and efforts to get out the vote.

Outside of election campaigns, interest groups also address specific issues that may be coming to a vote in Congress, such as Social Security or Medicare. Conducting mass-publicity campaigns, interest groups use direct mail and television, newspaper, and radio advertising to arouse public opinion.

Because of their potential influence, reformers seek to control these interest groups, but the First Amendment, which protects free speech and the right to petition the government, limits what can be done, and politicians are unwilling to limit the activities of an important source of money and other campaign help. The Federal Regulation of Lobbying Act (1946) required lobbyists and interest groups to register with the House and Senate, but because of vague wording the law has not been too effective and no stronger law has been put in its place.

Whether interest groups are good for democracy has been much debated. Some argue that the conflicting groups balance one another rather than control the system. Others point out that these groups often prevent government from acting and that they tend to represent the middle and upper classes rather than the lower. Furthermore, the stands taken by interest groups sometimes represent a powerful leadership group rather than the members as a whole. Whatever their faults and limitations, however, interest groups will likely be a part of the American political system for some time to come.

Analysis of Sample Essay Scoring 7 to 9 (Question 4)

The first paragraph gives a good definition of interest groups, including a distinction between those advocating "private" and those advocating "public" concerns. It also notes single-issue groups. It illustrates each of these groups by giving generalized examples—"business, labor or professional needs." Although names of specific groups would be good, time constraints prevent such a listing.

The second paragraph discusses lobbying, identifying some of the specific ways that it is done. It also notes the role of former government employees, some potential problems relating to them, and restrictions on their activities.

The third paragraph discusses the use of money. In addition to identifying specific ways that money is used, it also examines the development of federal law. It clearly distinguishes between the two types of PAC activities, contributions to candidates and "independent" campaigning. The following paragraph also specifies ways in which single-issue groups work.

The fifth paragraph examines the effort to control the political activities of these groups, discussing both why reform has been desired and, more fully, the First

Amendment issues and federal law. The concluding paragraph outlines major points of view regarding the role of interest groups in American democracy. It might be strengthened by making a brief reference back to the definition of interest groups introduced in the first paragraph, thereby pulling the whole essay together.

AP EXAMINATION IN
United States Government & Politics

PRACTICE TEST 2

AP EXAMINATION IN
UNITED STATES GOVERNMENT AND POLITICS

Test 2

Section I

TIME: 45 Minutes
60 Multiple-Choice Questions
50% of Total Grade

(Answer sheets appear in the back of this book.)

DIRECTIONS: Read the following questions and incomplete sentences. Each is followed by five answer choices. Choose the one answer choice that either answers the question or completes the sentence. Make sure to use the circles numbered 1 through 60 when marking your answers on your answer sheet.

---

1. The electoral college system is biased in favor of

    (A) states that support the Republican Party.

    (B) states dominated by one political party.

    (C) states with small populations.

    (D) candidates with a college education.

    (E) the industrial northeast.

2. A successful candidate for president must receive

    (A) a majority of votes cast by the public.

    (B) a majority of votes cast by the electoral college.

    (C) a plurality of votes cast by the public.

(D)   a plurality of votes cast by the electoral college.

(E)   a majority vote of the public and of the electoral college.

3.   The most important reason why George Bush was elected President in 1988 was

(A)   his forceful personality and public speaking ability.

(B)   the economy was in good condition.

(C)   his selection of Dan Quayle as a running mate.

(D)   his interest in education.

(E)   he was the incumbent.

4.   The most accurate way to measure public opinion is generally through

(A)   a stratified or quota sample.

(B)   a study of letters to the editor.

(C)   a random sample.

(D)   a mailed survey.

(E)   talking with your neighbor.

5.   Each of these persons was a leading figure in the adoption of the Constitution EXCEPT:

(A)   Thomas Jefferson   (D)   James Madison

(B)   Alexander Hamilton   (E)   John Jay

(C)   Patrick Henry

Cross-National Rankings of Health Care Expenditures and Measures of Health Status, 1985

	Health Care Expenditures as Percentage of GDP	Rank	Patient Access to Specialists	Health Status Indicator: Male Infant Death Rate	Rank
United States	10.7	1	Uncontrolled	12.8	6
Sweden	9.4	2	Uncontrolled	7.1	1
France	8.6	3	Uncontrolled	11.2	4
Netherlands	8.3	4	Referral only	9.2	2
West Germany	8.2	5	Uncontrolled	10.6	3
Britain	5.7	6	Referral only	12.2	5

From OECD, *Financing and Delivering Health Care* (Paris: OECD, 1987) at pp. 36 and 55.

6. According to the table, which of the following statements is correct?

    (A) The quality of health care is consistently related to the level of expenditures.

    (B) Uncontrolled access to health care, rather than controlled access, is more likely to improve the health status index of a country.

    (C) The Health Status Index is based upon longevity of adult females.

    (D) The U.S. spends a lower percentage of its Gross Domestic Product (GDP) on health care than other societies but, because it is larger, it actually spends more money.

    (E) The U.S. has a relatively poor Health Status Index, but expends a greater percentage of GDP on health care than the Netherlands.

7. Under a federal system of government,

    (A) power is concentrated in the central government.

    (B) power rests primarily in subnational units which control the national budget.

    (C) the national government and subnational units would share power.

    (D) each state has a veto over national policy in areas such as defense policy.

    (E) states would typically have no power over local matters such as schools, roads, and police services.

8. All of the following concepts are found in the Constitution EXCEPT

    (A) inalienable rights to life, liberty, and property.

    (B) federalism.

    (C) checks and balances.

    (D) indirect elections.

    (E) implied powers.

9. In addition to formal amendments, the U.S. Constitution has been changed by

    I. custom and tradition.

    II. judicial interpretation.

    III. statutory enactment by states.

(A)   I   (D)   I and III

(B)   I and II   (E)   I, II, and III

(C)   II and III

10.   The Constitution places legislative power in Congress and Executive power in the President. This is an example of

(A)   federalism.   (D)   fundamental rights.

(B)   checks and balances.   (E)   separation of powers.

(C)   constitutional interpretation.

11.   The term "New Federalism" has been applied to describe

(A)   a process for admitting new states into the union.

(B)   reduced rate of growth in federal financial assistance to states.

(C)   the breakup of the Soviet Union.

(D)   the resurgence of congressional power in the 1990s.

(E)   the Twenty-Eighth Amendment to the Constitution.

12.   Which of the following Amendments to the Constitution were adopted in the immediate aftermath of the Civil War?

I.   The Fourteenth Amendment

II.   The Nineteenth Amendment

III.   The Twentieth Amendment

(A)   I   (D)   I and III

(B)   I and II   (E)   I, II, and III

(C)   II and III

13.   The two leading American political parties

(A)   originated in the early twentieth century.

(B)   are the Whigs and the Federalists.

(C)   are equal in size.

(D)   have a legal monopoly on political power.

(E)   are pragmatic rather than ideological.

14. All of the following are recognized functions of the major political parties EXCEPT:

    (A) recruiting candidates for public office.

    (B) aggregating interests into electoral alliances.

    (C) establishing channels of communication between public and government.

    (D) providing personnel to staff elections and run the government.

    (E) articulating interests.

15. Which of the following persons would be most likely to vote?

    (A) A black factory worker living in the South

    (B) A white middle-aged attorney from the West

    (C) A 19-year old from the Midwest

    (D) A 30-year old female secretary with three children from the Northeast

    (E) A high school dropout from the Northeast

16. Voter turnout in the U.S., compared to other developed, industrialized democracies, is

    (A) one of the lowest.

    (B) the highest, reflecting our role as the world's leading democracy.

    (C) about average.

    (D) above average.

    (E) slightly below average, but improving.

17. The "Bill of Rights" is found in

    (A) the Declaration of Independence.

    (B) the Third Article of the Constitution.

    (C) amendments to the Constitution.

    (D) bills passed by Congress.

    (E) state constitutions only.

18. During the period just before adoption of the Constitution, an outbreak of violence known as _____ may have made national leaders more receptive to political change.

    (A) The Battle of Gettysburg

(B)   The Battle of Concord and Lexington

(C)   The Revolutionary War

(D)   Boston Tea Party

(E)   Shay's Rebellion

19.   A parliamentary system differs from a congressional or presidential system because in a parliamentary system,

(A)   the executive branch controls the legislative branch.

(B)   the executive branch is selected by and frequently belongs to the legislative branch.

(C)   elections are held in alternate years.

(D)   there is no written constitution.

(E)   parliament elects congress.

Executions by State

From 1976 through June 1989 Total: 111

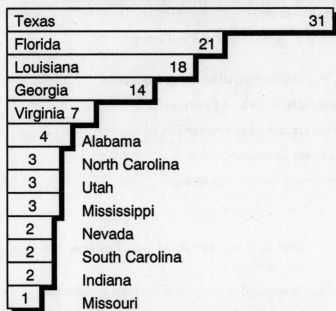

State	Executions
Texas	31
Florida	21
Louisiana	18
Georgia	14
Virginia	7
Alabama	4
North Carolina	3
Utah	3
Mississippi	3
Nevada	2
South Carolina	2
Indiana	2
Missouri	1

Source: NAACP Legal Defense and Educational Fund Inc. As published by *The New York Times,* June 1989.

20.   On the basis of the graph above, one can conclude that

(A)   most people who are executed are poor.

(B)   most executions have taken place in Republican-controlled states.

(C)   most executions have taken place in the South.

(D)   most murderers have been executed.

(E)   blacks are more likely to be executed than whites.

21.   Which of these important Supreme Court decisions established the doctrine of judicial review?

(A)   *Barron vs. Baltimore*   (D)   *Gideon vs. Wainwright*

(B)   *McCulloch vs. Maryland*   (E)   *Roe vs. Wade*

(C)   *Marbury vs. Madison*

22.   Political scientists classify governments as unitary, federal, or confederal. A *unitary* form of government

(A)   is less common than a federal system.

(B)   is the form used in the United States, Canada, and Mexico.

(C)   has power concentrated at the national level.

(D)   is more democratic.

(E)   is found only in the largest political systems.

23.   Under the U.S. Constitution, all states are required to

(A)   have a republican form of government.

(B)   adopt the Equal Rights Amendment.

(C)   have a strong Democratic Party.

(D)   elect governors for two year terms.

(E)   maintain balanced budgets.

24.   Which of the following is an example of the "Privileges and Immunities" clause of the Constitution?

(A)   New Jersey is required to accept garbage from out of state.

(B)   A citizen from New York is able to sue someone in a Massachusetts court.

(C)   A marriage performed in one state is legally valid in another.

(D)   A nonresident is required to get an Oregon fishing license.

(E)   A requirement is issued that school aged children be immunized against various diseases.

25. Which of the following is an example of the "Full Faith and Credit" clause of the Constitution?

   (A) New Jersey is required to accept garbage from out of state.

   (B) A citizen from New York is able to sue someone in a Massachusetts court.

   (C) A marriage performed in one state is legally valid in another.

   (D) A nonresident is required to get an Oregon fishing license.

   (E) A requirement is issued that school age children be immunized against various diseases.

26. The General Accounting Office performs all of the following functions EXCEPT

   (A) auditing government spending.

   (B) trimming agency budget requests.

   (C) preparing the Annual Budget document.

   (D) advising the president on budget matters.

   (E) submitting reports to Congress on agency budget performance.

27. When legislative district boundaries are drawn in such a way that it benefits one political party over another, this is commonly known as

   (A) philandering.   (D) campaign reform.

   (B) filibustering.   (E) illegal and unethical.

   (C) gerrymandering.

28. In the early years of the twentieth century, the Speaker of the House of Representatives

   (A) was usually elected to the presidency.

   (B) lost power to appoint committee and subcommittee chairs.

   (C) chaired the committee that approved nominations to the Supreme Court.

   (D) had to approve all legislation passed by Congress.

   (E) was Thomas P. "Tip" O'Neill.

29. Which of the following statements about the national debt is true?

   I. The national debt is over one trillion dollars.

II. The debt has increased at more than 200 billion dollars annually in some recent years.

III. It currently takes more than 10 per cent of the federal budget to pay the interest on the debt.

(A) I only

(D) I and II only

(B) II only

(E) I, II, and III

(C) III only

30. Which of the following is not a power that belongs to the President of the United States?

(A) Pocket veto

(D) Impoundment

(B) Address congress

(E) Executive agreement

(C) Item veto

31. Which of the following forms of federal aid imposes the greatest restrictions upon the recipient states?

(A) Categorical grant

(D) Grants-in-aid

(B) Block grant

(E) Social Security

(C) Revenue-sharing

32. The key Supreme Court case that established national supremacy by refusing to allow the states to tax the federal government was

(A) *Marbury vs. Madison.*

(D) *Brown vs. Board of Education.*

(B) *Roe vs. Wade.*

(E) *McCulloch vs. Maryland.*

(C) *Gibbons vs. Ogden.*

33. James Madison, one of the authors of the *Federalist Papers,* believed that the best opportunity to preserve liberty would be

(A) to elect a Federalist President.

(B) to create a unified government with all power concentrated in the hands of a strong president.

(C) found in the diversity of interests or "factions" in American society.

(D) to continue to operate under the Articles of Confederation.

(E) to organize the Republican Party.

Index of Expenditures for Medicaid, Medicare, Government-Financed Personal Health Care Expeditures, and All Personal Health Care Expeditures, 1966-1990
(1966 = 100)

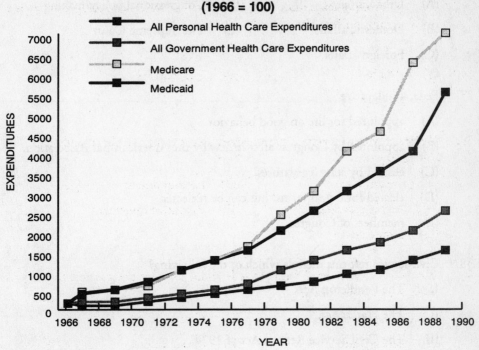

Source: U.S. Department of Health and Human Services. Health Care Financing Administration. As published in *Intergovernmental Perspectives*, Spring 1992, p. 6.

34. According to the figure above

    (A) Medicare expenditures exceed expenditures for Medicaid.

    (B) medical expenditures have actually declined since 1970.

    (C) Medicare and Medicaid expenditures have grown more rapidly than personal health care expenditures.

    (D) the U.S. spends too much on medical care.

    (E) U.S. medical expenditures exceed that of most other countries.

35. The "pluralist" theory of American democracy contends that

    (A) everyone has about the same amount of political power.

    (B) everyone should have about the same amount of power.

    (C) a small elite rules.

    (D) a number of elites compete for power.

    (E) power should be divided between Congress, the president, and the Courts.

36. American presidents tend to have the most power in which of the following arenas?

    (A) Urban affairs   (D) Congressional policy-making

    (B) Domestic affairs   (E) The Supreme Court

    (C) Foreign affairs

37. Federal judges are

    (A) appointed for life on good behavior.

    (B) appointed by Congress after review by the American Bar Association.

    (C) elected by state legislatures.

    (D) elected for 6 year terms, but can be reelected.

    (E) members of Congress.

38. Civil service reforms include which of the following?

    I. The Pendleton Act

    II. The Hatch Act

    III. The Civil Service Reform Act of 1974

    (A) I   (D) II and III

    (B) I and II   (E) I, II, and III

    (C) I and III

39. Oliver Wendell Holmes, late Supreme Court Justice, once wrote "I do not think the United States would come to an end if we lost our power to declare an act of Congress void. I do think the union would be imperiled if we could not make that declaration as to the laws of the several states." Based on that statement, Holmes would most likely have opposed

    (A) a decision allowing states to decide whether federal courts could review state actions.

    (B) a decision prohibiting federal courts from overturning Congressional actions.

    (C) a decision allowing federal courts to review any state case raising a federal issue.

    (D) a decision prohibiting abortions.

    (E) a decision requiring a major company to pay damages to another company for breach of contract.

40. In general, over the past two hundred years, in terms of the balance of power between the states and the national government, the national government has

    (A) grown significantly weaker than the states in all areas.

    (B) lost power to the states, particularly over economic matters.

    (C) experienced no change in power.

    (D) grown relatively stronger, particularly in economic matters.

    (E) completely displaced the states in matters dealing with health, welfare, and education, but not the economy.

41. An Act of Congress tying federal highway aid to the states to the adoption of certain speed limits specified by Congress is most likely based upon which constitutional power of Congress?

    (A) The power to tax

    (B) The power to regulate *inter*state commerce

    (C) The power to set speed limits

    (D) The power to spend for the public benefit

    (E) The power to regulate *intra*state commerce

42. If the United States were operating today under the Articles of Confederation instead of the Constitution, a problem like air pollution or the preservation of endangered species would most likely be handled by

    (A) Congress, acting through the Speaker of the House and the President of the Senate.

    (B) the Supreme Court.

    (C) the President.

    (D) the individual states.

    (E) the Senate natural resources committee.

43. Presidential Primaries are

    (A) required by the Constitution.

    (B) used in all states.

    (C) used to select members of the Electoral College.

    (D) an alternative to the use of "caucuses" to select delegates to national party conventions.

    (E) used only in the Republican Party.

44. In the six presidential elections held from 1968 to 1988, the Democrats

    (A) won all elections.

    (B) won all but one election.

    (C) won half of the elections.

    (D) won only one election.

    (E) lost each election in the electoral college, but won the popular vote in each election.

45. Which of the following governmental agencies is not a cabinet-level department?

    (A) Veterans

    (B) Housing and Urban Development

    (C) U.S. Postal Service

    (D) Defense

    (E) Education

46. If, in reaching a judicial decision, a court relies upon the reasoning in an earlier case, the court has relied upon

    (A) precedent.   (D) a statute.

    (B) the Constitution.   (E) the Chief Justice.

    (C) common sense.

47. Which President did not serve as a state governor before becoming President of the United States?

    (A) Jimmy Carter   (D) Ronald Reagan

    (B) Harry Truman   (E) Franklin D. Roosevelt

    (C) Woodrow Wilson

48. "Political socialization" is a term that best refers to

    (A) the policies of the Democratic Party.

    (B) the policies of the Republican Party.

    (C) the process by which people decide to become Democrats or Republicans.

(D)   political attitudes and values held by the public.

(E)   the process by which people acquire political attitudes and values.

49.   Based on the Seniority system as it is presently used in the House of Representatives, which of the following persons on a Committee would serve as Chair?

(A)   Representative Brown, Democrat, age 43, in Congress for 12 years, member of Committee for 10 years

(B)   Representative Green, Republican, age 67, in Congress for 17 years, member of Committee for 14 years

(C)   Representative White, Democrat, age 51, in Congress for 8 years, member of Committee for 5 years

(D)   Representative Black, Democrat, age 81, in Congress for 21 years, member of Committee for 8 years

(E)   Representative Smith, Republican, age 45, in Congress for 15 years, member of Committee for 15 years

50.   The Rules Committee of the House of Representatives

(A)   determines committee assignments for members of the House.

(B)   determines how bills will be handled in House debate.

(C)   negotiates compromises with the Senate.

(D)   has grown increasingly important in the twentieth century.

(E)   selects the Speaker of the House.

51.   Former Chief Justice Warren Burger has crusaded for which of the following as a means to ease the workload of federal courts?

(A)   Creating a new court of appeals to decide cases involving conflict between other appellate courts

(B)   Making it easier for decisions in state court to be reviewed in federal court

(C)   Abolishing diversity jurisdiction of federal courts

(D)   Referring most cases to arbitration or mediation

(E)   Eliminating federal district courts

Questions 52 and 53 refer to the following passage:

"We come then to the question presented: Does segregation of children in public schools solely on the basis of race, even though the physical facilities and other 'tangible' factors may be equal, deprive the children of the minority group of equal educational opportunities? We believe that it does ... We conclude that in the field of public education, the doctrine of separate but equal has no place. Separate educational facilities are inherently unequal." [*Brown vs. Board of Education,* 1954]

52. The viewpoint which is closest to the meaning of equality in the passage above is the viewpoint that

    (A)   life, liberty, and the pursuit of happiness is important.

    (B)   everyone should pay an equal amount in income taxes.

    (C)   different people should be treated differently.

    (D)   equality requires the elimination of signs of inferiority such as separation on the basis of race.

    (E)   as long as people get a good education it should not matter whether they go to an integrated or segregated school.

53. The passage would most clearly support a subsequent decision to

    (A)   prohibit homosexual marriages.

    (B)   permit single-sex educational institutions.

    (C)   ban restrictive covenants in property deeds that would restrict the sale of single-family homes on the basis of a purchaser's race.

    (D)   require public schools to mainstream handicapped students.

    (E)   require integration of other public facilities, such as restaurants and swimming pools.

54. A "concurring opinion" by a judge means that

    (A)   the judge supports the president.

    (B)   the judge strongly opposes the court's decision.

    (C)   the judge agrees with the majority reasoning, but rejects their conclusion.

    (D)   the judge agrees with the majority's conclusion but rejects their reasoning.

    (E)   the judge has refused to write an opinion on the case.

55. Regulatory agencies must give advance notice of rules that they propose to adopt, which is a requirement found in

    (A)   *Brown vs. Board of Education*   (D)   The Constitution

    (B)   The Hatch Act   (E)   The Civil Rights Act of 1964

    (C)   The Administrative Procedures Act

56. Approximately how many people work for the national government?

    (A) one million

    (B) five million

    (C) ten million

    (D) 20 million

    (E) 100 million

57. Modern presidents have been less dependent on the advice of career diplomats in the foreign service than their predecessors because of changes in

    (A) the Constitution.

    (B) laws adopted by Congress.

    (C) transportation and communications technology.

    (D) public opinion.

    (E) the role of the vice president.

58. Which of the following is generally regarded as a key feature of the "Reagan Revolution"?

    (A) Democrats lost control of the House of Representatives

    (B) Sharp increases in defense spending

    (C) Greater attention to education at the national level

    (D) Significant decreases in domestic spending

    (E) The appointment of more liberal federal judges

59. During "midterm" congressional elections, how likely is the President's party to increase the number of seats in Congress that it holds?

    (A) Always increases

    (B) Almost always increases

    (C) Usually increases

    (D) About as likely to increase as to decrease

    (E) Less likely to increase than to decrease

60. All of the following statements about modern congressional staffs are true EXCEPT

    (A) staff members have grown increasingly important.

    (B) the number of staff members has increased dramatically since the 1950s.

    (C) members of Congress are increasingly dependent on their staff.

(D)   only a few members of Congress have full-time staff working in their home states and districts.

(E)   staff members are appointed politically.

STOP

This is the end of Section I.
If time still remains, you may check your work only in this section.
Do not begin Section II until instructed to do so.

Section II

TIME: 100 Minutes
4 Free-Response Questions
Approx. 50% of Total Grade

DIRECTIONS: Write an essay based on each of the following four questions. Be sure to pace yourself by allotting about one-fourth of your time, or 25 minutes, for each question. Where appropriate, use substantive examples in your answers. Your essays should be numbered to correspond with the questions to which you are responding.

---

1. Since about 1970 there has been an effort to shift power from the federal government to the states. Discuss the constitutional relationship of the federal and state governments, the reasons why there has been an effort to shift power in recent years, and explain some of the specific means by which the shift has been attempted.

2. Currently the constitutional and legal validity of affirmative action is being widely discussed. Explain why affirmative action was begun in the 1960s and the constitutional and legal issues that have been debated since that time.

3. Federal Budget Outlays (in billions of dollars)

	1970	1989 (est.)	Percent Increase 1970-1989
Fixed Costs	120.3	865.1	719.12
Variable Costs	83.8	306.3	365.51

For the purpose of this question, fixed costs are those over which the President has relatively little control. These are costs that can be adjusted only by an act of the U.S. Congress. Variable costs are those that can be changed by Presidential decision. Fixed costs include entitlement programs, interest on the deficit, and other programs approved by Congress. Variable costs include defense spending and other executive branch programs.

a) From the information in this table, how much responsibility does the Presidency bear for the growth in federal spending?

b) Since politics in the real world is more complicated than a simple table, what might have to happen before federal spending is reduced?

4. "While people complain about negative political advertisements as harmful to the political process, there is no concrete evidence that negative political campaigns have any effect on voter turnout or citizens' attitudes towards government and politics in general. What we do know is that negative political advertising has been used as long as there have been campaigns. Since politicians running for office want to appeal to as many voters as possible and are reluctant to state their specific positions on an issue, negative ads are often the only source for information about a candidate's position and action on an issue."

This claim by a political scientist seems to contradict the conventional wisdom that negative political campaigns somehow degrade the political process.

a) Explain why negative advertisements might, in fact, help voters make a more informed election decision.

b) Given what you know about campaigning, criticize the author's favorable position on negative political advertising.

END OF EXAM

UNITED STATES GOVERNMENT AND POLITICS

TEST 2

ANSWER KEY

1.	(C)	16.	(A)	31.	(A)	46.	(A)
2.	(B)	17.	(C)	32.	(E)	47.	(B)
3.	(B)	18.	(E)	33.	(C)	48.	(E)
4.	(A)	19.	(B)	34.	(C)	49.	(A)
5.	(C)	20.	(C)	35.	(D)	50.	(B)
6.	(E)	21.	(C)	36.	(C)	51.	(A)
7.	(C)	22.	(C)	37.	(A)	52.	(D)
8.	(A)	23.	(A)	38.	(E)	53.	(E)
9.	(B)	24.	(B)	39.	(A)	54.	(D)
10.	(E)	25.	(C)	40.	(D)	55.	(C)
11.	(B)	26.	(B)	41.	(B)	56.	(B)
12.	(A)	27.	(C)	42.	(D)	57.	(C)
13.	(E)	28.	(B)	43.	(D)	58.	(B)
14.	(E)	29.	(E)	44.	(D)	59.	(E)
15.	(B)	30.	(C)	45.	(C)	60.	(D)

DETAILED EXPLANATIONS
OF ANSWERS
TEST 2

Section I

1.   **(C)**   The electoral college system does not directly favor the Republican Party (A), Democratic Party (B), or northeast as a region (E), but instead favors states with small populations (C) because each state is given electoral college votes equal to the number of Representatives and Senators from that state. Small states are over represented by this formula since all states, regardless of population, have two senators. The electoral college selection process has nothing directly to do with the education of candidates (D).

2.   **(B)**   To be elected president a person must receive a majority of electoral college votes. To win the presidency a candidate need have neither a majority (A) nor a plurality (C) of the popular vote. Since that is so, (E) is also incorrect. Although unlikely, it is possible to obtain a majority of the electoral votes without winning the popular vote. In the absence of an absolute majority of the electoral college vote (D), the election is thrown into the House of Representatives, where the plurality winner in the electoral college could lose.

3.   **(B)**   Any selection of "the most important" reason is open to challenge, but (B) is clearly the best choice. Traditionally, it is difficult to defeat the party in office when economic conditions are regarded as favorable, as they were during most of 1988. Bush is not known for having either a forceful personality or strong public speaking skills (A). His running mate (C) was widely regarded as a liability, and education (D) was only a peripheral issue in the campaign. Although he had served as vice president, Bush was not the incumbent (E) President when he ran for office.

4.   **(A)**   A stratified or quota sample (A) selects survey respondents randomly within identified segments (or strata) of the population in proportion to what the segments share of the total population. Such surveys can be quite accurate with 1000-1500 respondents. A random survey (C) would have to be much larger (and more expensive) to achieve the same accuracy. Letters to the editor (B) and mailed surveys (D) are often heavily biased because people who feel strongly about issues but whose attitudes are not necessarily representative of the majority, are more likely to write letters or return mailed

surveys. Talking with your neighbor (E) is obviously far too limited to accurately represent the population.

5. **(C)** Patrick Henry was a strong advocate of independence but an opponent of the Constitution because he was suspicious of a central government. Each of the others was a major figure favoring the Constitution. Although out of the country at the time, Jefferson (A) was in correspondence with other national leaders. Hamilton (B), Madison (D), and Jay (E) were vigorous public advocates, writing many of the essays later collected as *The Federalist Papers.*

6. **(E)** The quality of health care is not consistently related to the level of expenditures (A); otherwise the ranking would be essentially identical on both factors. (B) is incorrect because there is also no consistent difference in the Health Status Index based on whether access is controlled or uncontrolled (average rank is 3.5k for controlled and uncontrolled access). The Health Status Index is based upon male infant mortality, not the longevity (C) of adult females. (D) is incorrect because the U.S. actually spends a higher percentage of its Gross Domestic Product on health care than any other country listed on the table.

7. **(C)** In a federal system power is shared. A system with power concentrated at the national level (A), or in which states have no power over local matters (E), is unitary; one with power concentrated in subnational units, particularly if those units controlled the national budget (B) or where subnational units (D) had veto power would be a confederal system.

8. **(A)** The correct answer is (A) because inalienable rights are mentioned in the Declaration of Independence, which many scholars regard as a much more radical document than the "conservative" Constitution. The Constitution sets out a framework for distributing power between the states and national government based on federalism (B), checks one power against another (C) by, for example, giving the President the power to nominate members of the Supreme Court, but requiring Senate approval, providing for the indirect election (D) of the President by the electoral college, and has been interpreted to contain implied powers (E) beyond those specifically listed.

9. **(B)** The constitution has been changed by custom, tradition (I), and judicial interpretation (II). Examples include the two-term limitation (only added as a formal amendment in the twentieth century), emergency powers of presidents and the interpretation of the "equal protection" clause. State statutes (III) do not directly affect the meaning of the Constitution.

10. **(E)** The distribution of governmental powers between the branches is known as "separation of powers." A related concept, "checks and balances" (B) most frequently refers to situations where power is "shared," and is therefore "checked" by the power of another branch. Federalism (A) refers to the distribution of power between levels of government (state, national), while constitutional interpretation (C) could refer to any

aspect of the constitution, not simply to the distribution of governmental power. The notion of fundamental rights would refer to basic liberties such as freedom of press and speech.

11. **(B)** New Federalism, closely associated with the Reagan and Bush administrations, involves reduced dependence of states upon federal financial assistance. Despite criticism from many state leaders, it has been one way to limit the growth of federal spending generally. As used here, the term has nothing to do with Soviet politics (C) nor with the admission of states (A) to the Union. The growth of Congressional power (D) to the extent that it may exist, would be an example of changes in the separation of powers within the national government, rather than changes in the federal system. There is no Twenty-Eighth Amendment to the Constitution.

12. **(A)** The Thirteenth, Fourteenth (I), and Fifteenth Amendments were adopted between 1865 and 1870 to deal with issues of slavery, citizenship, and the right to vote, primarily for black Americans. The Nineteenth (II) and Twentieth (III) Amendments, adopted in 1920 and 1933, respectively, dealt with the right of women to vote, and with moving the beginning and ending dates for presidential and congressional terms of office from March to January.

13. **(E)** American parties are pragmatic organizations, dedicated more to winning elections than promoting a particular ideology. Thus, their ideological positions tend to be moderate. There are many legally organized political parties (D), although most have only a handful of members. The Democratic Party and the somewhat smaller Republican Party (C) trace their origins into the early and mid-nineteenth century (A). The Whigs and Federalists (B) were early parties that no longer exist.

14. **(E)** Articulating interests is generally thought of as the special task of interest groups. Parties, on the other hand, bring together or "aggregate" interests (B) in order to create a working majority to run government. Parties also play a significant role in recruiting candidates (A), serving as channels of communication (C), and staffing elections (D).

15. **(B)** On the average a white, middle-aged attorney would be the most likely to vote. Except for the South, region is not a significant vote predictor. Younger people (C), those who are less educated (E), those with lower paying occupations (D), and those from minority groups (A) are less likely to vote. Overall, women are only slightly less likely to vote than men, a fact offset by their greater numbers in the electorate. Here the age and probable education level of the secretary (D), rather than sex, make her a less likely voter than the attorney, whose sex is not identified.

16. **(A)** Election studies consistently show low and declining voter turnout rates in the United States compared to other developed industrialized democracies around the world. According to one study by the Congressional Research Service (Library of

Congress), the U.S. had the lowest rate of 28 western democracies during the 17 years preceding the study.

17. **(C)** The Bill of Rights is found in the first ten amendments to the Constitution. The Declaration of Independence (A) speaks about some very important rights, as do state constitutions (E) and, on occasion, acts passed by Congress (D), but the term has come to be applied specifically to the constitutional amendments identified above. The Third Article of the Constitution (B) describes the structure and power of the judiciary, which plays an important role in interpreting the Bill of Rights, but does define those rights. Although state constitutions frequently contain a Bill of Rights, the fact that they are not the sole source of such rights makes (E) an incorrect response.

18. **(E)** Shay's Rebellion showed the weakness of the Articles of Confederation. The other options listed either occurred before the Articles of Confederation were adopted or many years after the adoption of the Constitution. The Boston Tea Party (D) and the Battle of Concord and Lexington (B) took place earlier, either before or during the Revolutionary War (C) which preceded the Articles of Confederation. The Battle of Gettysburg (A), which took place during the Civil War, occurred over 70 years after the Constitution was adopted.

19. **(B)** Characteristically in a parliamentary system, voters elect a legislature which then selects the executive from among its members, thereby ensuring that the institutions are joined together rather than separated. (A), (C), and (D) may be correct in a particular system but are not generally characteristic of parliamentary systems. Answer (E) simply confuses the legislative bodies in a parliamentary system with that of a congressional system.

20. **(C)** Of the 111 executions from 1976 through June 1989 indicated on the graph, all but seven occurred in the states of the old Confederacy. The data presented in the table simply does not indicate whether those who were executed were poor (A) or black (E). (D) is incorrect because only a small percentage of murderers have been or are ever likely to be executed. Although the Republican Party has become more influential in the formerly Democrat-controlled "solid South," it is not accurate to characterize the states on the graph as "Republican-controlled" (B).

21. **(C)** *Marbury vs. Madison* is the correct choice. The *Barron* decision (A) determined that the Bill of Rights did not apply to the states. (B) is best known for the "implied powers" doctrine and (D) was the mid-twentieth century decision that gave poor people the right to state-provided legal representation in criminal cases. *Roe vs. Wade* (E) is the controversial abortion rights decision.

22. **(C)** The unitary form is the most common type and is found in both large and small states, therefore (A) and (E) are incorrect. The U.S., Canada, and Mexico (B) are among the handful of federal systems in the world today, and are not unitary.

Governmental structure (unitary, federal, confederal) is not consistently related to the democratic character (D) of a political system.

23. **(A)** Although we commonly use the term "democratic" today to describe our government, that term is not used in the Constitution, which instead requires each state to have a "republican" form of government. As used in the constitution, "republican" meant roughly a "representative" government. State law, not the federal constitution, determines whether states adopt the ERA (B), elect governors for two year terms (D) or maintain balanced budgets (E). There is no constitutional requirement, state or federal, with regard to having political parties.

24. **(B)** Rights available to a citizen of one state must be made available to citizens of other states as well. Since a resident of Massachusetts can sue in Massachusetts courts, so too can nonresidents from New York or elsewhere. There are exceptions for benefits such as fishing licenses (D) that are paid for by the taxpayers of a state. (A) is an example of the "commerce clause" in operation, while (C) refers to the "Full Faith and Credit" doctrine. There is no constitutional requirement regarding immunization against disease (E).

25. **(C)** "Full Faith and Credit" would require that a valid marriage performed in one state be recognized as such elsewhere, a concept somewhat different from the idea of "privileges and immunities," which refers to making the rights, such as the right to sue (B) available to a citizen of one state available to citizens of other states as well. (D) is an exception to the "Privileges and Immunities" clause, while (C) concerns the "Commerce" clause. There is no constitutional requirement, state or federal, regarding immunization against disease.

26. **(B)** The GAO, which reports to Congress, performs all of the other functions listed. It is not involved with formulation or trimming budget requests coming from the agencies. That is a function performed by the Office of Management and Budget, an executive agency under the direction of the President.

27. **(C)** The correct answer is "gerrymandering," a term derived from the name of Elbridge Gerry, an early American politician who drew district boundaries in a manner that benefited his party. (A) is incorrect since it refers to sexual misadventures. Gerrymandering is not illegal and at least arguably not unethical (E), but it hardly qualifies as a campaign reform (D) effort. Filibustering (B) refers to the practice of making exceedingly long speeches in Congress and has nothing to do with the drawing of political boundaries.

28. **(B)** A powerful Speaker who abused his appointment power was eventually deprived of that power in the early years of the twentieth century. Speakers are selected to the Presidency (A), although Senators have more frequently achieved that position. The Speaker has no role in Supreme Court nominations (C), since the power to approve rests with the Senate. Like all members of Congress, the Speaker has only one vote and

legislation can pass without approval from the Speaker (D). Tip O'Neill (E) was a colorful and powerful Speaker of the House during the 1980s.

29. **(E)** All of the statements are true. In fact, the national debt is substantially in excess of one trillion dollars, has been accumulating at more than 200 billion annually, and it takes closer to 20 percent of the budget to pay interest on the debt.

30. **(C)** Unlike many governors, a president may not veto individual items [an "item veto"] in a piece of legislation, but must instead veto the entire bill if he is dissatisfied. Presidents can, however, exercise a "pocket" veto (A) by failing to sign a bill adopted by Congress in the closing days of a legislative session, address Congress (B), impound or refuse to expend funds (D), and enter into executive agreements (E) with foreign governments.

31. **(A)** Categorical grants are made available for specific, narrow purposes (highway grants, energy assistance, housing). Block grants (B) is incorrect because such grants may be used for broader purposes and hence give state and local governments more control over the use of grant funds. Similarly, (C) is incorrect because revenue sharing funds, although mostly eliminated today, were provided to states through formulae based on population and "tax effort," with few strings attached to the use of those funds. (D) is incorrect because it is a generic term used to refer to all types of grant programs, and would be equally applicable to describe (A) and (B), and possibly (C). Social Security (E) payments are made directly to beneficiaries rather than to the state, and are therefore not considered a form of aid to states subject to restriction.

32. **(E)** *McCulloch vs. Maryland* involved the question of whether the state of Maryland could tax a federally chartered bank. The Court held that it could not, because to do so would infringe on the power of the national government. (A), (B), (C), and (D) are all well-known cases, but their importance is based upon other issues. (A) is incorrect, although important, because it established the principle of "judicial review." Similarly, (C) is an important early case involving the meaning of the "Interstate Commerce" clause. Although important, (B) involves abortion rights and (D) is a contemporary case dealing with the question of segregation in public schools.

33. **(C)** Madison felt that the diversity of economic and political interests in American society, coupled with a federal form of government and a system of checks and balances among the branches of the national government, would ensure that no single group could dominate over others. Although Madison was an author of the *Federalist Papers,* (A) is incorrect because Madison was not supportive of the strong national government and strong chief executive advocated by the Federalist Party, a group organized around Alexander Hamilton. (B) is incorrect because Madison found liberty in diversity, rather than strong, centralized leadership. On the other hand, (D) is also incorrect because Madison clearly wanted to replace the weak government of the Articles of Confederation with a stronger, but not overbearing national government. (E) is

incorrect since Madison had nothing to do with creating the Republican Party, an organization that did not come into existence until the mid-1850s.

34. **(C)**   The figure portrays indexed expenditures (with expenditures in 1966 set at the base rate of 100), not the actual dollar amount spent. On the basis of index figures alone, one can only determine relative rates of growth, not whether actual dollar amounts spent on Medicare exceed expenditures for Medicaid (A). (B) is clearly incorrect since all expenditure categories have shown increases. (D) is a value statement which cannot be directly inferred from the figure. Similarly, (E) is incorrect because there is no data presented on comparative medical expenditures.

35. **(D)**   Pluralist theory, sometimes called "plural elitism," argues that multiple elites contend for power and that the essence of democracy is preserved by their need to compete for mass support. (A) is incorrect and corresponds to a simple classical concept of democracy that exists, if at all, in small communities. (B) is a value statement about what ought to be, but does not necessarily reflect the view of pluralists who see both necessity and value in elites' competition. (C) is incorrect since it is a belief held by "elitists," whose views are in sharp contrast to those of the "pluralists." (E) is a statement about separation of powers, not pluralism, and is therefore incorrect. Although compatible with a pluralist viewpoint, it is not a necessary component of that perspective.

36. **(C)**   Presidents exert the most power in foreign affairs for a number of reasons including their expansive constitutional powers as commander-in-chief and chief diplomat. Presidents exert much less power in domestic affairs (B) because Congress has substantial powers there, including the power to regulate interstate commerce, tax, and spend. (D) is incorrect since Congress is a co-equal branch of government, whose actions are not directly controllable by the President. (A) is incorrect because in our federal system control of urban affairs is largely a function of state and local governments. (E) is incorrect since the President has no control over the Supreme Court other than the power to nominate its members.

37. **(A)**   Federal judges are appointed for life on good behavior, and may be removed only by impeachment, death, or resignation. (D) is clearly incorrect, since there is no specified term and (C) is incorrect since federal judges are not elected. (B) is incorrect since judges are not appointed by Congress nor is there any official role for the American Bar Association. Members of Congress (E) are prohibited by the doctrine of separation of powers from simultaneously holding a position in either the executive or judicial branches of government.

38. **(E)**   Each of the listed acts has played an important role in the history of the civil service. The Pendleton Act (I) in the late nineteenth century established the civil service. The Hatch Act (II) limits political activity of public employees in an effort to prevent the use and abuse of public employees for partisan purposes . The 1974 reforms (III)

established the federal executive service. Since each alternative has been important, (A), (B), (C), and (D) are incorrect because they eliminate one or more of these key legislative acts.

39. **(A)** Holmes was more concerned to protect the courts power to regulate the states than to regulate Congress. (B) is incorrect since it involves regulating Congress, while (C) is incorrect because Holmes should support such a decision. (D) and (E) are incorrect since there is simply no basis provided by the quotation for determining his view on a policy issue like abortion or the merits of a contract action.

40. **(D)** The national government has seen its power grow substantially over the past two hundred years relative to that of the states. Nowhere has that growth of power been more dramatic than in economic affairs. (E) is incorrect because states still retain significant power in our federal system, especially in areas involving health, welfare, and education. (A), (B), and (C) are inconsistent with the reality of growing national government power and directly contradict our historical experience.

41. **(B)** Congress has based its requirement for states to adopt speed limits upon its power to regulate interstate commerce, defined as commerce between the states. (C) is incorrect because there is no specific federal power to regulate speed limits. Although Congress does have the power to spend, (D) is a less appropriate answer because spending must be exercised in conjunction with another power given to the national government. The power to tax (A) is not directly involved, nor would (E), the regulation of commerce solely within a single state ("intrastate"), be an appropriate response since that remains under state control.

42. **(D)** The Articles of Confederation created a very weak national government, leaving the individual states to handle almost all matters. (A), (B), (C), and (E) are incorrect since each would be based upon action by some part of the national government. In addition, (A) would be incorrect since there was only one chamber in Congress under the Articles of Confederation. Similarly, (B) is incorrect since the Articles provided for no Supreme Court and (C) is incorrect because it provided for no President as we know that office today. Finally, since there was no Senate in the Congress of the Articles of Confederation, there would also not have been a Senate natural resources committee (E).

43. **(D)** Primaries and caucuses are the two alternative methods used to select delegates to the national conventions for the two major political parties. (A) is incorrect since primaries are neither mentioned nor required by the Constitution. (B) is incorrect since primaries are used in many but not all states. (C) is incorrect since primaries play no direct role in the selection of electors. (E) is incorrect because primaries are also used by the Democratic Party.

44. **(D)** Although more Americans identify themselves as Democrats and Democrats have consistently controlled one or both houses of Congress, the Democratic Party

won only one presidential election in the 20 years between 1968 and 1988: the 1976 election of Jimmy Carter. Therefore (A), (B), and (C) are clearly incorrect. (E) is incorrect for the additional reason that the popular vote winner in each of the six elections, whether Democrat or Republican, also won the electoral college majority.

45. **(C)** The United States Postal Service, formerly the Post Office Department, lost its Cabinet status in the 1970s. The newest Cabinet department is Veterans (A), while (B) Housing and Urban Development and (D) Defense have been Cabinet departments for some years and (E) Education was elevated to the Cabinet in the 1970s.

46. **(A)** Precedent means to follow the rule in the "preceding" case, hence (A) is the correct response. Following the decision in an earlier case is a "rule" of the courts themselves, but is not required by the Constitution (B), nor by a statute (D), a law enacted by the legislative branch. (C) is incorrect since a major reason to follow earlier cases is consistency, rather than "common sense." (E) is incorrect, because the Chief Justice may or may not have agreed with the earlier decision.

47. **(B)** Truman's career included serving as a local governmental official, Senator and Vice President of the United States. Jimmy Carter (A) had been Governor of Georgia; Woodrow Wilson (C), who also served as President of Princeton University, was Governor of New Jersey; Ronald Reagan, best known for his film and television career, served two terms as Governor of California; and Franklin D. Roosevelt (E) had been Secretary of the Navy and Governor of New York before being elected to the Presidency.

48. **(E)** Political socialization is the process by which political attitudes and values of all kinds are formed. (C) is incorrect because it is only one aspect of political socialization: party identification. (D) is incorrect because it refers to political culture: the content of which is learned through the socialization process. (A) and (B) are irrelevant responses.

49. **(A)** Committee chairmanships in the House of Representatives are generally given to the member of the majority party (Democratic) that has served the longest on the particular committee, in this case (A). (B) and (E) are incorrect because they are not Democrats. (C) and (D) are incorrect because seniority is not based upon age, but on length of service to the committee.

50. **(B)** The Rules Committee determines the rules for house debate on most bills, giving it substantial power. (A) is incorrect since the Rules Committee does not make committee assignments and (C) is incorrect because negotiating compromises is a function of conference committees, not the Rules Committee. (D) is incorrect because the Rules Committee, although still powerful, has declined in importance in recent decades. Selection of a speaker (E) is done by the majority party caucus and is not a function of the bi-partisan Rules Committee.

51. **(A)** Chief Justice Burger has been a strong advocate of a new intermediate appellate court to resolve disputes between the judicial circuits. (B) is incorrect since making it easier for state court decisions to be reviewed in federal court would further clog the system. Although (C) and (D) might reduce the federal court workload, Chief Justice Burger has not been closely identified with those positions. No responsible individual has proposed the drastic step of eliminating the federal district courts (E), which are the federal trial courts.

52. **(D)** An important aspect of the Court's argument in *Brown* was that the intangible badge of inferiority that accompanied segregated schools deprived children of equal educational opportunities and made separate educational facilities "inherently" unequal. The passage expresses the view that segregation itself, rather than the quality of education narrowly defined, is the issue. Therefore (E) is incorrect. The statement makes no reference to how "different" people (C) should be treated, except to indicate that treatment should not differ on the basis of race. Answers (A) and (B) are not responsive. (A) does not refer directly to equality and (B)'s reference is to an aspect of equality that is remote from the issues of race.

53. **(E)** Within a few years after the *Brown* decision, the Court handed down decisions requiring the integration of other public facilities. Racial discrimination, unlike discrimination based upon sex (B), sexual preference (A), or the physical/mental capabilities (D) of students, is clearly prohibited by the Fourteenth Amendment. Protections against other forms of discrimination is less certain. Although racially restrictive covenants (C) are banned in a manner consistent with the results in *Brown*, the reasoning was different because it involved private discrimination. Equally important, the Supreme Court decision on restrictive covenants predated the *Brown* decision by several years.

54. **(D)** In a "concurring opinion" the judge "concurs" or agrees with the majority conclusion but bases his or her answer on different reasons. (C) is incorrect because it reverses what the opinion concurs with, while (B) describes a "dissenting opinion," not a "concurring opinion." (A) is incorrect since it is in agreement with the rest of the court, not the President that is the issue. (E) would refer to an abstention, not a "concurring opinion" which would necessarily be in writing.

55. **(C)** The Administrative Procedures Act deals with the procedural rights of citizens, including the right to notice of administrative rules being adopted by regulatory agencies. The historic 1954 desegregation decision (A), the act which limits political activity of government employees (B), the Constitution (D), and the Civil Rights Act of 1969 (E) are all important, but do not directly deal with notice requirements in rule making.

56. **(B)** Approximately five million people, including those in the armed services, work for the national government. (A) substantially understates the scope of federal

employment, while (C), (D), and (E) substantially overstate it. There are approximately 100 million people in the entire workforce, nationally.

57. **(C)**   Changes in transportation and communications technology have made it possible for heads of state to deal more directly with each other than was possible in an earlier era. There have been no changes in the Constitution (A), laws adopted by Congress (B) or the role of the vice president (E) that have had a substantial impact on a president's relation with the foreign service. Similarly, public opinion (D) has only an indirect impact on presidential behavior and would not account for a change in a president's reliance on career diplomats.

58. **(B)**   The Reagan administration advocated significant increases in defense spending. Although domestic spending (D) was downplayed, those expenditures also grew under Reagan. (A) is incorrect since the Democrats retained control of the House throughout the Reagan administration, although Republicans captured control of the Senate for several years. Education (C) was not a priority of the administration and Reagan advocated the appointment of conservative, not liberal judges; hence, these responses are also incorrect.

59. **(E)**   During a presidential election year, the "coattail effect" of the presidential winner usually means that the president's party gains some seats at that time which it may not be able to retain two years later at a "midterm" election when the president is not running. Therefore, (A), (B), (C), and (D) are incorrect because it is less likely that the president's party will increase the number of seats held in Congress than it will experience some decrease.

60. **(D)**   This answer is correct because it is the only statement which is not true. Actually most members of Congress have full-time staff working in their home states and districts. The size (B) and importance (A) of staff has increased as members of Congress have become increasingly dependent (C) on the knowledge and expertise of these political appointees (E).

Section II

Question 1–Sample Essay Scoring 0 to 3

According to the United States Constitution, power is shared between the national, state, and local governments. The distribution of power has always been a matter of contention and its formulation has changed over time. In addition to specific powers granted by the Constitution, the national government has gained power throughout United States history, often at the expense of the states, which has been supported by Supreme Court decisions.

In the twentieth century the national government has gained expansive regulatory power over such areas as the economy, the environment, and civil rights. These regulations restricted, for example, the actions of business owners in the use of their property and their relations with both employees and customers. Such restrictions aroused much criticism that has resulted in increasing efforts to reduce the power of the federal government.

Since the early 1970s there have been efforts, particularly in the Reagan administration, to dismantle some government regulations or simply not enforce them. But the major attempt has been to shift power from the national to the state governments through the movement of funds. Revenue sharing, begun by Richard Nixon, and various other programs have sent money from Washington to the states. Probably the most significant example of this effort is the recently passed welfare reform bill which discontinued the national welfare program, putting in its place state designed and operated programs which would receive grants from the federal government.

Although there have been calls from President Clinton and others to reduce the size of the national government and simplify its regulatory system, to date there have been mixed results.

Analysis of Sample Essay Scoring 0 to 3 (Question 1)

This essay jumps into a description of the Constitution without relating it to the theoretical framework of federalism. As a result, the essay does not have a central thesis that holds the parts together. The description of the Constitution is generalized, lacking the specificity of detail that characterizes excellent essays.

The second paragraph gives a historical perspective, but again it is highly generalized and says nothing regarding why the power of the national government grew. It comments somewhat offhandedly when it refers to restrictions on the actions of business owners, mentioning why opposition arose to this growth of power but does not state the issue clearly.

The third paragraph is somewhat better, making specific references to the Reagan and Nixon administrations and briefly describing the welfare reform bill. But it only vaguely defines revenue sharing and does not discuss specifically the various ways that money has been shifted to the states. The concluding sentence of the essay is again highly generalized.

Question 1–Sample Essay Scoring 4 to 6

A federal governmental system is one in which power is shared by several entities. In the United States this sharing takes place between the national or central government and the state governments. American history has been replete with debates over this relationship.

According to the Constitution the national government has certain powers, including such things as taxation, the coinage of money, and naturalization rules. Over time the Supreme Court has expanded these powers through "broad construction" of the Constitution, which allows the national government to do anything that is not prohibited by the document.

The major growth of national governmental power has come in the twentieth century, particularly with the New Deal of the 1930s and the Great Society of the 1960s. Under these programs, the national government entered into social and economic arenas and in some cases, particularly civil rights, took over areas that had formerly been under the states. Subsequently, the national government also moved extensively into environmental regulation.

Not surprisingly, criticisms of the enhanced power of the national government also emerged. Critics pointed to the increasing national debt, loss of state powers, and negative economic impact. Richard Nixon announced a "New Federalism," the key feature of which was "revenue sharing," which turned over money to the states as unrestricted grants. This program continued until 1986, when it was discontinued because it was regarded as ineffective in terms of both economic impact and redistribution of government responsibilities.

Critics of the growth of government power have sought, with mixed success, to reduce the vast array of national government regulations. The Reagan administration, faced with a Democratic Congress, primarily reduced enforcement of existing regulations. With the Republican takeover of Congress in 1995, however, there has been a determined effort to dismantle much of the regulatory environment, but this effort has met little success because of both disagreement among the Republicans themselves and the opposition of a Democratic president, Bill Clinton. Welfare reform, however, returned most of the welfare system to the states along with money to support it.

The contemporary mood seems to support reduction of national government power and enhancement of state power. But the specific way that power is shared and the balance between the national and state governments will always be subject to the specific social and economic issues the nation faces.

Analysis of Sample Essay Scoring 4 to 6 (Question 1)

This essay begins with a brief statement regarding federalism. The statement would be improved by going into more detail. Similarly, the next paragraph discusses the Constitution, referring to various powers given to the national government and the Supreme Court's role in expanding those powers. But it lacks specific references to the relevant parts of the Constitution or to Supreme Court decisions.

The third paragraph gives a generalized history of the growth of the national government in the twentieth century but would be strengthened by specific references to legislation. The following paragraph does a good job of identifying some of the points made by critics and discusses revenue sharing in fairly specific terms. Similarly the fourth paragraph discusses in some detail further efforts to reduce the size of the federal government. Both the third and fourth paragraphs, however, need to go into further detail regarding the three types of grant programs which sent money to the states and the welfare reform bill.

The final paragraph returns to the theme of the first paragraph—the changing relationship of national and state governments. This gives the essay a sense of completeness.

In short, this essay has thematic unity but is less than excellent because it lacks detail in developing its points.

Question 1—Sample Essay Scoring 7 to 9

Under the United States Constitution, governmental power is shared by the national government and state governments. Local governments—including county, city, school districts, transportation districts, and others—provide a third layer of government. This system of shared power is called the federal system or federalism. Throughout American history, there has been continual struggle over how this power is to be shared.

The Constitution specifies that the national government has certain specific or *enumerated* powers (Article 1). The Supreme Court has also concluded that the national government has *implied* powers (*McCulloch v. Maryland*, 1819) and *inherent* powers (*U.S. v. Curtiss-Wright Export Corporation*, 1936). Finally, the national government has *concurrent* powers, such as taxation, that it shares with the states and local governments. Thus the power of the national government is extensive and changing.

Today debate centers on what is popularly called "big government." Franklin Roosevelt established Social Security (1930s) and Lyndon Johnson obtained civil rights legislation and Medicaid (1960s) directed at social problems. National government power has also grown through its expanding regulatory powers such as the Clean Air Act (1970) and the Clean Water Act (1983), which sought to achieve national environmental standards.

Beginning with Richard Nixon (1969-1974), presidents have attempted to reduce the power of national government and turn more responsibility over to the states. Money has been returned to the states in the form of grants, which include: (1) block grants for "broad functional" areas such as health care and community development, (2) categorical grants for specific purposes, Medicaid and Food Stamps being two examples, and (3) general purpose grants which largely can be used by the recipients as they see fit. Revenue sharing, used between 1972 and 1986, has been the major example of general purpose grants.

The national debt, limits on the freedom of states, local governments, and individual citizens, and social problems such as poverty and crime have prompted considerable criticism of big government. As a result, there have been repeated efforts to reduce the regulatory burden of the federal government. In 1995 the Republican dominated Congress frequently clashed with the Clinton administration over such issues as cost-benefit analysis of regulations and reduction of environmental legislation, but they did agree on speed-limit repeal and telecommunications reform (1996). The leading example of the effort to return power to the states is the welfare reform bill (1996) which replaced the Aid to Families with Dependent Children program with block grants to the states which could then develop and operate their own welfare programs with little interference from Washington.

It is unlikely that the limits of national government power will ever be strictly defined. As long as state and local governments have problems for which their resources are inadequate, they will look to the national government for help. But that help will always bring with it intrusiveness and standardization that will never be entirely acceptable to other entities that desire a degree of independence.

Analysis of Sample Essay Scoring 7 to 9 (Question 1)

This essay begins with a good definition of federalism, noting that it includes local governments as well as the national and state governments. It also presents the thesis that there has been continual struggle over the sharing of power throughout American history.

The second paragraph details the specific powers of the national government, including those that it shares with the states, and describes the role of the Supreme Court in expanding the power of the national government. This paragraph also includes specific references to relevant sections of the Constitution and Supreme Court decisions.

The third paragraph notes the nature of the current debate over national government power and gives a brief historical description of the growth of this power in the twentieth century. It supports this description with references to specific legislation.

The fourth paragraph describes the effort to reduce the power of the national government and outlines the three kinds of grants and gives examples of each. The following paragraph continues this description chronologically, noting some of the reasons for criticism of "big government" and referring to specific examples of legislation and the type of grant established by the welfare reform bill. The final paragraph returns to the theme of change and struggle introduced in the first paragraph and explains why this situation is likely to continue into the future.

Overall, this essay gives the reader a sense that the author not only understands the subject being written about, but knows a lot more than there was time to write. At the same time, the author had control over the material presented, offering ideas and supporting detail in a well-structured essay.

Question 2–Sample Essay Scoring 0 to 3

The term "affirmative action" refers to programs which promote the hiring and promotion of individuals because they are members of a racial minority or, more recently, women. It has become controversial in recent years because Caucasian males have argued that such programs constitute "reverse discrimination," believing that the former discrimination against people on the basis of their skin color or being female has now been transferred to them and is equally wrong.

These affirmative action programs began in the 1960s as the civil rights movement succeeded in doing away with legalized discrimination. Wanting to go beyond simply making discrimination illegal, many employers and universities began to give special attention to minorities, particularly African Americans. Employers hired and promoted African Americans and Hispanics while colleges and universities accepted such students despite often inferior academic records. Some affirmative action programs established fixed percentages or numbers of minorities to be advanced.

Many Caucasians protested against these practices. Eventually, a student seeking acceptance at a medical school in California who was denied because he was white, sued the university. When the suit went to the Supreme Court, it ordered the school to accept him. From this point in the late 1970s, the policy of affirmative action became increasingly controversial.

Although affirmative action continues to be widely practiced, the conservative political direction of the country in the 1980s and 1990s has undermined its support. In California, for instance, the University has decided to end its affirmative action program. Such decisions appear to be taking place elsewhere as well.

Analysis of Sample Essay Scoring 0 to 3 (Question 2)

The first paragraph gives both a brief definition of affirmative action and the reason why it has become increasingly controversial. Both statements are very general and make no reference to the Constitution. They also do not present a thesis.

The second paragraph gives a brief historical account of affirmative action but does not go into specifics, such as legislation. Similarly, the third paragraph describes the challenge to affirmative action but makes no reference to the Constitution nor does it specifically identify the Bakke case. The final paragraph describes the current situation but again in highly general terms, making no reference to constitutional issues. Because no thesis was stated in the first paragraph, there is not much that the closing paragraph can refer back to.

Question 2–Sample Essay Scoring 4 to 6

The Civil Rights movement of the 1950s and 1960s, which called for an end to racial discrimination, provided the stimulus for affirmative action. Although the civil rights laws of the mid-decade forbade discrimination, many rights advocates believed more needed to be done to overcome the effects of more than a century of slavery and discrimination.

The first affirmative action program came early in the presidency of John F. Kennedy. Essentially he said that the Federal government would not hire contractors unless they both hired and promoted minority groups. During the late 1960s, many colleges and universities began giving minority groups preference in their admissions and employers began following a similar practice in hiring.

In the early 1970s, Alan Bakke applied to the medical school at the University of California at Davis. When he was turned down, despite having better grades and test scores than several minority students who were accepted, he sued on the grounds of reverse discrimination. A few years later his suit reached the Supreme Court, which said that he must be accepted by the medical school but that minorities could be given special preference as long as no rigid quotas were established.

The Supreme Court tended to uphold affirmative action programs, which by this time included women as well as racial minorities, until the late 1980s when it began making discrimination suits against employers more difficult. These decisions became a political issue, resulting in the passage by Congress of a bill making such suits easier.

With the more conservative drift of the country politically, however, the issue of affirmative action continues to draw attention. The University of California system has decided to end its affirmative action program and the federal court has ordered the law school at the University of Texas to ignore race as a basis for admissions. These are only the most prominent of several such reversals.

Affirmative action seeks not only to establish equality but to right the wrongs of the past. It will continue to generate controversy, in part, because the current generation does not feel responsible for the actions of previous generations. While equality of opportunity is a worthwhile goal, many people now believe that the equality of result sought by affirmative action is neither justifiable nor reachable.

Analysis of Sample Essay Scoring 4 to 6 (Question 2)

The opening paragraph ties affirmative action to the civil rights movement and thereby offers a historical context for the following discussion but it does not define the term. The references to civil rights laws are generalized rather than specific. The following paragraph describes the first affirmative action program but does not relate subsequent efforts to the 1964 Civil Rights Act.

The third paragraph describes the Bakke case but says only that the grounds were "reverse discrimination," making no reference to the constitutional and legal issues. The following paragraph notes that women were now included in affirmative action programs, but it does not go into detail regarding Supreme Court decisions.

The fifth paragraph briefly describes the current movement against affirmative action, but does not tell us when the California and Texas decisions were made. The final paragraph provides a conclusion but only describes how many Americans currently feel about affirmative action. It therefore fails to relate the essay to the constitutional and legal issues that the question asked it to address.

Question 2–Sample Essay Scoring 7 to 9

Affirmative action—programs to compensate for past discrimination by favoring minorities—arose out of the demand, first from African Americans in the 1950s and 1960s, for equal treatment by the legal system and social institutions. Legalized segregation in the south and discrimination against African Americans elsewhere in the United States were increasingly challenged after the 1954 *Brown v. Board of Education* decision that declared school segregation unconstitutional on the basis of the Fourteenth Amendment guarantee of equal protection of the laws. The Montgomery Bus Boycott (1955-56), Sit-ins and Freedom Rides (beginning 1961), and the March on Washington (1963), led to the Civil Rights Act (1964) and Voting Rights Act (1965), which dismantled legalized segregation.

Within this context, President John F. Kennedy issued an order in 1961 that prohibited contractors hired by the federal government from discriminating against minority groups. He further instructed these contractors to hire and promote minorities. After passage of the 1964 Civil Rights Act, many employers and universities developed affirmative action programs that gave preference to minorities, later extended to women, in hiring or admissions. It was hoped that such an approach would make up for past discrimination and move society more quickly toward equality of both opportunity and results.

Almost immediately critics charged that such affirmative action programs constituted "reverse discrimination" that was illegal under both the Fourteenth Amendment to the Constitution and the 1964 Civil Rights Act. Alan Paul Bakke, who had applied to the medical school of the University of California at Davis, was denied admission even though minority students with lower qualifications were admitted. He sued the university on the grounds that he had not been accepted because of his race. In 1978 the Supreme Court ordered, citing the Fourteenth Amendment, that the University admit Bakke but at the same time stated that special preference could be given to minorities as long as no quotas were established.

Over the next several years the Court generally upheld affirmative action programs. By 1987 it stated that even when there is no evidence of past discrimination, an employer may promote women and minorities over white males. Shortly thereafter, however, it began moving in a more conservative direction and through a series of decisions made discrimination suits against employers increasingly difficult. A 1991 civil rights bill essentially reversed these rulings, as civil rights advocates turned to the legislature in the face of an unsympathetic Court.

The debate over "reverse discrimination" has not been resolved, although the arguments remain much the same. In 1995 the University of California decided to ban racial and sexual preferences beginning with admissions for the 1997-98 academic year (later delayed to 1998-99). About the same time, a federal court struck down a race-based admissions policy at the University of Texas School of Law. Similar reversals of affirmative action programs took place at other institutions.

Although opposition to affirmative action appears to be increasing, the Fourteenth Amendment to the Constitution and federal civil rights laws ensure that the issue will continue to be a live one. How to balance the need to help historically oppressed minority groups with the need to avoid "reverse discrimination" will be an ongoing struggle.

Analysis of Sample Essay Scoring 7 to 9 (Question 2)

This essay begins with both a definition of affirmative action and discussion of its historical background. Although a thesis could be more clearly stated, the essay implies that affirmative action is tied to both the Fourteenth amendment to the Constitution and to civil rights legislation.

The second paragraph describes the first affirmative action programs, referring specifically to President Kennedy's 1961 order and the response of employers and universities to the 1964 Civil Rights Act. It also explains why people turned to affirmative actions.

Paragraph three turns to the challenge to affirmative action, describing the Bakke case in some detail. In particular it notes that the successful challenge was based on the Fourteenth Amendment. The essay continues in the following paragraph to describe the Supreme Court's continuing support of affirmative action through the high point of 1987, to which the essay makes a specific reference. It then makes a general statement regarding the change in the court's position and describes the 1991 bill that reversed these rulings. Although more detail might be desired in this paragraph, the author provides the necessary information within the allowed time constraints.

The fifth paragraph describes the current moves against affirmative action with specific references to the situations in California and Texas. Although it makes no specific reference to constitutional and legal issues, it states that "the arguments remain much the same," referring to earlier statements in the essay.

The final paragraph refers to both the Fourteenth Amendment and civil rights laws, thereby returning to elements introduced in the first paragraph and indicates the effect these will have on future discussion. As with all good essays, this essay combines both general statements and supporting details. It would be strengthened with a clearer thesis statement in the first paragraph.

Question 3–Sample Essay Scoring 0 to 3

The data clearly illustrates that the President bears less responsibility for the increase in spending than Congress. Congress controls the major portion of the budget, and this portion has gone up tremendously in the past three decades.

The only way to solve this problem is by voting out the incumbents. The Congress needs new people who will change the way the budget is written, and cut spending. There is no way the current members of Congress will cut spending, and we need to elect representatives who will honor their promise to cut spending.

The government wastes so much money that reducing spending would not be hard if politicians really wanted to cut spending. It seems that every year, no matter who is in office, the government is spending more money. In order for this to stop, the President must not approve any budget that has any spending increases at all.

However, the government spends money on some important things, so we need to make sure that they don't cut these things.

Analysis of Sample Essay Scoring 0 to 3 (Question 3)

This essay begins by correctly answering the first part of the question. In fact, the first paragraph is an adequate introduction for the essay. However, there is no thesis statement here. What looks like a thesis statement opens the second paragraph. Voting out incumbents is suggested as a way to solve the problem. But this solution does not engage the data or the question in any depth.

No evidence is given that it is the particular members of Congress who are responsible for a pattern which has endured for 30 years or more. In fact, the stimulus data seem to suggest that the pattern is a result of institutional arrangement rather than the individual members of those institutions. Even if the author does not believe that the institutional arrangements are at the root of the problem, this aspect of the issue needs to be addressed.

The author also states that it would be easy to cut spending. But there is no specific evidence offered to make the case. The other solution proposed is that the President should veto any budget that contains spending increases, demonstrating no understanding of the possible ramifications of such an inflexible political position.

The final paragraph is hardly adequate as a paragraph at all since it only contains one sentence. In addition, this sentence seems to contradict much of the essay, and bears little, if any, relation to what has already been written. Rather than amplifying and restating the thesis, this sentence contradicts the already weak points of the essay.

Question 3–Sample Essay Scoring 4 to 6

From the evidence presented in the table, it seems that the President bears about one third of the responsibility for the increase in the size of the federal budget. While clearly, both the Congress and the President need to curtail federal spending, striving for a balanced budget, the Congress has further to go. Congress must take on the task of reducing spending, because they are responsible for most of the budget. The President has direct control over only a small part of the budget.

Given current political realities, it seems unlikely that Congress will be able to do anything about the budget, unless there is a change in their attitude toward federal spending. An amendment to the Constitution to balance the budget might force the Congress to eliminate unnecessary spending, but amending the Constitution is a very difficult and lengthy process.

Another solution might be to raise taxes, but this is always politically unpopular, and the members of Congress do not want to do this as it may hurt their chances to get re-elected. What needs to happen is that voters need to realize that Congress, not the President controls most of the budget, and demand that their Representatives and Senators do something about spending. It seems that for any improvement at all to take place, people in government need to work together with a genuine commitment to cutting spending.

Analysis of Essay Scoring 4 to 6 (Question 3)

The thesis of this essay needs to be both more precise and more explicit. The first paragraph answers the first part of the question, and this answer does imply what follows in the rest of the essay. However, it ultimately does not give the essay enough direction. It does summarize the data, but does not provide a solid interpretation around which to build the essay.

The second paragraph suggests a solution to the increase in spending, and also presents a possible objection to that solution. However, neither the solution nor the objection is developed well enough. While the objection offered is a valid one, there are other, more important objections to a balanced budget amendment. For instance, it might place restrictions on spending needed in an emergency situation, and a require-ment that a budget be balanced limits the ability of the government to apply Keynesian economic principles of increasing government spending in order to stimulate a slow economy.

The third paragraph offers an alternative solution to the budget crisis, but this solution does not address the issue of spending. The question and data are not about the budget deficit, but rather federal spending. These issues are not unrelated, of course, but it is important, especially given the time provided, for the essay to directly answer the question asked. The last solution offered, that citizens themselves need to do something about the budget deficit, is interesting and compelling. However, the author does not go into enough detail as to what citizens can do to slow the growth of spending. The final sentence concluding the essay is adequate, but it would have been more effective if this statement was amplifying an explicit thesis.

Question 3–Sample Essay Scoring 7 to 9

While the President has control of a significant portion of the federal budget, the growth in federal spending cannot be attributed solely to the President. In fact, most of the growth in federal spending is a result of either acts of Congress, or other items over which the President has little or no control. In fact, over the past 30 years or so, while both kinds of spending have grown considerably, the portion of the budget over which the President has relatively less control has grown twice as fast. In order for this growth to be curtailed (if one assumes that federal spending is too high), some change in how budgets and spending are approved would most likely have to occur.

It is too simplistic to say that Congress should just limit spending. If the answer were as easy as that, it seems likely that the federal budget would not have grown so much in the first place. Over the years, various Presidents have suggested means by which they could gain more control over the budget, and supposedly cut wasteful spending and programs.

One popular suggestion has been a "line item veto," a device by which the President could veto, or reject, parts of a bill, in this case, the federal budget, rather than being forced to choose to either accept or reject the bill in full. This would give the President the ability to cut programs that the President does not think would benefit the nation as a whole. Some argue, however, that this change would violate the Constitution and the doctrine of separation of powers.

Congressional opponents of the line-item veto brought their case to the U.S. Supreme Court in the belief that the shift in power brought about by the veto authority would change "the legal and practical effect" of their votes. Thus, the lawmaking procedure set forth in the Constitution would, in effect, have the rug pulled out from under it. But the high court, in a decision read from the bench by Chief Justice Rehnquist, said members of Congress "are not the right people to bring this suit" because they lack legal standing to do so. Ironically, the court noted that the requirement for legal standing stemmed from the general principle of separation of powers among the three branches of government.

But back on the legislative front, there is growing reason to be cautiously sanguine about the prospects for bringing federal spending under control. In July 1997, with both Republicans and Democrats practically falling over each other to claim victory and credit, the House overwhelmingly approved landmark legislation to balance the federal budget by 2002. The Senate was expected to follow suit. This kind of bipartisan effort, the result of tortuous negotiations, is encouraging in and of itself. But at the same time, one needs to take note of the uncontrollable urge a lawmaker must feel to attach himself or herself to such legislation. To vote against a package that combines long-promised tax cuts with a balanced budget is politically suicidal. The bill's most worrisome aspect is its so-called backloading, whereby tax breaks are planned to bring about the greatest revenue losses after 2002. Add to that the fact that legislators avoided dealing with the hydraheaded issue of medical or pension cost containment, and you have a potentially explosive witch's brew of budget busters.

Ultimately, if politicians or citizens want to decrease public spending, there will have to be a change in the way federal budgets are developed, either through a formal change in law, or in the informal way Congress and the President draw up a budget agreement. But the issue of whose ox is being gored can never be expected to be far from the surface.

Analysis of Essay Scoring 7 to 9 (Question 3)

This essay presents a balanced and thorough understanding of the question and the data presented. It has a strong thesis statement and develops this line of argument well. The first paragraph introduces the topic and summarizes as well as interprets the data. This is important, because the author's summary highlights the aspect of the data which will form the basis of the rest of the discussion. To conclude the introductory paragraph, the author offers the thesis statement, which both addresses the question and the stimulus. All of this paragraph presents a balanced understanding of the issue.

The author develops the argument in the second paragraph by outlining why an alternate suggestion is not likely to decrease budget growth. Here, the author uses the evidence provided in the chart which in fact shows that, historically, Congress has been even less reluctant than the President to slow the growth in government spending. The author then goes on to state that Presidents have offered that more control by the executive branch over federal spending would be a more effective way to slow growth. Ideally, this paragraph would contain some specific evidence of the failure of Congress to slow its own growth, such as the failure of the Gramm-Rudman bill to slow deficit spending, but this is a minor point given the context of the rest of the essay.

The final paragraph describes the, as of yet, untried solution of the line item veto. The author offers an adequate description of how it would work and why it might decrease growth in federal spending. This discussion is balanced with some criticisms of the change, and this demonstrates a rich and coherent understanding of the topic. Finally, the conclusion reinforces the main thesis, and while offering no definite answers, confronts both the question and the stimulus.

Question 4–Sample Essay Scoring 0 to 3

Negative advertising is being used more and more in elections. Candidates use them because they think they will help them get elected. I also think that candidates use them because they do not have a positive message, and can only attack their opponents.

The paragraph above says that negative political advertisements may contain important information. This information may be important but voters should not always believe campaign ads, since the information they contain might not be true. Negative advertising does not help voters make a choice, because they want objective information.

Candidates should try to get elected based on their own qualifications and issue positions, not by insulting their opponent. These insults only end up insulting the voter, and turning them off to the political process.

Analysis of Sample Essay Scoring 0 to 3 (Question 4)

This essay does not actually answer the question asked, except in criticizing negative political advertising. However, even here, it does not address the issues brought up in the stimulus paragraph. Another problem is that there is no identifiable thesis statement. It is clear the author does not approve of negative political campaigns, but there is little demonstration of any analysis of the issue. Grammatical flaws also mar the first paragraph, as the writer, perhaps hurrying to get something on paper, fails properly to match the direct objects ("them") in the second and third sentences to their antecedent ("advertising") in the first sentence.

Much of the essay is little more than judgmental criticism of negative advertising, with no evidence to back up these statements. Also, there is no coherent line of criticism, no development of an argument. None of this is necessarily incorrect information, but it is presented in such a way as to make statements with little substantiation.

The essay is unbalanced, making no acknowledgment of the possible benefits of negative political advertisements. The connection made between negative campaigns and voter dissatisfaction is a good one. However, it needs to be developed more in order to form the basis of a more compelling argument, one which balances the author's point with the information provided in the stimulus paragraph.

The second paragraph highlights issues ignored in the stimulus paragraph. This is important, solid information, and directly engages the question. Negative advertisements do present information, but that information is not really useful if it is inaccurate or biased. This is a necessary caveat to the stimulus paragraph.

The final paragraph draws some speculative criticisms of the stimulus paragraph, about the potential these ads have for having a negative impact on the political process as a whole. This paragraph is both balanced and reasonable, formulating a plausible counter-argument to the stimulus paragraph. The concluding lines tie the essay together, placing the claims of the stimulus paragraph in a broader context. But unfortunately, the author's line of reasoning is never fully developed.

Question 4–Sample Essay Scoring 4 to 6

Negative political campaigns have been around as long as there has been politics. It seems unlikely that there will ever be a major political campaign where there is not some kind of negative advertising. The whole point of a campaign is to make one candidate look better than the other, and negative advertisements have been shown to be fairly effective in doing so.

Negative advertisements give information about a candidate that the voters wouldn't get from the candidate themselves. Thus, they are an important source of information. Nevertheless, the advertisements themselves may be misleading, and therefore, less useful. It is difficult for a candidate who has been attacked unfairly to try to get his or her message out while at the same time defending him or herself from attacks. Sometimes, candidates are prevented from getting their message out, because they are busy defending themselves. It is possible that the candidate who has new and interesting ideas may not get to explain them to the voters if the candidate is constantly attacked by negative advertisements.

Ultimately, the voters have to pay attention and not be fooled by misleading and inaccurate campaign information. Campaign advertisements of any kind cannot always be taken at face value.

Analysis of Sample Essay Scoring 4 to 6 (Question 4)

The introduction, while making a concise statement about the purpose of negative advertising, does not really engage the stimulus paragraph. There is not an identifiable thesis statement, and the essay overall lacks a balanced structure. The first instance of this is when the author does not distinguish among the different kinds of negative political advertisements. While what is presented in the first paragraph might introduce the topic well in a longer essay, time does not permit such a general introductory paragraph.

The second paragraph does begin to address the stimulus paragraph and the question. However, the focus is lost here as the author begins to discuss how a negative campaign might harm the target of the campaign. Again, the essay does not clearly address the question, nor is it directly replying to the stimulus paragraph. This information could be expanded and, in a way, is leading to an important criticism of negative campaigning, that is, if a candidate must defend him or herself from attacks, then voters may be less likely to get a chance to evaluate the candidate's actual campaign platforms. As a result, a negative campaign may not result in a more knowledgeable electorate, which contradicts the stimulus paragraph's main point.

Finally, the conclusion, while offering good advice which applies to all campaigning, does not really tie the rest of the essay together. It does attempt to put negative advertising in the broader context of campaigning in general, but it is not responding to the question, nor does it further the analysis of the essay.

Question 4–Sample Essay Scoring 7 to 9

In evaluating negative advertisements, one has to take into account what exactly about the candidate is being criticized. Some negative advertisements can inform voters about important positions and activities of the candidate. However, some negative ads are less than helpful, especially those which attack the candidate's character, rather than his or her politics. The information on issues is important for voters, because candidates themselves, in an effort to appeal to all voters, will say that they are against crime, but may be reluctant to say that their program to eliminate crime includes specific proposals—like gun control—that are unpopular with many voters. In this case, a negative ad stating the candidate's specific position on an issue can be helpful to voters. Nevertheless, there are problems with relying on negative ads for information.

Often, if not usually, the information in such an ad is presented in a biased and possibly misleading way. That is, an opponent will cast a candidate's policy stand in as unappealing a way as possible, in order to alienate as many voters as possible. This might border on presenting inaccurate information. In fact, it is often difficult for voters to check the accuracy of any statement provided in a campaign advertisement.

At the very least, negative ads often lack the kind of context that would enable voters to make an informed choice. Such ads can be extraordinarily powerful in the way they play upon emotions, as witness President Johnson's anti-Goldwater ad featuring a little girl picking daisies in the foreground as an explosion occurs and an atomic mushroom cloud appears behind her. This ad was so controversial—its implication being that Barry Goldwater was capable of plunging the United States into nuclear war—that it ran only once. And by then, of course, it had already achieved its purpose: planting doubt.

Today's negative ads are more "hot-button" oriented, appealing to what voters tell pollsters would most upset them to learn about a candidate. If the advertising messages come across as *ad hominem* attacks, negative advertisements can damage the credibility of both candidates, increasing the level of voter dissatisfaction with all politicians. This can result both from the content of the ads and from the rising frequency of such advertising in recent years: the sheer amount of it risks turning the public off to the whole political scene, causing a spiraling decrease in voter turnout. Such ads from opposing camps can end up, in effect, canceling each other out, and voters may stay away from the polls, frustrated that they can't find a reason to vote *for* someone.

While the author of the passage claims that there is little empirical evidence of actual damage, it does not seem that these negative effects would be easy to measure. Moreover, by the time one could gauge the harm that these ads do, it might, in essence, be too late. It seems likely that if both candidates are attacked, that in the end, voters will think a little less of both of them, even if they end up supporting one or the other. Negative advertisements may be a good source of information, but that information may come at a price.

Analysis of Sample Essay Scoring 7 to 9 (Question 4)

The essay presents a thesis statement after refining the position provided in the question. The author shows an understanding of the political scientist's statement in the question, but then goes on to criticize it. The transition to the thesis statement is somewhat abrupt and a bit clunky, but the writer's first paragraph does demonstrate a balanced understanding of the issue of negative advertising. The essay is refined by an extended analysis that points out an important distinction between advertisements that are personal attacks and those which give information about issue positions.

Specific examples—like the discussion of LBJ's anti-Goldwater ad—illustrate the points well. By showing the extremes to which negative advertising could lead, the writer presents a cautionary note to challenge the notion set out by the political scientist that this kind of advertising necessarily transmits useful information about a candidate's positions.

As a whole, the essay supports the thesis statement in a fluid, well-organized manner. The author comes across as confident, informed, and logical.

AP EXAMINATION IN
Comparative Government & Politics

PRACTICE TEST 3

AP EXAMINATION IN
COMPARATIVE GOVERNMENT AND POLITICS

Test 3

Section I

TIME: 45 Minutes
60 Multiple-Choice Questions
50% of Total Grade

(Answer sheets appear in the back of this book)

DIRECTIONS: Read the following questions and incomplete sentences. Each is followed by five answer choices. Choose the one answer choice that either answers the question or completes the sentence. Make sure to use the circles numbered 61 through 120 when marking your answers on your answer sheet.

---

1. In theory, representative democracy is superior to direct democracy for all of the following reasons EXCEPT

    (A) representative democracies are more practical for large countries.

    (B) representative democracies give policymakers more time to specialize in the art of decision making.

    (C) representative democracies guarantee a higher level of popular participation in politics.

    (D) representative democracies encourage deliberative decision making and discourage emotional mob rule.

    (E) representative democracies encourage the selection of the most knowledgeable and worthy candidates.

2.   Proportional representation schemes tend to

(A)   under represent majority parties.

(B)   promote the development of multiparty systems.

(C)   limit presidential power.

(D)   promote two-party legislatures.

(E)   reduce coalition politics.

3.   A political system marked by broadly representative and participatory institutions in which a variety of interests vie for favorable attention is best described by which of the following types of political culture?

(A)   Centrist

(B)   Parochial

(C)   Traditional

(D)   Civic

(E)   American

4.   In comparing old nation-states of Europe and the Americas to states that achieved independence in the twentieth century, in which of the following ways are the new states likely to differ from the old ones?

(A)   New states are likely to be less economically developed.

(B)   New states are likely to be bigger in geographical area.

(C)   New states are likely to be more stable.

(D)   New states are likely to be more democratic.

(E)   New states are likely to exhibit greater governmental continuity.

5. Which of the following is NOT necessary to the legal concept of the state?

    (A) Territory

    (B) Population

    (C) Common history, traditions, ethnic background, and language

    (D) Recognized independence

    (E) A government

6. Constitutions written in the eighteenth century differ from those written in the twentieth century in which of the following ways?

    (A) Eighteenth century constitutions were preoccupied with declaring and specifying individual rights.

    (B) Eighteenth century constitutions were less interested in establishing government machinery.

    (C) Eighteenth century constitutions were more interested in consolidating central government control over the economy.

    (D) Twentieth century constitutions were less interested in government planning and social welfare policy.

    (E) Twentieth century constitutions were shorter, simpler statements of political philosophy.

7. The two-ballot system in France is likely to lead to all of the following EXCEPT

    (A) coalition building among parties in both the right and left blocs.

    (B) strict voter-party identification.

    (C) a right/left ideological split in the National Assembly.

    (D) few candidates gaining a majority vote on the first ballot.

    (E) a Communist Party member voting for a Socialist Party candidate on the second ballot.

8. Democratic centralism as practiced by the former USSR meant that

    (A) elections would be held only for central government offices.

    (B) suggestions for policy might be made from the grass roots, but once decisions were made by a higher authority, obedience was expected.

    (C) each socialist republic could determine the means by which it centralized its work.

    (D) autonomous republics were free to hold democratic elections, so long as centralized administration was preserved.

    (E) the Russian Soviet Federated Socialist Republic, as the most democratic republic, would remain the center of power.

9. Which of the following statements about Cabinet government in Britain and France is NOT true?

    (A) In both countries, the Cabinet exercises executive responsibilities.

    (B) In both countries, the Cabinet is responsible to the legislative body.

    (C) In both countries, Cabinet members sit as voting members of Parliament while serving in executive posts.

    (D) In both countries, the prime minister and Cabinet establish the direction of public policy, although in France the president may, and often does, take charge.

    (E) In both countries, Cabinet members take responsibility for national ministries.

French Legislative Elections				
	Socialists		Gaullists	
Year	# of voters (in 1,000s)	# of seats in Parliament	# of voters (in 1,000s)	# of seats in Parliament
1958	3,176	40	4,011	196
1962	2,319	65	6,581	256
1967	4,224	117	8,449	233
1968	3,660	57	9,664	349
1973	4,523	102	8,243	270
1978	6,413	113	6,330	154
1981	9,432	270	5,231	83

10.   The above table illustrates which of the following trends in French politics?

(A)   Socialist Party influence has declined since 1958.

(B)   The percentage of votes won has had little effect over the years on the number of parliamentary seats.

(C)   The Gaullists have done consistently worse than the Socialists, especially in number of legislative seats.

(D)   Gaullist influence in parliament rose to a high in the late 1960s and has since declined as Socialist influence increased.

(E)   The Socialist Party strength has been gained at the direct expense of the Gaullists.

11. Which of the following is NOT part of the French political culture?

   (A) Distrust of the state

   (B) Positive and active support for government institutions

   (C) The tendency to ideological argument

   (D) Revolutionary traditions

   (E) Development of local and family ties to offset state influence

12. In France, the largest class of people consists of

   (A) the middle class.

   (B) industrial workers.

   (C) farmers.

   (D) clerics.

   (E) landed elites.

13. Changes in the French class structure over recent decades include all of the following EXCEPT

   (A) fewer people than ever before now live in small villages.

   (B) growing technology has led to an increase in white collar workers.

   (C) workers have become increasingly impoverished and revolutionary.

   (D) farmers are both less numerous and less tied to traditional values.

   (E) a new elite of technocrats has largely displaced the old landed aristocracy.

14. The Constitution of the Fifth Republic in France was explicitly intended to correct the failings of the Fourth Republic. These failings included all of the following EXCEPT

  (A) too many conflicting parties.

  (B) interest group politics that prevented consensus.

  (C) weak governmental leaders.

  (D) tyrannical political control by stable coalitions.

  (E) high levels of alienation of the people from the government.

15. Powers of the French president in the Fifth Republic include all of the following EXCEPT

  (A) naming the prime minister.

  (B) dissolving the National Assembly.

  (C) extensive emergency powers.

  (D) carrying issues directly to the people for referendum.

  (E) amending the constitution.

16. The constitution of Great Britain is characterized by which of the following?

  (A) An uncodified set of customs, acts of Parliament, and court decisions

  (B) A Federal system of divided authorities

  (C) The people, not Parliament, are sovereign

  (D) Great inflexibility and rigidity

  (E) Individual ministerial responsibility to Parliament

17.	Political culture in Great Britain is best described as

    (A)	highly revolutionary.

    (B)	ideologically motivated.

    (C)	authoritarian.

    (D)	consensual and evolutionary.

    (E)	radically democratic.

18.	The effect of social class on voting behavior in Britain is best reflected in which of the following statements?

    (A)	A middle class voter is more likely to vote Labour than a working class voter.

    (B)	The Labour party consistently wins control of Parliament because 50 percent of the British are working class.

    (C)	Regardless of their actual class status, almost half of British voters view themselves as middle class, including workers who increasingly defect from the Labour party.

    (D)	Upper income and upper class elements are more heavily represented in the Labour party than the Conservative party.

    (E)	Upward mobility predisposes the Asian immigrant classes in Britain to support the Conservative party.

19.	Which of the following is NOT true of the role of the opposition in the British parliament?

    (A)	It is organized to challenge the standing government's policies.

    (B)	It is representative of party followers throughout the country.

    (C)	It is not permitted to publicly voice its criticism of majority party policy.

    (D)	It provides the alternative government should the standing government fall.

    (E)	It may seek to undermine the legitimacy of majority party policy through debates in the House of Commons.

20. The prime minister in Great Britain is all of the following EXCEPT

   (A) leader of the majority party in Parliament.

   (B) leader of and representative of the British nation.

   (C) chair of the cabinet.

   (D) chair of the House of Lords.

   (E) a major actor in foreign policy.

21. Stalin's efforts to ensure the success of "Socialism in One Country" led to a modernization policy based upon all of the following EXCEPT

   (A) priority was given to heavy industry in order to enhance the military capacity of the state.

   (B) agriculture was to be collectivized and mechanized.

   (C) excess urban labor was to be sent into rural areas to help operate collective farms.

   (D) education was centralized to ensure growth in the numbers of skilled workers and scientists.

   (E) persons who opposed modernization were considered enemies of the people and subject to execution, imprisonment, or banishment.

22. The success of the Bolshevik Revolution under Lenin can be attributed to all of the following factors EXCEPT

   (A) no capitalist state made any effort to overthrow the Bolsheviks or to support their opposition.

   (B) Lenin promised peace to Russian soldiers who were increasingly disgruntled about Russia's participation in World War I.

   (C) peasants were promised land by the Bolsheviks and were encouraged to expropriate it for themselves.

   (D) workers were promised bread and encouraged to engage in strikes.

   (E) the Bolsheviks deftly gained influence over local soviets in military units, villages, and cities to overthrow the Provisional Government.

23. The political changes in the former Soviet Union before its collapse were attributable to all of the following EXCEPT

(A) non-Russian ethnic resentment of Russian dominance and lingering sentiments of ethnic self-determination.

(B) robust growth in Soviet trade with the West, which prompted rising economic growth and consumer expectations.

(C) the debilitating economic effects of extensive Soviet military intervention throughout the world.

(D) the realization by reformers, like Gorbachev, that socialist economic principles were stifling economic incentive and productivity.

(E) the overbalance of expenditures on national security and under-investment in the consumer economy.

24. The principal difference between a collective farm (*kolkhoz*) and a state-owned farm (*sovkhoz*) in the former Soviet Union was that

(A) on the *kolkhoz* peasants owned no land and were paid by the state; on the *sovkhoz*, peasants could work their own land.

(B) on the *sovkhoz*, unlike the *kolkhoz*, peasants could own their own garden plot.

(C) the *sovkhoz* farms were much smaller than the *kolkhoz* farms and received less state support.

(D) on the *kolkhoz*, peasants could own private garden plots; while on the *sovkhoz*, farmers were treated as salaried workers.

(E) the *kolkhoz* was less productive and far more exploitive because peasants could hire out work at slave wages on their private plots.

25. The reforms proposed by Soviet General Secretary Mikhail Gorbachev from 1985 to 1991 were designed to

    (A) end the political monopoly of the CPSU.

    (B) end the Cold War while maintaining the Soviet military presence in Eastern Europe.

    (C) bring a command economy and state socialism to the Soviet Union.

    (D) limit political repression and decentralize economic decision-making while maintaining the CPSU monopoly on political power.

    (E) break up the Soviet Union in favor of a more manageable, independent Russian Federation.

26. The Mandate of Heaven concept in Chinese politics refers to

    (A) the People's Liberation Army nuclear strategy.

    (B) the notion of divine support for imperial rule, which if withdrawn, could justify revolt.

    (C) the Maoist policy of encouraging constant cultural revolution.

    (D) Deng Xiaoping's economic modernization program.

    (E) the Communist party's control over national elections.

27. Mao's legacy of Cultural Revolution in China has been repudiated in which of the following ways?

    (A) The Gang of Four has been elevated to more important positions.

    (B) Red Guards now dominate the Army.

    (C) The Communist Party has reasserted its control over politics.

    (D) Openness has given way to hyper-isolationism in global affairs.

    (E) Criticism and self-criticism is expected of party officials.

28. Which of the following is NOT characteristic of the Communist party of China?

    (A) The Standing Committee of the Politburo is the greatest influence in party decision making.

    (B) The basic unit of the party is the branch committee which provides surveillance over government officials at all levels.

    (C) The People's Liberation Army is controlled by the party's Military Affairs Commission.

    (D) The party is less powerful than the formal government apparatus.

    (E) The chairman of the Central Committee is the most prestigious office in the party organization.

29. The concept of the mass line in Chinese political doctrine refers to

    (A) the effort by party officials to keep the masses in line.

    (B) the notion that party cadres must maintain close contact with common people and integrate mass public opinion into the policy-making process.

    (C) the effort by the party to ensure successful propaganda mechanisms to preserve a pliant population.

    (D) the need for continuous influence by the masses over the party through active recruitment of party members from the masses.

    (E) the reeducation campaign through which party leaders are made more sensitive to mass attitudes.

30. Which of the following is NOT a fundamental tenet of Maoism?

    (A) Conflict and disorder are to be valued, not abhorred.

    (B) The human spirit conquers over matter and machines.

    (C) The people should learn to be dependent on the state.

    (D) Specialization and intellectualism is bad.

    (E) Rural values are superior to the corrupt influences of urban life.

31. The French political system differs from the British system in which of the following ways?

    (A) The French have a federal system and the British have a unitary one.

    (B) The French prime minister is less powerful than the British prime minister.

(C)   The French Parliament consists of two parties while the British Parliament is fragmented into many parties.

(D)   The French president is a figurehead, unlike the British head of state.

(E)   The French National Assembly is more powerful than the British House of Commons.

32.   Which of the following best explains why the earlier Soviet movement toward democracy succeeded while the Chinese democratic movement failed?

(A)   Elder leaders of the Chinese Communist Power still retain control of the party, while younger reformers have dominated in the Soviet Union.

(B)   The number of student participants in China's democracy movement fell far short of the numbers of Soviet students agitating for change.

(C)   The military in the Soviet Union was agitating for rapid democratic reform, whereas in China the military was against reform.

(D)   China's conservative Red Guards were more successful in convincing the public not to tolerate reforms, while the KGB openly supported change in the Soviet Union.

(E)   The party lost control of the state apparatus in China and could no longer enforce democratization, while in the Soviet Union the party continued to control and reform the state machinery.

33.   Which of the following statements is most true of the difference between the electoral systems in France and Britain?

(A)   French elections are one-time elections, whereas in Great Britain, there are first and second ballots.

(B)   In France, candidates run without regard to party affiliation, whereas in Great Britain, they run on a party list.

(C)   French elections employ a proportional representation scheme with party lists, whereas in Great Britain, candidates must win a single member district election.

(D)   Elections in France tend to encourage a two-party system, whereas in Great Britain, they ensure multiple parties.

(E)   Unknown politicians without party affiliation are more likely to win in France than in Great Britain.

34.   China and the former Soviet Union were similar in all of the following ways EXCEPT

(A)   both countries were dominated by communism for several decades.

(B)   both countries experienced relatively bloody revolutions.

(C)   leaders in both countries resorted to "cult of personality" tactics in order to consolidate national power.

(D)   the Communist party in both countries was dominated by workers.

(E)   the prerevolutionary economies of both countries were largely agricultural and nonindustrial in character.

35.   Which of the following factors distinguishes leadership in Communist systems, such as those which have existed in the former Soviet Union and China, from democratic systems such as those found in France and Great Britain?

(A)   Leaders of Communist systems do not have to balance competing interests, as do leaders of Democratic systems.

(B)   Leadership transitions in Communist systems are more uncertain and destabilizing than in Western democracies.

(C)   Leaders of Communist systems are more likely to be recruited from the masses than in Democratic systems.

(D)   Leaders of Communist systems rely more heavily on the support of public opinion than do Western leaders.

(E)   Leadership in Communist systems requires charismatic personalities, whereas this is not true of Democratic systems.

36.   Which of the following distinguishes a Communist political system from a pluralistic one?

(A)   Pluralistic societies generally exhibit stronger and more inflexible central control of the economy.

(B)   Communist systems are usually marked by more rapid and sustained economic growth.

(C)   Pluralistic systems tend to encourage less popular participation.

(D)   Communist systems are inherently more stable.

(E)   Change in Communist systems is often more abrupt and violent.

Percentage of seats in the Parliament				
42%	35%	12%	8%	3%
Party A	Party B	Party C	Party D	Party E

37.   Based on the above graph, assume that you are the leader of Party A. You want to build a government coalition at minimal cost to your party, but

enough to capture a majority of seats to control Parliament. Which party or parties are you most likely to seek a coalition with?

(A) Party B

(B) Party C

(C) Party D

(D) Parties D and E

(E) Parties C and E

38. The decline of the Communist party in France since the 1970s can be attributed to all of the following factors EXCEPT

(A) their close support for policies of the Soviet Union.

(B) their inability to attract and maintain the support of younger voters.

(C) the authoritarian control exerted by top party officials over the rank and file.

(D) their refusal to work with the Socialist party, which, because of its accommodationist tactics, was viewed by the Communists as a sellout to right-wing politics.

(E) the emergence of a very young and inexperienced party leadership that failed to sustain the advances made by older, but retiring party leaders.

39. Charles de Gaulle's influence on French political thinking is expressed as a philosophy called Gaullism, which includes all of the following ideas EXCEPT

(A) support for many of the policies of the Communist left.

(B) national independence from foreign influences.

(C) a self-sufficient defense posture.

(D) central direction of the national economy, while broadening the nationalized sector.

(E) a determination to secure and maintain France as a major world power.

40. The French civil service is like that of Great Britain in all of the following ways EXCEPT

(A) competitive exams are used to recruit senior members of the civil service.

(B) civil servants may run for political office while remaining in the civil service.

(C) civil servants are a permanent body of administrators that do not lose their positions with the election of new governments.

(D)   the civil service is at the discretion of elected government officials and work under their direction.

(E)   the civil service is divided into ministries and bureaus.

41.   In France, when the president and the prime minister come from different parties, the period of dual executive responsibility is referred to by which of the following terms?

(A)   The rule of incompatibility   (D)   Cohabitation

(B)   Divided government   (E)   Unconstitutionality

(C)   Mixed government

42.   As Prime Minister of Great Britain, Margaret Thatcher

(A)   represented the Labour party.

(B)   supported British acceptance of monetary union with the European Communities.

(C)   favored broader constitutional rights for criminals and the accused.

(D)   favored a free market economy and private ownership of property.

(E)   favored extensive government spending and public welfare programs.

43.   In contrast to Joseph Stalin, Nikita Krushchev

(A)   aggressively pursued diplomatic ties with the Third World and initiated widespread foreign aid programs.

(B)   was principally concerned with consolidating the success of socialism in the Soviet Union.

(C)   refused to negotiate with Western leaders.

(D)   ruled with an iron fist and refused to tolerate disagreement with his policies.

(E)   abandoned efforts to counter the presence of NATO in Europe.

44.   The Labour party in Great Britain is characterized by all of the following EXCEPT

(A)   a tendency to split between left-wing extremist groups and a moderate center favoring gradualism.

(B)   strong support from union organizations.

(C)   consistent and unqualified support of British entry into and full participation in the European Common Market.

(D)   support for nationalization and public regulation of key industries.

(E)   support for progressive tax policy and universal social welfare services.

45.   Upward social mobility in the former Soviet Union was based principally upon which of the following factors?

(A)   Non-Russians enjoyed a substantial advantage over Russians in upward social mobility

(B)   Political loyalty to the Communist Party and/or technical competence

(C)   Peasant and working class origins improved one's chances for advancement because these groups are favored by communist ideology

(D)   Nonpolitical careers guarantee higher status, but are open to fewer people

(E)   Athletics provided the only significant alternative besides politics

46.   The strong resurgence of extreme right-wing politics in France led by Jean Marie La Pen, can be accounted for by all of the following EXCEPT

(A)   the tremendous recent growth of communist support which has excited a right-wing reaction.

(B)   growing opposition to liberal immigration policy.

(C)   the growth of racial sentiments.

(D)   concern among lower middle class and blue collar workers about losing jobs to foreigners.

(E)   a resurgence of French nationalist sentiments.

47.   The views and policies of the National Front in France most closely resemble those of the

(A)   Liberal Democrats in the Russian Federation.

(B)   Conservative Party in Great Britain.

(C)   Chinese Communist Party.

(D)   Republican Party in France.

(E)   Labour Party in Great Britain.

48.   The role of the monarch in the British political system is marked by all of the following EXCEPT

(A)   the right to open Parliament with a Speech from the Throne.

(B)   the right to invest the prime minister.

(C) the only authority capable of dissolving Parliament.

(D) the right to enact legislation approved by Parliament.

(E) the right to veto legislation approved by Parliament.

49. All of the following statements are true of Britain's House of Lords EXCEPT

(A) it has the power to delay money bills for a month.

(B) it has the power to delay legislative proposals enacted by the House of Commons for a year.

(C) after a year, the House of Lords may amend or veto proposals and return them to the House of Commons.

(D) it is Britain's final court of appeal.

(E) it consists of hereditary peers as well as life peers appointed by the Crown.

50. Prior to the recent collapse of the Soviet Union, the Supreme Soviet retained all of the following formal powers and functions, EXCEPT

(A) amending the Constitution.

(B) admission of new republics to the Soviet Union.

(C) electing the general secretary of the Communist Party.

(D) electing a Presidium to serve as a permanent organ of state power and a collective head of state.

(E) forming a Council of Ministers to implement government policy.

51. Deng Xiaoping's policy approaches differed from those of Mao Zedong in all of the following ways EXCEPT

(A) Deng accepted the need for concrete rewards to motivate the Chinese, rather than Mao's emphasis on ideology.

(B) Deng was willing to tolerate greater inequality than Mao in exchange for a higher degree of prosperity.

(C) unlike Mao, Deng distrusted intellectuals and preferred the peasant culture.

(D) unlike Mao, Deng tolerated greater decentralization of economic planning.

(E) Deng was more open to establishing and strengthening ties with foreign countries.

52. The Four Modernizations campaign in China included all of the following EXCEPT

   (A) developing foreign aid policy.

   (B) developing the agricultural sector.

   (C) developing the industrial sector.

   (D) developing the educational system.

   (E) developing the national security capacity.

53. The "Red versus Expert" debate in China focused on the problem of

   (A) how to balance the need for quality education to achieve modernization with the goal of equal, mass education.

   (B) how to discourage ideological training for peasants.

   (C) how to reduce the technical training of Communists to ensure their ideological commitment.

   (D) how to reduce access to higher education in order to ensure that only a qualified elite could gain entrance.

   (E) how to get college graduates out of the Communist party.

54. Which one of the following is most likely to exercise a great deal of influence within the Chinese political system?

   (A) A vocal minority party, such as a student movement

   (B) An independent local government, such as the mayor of Shanghai

   (C) An independent judiciary, such as a judge in Beijing

   (D) The military hierarchy, including top officers of the People's Liberation Army

   (E) The National People's Congress

55. Which of the following statements best describes France's bicameral legislature?

   (A) The Senate completely dominates the National Assembly in legislative matters.

   (B) The Senate alone may overthrow the government.

   (C) The Senate is indirectly elected while the National Assembly is directly elected by the people.

(D)   No piece of legislation may be enacted without the explicit consent of both houses.

(E)   Together, the Senate and the National Assembly dominate the government of France.

56.   Legislative committees in Britain's House of Commons

(A)   control the fate of government bills through the power of refusal to report them to the floor of the House.

(B)   consist of Standing Committees which may discuss and suggest amendments, and Select Committees which conduct ad hoc investigations and hearings for the government.

(C)   take the first vote on bills submitted to the House of Commons.

(D)   are unimportant rubber stamps because they may not suggest substantive amendments to bills.

(E)   may consider bills only after the third reading on the floor of the House of Commons.

Steve Raper

57.   The political cartoonist is most strongly making the point that

(A)   Gorbachev never really favored either *glasnost* or *perestroika.*

(B)   Gorbachev's reforms were implemented too slowly to be effective.

(C)   Gorbachev believed that the Russian Republic would be better off economically and militarily by leaving the Soviet Union.

(D)   once implemented, reform measures proved difficult for the CPSU to control.

(E) the attempted August 1991 coup pushed Gorbachev into moves with which he was not comfortable.

58. In Great Britain, delegated legislation made by government agencies outnumbers regular acts of Parliament by twenty to one. Which of the following does not account for this?

(A) Parliament does not have enough time to enact detailed legislation.

(B) Technical questions must often be ironed out after the passage of parliamentary acts.

(C) Unforeseen contingencies often arise during the implementation of acts.

(D) Emergencies often call for immediate administrative response.

(E) Parliament prefers to minimize administrative flexibility.

59. The Gang of Four in China were

(A) the ministers in charge of the Four Modernizations.

(B) long-time members of Deng Xiaoping's inner circle.

(C) radicals associated with the Cultural Revolution who were jailed and punished by Hua Guofeng after Mao's death.

(D) the Army officials responsible for the Tiananmen Square massacre.

(E) liberal reformers who desired strong ties with the West.

60. Leonid Brezhnev's policies in the Soviet Union aimed at all of the following EXCEPT

(A) achieving massive growth in Soviet military power.

(B) giving priority to the consumer economy by increasing domestic production and consumption of consumer goods.

(C) intervening, with military support, on behalf of Marxist regimes in the Third World.

(D) pursuing arms control with the West without constraining Soviet military development.

(E) seeking detente with the West to encourage greater commercial and trade ties, while expanding influence into the Third World.

STOP

This is the end of Section I.
If time still remains, you may check your work only in this section.
Do not begin Section II until instructed to do so.

Section II
Part 1

TIME: 45 Minutes
1 Free-Response Question
30% of total grade

DIRECTIONS: Write an essay based on ONE of the following two questions. Make sure to choose the question that you are most prepared to answer in the time allotted. Your essay should be numbered the same as the question you choose.

---

1.   A distinctive dichotomy often used to describe political systems involves whether they reflect a parliamentary or a presidential form. In examining this issue, how has the former Soviet Union OR France diverged from the forms exhibited by India, Mexico, OR Nigeria?

2.   In various political systems the representation of specific groups, issues, and interests are largely performed by political parties. Compare and contrast how the interest aggregating mechanism of political parties operates in EITHER the former Soviet Union OR Great Britain and in ONE of the following countries—Mexico, India, OR Nigeria.

Part 2

TIME: 30 Minutes
1 Free-Response Question
20% of total grade

DIRECTIONS: Write an essay based on ONE of the following four questions. Make sure to choose the question that you are most prepared to answer in the time allotted. Your essay should be numbered the same as the question you choose.

---

3. Discuss how Mexico's political and economic development have been influenced and shaped by its geographical proximity to the United States. Provide specific examples in your answer.

4. Assess and analyze the effects and extent to which the peace settlements in Europe at the end of World War I became causes of World War II.

5. In a descriptive and factually explicit essay, discuss the definition of totalitarianism in the Soviet Union under Stalin and Germany under Hitler. Are they interchangeable examples of totalitarianism?

6. In a descriptive and factually explicit essay, explain to what degree the United States' geographical location affected its role in the European theater during World War II?

END OF EXAM

COMPARATIVE GOVERNMENT AND POLITICS

TEST 3

ANSWER KEY

1.	(C)	16.	(A)	31.	(B)	46.	(A)
2.	(B)	17.	(D)	32.	(A)	47.	(A)
3.	(D)	18.	(C)	33.	(C)	48.	(E)
4.	(A)	19.	(C)	34.	(D)	49.	(C)
5.	(C)	20.	(D)	35.	(B)	50.	(C)
6.	(A)	21.	(C)	36.	(E)	51.	(C)
7.	(B)	22.	(A)	37.	(B)	52.	(A)
8.	(B)	23.	(B)	38.	(E)	53.	(A)
9.	(C)	24.	(D)	39.	(A)	54.	(D)
10.	(D)	25.	(D)	40.	(B)	55.	(C)
11.	(B)	26.	(B)	41.	(D)	56.	(B)
12.	(A)	27.	(C)	42.	(D)	57.	(D)
13.	(C)	28.	(D)	43.	(A)	58.	(E)
14.	(D)	29.	(B)	44.	(C)	59.	(C)
15.	(E)	30.	(C)	45.	(B)	60.	(B)

DETAILED EXPLANATIONS
OF ANSWERS
TEST 3

Section I

1. **(C)** Although representative democracies permit citizens to participate in politics through voting, working for parties, communicating with legislators, campaigning for office, and so forth, the vast majority of citizens rarely participate beyond voting in elections, and many even choose not to engage in this most elementary act of participation. Thus, there is no guarantee that citizens of representative democracies will participate more in politics, than those in the direct democracy model. Therefore, (C) is correct. (A) is incorrect because direct democracies have flourished in only the smallest of political systems, such as the Greek or Italian city-states or in contemporary town meeting contexts. (B) is incorrect because full-time public officials in the representative model have more time to specialize in the art of decision making, allowing them to make better decisions than the public can. (D) is incorrect because representative democracies are better insulated from public passions and are more likely to make good decisions. In direct democracy, the least educated and most poorly informed elements of society can have an equal input into decision making. (E) is incorrect, because representative democracy should, in theory, place more knowledgeable and trustworthy individuals in positions of authority. Moreover, if elected officials prove unequal to the task, they can be voted out of office and replaced by more trustworthy individuals.

2. **(B)** In proportional representation schemes, seats in the legislature are allocated by the percentage of the nationwide vote won by a particular party, rather than by the number of party members that win local elections for particular seats. Although smaller parties may fail to win a majority of the vote in any one district or part of the country, they might, for example, gain 10 percent of the overall national vote, and thus be entitled to 10 percent of the seats in the legislature. This permits the growth of numerous parties representing a broad spectrum of ideologies and programs. Making (B) the correct choice. (A) is not correct. Majority parties, like all parties in proportional representation schemes, are represented in the legislature in rough proportion to their electoral success, thus being neither over- nor under-represented. (C) is incorrect because the power of a president is usually determined by the constitution of the country. Proportional representation schemes have little direct influence on presidential authority and power. Proportional representation tends to promote the development of many parties, thus

working against the maintenance of two-party systems (D). In proportional represen-tation systems many parties have a portion of legislative seats, and often no single party has a majority of seats in the legislature. To form a government, it is necessary to have a majority of votes in the legislature; this stimulates parties to engage in coalitions to build the necessary majority. It follows that proportional representation schemes encourage rather than discourage coalition politics (E).

3.   **(D)**   Civic political culture is marked by pluralistic and participatory institutions, popularly elected legislative bodies, and considerable interest group and party compe-tition. Centrist political cultures (A) are based on authoritarian leadership, centralized planning, governmental control over the media, and usually by restrictions on individual rights to association and expression. (D) is the right answer. Parochial political cultures (B) are found in societies where the common people are reluctant to participate in politics, preferring instead to give loyalty to local political and economic elites. Interests are viewed in terms of local calculations by paternalistic rulers over politically inactive populations. Traditional political cultures (C) tend to be parochial in character, although in many of them some popular participation in decision making does occur. (E) is not the correct answer because the American political culture is but one example of a civic culture and does not constitute a type of political culture.

4.   **(A)**   Most of the countries achieving independence in the twentieth century were in Africa, Asia, and the Central and South Pacific, where high degrees of poverty exist, so (A) is correct. (B) is incorrect because some of the recently independent countries are very large, but many others are very small in geographical area; new states are likely to be neither bigger nor smaller than older ones. (C) is incorrect because the new states have proven to be significantly less stable than established states. Although many of these countries adopted democratic constitutions (D) initially, their instability has caused many of them to revert to authoritarian forms of rule. (E) is incorrect because many of these countries have experienced revolutions, coup d' états, and other breaks in continuity of government.

5.   **(C)**   A state is a legal entity possessing a territory (A), a population (B), and a government (E) that is recognized as having independent authority over its territory and population (D). The state's population may or may not have a common history, tradition, ethnic background, or language (C). These attributes are ascribed to nations as groups of people, not to states as legal entities. A state can exist even where these shared or common values and characteristics are not present. Also, a nation of people with such characteristics may exist without a formal state

6.   **(A)**   As compared to twentieth century constitutions, most constitutions written in the eighteenth century were statements of individual rights and first principles, so (A) is correct. (B) is not the correct answer, because in addition to stating individual rights and first principles, eighteenth century constitutions were equally interested in estab-lishing government machinery. (C) is incorrect because eighteenth century constitutions generally reflected a laissez-faire attitude toward government involvement in the

economy. (D) is incorrect because in the twentieth century, constitutional framers shifted to emphasizing comprehensive systems of social and economic control by governments, especially as many former colonies attained their independence facing substantial economic hardship and social instability. (E) is incorrect because twentieth century constitutions tend to be long, comprehensive, and detailed plans rather than skeletal blueprints for future action.

7.   **(B)**   The correct choice is (B). Under the two-ballot system, the two candidates gaining the highest vote totals on the first ballot will appear in a run-off on the second ballot. Often, French voters are forced to choose between two second-ballot candidates for whom they did not vote on the first ballot. Thus, voter-party identification is flexible and pragmatic, not strict. It is rare that any one candidate gains a majority on the first ballot—in which case no second ballot would be necessary. The system has also encouraged a left/right political split: Socialists, Communists, Greens on the left; Neo-Gaullists, Republicans, and National Front on the right. Commonly no single party receives a majority of seats in the National Assembly, calling for a left or right bloc coalition in the legislature.

8.   **(B)**   Democratic centralism as practiced by the USSR encouraged discussion and debate in the formulation of policy, but demanded rigid adherence to policy once a decision was made by the highest authorities. Elections (A) were not part of the democratic centralism model of policy-making, but were used rather as a formal means of acknowledging Communist Party candidates' legitimacy for office. (B) is the correct choice. (C) is not the answer because each republic was basically organized along the lines dictated in the Soviet Constitution. Genuine free and democratic elections (D) were not permitted, in autonomous republics or elsewhere. The Communist Party controlled the outcome of all elections. (E) is incorrect because what is known today as the Russian Federation was no more democratic than any other republic.

9.   **(C)**   While cabinet members in Great Britain serve simultaneously as members of both the executive and the Parliament, in France the principle of incompatibility prohibits cabinet members from serving this dual role. Cabinet members must resign their legislative seat to serve in the government. They may sit in Parliament and defend government measures there, but they may not vote. Therefore, (C) is the right answer. The cabinet's principal role is to serve as the executive arm of government (A). The cabinet is responsible to the Parliament (B), which can force the government (cabinet and prime minister) to resign, and call for new parliamentary elections. Public policy in both countries is initiated under the authority of the prime minister and cabinet (D). In France, the president has constitutionally asserted primacy in establishing policy, thus usurping a role otherwise normally held by the prime minister and cabinet. Cabinet members do lead specific ministries in national government, such as Foreign Affairs, Treasury, Defense, and Justice (E).

10. **(D)** The table documents the Gaullist rise and decline, and the Socialist Party's rise in influence in the 1960s, so (D) is correct. (A) is not correct. The data clearly show an increase in Socialist party influence. (B) is incorrect because the data show that there is a rough relationship between the percentage of votes a party wins and the number of seats it holds. (C) is also incorrect. The Gaullists did better in all but the 1981 election, compared to the Socialists. (E) is not the answer since it is not possible to know from the information in the table alone whether Socialist party strength increased directly at the expense of the Gaullists since 1968. To draw this conclusion one would need to know how other parties fared.

11. **(B)** French political culture is dominated by a strong distrust of state policies and an equally strong individualism. This distrust leads most Frenchmen to not actively support or participate in national level political activities. (B) is the right answer. The French do distrust the state (A). French politics is marked by a high degree of abstraction and ideology (C). Pragmatic, solution-oriented politics are rejected in favor of highly principled, intellectual, and ideological discourse. France does have a tradition of revolution (D) and political upheaval. The French have historically developed strong family ties and local networks to offset the central control of the state (E).

12. **(A)** The French middle class, consisting of salaried engineers, white collar workers, civil servants, teachers, and non-salaried members of various professions, numbers about 9 million and constitutes 40 percent of the work force. (A) is correct. Industrial (blue collar) workers (B) account for about 7 million people. Farmers (C) account for only about 2 million people. Clerics (D) are a very small minority. Elites (E) are a tiny minority of the population.

13. **(C)** Workers in France have, in fact, enjoyed rapid and substantial rises in wages and benefits; this class is not revolutionary. Rather it has a stake in preserving the system that has been so beneficial for it. Thus, (C) is the correct choice. France is a society that is becoming increasingly urban and less rural (A). The number of white collar workers has increased (B), and much of this increase is due to technological advances. Since the number of farmers has declined and because farmers are better educated and less traditional than in the past (D) is incorrect. (E) is incorrect because political influence has gravitated from rural, land-owning aristocrats to white collar, urban technocrats.

14. **(D)** Far from experiencing tyrannical control by stable coalitions, the French Fourth Republic witnessed changes in government, on average, every eight months. This lack of continuity was a major problem (D). Too many political parties and interest groups vied for influence (A), and none enjoyed a majority, thus making government difficult. (B) is incorrect because the existence of so many different organized interests prevented consensus. The weakness of the presidents and of prime ministers (C) contributed further to the inability to govern effectively. The constant and unstable coalition politics that marked the Fourth Republic led to governmental immobility and this led to popular disillusionment with politics (E).

15. **(E)**   The presidents of the two countries share all of the powers listed except (E), the power to amend the constitution.

16. **(A)**   The British constitution, unlike most modern constitutions, has evolved over a long period of history. This evolution has meant that no single document serves as the constitution. Rather, acts of Parliament, taken together with customs, conventions, and court decisions, comprise the constitution of Britain, so (A) is correct. Great Britain is not a federal system (B). Parliament, not the people, is sovereign. (D) is not correct because the constitution tends to be quite flexible, rather than rigid. (E) is incorrect because cabinet ministers are collectively, not individually, responsible to Parliament.

17. **(D)**   The people and political institutions of Great Britain reflect a strong tendency toward gradual evolution rather than drastic or rapid change. They also reflect a desire to gain consensus so that order and stability prevail, rather than anarchy and revolutionary opposition. (D) is the best answer. (A) is incorrect because Great Britain's political culture is marked by gradualism and incrementalism rather than radical change. (B) is incorrect because the British tend toward pragmatism rather than ideology. (C) is incorrect because British politics is marked by democratic limitations on authority rather than authoritarian government. (E) is not the answer because although it has a democratic tradition, Britain's experience with democracy cannot be described as radical.

18. **(C)**   Since the 1970s, less than half of the working class has supported the Labour party. Before then, Labour could count on significant working class support. But increasingly the British people—even workers—view themselves as middle class regardless of their actual income and occupation status. (C) is correct. (A) is incorrect because middle class voters tend to support Labour less than working class voters. (B) is incorrect because despite the fact that 50 percent of British voters are members of the working class, working class support for the Labour Party has declined, especially among those who should be most inclined to support it. Indeed, Labour has failed to gain control of Parliament in recent British elections. (D) is not correct because upper income and upper class elements are more heavily represented in the ConservativeParty rather than in Labour. (E) is not correct. Asian and immigrant populations face substantial prejudice in Britain and do not have significant opportunities for upward social mobility; Labour has tended to be more sympathetic to their situation.

19. **(C)**   The opposition in Britain has every right both to publicly criticize and to seek changes in the policies proposed by the majority party. (A) is true because the opposition party may challenge the standing government's policies and forthrightly oppose them. (C) is correct. The opposition represents the interests of its supporters (B), and seeks to exploit any divisions that might appear in the ranks of the majority party, while attempting to build a winning coalition of its own for the next election. The

opposition is continuously organized; it monitors majority party policy, seeks to modify it, and exposes errors in policy, often through heated debate; if the existing government falls, it will be ready to stake a claim to government (D) by winning the parliamentary elections. The opposition may destabilize support for the majority (E), appeal to its constituents, openly challenge majority party policy in parliamentary debates, and build public support to defeat the majority party in a subsequent election.

20. **(D)** The prime minister is not the "chair" of the House of Lords, although he or she is the leading figure in the House of Commons. (D) is the best answer. The prime minister is the head of the majority party (A). The prime minister does serve as the leader of the nation and as its main representative to other nations (B). The prime minister does chair meetings of the cabinet (C). Although a foreign minister is named by the prime minister to handle foreign policy, prime ministers have historically assumed a great deal of responsibility for foreign affairs themselves (E).

21. **(C)** Stalin's modernization policy called for, or led to, all of the points raised, with the exception of (C). In fact, the collectivization of agriculture was intended to increase production of food, thereby making it possible to free up rural labor which then could be drawn into the urban areas as industrial workers. This would help support the primary goal of increasing industrial production and military might. Thus, the object was not to get urban workers onto the farms, but the opposite. Priority was to be given to heavy industry (A). Mechanization and collectivization of the farms (B) was a key element of the plan. Modernization could only happen through an extensive reform of the educational system, which under Stalin's plan was devoted to producing well-trained technicians, scientists, and skilled workers (D). To achieve this policy of modernization, Stalin increasingly concentrated power in his own hands, and opponents to himself or his policies were ruthlessly eliminated (E).

22. **(A)** The Bolshevik Revolution, which began in 1917, faced considerable opposition both from inside and outside of Russia. For three years Bolsheviks fought the White Russians to establish full control over the country; American forces supported the White Russians in Siberia, as did other European nations opposed to Lenin's Communist revolution. The best answer is (A). Lenin's promise of peace for the soldiers (B) was an important factor in his ultimate success. Lenin did promise land for the peasants (C) who in turn supported the revolutionary cause. Lenin's promise of bread for the workers (D) further galvanized popular support for the Bolshevik cause. The revolutionary committees, or soviets, that had sprung up around the country gradually came under Bolshevik influence (E). The provisional government, which had previously overthrown the tsar, buckled under the pressure of Lenin's strategy.

23. **(B)** Although the Soviet Union experienced a modest increase in trade with Western capitalist nations in the last years of its existence, there were substantial impediments to a significant growth in trade. The Soviet currency, the ruble, was not regarded by capitalist countries as a strong or reliable asset to resolve trade accounts, and the Soviet Union lacked the hard currencies of other countries. This minimal trade did

little to stimulate economic growth or enhance consumer confidence in the Soviet Union, or to cause the dramatic political changes of the late 1980s and 1990s. Thus, (B) is correct. Ethnic nationalism in the non-Russian republics (A) was a driving force in the Gorbachev reforms. The expensive military adventurism of the Soviet Union in the 1970s and early 1980s deprived the domestic economy of resources (C). The Gorbachev reform programs, designed to provide greater economic incentives, were instrumental in precipitating the changes that ultimately led to the dissolution of the Union of Soviet Socialist Republics (D). The dismal performance of the national economy was related to the over-investment in military spending as well as inattention to the consumer economy (E).

24. **(D)** The chief difference between the *kolkhoz* and *sovkhoz* is that the former does allow peasants to own their own homes, some livestock, and a private garden plot, which can be used to grow produce for the open market. In turn, the peasant is required to work on collective lands. The *sovkhoz* are state-run enterprises where the farm workers are paid to work on state-owned land. The workers may own no land of their own. (D) is the best choice. (A) is incorrect because peasants may own land on a *kolkhoz* while they may not on a *sovkhoz*. (B) is incorrect because peasants on a *sovkhoz* may not own a garden plot. (C) is incorrect because the *sovkhoz* are typically three times larger than the *kolkhoz*. (E) is incorrect because the *kolkhoz* system is neither less productive nor more exploitative than the *sovkhoz* system. Both the collective and state farms are less productive than the tiny private plots permitted in the *kolkhoz* system.

25. **(D)** *Glasnost* was originally envisioned as a limited form of freedom of expression as well as a mandate to clear the *gulags* of political prisoners. Democratization, however, inevitably led to greater political pluralism, and by February 1990, a multi-party system was legalized in the USSR, thus ending the CPSU's monopoly of power. Put another way, once the Gorbachev reforms were unleashed, they came to take on a life of their own. Gorbachev never intended to end the CPSU's political monopoly or to dissolve the Soviet Union. Rather, *glasnost* and *perestroika* together were aimed at making the USSR more efficient.

26. **(B)** The Mandate of Heaven idea is part of the political culture of China. As long as a ruler and his subjects enjoyed peace, successful military efforts, good harvests and prosperity, the ruler enjoyed support from heaven. However, in the event that heaven would become displeased, resulting in calamities, the Mandate of Heaven was revoked and the people had a right to revolt. (B) is correct. PLA nuclear strategy (A) is not linked to this concept. (C) is incorrect because the Mandate of Heaven concept predates Maoist ideology and is largely unrelated to it. Deng's modernization strategy (D) is not related to this concept. The Communist party's control over national elections (E) is irrelevant to the existence of the Mandate of Heaven tradition.

27. **(C)** During the Cultural Revolution, Mao attempted to shake Communist party control of Chinese politics by calling for permanent revolution. When Deng Xiaoping gained power, he reasserted the party's central role in the policy-making process. This signified a major rejection of Maoist theory. The best answer is (C). The Gang of Four (A), which had been influential during the Cultural Revolution, were imprisoned and punished for crimes committed during that period. The Red Guards (B), who had been at the forefront of change in the Cultural Revolution, were later eliminated as a source of policy-making and the regular army elevated to its traditional seat of influence. (D) is incorrect because China, far from growing hyper-isolationist after Mao, began instead to seek an accommodation with the outside world even before Mao's death. The criticism/self-criticism movement (E) that flourished under Mao, lost both its novelty and its currency in later years.

28. **(D)** It is the party rather than the government apparatus in Communist China that possesses the greatest influence. Party officials hold the important positions in government, and their highest obligation is to the party itself. So, (D) is correct. The Standing Committee of the Politburo is the most influential organ of the Communist party (A). The party branches do help to ensure that party members are following the party line in their official government capacities. Thus, the party keeps active surveillance over its members and over government officials (B). The party does provide direction to the Army through its Military Affairs Commission (C). Although the Standing Committee of the Politburo is the most influential organ of the party, it is the chairman of the Central Committee (E), who also serves on the Politburo, who occupies the most prestigious office in the party.

29. **(B)** The mass line is a version of democratic centralism that calls upon the party to take into account the attitudes and opinions of common people as they make policy for the country. Once policy is made, lower level government officials and the people as a whole are expected to obey. (B) is the best choice. The mass line is not intended primarily to impose order on the masses (A), but to encourage their participation at the earliest and lowest levels of decision making. The mass line is not primarily a vehicle for propaganda and regulation of mass behavior (C). The mass line is not intended to be a recruiting device for Communist party members (D). Although the party has engaged in reeducation programs for high-level officials—especially during the Cultural Revolution—the mass line idea does not require political reeducation (E).

30. **(C)** Far from becoming dependent on the state, Mao argued that the people should learn self-reliance. This self-reliance would end the Chinese tendency to defer to authority and wait for orders from traditional rulers. It would encourage initiative and productivity. (C) is the best answer. For Mao, the traditional deference to authority and preference for order (A) should be rooted out in favor of conflict, struggle, and change. Mao believed that the human spirit could conquer all things. Material wealth, scientific knowledge, and mechanical virtuosity are inferior. Human work is better than reliance on machines (B). A backward, agricultural society can make great leaps forward without

major industrial development. Mao distrusted intellectuals and over-specialization because the latter leads to dependency on others and prevents self-reliance. Mao believed in the traditional moral values of the rural people (E). Their basic honesty was to be preferred over the corrupt influences that pervade urban life.

31. **(B)** The correct answer is (B). The prime minister in the French system is nominated by the president and works for the president's programs, whereas in the British system the prime minister answers to no higher political authority. (A) is not correct because both France and Great Britain have unitary systems. (C) is incorrect because the French Parliament includes many parties, while the British House of Commons has been dominated historically by two parties, with only recent challenges from significant third parties. (D) is incorrect because the French president is the most powerful figure in the government, rather than a figurehead, while the head of state in Britain, namely the monarch, plays a symbolic role. (E) is incorrect because in Britain, ultimate sovereignty lies with Parliament and the prime minister is accountable to Parliament. In France, the president, as the head of the government, operates independently of the French National Assembly and has significant rule-making capacities that do not fall under the Assembly's legislative authority.

32. **(A)** Generational factors often play a role in reform. China is still governed by a powerful and relatively old set of leaders who are resistant to rapid reforms. Gorbachev and other younger Soviet leaders, by contrast, were prepared to advance a program of rapid and extensive reforms. Therefore, (A) is the best answer. (B) is not correct because students were the drive behind China's democracy movement. Students in the Soviet Union may have supported democracy, but Gorbachev led the way. (C) is incorrect because the Soviet military resisted reforms, while the military in China, though generally opposed to rapid reform, was divided over how to respond to student demands. Red Guards (D) were not involved in China's democracy movement and had no influence on public attitudes, while the KGB represented a conservative force in the USSR. (E) is not correct because the Chinese Communist party continues to enjoy control over the state apparatus.

33. **(C)** The chief difference between elections in Great Britain and France lies in proportional representation versus single member district approaches. In the French proportional representation system, the number of parliamentary seats won by a party depends on how many votes it receives in each department. In Britain, to become a member of Parliament a candidate must win a plurality of votes in a winner-take-all election. (C) is the best answer. (A) is incorrect because the reverse is true: France has two-step or two ballot elections and Britain a single election. (B) is not correct because candidates in French elections are placed on party lists while in Britain candidates are identified by party. (D) is not correct because the proportional representation system in France does promote the existence of several parties, while the single member district system in Britain tends to inhibit the emergence of strong third parties. (E) is not correct because parties in both countries determine who represents them on the ballot.

34. **(D)** The leadership in the Communist parties of both countries is dominated by intellectuals, party functionaries, and bureaucrats rather than by workers or peasants. (D) is the correct response. (A) is not the answer because both countries have indeed been ruled by Communist parties—China since 1949 and the Soviet Union from 1917 until only very recently with the sudden collapse of the USSR. Both countries had revolutions fought over several years and with much bloodshed (B). The "cult of personality" (C) has in fact been employed in both countries, most notably by Stalin in the Soviet Union and by Mao in China. Both countries were agriculturally oriented prior to their respective revolutions (E). China remains so, while the Soviet Union, only after decades of effort, achieved significant industrialization.

35. **(B)** One of the fundamental traits of communist systems is the power struggles that occur whenever a leader dies or begins to weaken. Since there are no elections to determine a successor, contenders often engage in very destabilizing contests to determine who is the strongest. So, (B) is the best answer. (A) is not the answer because even though interest group activity is clearly more open and widespread in democracies than in Communist systems, there are different interests in the latter that compete for control over policy, including such groups as the army, party theoreticians, bureaucrats, technocrats, intelligence agencies, and regional representatives. (C) is not the answer because leaders tend to be drawn from elite classes in both Democratic and Communist systems. In Communist systems public opinion (D) is rarely consulted, except through the highly controlled party apparatus. (E) is not the answer because charismatic leaders are found in both systems, and so are non-charismatic leaders. If anything, more charismatic leaders are to be found in democracies because they have to appeal to voters to win elections.

36. **(E)** Change does not happen perhaps as often in Communist systems as in pluralistic ones, but when it does occur it is often more violent and revolutionary in nature. (E) is the answer. (A) is not correct because pluralistic societies generally permit private groups to have considerable freedom in pursuing economic gains, whereas Communist ones severely limit or eliminate private economic activity. (B) is not correct because although many pluralist systems have not achieved sustained and rapid economic growth, neither have many Communist systems. Indeed, most Communist systems have collapsed while pluralist systems continue to survive and adapt better to economic stress. (C) is incorrect because pluralist systems by definition encourage greater participation and initiative than do Communist ones. (D) is incorrect because Communist systems, though superficially more stable, have less capacity to adapt to economic and political changes. Recent events in the Soviet Union and Eastern Europe demonstrate their fragility in comparison to pluralistic systems.

37. **(B)** By allying with Party C, Party A ensures a 54 percent control of Parliament, while both minimizing the number of parties in its coalition and the size of the party in coalition with it. (B) is correct. (A) is not the answer because Party B is the main competitor and very large in size; Party A would have to make too many concessions in order to rule. (C) is not correct, because Party D would only give Party A 50 percent of

the seats, which is not a majority and not enough to control the Parliament. (D) is not the answer, because although Party A could choose to ally with Parties D and E and get 53 percent control, building and maintaining coalitions between three parties is more difficult than with two parties, and also because this results in fewer seats than a coalition with party C. (E) is incorrect because although this coalition would give Party A a 57 percent majority, it involves the unnecessary inclusion of Party E; with Party C alone, Party A can rule the government with a 54 percent majority, and Party E's participation becomes superfluous.

38. **(E)**   The Communist party has declined not because of youthful leadership, but because of an aging leadership that alienated the young and lost touch with trends in French public attitudes. Thus, (E) is the best answer. French voters distrusted the party's seemingly slavish adherence to the Soviet line (A), which contributed to the party's eventual decline. Conservative trends among younger voters made party policy less attractive (B). The rigid control in Communist Party leadership did alienate younger party members (C), which split the party and caused defections to the Socialists. Old and rigid Communist Party leaders refused to move with Socialists toward a more moderate policy outlook (D). The Socialist party benefited from this moderation of ideology, while the Communists continued to alienate its own younger members and the electorate as well.

39. **(A)**   The correct response is (A). Far from embracing communist principles, de Gaulle deeply distrusted and opposed the policies of the left, especially of the Communist party, toward which he was openly hostile. De Gaulle did hope to reduce French dependence on all external influences (B). Part of reducing dependence on foreign influences included reducing reliance on other countries for its defense (C). De Gaulle pulled out of NATO for this reason. De Gaulle did want greater central control of national economic policy, but he also supported the major tenets of capitalism and opposed extensive nationalization of the private sector (D). De Gaulle and his supporters were very concerned with maintaining French prestige and power in global affairs (E).

40. **(B)**   In France, civil servants may run for elective offices at the local, departmental, and national level while retaining their civil service positions. British civil servants may not do so. (B) is the right answer. In both Britain and France, competitive exams are used to recruit for the highest civil service positions (A). The civil service does remain intact while political leaders come and go with the electoral fortunes of competing political parties (C). In both countries the civil service does work for the political head or minister (D); often they are more skilled in the routines of ministerial administration than the minister. In both Britain and France administrative duties are divided into ministries which are in turn subdivided into more specialized bureaus (E).

41. **(D)**   The best answer is (D) because the cohabitation strategy assumes that the president and prime minister will agree to "live together" rather than engage in constant confrontation. Cohabitation worked in the 1980s, when the French elected a president

of one party and had legislature dominated by another. The rule of incompatibility (A) refers to a minister's obligation to resign his voting seat in the National Assembly while serving in the Cabinet. Divided government (B) refers to the legislature being controlled by one party and the executive branch in the control of another. In the case of France, the prime minister, though the controlling figure in the majority legislative party, is also a member of the executive branch, along with the president. Mixed government (C) usually refers to the existence of democratic, oligarchic, and monarchical principles built into various institutions of government. (E) is not correct because the French constitution permits a president and prime minister to come from different parties.

42. **(D)** Thatcher's conservative political philosophy called for less government involvement in the economy and greater individual initiative. (A) is incorrect because Thatcher led the Conservative or Tory party, not Labour. The best answer is (D). Thatcher was a strong opponent of monetary union with the rest of Europe (B). (C) is incorrect because Thatcher favored a tough law and order policy. Although spending on the National Health Service and unemployment compensation actually increased during Thatcher's term in office, her goal was to reduce government spending, and she was successful in trimming education and housing subsidies and holding the line on further expansion of welfare benefits (E).

43. **(A)** Stalin was preoccupied with securing the economic development of the Soviet Union and did not pursue extensive ties with Third World nationalists. Krushchev altered this isolationist attitude with a decidedly internationalist strategy of improving ties with other countries, particularly in the emerging Third World. Therefore, the best response is (A). Consolidating the success of Socialism (B) was Stalin's principle concern, whereas Krushchev pursued a more expansionist diplomatic, political, and economic strategy. (C) is incorrect; both Krushchev and Stalin negotiated with Western leaders. (D) is also incorrect. Stalin ruled with an iron fist, accusing all personal opposition of being enemies of the state, subject to harsh punishment. Krushchev scrapped the enemy of the state idea, and refused to jail or execute even party enemies who attempted to overthrow him. (E) is incorrect because it was under Krushchev that the Warsaw Pact Alliance was developed with Eastern European countries to counter the NATO military presence.

44. **(C)** Labour support for the Common Market has been neither consistent nor unqualified. (C) is correct. Traditional tensions between left-wing and moderate Labourites have always existed (A). Tensions between the left-wing, which grew increasingly influential in the 1970s, and moderate parliamentary party leaders led eventually to the defection of several right-wing members in 1981, and to the formation of a new Social Democratic party. Labour has always enjoyed strong support from Union organizations (B), although not always the support of rank and file members. Support for nationalization and public regulation of industry (D) has been a consistent goal of Labour. Broader social welfare policy and a fairer tax system (E) have always been key Labour goals.

45. **(B)** The best response is (B) since most people advancing into positions of significant authority and status in the Soviet Union do so through pursuing political careers as loyal Communist Party members or by virtue of having important technical skills, or both. (A) is not correct because Russians actually compose a higher percentage of the Soviet Union's intelligentsia than they do of the overall population. (C) is not correct because the educational backgrounds of most working and peasant class individuals place them at a great disadvantage compared to the children of existing educated elites. (D) is incorrect because nonpolitical careers are more numerous than political ones, and because political careers, though more risky, offer higher rewards. (E) is incorrect because numerous nonpolitical careers, including literature, science, medicine, foreign languages, academic studies, and art offer substantial opportunities for advancement and recognition.

46. **(A)** Popular support for the Communist Party in France has been declining rather than increasing for several years. La Pen's support is not related to fears about greater Communist influence. (A) is correct. Immigration is the central concern of that portion of the French population which has supported La Pen (B). The racial factor in La Pen's success (C) stems from the fact that many immigrants are blacks or Asians. The fears of lower class Frenchmen that jobs will be lost to foreigners (D) is a major reason for their xenophobic attitudes and their support of a La Pen's promise to restrict immigration. Xenophobic attitudes are bolstered by strong feelings of French nationalism (E) among the classes most affected by immigration.

47. **(A)** La Pen's National Front party is most similar to Vladimir Zhirinovsky's Liberal Democratic Party in Russia. Thus, (A) is the correct answer. Both parties share strong ultra-nationalist views, including anti-immigration, pro-military stances.

48. **(E)** The best response to the question is (E). The monarch has no authority to initiate bills or to veto them. It is true that the Crown's assent to bills passed by Parliament is necessary for their enactment, but this assent is strictly formal and is always given. The King or Queen does open parliamentary sessions with a speech (A), although this speech is drafted by the cabinet. The Crown does invest a prime minister once a new government has been formed (D). The Crown may formally dissolve Parliament (C) after a vote of no-confidence in the government. The Crown ultimately enacts all law (D) even though this is a formal and not a substantive power.

49. **(C)** The House of Lords only has the power to delay legislation, and no capacity to amend or veto it. Hence, the House of Commons is the most significant parliamentary body. (C) is correct. The Lords do have the power to delay money bills (A). The Lords do have the power to delay legislation from the House of Commons (B). The House of Lords is Great Britain's highest tribunal and its final court of appeal (D). Only Law Lords appointed for life because of their judicial expertise hear appeals. Seats in the House of Lords are filled by hereditary right or by lifetime appointment (E).

50. **(C)**   Under the old regime in the Soviet Union, ultimate power resided in the Communist Party, not in the state apparatus. The General Secretary was not selected by the Supreme Soviet, but by the leadership of the Communist Party itself. The best answer is (C). Constitutional amendments were to be formally made by the Supreme Soviet (A). The Supreme Soviet was formally responsible for the admission of new republics (B). Formally, the Supreme Soviet did elect a Presidium (D), although the party informally dominated this process. While the party ultimately controlled Ministerial appointments, the Supreme Soviet technically formed the Council of Ministers (E).

51. **(C)**   The correct answer is (C). Mao, rather than Deng, distrusted intellectuals and preferred peasant culture. Deng praised scientific and technical expertise and was willing to emphasize the need for higher education, which invariably put the peasant class at a disadvantage. Deng was less ideologically oriented than Mao, and much more of a pragmatist (A). Deng did place greater value on economic prosperity than on enforcement of equality (B). Deng did favor greater decentralization of planning (D) whereas Mao staunchly insisted on the principle of socialist centralization of planning. Mao was distrustful of outside influences on China while Deng was less suspicious and more pragmatic in using foreign policy to enhance domestic goals (E).

52. **(A)**   Answer (A) is the best choice. The Four Modernizations focused on the domestic development of China, not on how it could either receive or give more foreign aid. How much foreign aid should be accepted as part of the modernizations was, of course, a question that needed to be addressed, but only as a means to attain the ends of the Four Modernizations. Agricultural development (B) was a vital part of economic modernization. Expansion of the industrial sector (C) was considered essential to modernization, especially in terms of strengthening national security. Expanded and improved education (D) was seen as essential to the achievement of economic modernization. Modernizing the national security sector (E) was considered a vital part of protecting and preserving Chinese interests.

53. **(A)**   The "Red versus Expert" debate centered around the problem of how to ensure that people would be both ideologically committed and technically skilled, and whether education should stress quality, thus producing well-trained students who could contribute to national economic development, or whether it should stress education for everyone (equality) at the expense of quality. (A) is the best choice. (B) is incorrect because it was always assumed that peasants should receive some ideological indoctrination. (C) is incorrect because the belief was that party members should strive for both technical expertise and ideological commitment. Reduced technical training was not a primary goal. (D) is also incorrect. Although population pressures made higher education opportunities highly competitive, the goal of Chinese policy was not to reduce opportunities or ensure that only elites got them. Removing college graduates (E) was not a primary goal of party officials.

54. **(D)** (D) is the correct answer, since the military has historically wielded influence within the CCP, from the "mass line" to the Cultural Revolution to the Tiananmen Square massacre. Local governments and judges are subservient to the CCP. The National People's Congress, while part of the CCP's "parallel hierarchies," is in reality little more than a debating forum for acts already decided by the party's politburo. A student movement may draw the attention of the CCP leadership, as occurred in 1989, but it is not likely to exercise considerable political influence.

55. **(C)** The best response is answer (C). The Senate is elected indirectly by municipal councilors, department councilors, and the National Assembly, whereas the National Assembly is elected directly by vote of the people every five years. (A) is incorrect because the National Assembly holds the prerogative of considering the budget first, has the last word on legislation, and retains the right to overthrow the government. This tips the balance in favor of the National Assembly. It is the National Assembly, not the Senate (B), that has the power to overthrow the government. (D) is incorrect because when compromise cannot be reached on legislation, the president may ask the National Assembly to rule definitively on government bills. (E) is incorrect because the Parliament under the Fifth Republic has been carefully circumscribed and presidential powers greatly enhanced.

56. **(B)** The correct answer is (B). The two kinds of committees found in the House of Commons are Standing Committees and Select Committees. The former discuss bills and propose amendments to them. The latter serve more specific, and often temporary, functions. (A) is incorrect because committees may not bottle up or pigeon-hole a bill. Bills go forward to the floor of Commons for final approval or rejection. (C) is incorrect because the first vote on a bill is taken by the House of Commons as a whole, before it is sent to committee. (D) is incorrect because the committees do have the power to suggest substantive amendments to bills. (E) is incorrect because committees consider bills after two readings on the floor of Commons. The third reading takes place after the committee has returned the bill to the floor of the House of Commons.

57. **(D)** The correct choice is (D). By 1990, Gorbachev attempted to slow down some aspects of *glasnost* and *perestroika*. However, the influence of the media and more moderate elements of the CPSU continued to push for reform. As Gorbachev was increasingly viewed as politically irrelevant following the August 1991 coup attempt, he signed the dissolution agreement for the Soviet Union on December 25, 1991, and resigned political office.

58. **(E)** Parliament desires administrators who execute the law to have some degree of flexibility. In order to have flexibility, they need to be able to create administrative regulations, as long as they retain the spirit of the original act. (E) is correct. Pressures on parliamentary time (A) are so great that members often leave the details of implementation to administrative agencies. The technical knowledge required for effective implementation of parliamentary acts (B) usually lies with the civil service and

ministries rather than with the MPs. Laws rarely anticipate all possible future problems (C), which is why Parliament allows flexibility. Emergencies are precisely the kinds of situations that call for administrative innovation (D).

59. **(C)**   The Gang of Four, including Mao's wife, Jiang Qing, had all risen to prominence during the Revolution and had all professed radical leanings. After Mao's death, Hua Guofeng, in an effort to consolidate his authority and after a reputed attempt by the Four to assassinate him, had them arrested. Answer (C) is the best choice. (A) is incorrect because the Gang of Four had no direct ministerial connection with the Four Modernizations. The Gang of Four were radicals who Deng opposed; they were never part of his circle (B). (D) is incorrect because the Gang of Four did not live to see the Tiananmen Square incident. The Gang of Four were not pro-Western (E), but Marxist radicals.

60. **(B)**   Brezhnev, though not unmindful of the need to cope with the domestic consumer economy, gave priority to military development and foreign policy expansionism. (B) is correct. Brezhnev placed high priority on military spending and weapons development (A). Brezhnev, both in theory and in practice, advocated Soviet military intervention in support of Third World Marxists (C). Brezhnev did pursue arms control efforts in order to limit Western arms development and thus keep the arms race within a tolerable level of expense (D). Brezhnev did seek relaxed tensions and greater economic ties with the West, while exploiting every advantage in the Third World (E).

Section II
Part 1

Question 1–Sample Essay Scoring 0 to 3

Political systems can generally be divided along presidential or parliamentary lines. Each one of these variants involves different kinds of political accountability, as well as different inter-governmental relationships between the executive and legislative branches. In France, the lines between a presidential and a parliamentary system are somewhat blurred due to the peculiarities of the Fifth Republic's institutional arrangements. Mexico displays a much more conventional presidential system, where the president exerts a dominant and powerful role. The characteristics of presidentialism or parliamentarianism in France and Mexico shed important insights into the political dynamics and the decision-making process of each country.

France's political system provides for a powerful head of state who holds an impressive arsenal of powers. As the central figure of the Fifth Republic, the President of the Republic presides over, guides, and directs the political system. Standing above the daily fray of partisan politics, the president symbolizes the unity and continuity of the French state. In this capacity, the president is much more than a figurehead. In fact, the president is given considerable constitutional authority to set and advance a national agenda by the way he uses his powers. His power to persuade, or his intimation that he would use or implement the full complement of his presidential powers, generally suffices to convince the head of government (Premier) and the parliament that compliance with his wishes is a more prudent course of action than risking a battle of political wills between the executive and the legislative branches.

A major feature of the French political system is the difficult role of the Premier, as the head of government, and his relationship to the legislative body, the National Assembly. In a sense, the premier has two masters to please. He must be careful not to offend or antagonize the president, whose support is vital, yet he must also cultivate and maintain a parliamentary majority in the National Assembly if his legislative program is to succeed. Situated between these two formidable forces, the Premier is clearly placed in a more vulnerable position than his stronger head of state counterpart, who serves a full seven-year term regardless of shifting alignments in the National Assembly. The Premier, therefore, is clearly the weaker partner of France's unusual "dual executive".

In contrast, Mexico's reliance upon a strong authoritarian president, who combines both the head of state and head of government functions, is the most prominent feature of its political system. The Mexican President is regarded as the national protector and guardian of the goals and aspirations of the Mexican Revolution. He is the guiding and directing force of the political system. Representing the Institutional Revolutionary Party (PRI), Mexico's dominant party, as its undisputed leader, the president is almost guaranteed automatic majority support in Mexico's compliant two-chambered Congress. Moreover, patronage and appointment to Mexico's Supreme Court, the judicial branch does not have an established tradition of independence from executive control.

Therefore, given a weak system of checks and balances and the acquiescence of the legislative and judicial branches to executive authority, the president is the dominant political force in Mexico.

The presidential/parliamentary variants of political systems reveal important insights into the internal dynamics of the French and Mexican political systems. The French dual executive provides for a highly unusual relationship between the two executives who share the head of state and head of government roles. Unlike a purely parliamentary system such as Britain, where the head of government (prime minister) is more powerful than the head of state (monarch), France reversed the process. Endowing the head of state with an imposing array of powers, the French president is clearly the more powerful executive figure. On the other hand, Mexico, rejecting any elements of parliamentarianism, established a strong authoritarian executive who exercises both head of state and head of government roles in a pure presidential system. Because of these distinct variations, France's and Mexico's political systems have evolved in meaningfully different ways

Analysis of Sample Essay Scoring 0 to 3 (Question 1)

Since the thesis centers on the differences between presidential and parliamentary systems, it is necessary for the writer to provide a clear and operational explanation of each variant and the characteristics reflected by each. While the presidential/parliamentary dichotomy is mentioned as a useful framework to compare and contrast political systems, no real effort is made to explain or delineate what the specific characteristics of presidential and parliamentary systems are. For example, what factors make a presidential system *presidential?* What factors make a parliamentary system *parliamentary?*

Only vague references are made to "peculiarities…arrangements" in France and a "conventional presidential system" in Mexico. Paragraph one is not a sufficiently developed introductory paragraph.

Any systematic understanding of the constitutional design and framework of the Fifth Republic should take into account the indispensable role played by Charles de Gaulle. The Fifth Republic is a creation that was designed to fit the unique personality and authoritarian flair of its controversial founder. But, in paragraph two, no reference is made regarding the genesis of the Fifth Republic (i.e., how or why it came about).

More seriously, however, this paragraph is flawed by errors of omission; it neglects to identify in greater detail the specific powers available to the president. A vague allusion to the president's "considerable constitutional authority" is unsatisfactory. The writer should elaborate on this more fully, perhaps discussing the powers of appointments, referendum, dissolution of the National Assembly, as Commander-in-Chief, and emergency decree.

Not mentioning the fact that the premier is appointed by the president is an unpardonable omission in paragraph three. De Gaulle, for example, disliking the popularity of his Premier Georges Pompidou, deliberately bypassed him after elections for the National Assembly and chose someone to replace him.

To illustrate and explain the compatibility and conflict dimensions of this unusual dual executive more fully, some reference to the party affiliation of the president and the premier should have been made. One could point out that when both president and premier are from the same political party, there is greater cohesion and harmony; if they are from different parties, a more conflictive relationship is not only possible, but probable.

Another defect in this paragraph involves the omission of a very significant challenge to the viability of France's dual executive. The uneasy "cohabitation" experiment between 1986-1988, involving the Socialist President Mitterrand and the Neo-Gaullist Premier Chirac, should have been discussed and examined. It wasn't even mentioned.

The lineal and historical development of the strong national caudillo emerging from Mexico's Hispanic tradition is not discussed in paragraph four. An explicit reference would reinforce Mexico's evolving pattern of authoritarianism and enhance the legitimacy of Mexico's strong presidency.

As the "guiding and directing force" of the Mexican political system and the "undisputed leader" of the PRI, specific mention should be made of some of the varied roles the Mexican president plays. A discussion of the roles of chief executive, chief legislator, Commander-in-Chief, and chief diplomat should be included.

While correct acknowledgment of the absence of an effective checks and balances system due to the weaknesses of the legislative and judicial branches is made, none of the president's formal constitutional powers are indicated, such as state of siege or federal intervention.

The concluding paragraph provides a lucid and persuasive summary. Unfortunately, the concluding paragraph is based upon the deficient body paragraphs.

Question 1–Sample Essay Scoring 4 to 6

Political systems can be characterized or differentiated in terms of whether they reflect a parliamentary or a presidential form. Each type possesses a specific combination of elements that provides a unique political infrastructure and system of practices that serve to distinguish one form from the other. The parliamentary system, for example, blurs the legislative and executive branches by fusing their roles in the head of government selected from the political party (or parties) that controls a majority of the seats of the unicameral system or the majority of the lower house of a bicameral legislative body. On the other hand, the presidential system usually presents a separate, distinct, and independent executive branch, created by a different electoral constituency than the legislative branch. The president in this system encompasses the roles of both head of government and head of state, while in parliamentary systems these roles are characteristically filled by two separate individuals. In both France and Mexico, the parliamentary and presidential features provide an interesting contrast and comparison. A better understanding of how these parliamentary and presidential factors operate in France and Mexico should provide a deeper insight into the political dynamics of both countries.

The legacy of Charles de Gaulle, and the creation of the Fifth Republic in 1958, conferred a rather unique system upon France. As the official head of state, the President of the Republic was invested with an impressive array of powers that would make other heads of state in parliamentary systems envious indeed. With considerable constitutional authority, the president presides over the entire political system without actually involving himself in the day-to-day operation of partisan politics or the intricacies of the legislative process. The president, as the guarantor of the independence and integrity of the state, can initiate referenda, dissolve the National Assembly, appoint the head of government, and exercise emergency decree powers in times of national crisis. Transcending the more politically vulnerable head of government, who has to constantly cultivate the support of a parliamentary majority to survive, the president is elected to serve a seven-year term, regardless of unpredictable political shifts in the parliament. In fact, the president not only symbolizes the continuity of the state, but is the linchpin of stability for the Fifth Republic.

The junior partner of the dual executive of the Fifth Republic is the premier. The premier, who can come from the same or a different political party or persuasion as the president, has a more traditional parliamentary role to play. Politically accountable to the National Assembly, the premier has to continually maintain the confidence of the legislative body if his legislative program is to succeed. Careful not to offend or antagonize the president, who can be a powerful rival and who, in the last resort, can use his vast powers to bypass or obstruct the head of government, the premier is constantly confronted with the problem of satisfying two different and, at times opposing, forces. Clearly, as the head of government, the premier's role is relegated to a secondary position in the political and institutional arrangements of the Fifth Republic.

Mexico, on the other hand, provides a clear example of a powerful, singular executive who towers over the political system. As Mexico's undisputed and dominant authority figure, the Mexican president enjoys a historical legacy as a benevolent and paternalistic leader who represents and personifies the whole nation. These traditional factors and expectations are combined with enormous constitutional authority. The Mexican president, in fact, initiates almost all legislation through his control of the dominant political party, the Institutional Revolutionary Party, through his powers of patronage, and through the lack of a meaningful checks and balances system. Even though the Constitution of 1917 provided for a formal separation of powers, a feature that is inherent in presidential systems, the Mexican Congress is generally subservient to presidential authority. The judicial system also has not developed a tradition of judicial independence. Consequently, the Mexican president remains as the central force in the Mexican political system.

France and Mexico present two very different examples of possible parliamentary/presidential combinations. France's quasi-presidential or hybrid system divides the executive function between two different offices. Its rather unique dual executive reverses the usual model of the nominal or symbolic head of state. Rather, the Fifth Republic has created a very powerful head of state while designing a less prominent role for the head of government. Mexico, conversely, has followed the more conventional and traditional singular executive model, combining the constitutional functions of head of state and head of government in one person. Unlike the French model, which reflects a presidential system with parliamentary features, the Mexican system is a model of pure presidentialism. Despite their differences, however, both nations have created a strong authoritarian executive that dominates their respective political systems.

Analysis of Sample Essay Scoring 4 to 6 (Question 1)

A conscious effort is made to distinguish the special characteristics of both the parliamentary and the presidential variants in paragraph one. A clear thesis is established at the end of the paragraph detailing why an examination of the parliamentary-presidential factor is important.

Only a passing reference is made about the genesis of the Fifth Republic and its founder and inspirational leader, Charles de Gaulle, in paragraph two. Additional data about the highly personal nature and design of the Fifth Republic would have been appropriate. Specifically, more information about the role of Charles de Gaulle would have provided a better contextual understanding of the origins of the Fifth Republic.

A fairly comprehensive exposition of the powers and prerogatives of the President of the Republic is presented.

While clearly identifying the premier as the weaker of the two French executives, insufficient attention is given to the inherently conflicting relationships between the president and the premier in paragraph three.

The revealing "cohabitation" episode (1986-1988) put the issue of France's dual executive under great public scrutiny and criticism. Yet this potentially explosive issue was not even broached when it should be explored in detail.

How Mexico's singular executive combines both head of state and head of government roles in the guise of one person should be more clearly presented as an example of a presidential system in paragraph four.

Explain more fully how the president has continued Mexico's "historical legacy as a benevolent and paternalistic leader." For example, identify and describe some of the historical antecedents that have contributed to the emergence of Mexico's strong authoritarian executive.

Specify some of the president's formal constitutional roles, such as chief executive, chief legislator, Commander-in-Chief, and chief diplomat, and indicate some of the president's formal constitutional powers (e.g., Article 29, Article 76).

Furnish a fuller explanation of why the Mexican Congress is "generally subservient to presidential authority." Why and how did this come about?

The concluding paragraph presents a clear contrast and comparison between the parliamentary-presidential dimension of the French and Mexican political systems.

While the concluding paragraph provides a lucid summary of the distinguishing features of each model, a conclusion is generally no stronger than the supporting details and evidence marshalled to generate it. Undoubtedly, additional detail would support the conclusion in a more convincing manner.

Question 1–Sample Essay Scoring 7 to 9

One of the key analytical terms used by political scientists to distinguish categories or types of political systems differentiates them into parliamentary or presidential variants. Each type of organizational form contains a specific group of political practices that shapes the formal political and institutional arrangements of that particular political system. A parliamentary system, for example, usually includes two separate individuals who serve as head of state and head of government, a fusion of powers between the executive and legislative branches, a majority or coalition party government, and legislative lines of executive accountability. Conversely, a presidential system has one individual who serves as both head of state and head of government, a separation of powers between the executive and legislative branches, a more diffuse and less cohesive role for political parties, and political accountability to the voting constituency from which the executive is elected. In this regard, while France and Mexico both share some important similarities in their undisguised admiration for a strong executive role, they also contain some meaningful and significant differences.

Under the French Constitution of 1958, which was inspired by the authoritarian inclinations of the legendary Charles de Gaulle, France was to develop a hybrid presidential-parliamentary system. The Fifth Republic could be regarded as a presidential system with clearly discernible parliamentary overtones; a system that, although designed and shaped for the personality of its founder, Charles de Gaulle, outlived its creator. The Fifth Republic conferred formidable powers upon the President of the Republic. The president is to be elected by direct popular vote to serve for a seven-year term, with no limitations on the number of terms he can serve. Provided with impressive authority, the president is the guarantor of the territorial integrity and the national independence of the state (Article 5), appoints the head of government, the premier (Article 8), has the power to submit referenda directly to the French people (Article 11), can dissolve the National Assembly in case of legislative "gridlock" and call for new elections within 20-40 days of a dissolution (Article 12), is Commander-in-Chief of the armed forces (Article 15), and can invoke emergency decree authority in cases of national crisis (Article 16). Elected by a national constituency, the president, as an extraordinarily empowered head of state, presides over the entire political infrastructure and is responsible to the nation at large for his actions. In short, the de Gaulle-designed presidency is the most important political force of the Fifth Republic.

The parliamentary anomaly of the Fifth Republic involves the creation of a unique type of "dual executive." Unlike most parliamentary systems in which the individual who plays the role of head of state is a symbolic figurehead, in France the powerful president towers over the more restricted premier, the head of government. Appointed by the president from the majority party or coalition majority, the premier is directly accountable and responsible for his actions and tenure to the National Assembly, which on a vote of no-confidence can force the premier and his government to resign. When the president and the premier share the same political ideology, there is a congruency based upon shared program goals that is reflected in a close cooperation and collaboration. However, when the president and the premier come from different political parties or philosophical mind-sets, there exists the potential for conflict and paralysis. Such a turn of events occurred during the uneasy 1986-1988 period of "cohabitation" between Socialist President Francois Mitterrand and Neo-Gaullist Premier Jacques Chirac. This political aberration or "blip" in the Fifth Republic exposed a major flaw in the dual executive system: the juxtaposition of a powerful head of state, accountable to the nation at large for a seven-year term, versus a less powerful head of government accountable and responsible to the National Assembly for a variable term of up to five years. With the distinct possibility of a major collision of egos between these two strong-willed incumbents, the Fifth Republic's stability entered upon an uncharted course. As it turned out, both men showed remarkable restraint in an uneasy power-sharing political truce in which neither man sought to test the delicate fabric of the Fifth Republic. While the 1988 elections ended the "cohabitation" experiment, the potential for future conflict was left unresolved, and the unpredictable possibility of another recurrence remains.

By contrast, the Mexican political system is predicated on a clearly defined presidential form of government in which the president, who is both head of state and head of government, is the sole executive endowed with enormous formal and informal powers. Emerging from the Spanish colonial legacy, the Mexican president has become a monarchical surrogate who perpetuates the Hispanic authoritarian tradition. A paternalistic figure, the Mexican president has reinforced the popular image of a *caudillo*-type national leader, especially since the Mexican Revolution of 1910. The Mexican Constitution of 1917 provided for a powerful president that was the chief executive, chief legislator, chief diplomat, and Commander-in-Chief of the armed forces. In addition, the president is also the head of the dominant, authoritarian political party, the Institutional Revolutionary Party, which has controlled Mexican politics since 1929. The president is independently and directly elected by all eligible voters to serve one six-year term. Empowered to initiate extraordinary or emergency powers, the president can declare a state of siege and suspend portions of the Constitution (Article 29), or promote federal intervention in a state to replace or remove a state government (Article 76). With his considerable powers of political patronage, the traditional deference accorded to presidential leadership and authority, and the submissive and compliant attitude of the legislative and judicial branches, the president remains the dominant political force in Mexico.

France and Mexico provide an interesting comparison and contrast of the presidential-parliamentary dichotomy. France has a hybrid, quasi-presidential system that includes some parliamentary features; combining elements of both models, France's political system is truly unique. Mexico, on the other hand, more closely parallels the Latin American tradition of a sole, powerful president. Elected under a different voting system than the legislature, the Mexican president holds an impressive array of formal and informal powers not subject to the constraints of a checks and balances system. In Mexico, the executive branch dominates the political system. In the final analysis, the French and Mexican political systems present two very distinct variants of the presidential-parliamentary configuration.

Analysis of Sample Essay Scoring 7 to 9 (Question 1)

A detailed description of the distinguishing criteria evidenced by both parliamentary and presidential systems is clearly and systematically presented in paragraph one. The thesis statement that France and Mexico "share some important similarities" as well as some "meaningful and significant differences" reveals the intended focus of the rest of the essay. The intent to draw an incisive comparison between and contrast of these two political systems is implicit.

The origins of the special executive features of the Fifth Republic's hybrid presidential-parliamentary system are recognized and acknowledged (e.g., the role and personality of Charles de Gaulle) in paragraph two. Specific facts regarding the formal constitutional authority and specific powers exercised by the president (e.g., Articles 5, 8, 11, 12, and 16) are presented. The dominance of the president as the more powerful of figure of the dual executive is persuasively presented. The discussion of the accountability of the president to the nation at large suggests that his preeminent role as the nation's top spokesman goes beyond the realm of narrow partisan politics and the persistent need to satisfy the wishes of a changeable parliamentary majority.

The dominance of the unusually powerful president over the premier is clearly expressed, as in the discussion of the dangers of more frequent or mercurial changes of support for the premier in the National Assembly in paragraph three. The problem of the conflict-cooperation factor between the head of state and the head of government is discussed critically. The "cohabitation" experience between 1986-1988, for example, is used to illustrate the real possibility of future political disharmony or disarray. The introduction of this example reflects a deep understanding of the political ramifications of France's unique dual executive.

Both the formal and informal powers of the Mexican president are recognized as being important (e.g., Articles 29 and 76) in paragraph four. The historic Hispanic tradition of the authoritarian leader is directly connected to the Mexican experience. This element reflects a deep cultural understanding of Mexico's political past and present.

Mention is made of the varied constitutional roles of the president and how they combine with his role as the head of the dominant political party.

That the president is both head of state and head of government, is independently elected for one six-year term, and is *not* formally accountable to the Mexican Congress for his actions and tenure, are clearly stated expositions of the presidentialist qualities of the Mexican political system.

The additional contention that there is a lack of an effective checks and balances system in Mexico is well stated. This enhances the assertion that the primary force in Mexican politics is played by the president.

The distinctive features of the presidential and parliamentary systems found in France and Mexico are summarized in a comparison/contrast format in this very strong conclusion. The wealth of evidence presented in the body of the essay reflects the depth of research and the recognition of the writer that a valid conclusion rests on a secure factual foundation.

Question 2–Sample Essay Scoring 0 to 3

The Soviet Union and Mexico both present very similar pictures regarding the nature of their political party systems. Both countries have political parties that have dominated their respective political systems. Moreover, both of these dominant political parties emerged from revolutionary legacies that produced an ideological legitimacy. This revolutionary heritage has conferred a continuing justification for each party to rule, to the detriment of any possible political opposition. As a result, both dominant parties, the CPSU of the Soviet Union and the PRI of Mexico, have exercised virtually unchallenged supremacy for over sixty years, and have become the primary political institutions through which various interests are aggregated.

The Soviet Union's dominant party, the Communist Party of the Soviet Union (CPSU), establishes the priorities of the Soviet system. Through a system of structured allocation of rewards and punishments, the CPSU effectively uses the power and machinery of the state to determine the direction of Soviet society. From the Five Year Plans implemented by the government to give direction and structure to various sectors of its command economy, to the massive militarization of Soviet society through its formidable military-industrial complex, to the use of the KGB to suppress political, ethnic, or economic dissent, the CPSU is the decision-maker.

Mexico also reflects the domination of a one-party system. The Institutional Revolutionary Party (PRI), the acknowledged heir of the Mexican revolutionary tradition, has become the focal point of interest aggregation in Mexico. Through a variety of cooptive, coercive, and traditional means, the PRI has been able to exercise a virtual monopoly over the political process, using the rewards of political patronage and distributing economic benefits to various contending groups. The prognosis for Mexico's immediate future suggests that the PRI's hold on the political system will continue unabated by virtue of its ability to manipulate the levers of power.

The Soviet Union and Mexico both present analogous examples of two different political systems that are dominated by one-party systems. The CPSU and the PRI both derive their legitimacy and their justification to rule from their revolutionary heritages. Moreover, both of these dominant political parties have placed themselves at the center of their respective political systems as the foci through which all meaningful economic and political demands must be processed. By continuing to use its ideological creed to promote its right to exercise power, both the CPSU and the PRI can expect to dominate their respective political systems for the foreseeable future.

Analysis of Sample Essay Scoring 0 to 3 (Question 2)

The basic thesis of this essay is very tenuous. The position adopted is oversimplistic and superficial, because it ignores real and subtle differences that exist between totalitarian and authoritarian systems. The assumption that both systems share common features understates and excludes meaningful differences that separate the two systems from each other.

The major flaw in paragraph two is that it ignores the fact that the Stalinist variant of Soviet totalitarianism has dramatically changed in the post-1953 period. Monolithic communism has shifted since Stalin's day to a form of collegial consensus and decision making, maintaining CPSU hegemony through a system of reciprocal privileges designed to preserve the perquisites and to assure the continued political survival of the CPSU.

The notion that a command economy orchestrated and directed by the CPSU dominates Soviet life ignores the fact that elements of free enterprise and a mixed-market economy also exist in the Soviet Union, in the form of "gray" and "black" markets in areas outside of the military-industrial complex.

Examples and specific details relating to "a variety of cooptive, coercive, and traditional means" are conspicuously absent in paragraph three. By the same token, those "various contending interest groups" need to be defined.

The vital role of the Mexican president as the nexus of Mexico's decision-making process is also unmentioned.

The functional sectors of the PRI (agrarian, labor, and popular) and the aggregation of these important segments of the Mexican population by the PRI are also not examined; and the recent challenges to the PRI's hold on the political system by a growing but embryonic opposition are not explored.

Most seriously, however, the conclusion is very subjective and oversimplistic, given recent destabilizing events such as the increasing alienation of the Mexican electorate, measured by lower voter turnouts, and the inroads made by the political opposition in the 1988 and 1991 elections. The PRI's position has been seriously eroded.

The conclusion's premise that the two systems are analogous seriously understates the idiosyncratic and unique historical, ideological, political, economic, and cultural features of each society. The implicit assumption that similarities outweigh differences, or that differences are not important, is questionable.

The prognosis for the future ignores some very serious underlying problems in both political systems. The political, economic, and social disintegration of Soviet society, the decline of the CPSU as the sole source of political authority, and the growing restlessness of various ethnic groups all reflect lack of cohesion and an enormous potential for future conflict.

In Mexico's case, while the situation is not as explosive as the Soviet one, the halcyon days of yesteryear are also gone. Mexico's struggle to overcome the impoverishment inherent in an underdeveloped country has still not been resolved. Here, as in the Soviet Union, the entrenched position of the dominant political party (the PRI) is beset by a host of challenges to its authority.

Question 2–Sample Essay Scoring 4 to 6

The Soviet Union and Mexico represent two different types of political party systems. Each has developed a unique pattern of interest aggregation largely based on the special nature of its own political party system. Democratic, authoritarian, and totalitarian political systems all reflect their own experiences which help to differentiate their peculiarities and features from those of others. Historical differences, ideological factors, and cultural traditions explain some of the reasons why the Soviet system differs from the Mexican. Nonetheless, the political party systems which have emerged in both cases display some common characteristics.

Until the Gorbachev era, the Communist Party of the Soviet Union (CPSU) was a totalitarian elitist party that formed the nucleus of the Soviet political system. It was responsible for guiding and directing the entire governmental structure, in which every level paralleled a corresponding level in the CPSU bureaucracy. In its official capacity as the only allowed political party, the CPSU determined the political, military, economic, and social priorities of the Soviet state. Once the inner circles of the party had reached a consensus, social mobilization of the population was pursued and usually achieved through a command economy favoring the military-industrial complex; the absolute control over the media and mass communications; and, as a last resort, the use of state coercion and repression. With the CPSU in command of the totalitarian state, the presence of independent interest groups (which is a characteristic identified with democratic systems) were simply non-existent. The Soviet citizen was merely a political subject who was acted upon rather than an independent actor who voluntarily and willingly participated in the political system. Such was the nature of the Soviet system, where power and authority emanated from the top to the bottom. In such a society, interest aggregation was carefully crafted, structured, and funneled through the auspices of the CPSU, which presided over the entire system.

Mexico, conversely, exhibits an authoritarian political system that is characterized by a strong presidential figure who towers over the political scene and who, by right, heads the dominant political party, the Institutional Revolutionary Party (PRI). Presidential priorities, combined with pragmatic political and economic needs, determine which interests and groups have a receptive and sympathetic ear during a given six-year presidency. The PRI has attempted to establish specific formal lines of representation through the internal mechanisms and structures of the party while providing access to other groups through more informal points of contact. Nonetheless, the PRI, by using its privileged position as the legitimate heir of the revolutionary legacy, has cultivated and developed a special mediating role in Mexican society. By becoming the most authoritative and visible instrument to process, resolve, and satisfy or reject the varied political and economic demands placed before it, the PRI has become the focal point in the Mexican interest aggregation process.

The Soviet Union and Mexico present a similar and a dissimilar pattern. Both of their dominant political parties, the CPSU and the PRI respectively, have evolved from revolutionary traditions that shaped the future course of their political development. Yet in each system there are significant historical differences, ideological factors, and cultural traditions that have affected the unique nature and role of their respective political systems. While the CPSU exercised a total and absolute control over the political system, allowing no official or formal opposition or independent interest groups, the PRI exercises a more permissive form of control, encouraging a somewhat more pluralistic profile that even includes a formal, but token, opposition movement. In the final analysis, the inherent features of the political systems of the Soviet Union and Mexico, whether totalitarian or authoritarian, shaped their emerging political institutions by their attempts to aggregate the varied interests, issues, and groups of their respective systems. To that extent, then, this important function ultimately stemmed from and reflects the basic character of the system itself.

Analysis of Sample Essay Scoring 4 to 6 (Question 2)

The thesis attempts to take into account how democratic, authoritarian, and totalitarian variants of political systems shape or affect the nature of their respective political party systems. Recognizing that while the Soviet Union and Mexico may have some common denominators regarding their political evolution, the distinction that there are meaningful differences between the two political systems is also acknowledged.

This represents a more sophisticated dichotomous analysis than that found in the previous essay.

The specific dynamics of how the CPSU reached a consensus are not clearly identified or spelled out in paragraph two. For example, a reference to and an explanation of the Leninists principle of hierarchical decision making (democratic centralism) would be relevant here.

The political status of the Soviet citizen, as a subject rather than a participant, is not systematically explored. For example, the long tradition of Tsarism, with its dependency on a paternalistic father figure, contributed significantly to an entrenched submissive attitude toward political authority. These attitudes proved to be compatible with the totalitarian-auhoritarian model of the Soviet one-party political system as exercised by the CPSU.

The strong presidential figure in Mexico is discussed, but an explanation of how he became such a formidable authority figure is lacking (e.g., the tradition of the caudillo, machismo, and paternalism in the Hispanic culture going back to the *patronato real* of the Spanish kings) in paragraph three.

Specific examples of formal and informal PRI structures used for interest aggregation are not given. Details and examples are needed to put "flesh on the bones." Richness of details will strengthen assertions by reflecting knowledge of the specific matters being examined. Good examples are the three functional sectors of the PRI, the "Monterrey Group," CONCANACO, CONCAMIN, technocrats/técnicos, the Church, etc.

One of the strong points of this essay is the writer's ability to draw a cogent and articulate comparison and contrast between two distinct political systems. Various attributes are recognized regarding the unique development of each political system, such as historical, ideological, and cultural factors.

The relative absence or presence of pluralism in Soviet and Mexican political life is a discerning feature and an interesting analytical dimension for differentiating between the two political systems.

Question 2–Sample Essay Scoring 7 to 9

The interest aggregation function of political systems is generally performed through a variety of institutional mechanisms, most notably by political parties. If political parties are too parochial or narrow in scope, they will not enjoy significant electoral success because their popular base and appeal will be too limited. A political party, unless it joins a coalition in a parliamentary system or is ensconced in a dictatorial one-party system, will generally not succeed in exercising power unless it encompasses a wide range of socioeconomic groups as its electoral base. The Soviet Union and Mexico provide two very striking examples of how a totalitarian elitist one-party system (Soviet Union) diverges from a dominant authoritarian one-party system (Mexico) in the exercise and implementation of this vital interest aggregating function, that exists to some extent in all political systems.

Prior to 1985, the Communist Party of the Soviet Union (CPSU) exercised a monopoly of power over the Soviet political system. Legitimized by the Soviet Constitution of 1977 (Article 6), the CPSU was recognized as the unchallenged guiding and directing force of the Soviet system. Monolithic in nature and hierarchical in structure, the CPSU's decision-making format closely followed Lenin's guideline of democratic centralism, a concept which promoted vertical decision making and one-party exclusivity in which no other political party could exist or compete for public favor. Theoretically, the CPSU represented the interests of the proletariat, but in practice the CPSU followed the self-serving function of institutional self-preservation. Representing the *apparatchiki* (party bureaucracy), the Soviet Armed Forces, the KGB, the formidable military-industrial complex, and large numbers of industrial and agricultural managers, among others, the CPSU became a party of privilege and conservatism dedicated to preserving the status quo. To perpetuate its privileges and its primary role in Soviet society, the CPSU institutionalized methods of political recruitment and elite renewal through the creation of the Young Leninist/Communist Leagues (Komsomols). These mass youth organizations were designed to continue CPSU control by instilling the necessary values in the next generation of Soviet leaders. The Soviet Union manifests a totalitarian elitist political party system where one-party elections occur devoid of any formal inter-party competition. The unique features of this top-heavy totalitarian model precluded the existence of competing autonomous interest groups vying for CPSU favor, but reflected a consensus of priorities that maintained the CPSU and its supporters in a mutually reinforcing web of power.

While sharing a revolutionary tradition with the Soviet Union, Mexico's political evolution took a somewhat different path. Emerging from the chaos and tumult of the 1910 Revolution, Mexico, under President Calles, instituted and formalized an official ruling party in 1929. In 1946, this new party (originally called the National Revolutionary Party and later the Party of the Mexican Revolution) became the centerpiece of the authoritarian one-party system and is now known as the Institutional Revolutionary Party (PRI). Enshrining the ideals of the Mexican Revolution and adopting a revolutionary mystique and posture, the PRI and its lineal predecessors have effectively exercised absolute power for over sixty years. By using a variety of cooptive techniques, electoral fraud, and repression, the PRI has developed a stable, authoritarian political system, predicated on a strong national executive (a *caudillo*-like figure) and a coalition of regional *caudillos* (state leaders), municipal *caciques* (local bosses), and the corporative leadership of the three functional interest groups established by the ruling party. Formalizing the internal structure of the PRI to include a broad popular base, the PRI co-opted the *capesinos* (peasants) through the National Peasant Confederation. Labor was organized through the Mexican Confederation of Labor and the middle class service sector and professional groups through the National Confederation of Popular Organizations. The aggregation of these interests through their formal representation and incorporation in the party structure endowed the PRI with an even greater claim to legitimacy, while creating even more obstacles for potential opposition parties to overcome. Yet even with these formidable barriers to opposition, the PRI's political hold on the electorate was shaken enough in the 1970s that the ruling party even established the illusion, if not the substance, of inter-party competition. The co-option of functional interest groups encompassed within the PRI were later augmented to include the co-option of its relatively meaningless political opposition through the granting of "bonus deputies" *(diputados de partido)*. The durability and longevity of the PRI's unbroken political tenure, therefore, is a result of its flexible response in meeting challenges to its continued authority. Its future success will similarly rest on its continued ability to meet such challenges in a resilient and creative way.

The interest aggregation function of political parties in the Soviet Union and Mexico clearly demonstrate different patterns. The intrinsic nature of the totalitarian system in the Soviet Union, in which an exclusive monopoly of power was exercised by the CPSU, exemplified clientelism, and a variety of shared values maintained the supremacy, prerogatives, and perquisites of the CPSU and its allied interest groups. Mexico, on the other hand, while also dominated by a single party that aggregated various societal interests and groups, different from the Soviet Union in that Mexico sought to maintain the illusion of a democratic facade to legitimize its right to rule. Moreover, unlike the CPSU in the Soviet Union, the PRI in Mexico tolerated and even encouraged the existence of a token political opposition. By officially allowing a greater degree of political pluralism, the PRI could parry the critics of Mexican democracy while continuing to legitimate its own preeminent role. In the final analysis, both the Soviet Union and Mexico evolved and developed two distinct types of political party systems— one predicated on exclusiveness in an emerging totalitarian system (CPSU), and one based on an authoritarian one-party system with limited but structured political pluralism (PRI).

Analysis of Sample Essay Scoring 7 to 9 (Question 2)

The universality of the interest-aggregation function, performed to some degree by all types of political party systems, is clearly stated. More important, however, is the argument that there are significant differences in the way this function is exercised that distinguish totalitarian from authoritarian political systems.

The unique totalitarian features of the CPSU prior to the Gorbachev era are clearly explained, and reinforced with supportive detail (Article 6, democratic centralism).

Important and prominent segments of the Soviet population that have significant representation in, and access to, the inner-circles of the CPSU are identified; the *apparatchiki*, the armed forces, the KGB, the military-industrial complex, etc.

The methods and techniques used by the CPSU to institutionalize its rule and to perpetuate its authority are presented, with the examples of the role of the Komsomols and the prohibition of formal opposition political parties.

The idea that the CPSU is primarily concerned with its own institutional survival and self-interest is logically and persuasively presented.

The revolutionary genesis of the PRI provides a deeper understanding of the special role the PRI and its predecessors have played in the formation of the Mexican political system.

The manipulative and regulatory techniques the PRI has employed to exercise an effective dominance over the political system are well presented.

A description of the network of authoritarian leadership from the preeminent role of the President of the Republic, to the state leaders, to the local bosses, provides a better picture of the vertical power structure of the PRI.

Part 2

Question 3–Sample Essay Scoring 0 to 1

Mexico's political and economic development has been shaped and guided more by its Hispanic authoritarian tradition and its indigenous heritage (deriving from the Pre-Conquest) than by its ongoing relationship with the United States. Mexico's political and economic evolution created by its unique hybrid legacy, in fact, relegates the United States to a marginal role at best. Therefore, it would be over simplistic to attribute Mexico's political and economic development as merely an outgrowth of its geographical proximity to the United States.

Mexico's political and economic development exhibits a singular independence from United States geo-political influence. For example, the development of the PRI, the dominant authoritarian one-party system that emerged, evolved from the revolutionary aftermath of the Mexican Revolution of 1910 and not from a slavish desire to emulate the American two-party system. Mexico's dominant political party developed as an indigenous creation to institutionalize (and ostensibly carry out) the ideals of the Mexican Revolution. While the presidential system with a formal separation of powers model was adopted (similar to the United States), the comparison ends there.

Mexico also has demonstrated that geographical proximity to the United States may not be as critical nor as influential as is often assumed. For example, in 1938 when Lazaro Cardenas nationalized the foreign petroleum holdings amid great furor and American opposition, Mexico clearly exhibited its economic independence from its northern neighbor. Similarly, Mexico's sympathetic foreign policy *vis-`a-vis* Fidel Castro and the Cuban Revolution has also frequently dismayed and piqued the American government. Mexico, in fact, refused to bow to intense U.S. pressure in the early 1960s to isolate and ostracize the Cuban government and instead vigorously maintained its independent stance to continue diplomatic relations. These events demonstrate Mexico's freedom of action unencumbered by its geographical relationship with the United States.

Finally, Mexico's adoption of a socialistic and communal form of land ownership, the *ejido*—also demonstrates Mexico's seeming lack of concern about placating its northern neighbor. The Mexican Revolution elevated the *ejido* as the form of land tenure that would provide the landless peasant with the quickest route to economic and social justice. Needless to say, the *ejido* caused great concern among not only Mexican *hacendados* (large landholders), but also among American landholders as well. Defying the American lobby seeking to prevent an effective land reform, President Cardenas, in particular, distributed large rural tracts of land in the form of the communal village *ejidos* to millions of landless peasants between 1934-1940.

In sum, while the geographical proximity to the United States has periodically played some role in the bilateral relations between Mexico and the United States, it has generally been of secondary importance. More frequently than not, Mexico's political and economic development have evolved because of the historical and nationalistic blend of factors that has allowed Mexico to create its own unique responses to its own unique problems. Mexico has been able to exercise untrammeled sovereignty over its own affairs in spite of its intrusive neighbor to the north.

Analysis of Sample Essay Scoring 0 to 1 (Question 3)

The thesis position of this essay begs/circumvents the question and entirely avoids confronting how geographical proximity to the United States has affected Mexico's political and economic development.

Using the "Mexican hybrid" argument as the primary means to explain Mexico's political and economic development ignores the powerful and, at times, telling role the United States has historically played in shaping Mexico's destiny.

The contention that Mexico has exhibited "singular independence" is greatly overstated if not moot.

From an alternative and more cynical point of view, Mexico's creation of the PRI was essentially to develop a stable political instrument to perpetuate the power and wealth of the Revolutionary Elites, not necessarily to carry out the selfless "ideals" of the Mexican Revolution.

The formation of the PRI, as an example of the institutionalized maturation of the Mexican Revolution, was partially a nationalistic response to "yanqui" imperialism—a fact that impinges upon the geo-political significance of the Mexican-United States relationship.

Cárdenas' action of seizing the foreign oil holdings represented an economic policy that has subsequently been reversed or de-emphasized in most other state-owned/nationalized industries, especially under the recent leadership of Carlos Salinas de Gortari (1988-1994). In fact, since 1940, and with only minor exceptions during the Echeverría presidency (1970-1976), Mexico has clearly moved in the direction of increasing privatization of property as a means of attracting foreign (American) capital investment.

Mexico's flirtation with Castro, on the other hand, merely reinforced Mexico's need to placate the Mexican Left, to re-legitimize Mexico's revolutionary credentials (and its own revolutionary mystique), and to symbolically maintain an independent foreign policy stance *vis-à-vis* the United States (i.e., to demonstrate that Mexico's foreign policy was not subservient to the needs/demands of the "Colossus of the North"). Again, in this instance, the writer underplays how geo-political factors regarding the Mexican-United States relationship were involved.

The *ejido* is a very insignificant part of the present land tenure system existing in modern-day Mexico and, as such, is not the best example. In fact, the *ejido* remains a highly inefficient economic form of ownership and has increasingly given way to small, medium, and large privately-owned and more capital-intensive forms of agriculture that have proven themselves more economically efficient.

Much of the *ejidal* holdings have languished due to the fact that most of the *ejidos* are of marginal quality because of infertility of soil, a lack of irrigation, and inadequate agricultural credit/capital.

More important, however, is the fact that export-oriented commercial agricultural markets are being encouraged to cater to the consumption needs of Americans rather than to the domestic consumption needs of Mexicans (e.g., rice, beans, cornmeal).

The writer's conclusion that Mexico has pursued its own course, generally ignoring its northern neighbor is an exercise in self-delusion. Mexico has never forgotten that half of its national territory was seized by the United States in the Mexican War (1846-1848)—or that it endured numerous U.S. interventions (economic, political, and/or military) since then.

At best, Mexico has steered a measured course in seeking to modernize its economy and to create a stale political system, but, uneasily, it has always had to look over its shoulder.

Question 3–Sample Essay Scoring 2 to 3

In a recent work on Mexico called *Distant Neighbors*, the author attempts to explain how Mexico's political destiny has been shaped by its relationship with the United States. Because of the geo-political dominance of Mexico's northern neighbor, Mexico's development has often reflected an ambivalent relationship with the United States. This historical legacy, no doubt a partial result of the United States stripping away one-half of Mexico's national territory, continues in various forms to the present day.

In a sense, shackled together by historical and geographical fate, Mexico and the United States have had a very tumultuous and mercurial relationship over the last century and a half. Enduring numerous military and political interventions, Mexico has learned the true meaning of Porfirio Díaz's (the dictator of Mexico from 1876-1911) famous dictum, "Poor Mexico! So far from God and so close to the United States." In sum, Mexico's sovereignty as an independent state, especially during the earlier period of Mexican-United States relations (1840s-1930s), was often compromised and subjected to the dictates of American "manifest destiny" (read as imperialism by Mexico).

Geographical proximity has also shaped Mexican-United States relations regarding bilateral economic relationships. Highly dependent upon the need for foreign investment capital, the concomitant need for reliable import and export markets, and the creation of a profitable tourist industry, Mexico has sought to cultivate a reliable economic partner in the United States. Starting with the *bracero* movement during World War II, Mexico was legally able to "export" its surplus (unemployed) agricultural workers to the United States up until 1964. Additionally, Mexico promoted export-oriented, capital-intensive, large scale, private farms in northern Mexico to meet the United States' demand for winter vegetables and fruit. In fact, as recently as 1989, Mexico depended on the United States to buy over two-thirds of its exports while Mexico purchased almost two-thirds of its imports from the United States. With the important growth of tourism, the appearance of *maquiladoras* (border assembly plants/factories), and the possible ratification of the controversial North American Free Trade Agreement (NAFTA)—which would eliminate most tariffs and trade barriers between Mexico, the United States, and Canada over the next 15 years—Mexico is being inextricably drawn into a regional economy dominated by the United States.

Finally, geographical proximity has also led to troubling bilateral relations regarding the burgeoning illicit drug trade and U.S. attempts at drug interdiction, as well as the flood of undocumented illegal aliens crossing the border to seek job opportunities in the United States. These difficulties simply underscore the question of how, and in what ways will the Mexican political system respond to American entreaties to monitor and enforce these mutually aggravating problems more rigorously. The unpalatable alternative is to risk threatening and undermining the stability of Mexico's political and economic institutions, as well as its continuing vital bilateral relationship with the United States. If the Mexican Government turns a deaf ear to U.S. grievances and complaints, the stability of the political system and the uninterrupted rule of the PRI could be severely jeopardized. Mexico, conversely, could also run a great risk of destabilizing its somewhat fragile and dependent economy by alienating its major trading partner and source of investment capital.

In the final analysis, as a lesser developed country, Mexico's independence of action is placed in a considerably more vulnerable position than its more developed and powerful northern neighbor. Mexico is still "so (or perhaps too) close to the United States" that if it attempts to exercise its full range of options, it does so at its own peril. Porfirio Díaz's dictum is still inescapably a part of the on-going Mexican-United States relationship.

Analysis of Sample Essay Scoring 2 to 3 (Question 3)

Reference to particularly relevant writings about the Mexican and U.S. relationship shows application of other knowledge and information to the question being raised.

The importance of the geo-political factor of proximity to the United States is explained in terms of an established, but ambivalent, historical legacy that forms the thesis position of the essay.

Specific reference should have been made about the Mexican War (1846-1848) being the factor responsible for the partition of Mexico.

The "special" Mexican-U.S. relationship is interpreted as essentially being characterized as one shaped by historical and geographical fate.

The highly asymmetrical relationship between Mexico and the United States is attributed to a stronger, expansionist power exploiting a weaker, less developed one.

Strongly implied, but not explicitly stated, is how the reservoir of ill-will Mexico still harbors towards the United States (because of the many U.S. incursions into its territory) finds expression in the present-day relationship between Mexico and the United States.

Lack of reference to specific interventions is an error of historical omission.

Geographical proximity is also used by the writer to help explain the reciprocal and highly interdependent economic relationship between Mexico and the United States.

Important factual information is provided as evidence regarding the many ways that the Mexican economy intersects and overlaps the American economy. Perhaps, however, more is less! Too many examples prevent an in-depth analysis. The *bracero* movement, for example, is outdated and could probably have been omitted.

The argument is cogently made that the growing regionalization of the U.S., Mexican, and Canadian economies would, more likely than not, provide increasing opportunities for Mexico's economic expansion.

The writer persuasively argues that the current bilateral relationship of Mexico and the United States is exacerbated by a host of mutually aggravating problems (e.g., drug trafficking and undocumented aliens).

The writer appropriately recognizes that continuing conflict over the resolution of these bilateral issues are of great importance to Mexico because failure to ameliorate them could result in serious political and economic consequences.

Unfortunately, the other prong of the Mexican dilemma is ignored by the writer. If the Mexican government appears to be too compliant in responding to U.S. pressure, the Mexican government becomes viewed as a "tool" of "yanqui" imperialists.

Mexico, it is correctly argued, has less independence of action because, as a lesser developed country, it is more vulnerable to the economic currents and political influence of its more powerful northern neighbor.

Question 3–Sample Essay Scoring 4 to 5

A recurrent theme in Mexican-United States relations has been the mutual interdependence that both nations share. The fact that Mexico and the United States have differences regarding their history, culture, race, and language only serve to complicate a very delicate and increasingly important relationship. Sharing a 2,000 mile border with the United States has, no doubt, caused Mexico serious problems in the past. The dilemma Mexico now faces, however, involves how it can maximize the economic benefits to be derived from a close geographical relationship with the United States without, at the same time, becoming (or being perceived as) an economic vassal or pawn of its northern neighbor. In fact, Mexico's historical relationship with the United States is still unfolding.

Mexico's long and traumatic relationship with the United States has often been characterized by friction and conflict. Subjected to an asymmetrical power relationship where Mexico has been the victim of numerous incursions against its sovereignty [e.g., the Mexican War (1846-1848), the period of Maximilian and Carlota (1862-1867), and during the Mexican Revolution (1910-1917)], Mexican political and economic development have been greatly influenced by its on-going relations with the United States. For example, in 1969 the United States attempted to crack down on drug trafficking along the U.S.-Mexican border with "Operation Intercept." This unsuccessful, unilateral action on the part of the United States to curtail the illicit drug trade (which was in part, caused by the Mexican government's passivity) resulted in a devastating economic setback for Mexican border towns dependent on U.S. tourism. In response, and under enormous domestic economic pressure, the Mexican government promised closer cooperation if the United States would lift its drug interdiction campaign (which it did shortly thereafter). The successful resolution of this crisis clearly revealed how closely enmeshed Mexico is/was to the changing demands of its northern neighbor.

Mexico's economy (and inevitably its political system) is also dependent on maintaining strong cordial relations with the United States. Not only has the United States exported many manufacturing jobs to assembly plants on the Mexican side of the border (*maquiladoras*) in such economic areas as textiles, electronics, and automobiles, but the

United States has also stimulated the Mexican economy by purchasing large quantities of Mexican exports, most notably petroleum and petroleum by-products. In fact, Mexico has become America's third largest trading partner. A serious political disruption provoking an alienation of American tourists, businessmen, or government officials could have catastrophic consequences on Mexico's present and future economic development. If a hostile political/economic climate were to be created, American tourists and investors would look elsewhere for a safer haven. To this extent, the Mexican political system is committed to maintaining its economic connection to the United States by fostering a closer, politically-collaborative relationship.

Finally, the staggering problem of tens of thousands of Mexican illegal (undocumented) migrants who stream into the United States each year has led to additional conflicts. Organized trade unions in the United States, ignoring the claims that Mexican "illegals" take menial and inferior jobs most American workers reject, contend that American jobs are being taken by foreigners. Unable to expand economically as rapidly as its population, Mexico has blinked at the problem. For Mexico, it is easier to "export" its surplus unemployed labor force to the United States than to have it become a nagging source of domestic political discontent.

In sum, Mexico has demonstrated that its geographical proximity to the United States is like a two-edged sword. In cutting both ways, that sword at times has served the needs of Mexico, and at other times the needs of the United States. Nevertheless, what is undeniable is that historical fate has forged an "odd couple" that shares a common border with both similar and disparate problems. How successful these "distant neighbors" will be in solving their mutual problems remains to be seen.

Analysis of Sample Essay Scoring 4 to 5 (Question 3)

The theme of mutual interdependence is appropriately recognized—despite historical, cultural, racial, and linguistic differences—as the present guiding principle of Mexican-U.S. relations.

Mexico's inherent political dilemma of needing the United States to help promote and expand Mexico's economic development without Mexico becoming subservient to American interests is insightfully noted as the thesis position.

Mexico's relationship with the United States is accurately portrayed as being an asymmetrical one (i.e., of a weaker power dominated by a stronger one).

Factual specificity identifying particularly relevant examples of U.S. domination is also evident.

The use of "Operation Intercept" provides an excellent microcosmic example of how conflicting Mexican and U.S. needs and demands were resolved.

The writer cites how Mexico's economy is integrally tied to maintaining a cooperative and collaborative relationship with the United States.

Appropriate examples of the prominent U.S. role in Mexico's economy are presented demonstrating that any serious disruption could lead to severe political and economic repercussions.

The writer appropriately addresses one of the major bilateral issues causing conflict between Mexico and the United States: the problem of undocumented migrants.

The writer perceptively illustrates a variable-sum game with positive and negative payoffs for both the Mexican and American participants involved (e.g., Mexico "exports" its unemployment problem, unemployed Mexican workers find jobs, American trade unions are threatened by foreign, non-union workers, and American businessmen can hire "illegals").

The adage "If Mexico (or the United States) sneezes, the other catches its cold" is clearly evidenced by the writer in his/her analysis and conclusion of how geopolitical factors have indelibly shaped the relationship between Mexico and the United States.

Question 4–Sample Essay Scoring 0 to 1

The Industrial Revolution had seen a tremendous increase in the manufacturing capabilities of Europe. This increase was seen not only in consumer goods but in the weapons of war. A true arms race had engulfed the nations of the Continent in the second half of the 19th century as arms, munitions, ever-larger guns and ships rolled off the assembly line. These were readily available to any nation possessing the financial resources to acquire them and believing, rightly or wrongly, that it required them to defend their honor. Moreover, not only were arms in greater supply than ever before, they were of a greater destructive nature than any previously used by man.

Beyond the mere presence of millions of men prepared to take up arms, there had come into existence a mind-set which seemed to both justify and indeed glorify war. Drawing upon the doctrines of Social Darwinism, there were those who argued that the battlefield was the ultimate proving ground upon which the merit of men and of their culture was tested: the strong survived, the weak perished. Further, as the people of Europe became more literate and as newspapers—as a consequence of the technological advances such as the rotary press, the linotype, and cheap paper from wood pulp—sprang up in ever increasing numbers, governments were not slow in using them for propaganda purposes. Through the press it was possible to inculcate in the peoples' minds the idea that their nation's cause was always correct. Nationalism, assuming the role of a secular religion, dictated that one must be prepared to fight and, if necessary, die, for the Motherland.

It was with this fanaticism that Germans, Frenchmen, Austrians, Russians, and others, after several decades of international tension, joyously marched to war in August of 1914, determined to defeat the foe in a "short little conflict." The realities of modern warfare quickly became clear: above all was the fact that the defensive tactics and tools of war had negated the possibility of a rapid and successful offensive war. Even a momentary breakthrough of the enemies' lines was rapidly closed as reserve troops could be quickly moved up via railroads to close the breach. As the western front settled down to trench warfare, the machine gun, barbed wire, endless barrages of heavy artillery, and poison gas demonstrated that sheer courage or even manpower could not bring victory: it was a lesson that cost millions of lives. On the eastern front, the Russian fate demonstrated the inadequacy of numbers if a nation lacked the industrial base to support them. Nor were the civilians spared, for even if they were not in the line of march of the armies engaged in battle, they could be made to suffer through blockades of food supplies as the submarines roved the seas or zeppelins or bombers struck from above.

Analysis of Sample Essay Scoring 0 to 1 (Question 4)

This essay fails to answer the questions at hand, and instead skirts the issue, going into specific detail about warfare tactics used in World War I. The information does not provide sufficient evidence as to what could have been the cause of the discontent in the post-war nations, and instead would have us believe that the Wars were fought because there was simply an over-abundance of munitions in land and power-hungry nations. The essay is disjointed and is a poor attempt at answering the question posed.

Question 4—Sample Essay Scoring 2 to 3

Several factors need to be understood concerning the events leading to World War II. First, there has been little debate over causes: Germany, Italy, Japan, and the U.S.S.R. were not satisfied with the peace settlement of 1919. They used force to achieve change, from the Japanese invasion of Manchuria in 1931 to the outbreak of war in 1939 over Poland. Hitler, bit by bit, dismantled the Versailles Treaty in central and eastern Europe. Responsibility has also been placed to some degree on Britain and France and even the United States for following a policy of appeasement which it was hoped would satisfy Hitler's demands.

Secondly, Britain and France as well as other democratic states were influenced in their policy by a profound pacifism based on their experience with the loss of life and devastation in World War I and by a dislike of the Stalinist regime in Russia.

Thirdly, while the U.S.S.R. was a revisionist power, it was profoundly distrustful of Germany, Italy, and Japan. The threat to their interests led the Soviet leaders to pursue a policy of collective security through the league of Nations (which they joined in 1934). Only after evidence of Anglo-French weakness did Stalin in 1939 enter an agreement with Hitler. This event, like the Great Purges, only heightened suspicion of Soviet motives and was later to become the subject of debate and recrimination in the Cold War that followed World War II.

Finally, Neville Chamberlain's policy of appeasement was not based on any liking for Hitler, whom he considered "half-crazed," but on a genuine desire to remove causes of discontent inherent is the Versailles settlement and thus create conditions where peace could be maintained. His error lay in his belief that Hitler was open to reason, preferred peace to war, and would respect agreements.

Using a Franco-Soviet agreement of the preceding year as an excuse, Hitler, on March 7, 1936, repudiated the Locarno agreements and reoccupied the Rhineland (an area demilitarized by the Versailles Treaty). Neither France (which possessed military superiority at the time) nor Britain was willing to oppose these moves.

The Spanish Civil War (1936–1939) is usually seen as a rehearsal for World War II because of outside intervention. The government of the Spanish Republic (established in 1931) caused resentment among conservatives by its programs, including land reform and anti-clerical legislation aimed at the Catholic Church. Labor discontent led to disturbances in industrial Barcelona and the surrounding province of Catalonia. Following an election victory by a popular front of republican and radical parties, right-wing generals in July began a military insurrection. Francisco Franco, stationed at the time in Spanish Morocco, emerged as the leader of this revolt which became a devastating civil war lasting nearly three years.

The democracies, including the United States, followed a course of neutrality, refusing to aid the Spanish government or to become involved. Nazi Germany, Italy and the U.S.S.R. did intervene despite non-intervention agreements negotiated by Britain and France. German air force units were sent to aid the fascist forces of Franco and participated in bombardments of Madrid, Barcelona, and Guernica (the latter incident being the inspiration for Picasso's famous painting which became an anti-fascist symbol known far beyond the world of art). Italy sent troops, tanks, and other materiel. The U.S.S.R. sent advisers and recruited soldiers from among anti-fascists in the United States and other countries to fight in the international brigades with the republican forces. Spain became a battlefield for fascist and anti-fascist forces with Franco winning by 1939 in what was seen as a serious defeat for anti-fascist forces everywhere.

Analysis of Sample Essay Scoring 2 to 3 (Question 4)

While well written and using excellent vocabulary, the essay lacks a clear and definite thesis statement, as well as a conclusion. Although the facts presented are both correct and accurate, the presentation is lacking and the topics covered are not expanded upon. Use of specific details is missing, such as explanations as to why the various treaties (e.g., The Treaty of Versailles, and the Treaty of St. Germain) were the source of so much discontent between the nations involved in World War I. The author does not elaborate on points enough to completely answer the question, but exhibits a fair effort nonetheless.

Question 4–Sample Essay Scoring 4 to 5

Described by wartime propaganda as the "war to end all wars," World War I was followed by peace settlements which promoted bitterness and disillusionment in Europe. In this way, the settlements may have themselves become causes of World War II.

Three treaties ended the war—the Treaty of Versailles with Germany and the Treaties of St. Germain and Neuilly with Austria and the Ottoman Empire. The Treaty of Versailles was criticized within Germany as the "imposed treaty," so called because it was not the treaty promised when Germany asked for a cease fire in November of 1918. Germany had been promised a negotiated treaty, but the Treaty of Versailles, written by Germany's enemies, had been forced upon Germany with the choice of signing the treaty or resuming hostilities.

Already embittered by a continuing British naval blockade of Germany in 1919, after the war ended—which, rightly or wrongly, was blamed by many Germans as the cause of starvation in the country—Germans were especially unhappy with some parts of the treaty. The German army was limited to 100,000 men; training was prohibited in tanks and planes; and Germany was required to pay an unspecified amount of reparations. To many Germans it appeared their nation was being blamed for starting the war and for all destruction resulting from the war.

The Treaty of Versailles opened the way for politicians such as Adolf Hitler, who argued that Britain and France were not to be trusted and their democracies were not to be emulated. Although Hitler's National Socialist party was never able to garner more than 34% of the vote, he probably spoke for many Germans when he dismissed the German government formed after the war, the Weimar Republic, as an expedient and weak government formed in hopes of gaining easier peace terms from Woodrow Wilson and his allies.

In order to convince many Germans that military force was necessary to roll back the hated treaty, Hitler also could point to two other parts of the peace settlements. Germany had lost much of mineral-rich Silesia to the recreated Poland, even though the majority of Silesians had chosen, in a referendum, to remain with Germany. Hitler also exploited the issue of the "Polish Corridor," a strip of formerly-German land awarded to Poland in order to give the Poles an outlet to the sea.

The treaties with Austria and the Ottoman Empire allowed the victorious allies to create a series of new nations in eastern Europe. The new nations were not particularly stable, struggling with internal divisions and bickering with their neighbors over borders and territory. In his book *Mein Kampf*, Hitler, an Austrian, looked at these areas as a natural direction for future German expansion.

Disillusionment over the peace settlement was not restricted to Germany. Britain and France had been promised a collective security agreement with the United States by Woodrow Wilson. When the United States, instead, withdrew from the European diplomatic system after the war, both European nations struggled to find new ways to make themselves secure. By the 1930s, many British citizens and some French citizens had come to believe that the Treaty of Versailles had been too harsh. The result, unfortunately, was a tendency to view Hitler as a mere statesman with valid grievances who needed to be "appeased."

It would be inaccurate to say the treaties at the end of World War I became the major causes of World War II. The major causes lay in the personality and ideas of Adolf Hitler. By helping Hitler's rise to power, and by failing to establish a stable diplomatic system to block him, the treaties were, however, a factor.

Analysis of Sample Essay Scoring 4 to 5 (Question 4)

The essay begins with a strong thesis statement, which is expanded upon throughout the remaining paragraphs. By citing the various treaties which ended the war, the writer is providing the factual evidence which lends credibility to the thesis. The reasons for the hostilities which were still felt by the various post-war nations are explained throughout, making a smooth transition to the writer's conclusion that these hostilities were actually a cause of World War II. The essay is well written and demonstrates good use of vocabulary and knowledge of comparative politics.

Question 5–Sample Essay Scoring 0 to 1

The similarities between the Soviet Union under Stalin and Nazi Germany under Hitler point to a very close relationship between Communist totalitarianism and its National Socialist counterpart. Both leaders ruled through fear and intimidation. But

Stalin's reign of terror was closely aligned (at least in his mind) to the purging of counter-revolutionary insurgents bent on sidetracking the Communist government founded by Lenin. Hitler, however, made little attempt to cloak his dictatorial methods with established ideology. Though the end result was often the same, it is incorrect to assume that German totalitarianism and Soviet totalitarianism were the same brand under different names.

Whereas Hitler was determined to create a juggernaut capable of invading and controlling all of Europe, Stalin was reined in by an ideology which stated that each country's workers must come to their own decisions to overthrow their governments and establish Communist regimes. Though a seemingly minor point, this basic ideological difference has a profound effect on how the two leaders governed. Stalin was able to take a great deal of time ferreting out dissidents and those opposed to his regime. Thousands of army officers and high-ranking government officials were killed in the purges of 1936-38 as Stalin eradicated all opposition. The trials of Bukharin, Zinoviev, and Kamenev, though obviously controlled by Stalin, were ways in which the Soviet government could be seen to be acting on ideological bases. Stalin, though in complete control, needed the trials to ensure that the public would at least ostensibly support his purges.

Hitler, however, had very little need to justify either his motives or actions. Following his election as Chancellor in early 1993, he was able to micro-manage the government to the extent that no other party or figure could gain control. Soon after, in March of that year, he was named by the Reichstag as both Chancellor and President and became Der Fuhrer, a complete and total dictator with all of Germany reacting to his every whim. In a sense, he was the perfect totalitarian, controlling by sheer will and backed by both the army and a private corps of the SS. Though there were plots against him, including the abortive assassination attempt in 1944, most plotters were easily discovered and summarily shot, with fewer still tried in public by mock courts.

In the end, the Soviet Union was a single-party totalitarian regime intent on solidifying Stalin's place in the government. Hitler, however, actively pursued an agenda which forced him into external conflicts which distracted him from the types of state and party purges more typical of the Stalin regime. Though they are extremely similar in methods, the two regimes were designed for different purposes and became increasingly dissimilar as they progressed.

Analysis of Sample Essay Scoring 0 to 1 (Question 5)

Little factual research and a general stance on the issue confuses the thesis here. The thesis does not completely answer the question. Instead, it charts the two men's careers in very general terms without placing them in clear cut historical context, i.e., why did Stalin have to try Bukharin, Kamenev, and Zinoviev; and, specifically, who masterminded and how did the assassination attempt against Hitler fail. Issues tantamount to supporting a thesis must be accompanied by the relevant facts. Without a clearly stated thesis and a systematic and logical argument, an essay of this nature remains patently unconvincing.

Question 5–Sample Essay Scoring 2 to 3

The phenomena of totalitarianism or all-embracing state is a distinctively new and unique, twentieth century development in the theory and practice of despotism. The Soviet Union, reshaped under Stalin in the 1930s, has long been coupled with the Nazi-Fascist government of Hitler under the general heading of "totalitarianism." In this light, they have been represented respectively, the Soviet totalitarianism of the "Left" and the German totalitarianism of the "Right," two different types of one and the same political genus. This is an incorrect assumption which confuses the methods of Stalin and Hitler, which were very similar, with very different ideological goals of the USSR and Germany.

It is true that the two regimes share the Fuhrerprinzip, the mass party accepting no opposition and extending its influence to all other organizations. They also share the aggressive ideology, the political use of mass communication to control the population, the threat of terror and imprisonment (especially concentration camps) and the penetration of the state into every sector of the compartmentalized society. Moreover, the governing practices of the two leaders, including the purging of government staff, were similar. Just as the abortive assassination plot against Hitler caused a massive restructuring of the German high command toward the end of World War II, Stalin's liquidation of his erstwhile colleagues in the Communist party and more particularly, his apocryphal struggle with Trotsky, allowed him to create an isolated and artificial society that would conform to his every wish.

Yet, with all the similarities between the two leaders, the basic nature of the two regimes differed widely. The Nazi party based its fascism on a nationalist platform, bolstered by the reemergence of Germany as the major European power. This was both the ideological aim of the party and its leader. In the USSR, the nature of Communism as put forth by V.I. Lenin did not specify Stalin's dictatorial regime. Stalinism was an offshoot of communism but under no circumstances was it the only development expected or desired. Lenin's system, a "revolution of the proletariat," was altered by Stalin in a process that involved, among other things, the repression of Lenin's Bolshevik party and the rise of Stalin's totalitarian autocracy. Stalin never permitted his new regime to be called "Stalinism" and maintained to the end the myth of complete continuity between his regime and the one created in the October Revolution. However, the differences are profound and show a very different USSR.

In effect, Nazism claimed that the state would operate in the people's interest to ensure a strong nationalistic power capable of righting the wrongs done to Germany following WWI. Hope for a better Germany in which its citizens could be proud was the hallmark of Hitler's speeches. Later, when he attacked Jews, gypsies, and other minorities, he did so with the excuse that they were trying to stop German development and empowerment. Stalin, on the other hand, founded a regime dedicated, at least in theory, to accomplishing the goals of the October Revolution and allowing the people of the Soviet Union to govern for themselves. By professing to continue the goals of Lenin, Stalin was forced to pay lip service to the Supreme Soviet and Communist party. Later, when both legislative and ideological bodies were completely cowed, he was able to purge both the government and the population at will. Yet, unlike Hitler, his methods were aimed at all of the Soviet Union.

The concept of totalitarianism is a vague and often misleading term to describe governments. As single-party leaders Stalin and Hitler were remarkably similar. As totalitarians, their goals were very far apart. Hitler's concern was directed toward outside threats, with the bulk of his plans going toward creating a purely German nation. The internal obsessions of Stalin further isolated the USSR. Though they may have started out with identical possibilities, Nazism exploded outward across Europe and was eventually destroyed. Stalinism erected the Iron Curtain, closing off the USSR from the rest of the world for decades.

Although the generic term of "totalitarianism" can apply to both the USSR under Stalin and Germany under Hitler, it also ignores countless other political systems which do not follow the dictates laid out by either of these two men. Left wing or right wing, the term also fails to address the many other examples of nationalist single-party systems including Turkey under Kemel Ataturk, Nationalist China under Chiang Kai-shek and Egypt under Nasser.

Analysis of Sample Essay Scoring 2 to 3 (Question 5)

This is a relatively strong essay which attempts to tie the aggressive nature of Hitler's totalitarian regime to his goals of world dominance by stressing his skills as an orator. Problems with the essay revolve around the lack of directly related factual evidence to support the claims. The essay does not explain Stalin's purges following his control of the Supreme Soviet and the Party or explain Hitler's tendency to ignore his advisors' advice. The essay presents a strong argument on how they operate, but would have been strengthened with specific examples of their actions. Again, factual evidence to support all claims is necessary.

Question 5–Sample Essay Scoring 4 to 5

Although we are inclined to think of totalitarianism as a twentieth-century phenomenon, one could reasonably assert that several Roman emperors tried to set up totalitarian states. Still, it is the twentieth-century that brought the "art" of totalitarianism to its peak. Both Stalin and Hitler commanded complete control over every aspect of political and social life in their countries. No form of opposition was tolerated. In that sense, both Stalin and Hitler can be considered the heads of successful single-party political systems. Each used terror and suppression of individual liberties to maintain that system. However, one might argue that certain personality differences between the two leaders led them to somewhat different styles of single-party rule.

What then were these crucial differences? One man (Stalin) was driven by paranoia; the other (Hitler) suffered from megalomania. Stalin was irrationally distrustful of the political figures under him, and he was convinced that conspiratorial enemy forces were operating at home and abroad. By contrast, Hitler was equally sure that he was a man of personal omnipotence and grandeur.

In 1928, when Stalin became the leader of the Communist party after Lenin's death, he did so amidst a fierce power struggle. His own victory was obtained through alliances with other party members. But once he had solidified his power base, Stalin set about to destroy these former allies. The trials of the party officials, particularly Bukharin's, have long been seen as the result of Stalin's paranoia.

By contrast, Hitler shunned all interparty alliances and held the reins over his entire staff, never allowing any single minister or officer to have complete control over a particular domain. The result was that Hitler ran the country by decree. For example, against the better advice of his military planners, he undertook the invasion of Russia. As early as 1941, General Halder had pointed out though the German Army was superior in arms and experience, time would favor the Russian Army. Hitler would not listen, and even though some three million Russian soldiers were killed, wounded or captured, the Germans were still far-outnumbered by the Russians. When the terrible winter had passed and the Germans marched on Stalingrad, the tank battle that followed crippled the Nazi Panzer Army. Hitler's later misjudgments, including D-Day, marked the beginning of the series of fatal errors that would eventually destroy his own power. He was NOT omnipotent.

Though both men commanded totalitarian regimes, Stalin had certain advantages over Hitler. Because the Soviet Union was geographically isolated from the rest of the world, Stalin could exert control over the media and the academic establishment in a unique way and suppress any suspicions about his actions. He managed to see that entire histories were systematically deleted from the press. He was able to establish official versions of events so that they could not be questioned. Even now, some forty years after his reign, we still do not know how many millions of people were killed under his orders.

By contrast, Hitler was never afforded the luxury of complete isolation, and by the spring of 1943, reports of the mass imprisonment of Jews were leaked to the Allied forces. Indeed, for most of his political life, Hitler was entangled in both internal and external conflicts. He had to adapt his goals to short-term aims, simply in order to survive as leader. Stalin had both the time and the discipline to be more methodical in working toward long-term goals.

Though both governments were totalitarian in structure, Hitler's drive for European supremacy set in motion a war machine that spun out of control as its own leader defied advice from his staff. Stalin's Soviet Union was an entity to itself, drawing upon some of the practices of Nazi Germany, but driven more by fear <u>of</u> rather than fanatical faith <u>in</u> its leader.

Analysis of Sample Essay Scoring 4 to 5 (Question 5)

A strong example of the interplay of theory and factual details. The author presents an interesting thesis and tries to support it by relating psychological traits to political actions. The essay works toward a conclusion that is more than a repetition of the opening statements.

Question 6—Sample Essay Scoring 0 to 1

The distance between North America and Europe was very influential on the type of U.S. participation in the war between the Allies and Germany. The difficulty in providing munitions and troop transport alone forced the United States to confront a number of logistical problems. The armed forces found it difficult to mobilize the appropriate number of men and were baffled by the very real problems of transportation and training. Adding to that were a number of minor problems from the construction of housing and training facilities to development of intercontinental communication systems linking the executive office to the military. The result of this was a hesitancy on the part of the United States' government which could have cost the Allies the war.

Since the largest number of U.S. troops ever transported was the deployment in England, a great deal of the armed forces' efforts went into the logistics of troop movement. Air fields and bivouacs were top priorities to the military planners and as a result, the more important questions of defense and attack were delayed allowing the German army to solidify its positions throughout Europe and Africa. America's isolation also brought a fresh sense of optimism to its soldiers, untouched by the hardships and deaths in the continent abroad. The sense of hope and determination cannot be overlooked as important factors in the war against Germany. The infusion of rapidly produced and readily transported weapons refueled the British war machine and made it possible for the Allies to plan and execute the successful invasion of Normandy.

Lastly, the Allies were much more readily able to replenish both supplies and troops, drawing as they did from the prosperous ranks of a country barely touched by the worldwide conflict. Once the draft was enacted and became a highly efficient and organized process, the continuing influx of fresh, well-trained troops was more than the German army, battered by harsh winters and an ever lengthening supply lines, could withstand. In the end, the United States was able to shift the balance of power by applying its superior numbers and uninterrupted research capabilities to the Western European theater of World War II. America's isolationist tendencies which had been an obstacle to joining the Allies during the early days of the war actually turned into an advantage when total commitment mobilized the most productive and unencumbered working force of the world

Analysis of Sample Essay Scoring 0 to 1 (Question 6)

This weakly constructed essay is not very convincing. Though logistics were a problem for the U.S., they were equally so for Germany in Africa and perhaps more important to Germany in Russia. Poor structure and lack of factual detail make this a pretty thin response to the question.

Question 6–Sample Essay Scoring 2 to 3

Geography played a crucial role for the U.S. during WW II in that America was well aware that it held two important advantages over all other international powers. It was sufficiently isolated so that it was free from the threat of invasion, and America had more than enough natural resources to meet the demands of a world conflict.

Beginning as early as 1939, U.S. airplane production rivaled that of Italy and France, though it was not engaged in active conflict. With no apparent threat of losing any planes in conflict, the U.S. was able to stockpile other armaments as well. When the U.S. joined the battle in North Africa, the British-led forces held an effective advantage over the Germans with some 20 times the number of tanks and aircraft, most of which were produced in America. How did the Americans manage this?

Though its power declined in world politics during the interwar years, the U.S. was the only large country to benefit from the Great War. It became the world's largest creditor nation in addition to being the largest producer of manufacturers and foodstuffs. In fact, the U.S. production output was greater than all six of the other great powers combined. These gains were possible because of geography. It is clear that when the U.S. entered the war in Europe following Germany's declaration, Churchill's prediction that "the proper application of overwhelming force" had begun. In fact, the U.S. had such vast monetary, natural resources, and production clout, it could afford to wage two large-scale conventional wars and invest the scientists, raw materials and money (about $2 billion) in the development of a brand-new weapon that might or might not work. The feat of developing the atomic bomb was a direct consequence of the United States' geographical advantage during the war.

These two factors, simple as they may seem, show that the United States' unique geographical advantage allowed production, financial, and resource superiority to be applied at will in ever increasing amounts to every theater of war. In Europe, the effects were most obvious in superior aircraft, especially long-range bombers which decimated cities such as Dresden and all but halted Germany's production of weapons. As the war progressed, it became clear to all involved that the United States' geographical isolation was perhaps its biggest asset.

Analysis of Sample Essay Scoring 2 to 3 (Question 6)

This is a good essay that utilizes facts relating only to the two major points: freedom from fear of invasion and abundant supply of resources. By narrowing the topic, the essay addresses the points completely and convincingly. Its weaknesses are that it does not address counter-arguments including the United States' reluctance to join the conflict, unfamiliarity with terrain, and lack of commitment to fighting a war similar to the Great War (many people were against fighting in the war because of the remembered hardships of that war). Although this is a strong essay, it could have benefited from a discussion of other factors related to geography.

Question 6–Sample Essay Scoring 4 to 5

Hitler's declaration of war against the United States in December 1941 pitted the most powerful nation in the world against the Axis powers in a battle of material that determined the fate of the world. Though industrial productivity alone could not guarantee military effectiveness, the declaration of war did reveal the unique strengths of the United States work force. The immense distance separating the United States from Europe brought three important advantages to the U.S.: (1) the level of production continued to rise throughout the war; (2) U.S. soldiers were afforded superior training and the opportunity to test and develop new weapons; (3) both the military and the civilians had continuously higher morale because the Europeans never imperiled their homeland.

When the U.S. began increasing the number of railroad cars, assembly lines, and labor forces, workers were able to work constantly, uninterrupted by the threat of air raids. It is true that in the critical years of the Battle of the Atlantic the allies lost a frightening number of ships. But by mid-1942, the U.S. was already launching vessels faster than the German U-boats could sink them. Tank production was also higher than the Germans by a considerable margin. But the most telling statistic was in aircraft construction where U.S. bomber and fighter production soared during the years between 1940 and 1944. Compared to the new German planes, U.S. planes were heavy and more heavily armored than any of the German aircraft.

The Germans were fighting a war on two fronts. As the Nazis spread out from Russia to Africa, they tried desperately to keep their troops supplied. All the while, U.S. soldiers were learning how to fly better-equipped and more maneuverable planes, fire more reliable weapons and meet the challenge of fighting on foreign terrain. German U-boats, once the rulers of the North Sea, were forced to withdraw by May of 1943 when the U.S. unveiled long-range Liberators, escort carriers and hunter-killer escort groups equipped with the latest radar, depth charges, and submarine detector devices. But the most striking advantage of distance from the front was the opportunity to develop the atomic bomb. In the deserts of New Mexico, thousands of miles from Berlin, the Manhattan project was the ultimate testament to the benefits of geographical distance from the European theater.

If the German army had the most disciplined officers and the most battle-hardened infantry, then the U.S. had the most enthusiastic soldiers, fighting in foreign lands with the best supplies and equipment available. Morale was high, and results were clear. Winston Churchill's prediction that the fates of Hitler, Mussolini and Japan were sealed was correct in every sense. The Axis powers could only delay the inevitable defeat at the hand of a larger, better-equipped, and more determined fighting force.

Analysis of Sample Essay Scoring 4 to 5 (Question 6)

This forceful, tightly-constructed essay addresses various aspects of the U.S. geographical position and its impact. The essay carefully builds up to the construction of the atomic bomb and provides enough detail at each step to make the conclusion sound and convincing.

Glossary of United States
and Comparative Terms
for Government and Politics

UNITED STATES

ABC Programs: those implemented by Franklin Delano Roosevelt during the Great Depression to give relief to the unemployed

Administrative Law: the rules and regulations that regulate administrative agencies

Admiralty and Maritime Law: the legal code as applied to navigation and commerce on the high seas as well as upon navigable waterways

Affirmative Action: programs designed to overcome past discriminatory actions such as providing employment opportunities to members of a group that were previously denied employment because of racial barriers

Amendment: the modification of the constitution or a law

Amicus Curiae: a third-party brief filed with the permission of the court to support a litigant

Anti-Federalist: persons opposed to the creation of a strong national government out of fear that individual and states' rights would be destroyed

Appeasement: the act of making concessions to a political or military rival

Appellate Court: courts that have the authority to review the findings of lower courts

Appellate Jurisdiction: the power to review the decisions of lower courts

Articles of Confederation: union of states created in 1781 in which the national government did not have the authority to act directly upon the people and antecedent to the Constitution

Assigned Counsel System: persons who are unable to obtain legal counsel will be provided, by the courts, suitable representation

Baker vs. Carr: the Supreme Court held that congressional district reapportionment may not be used to dilute representation of minorities

Bicameralism: a two-house legislature

Bill of Attainder: legislative act that inflicts punishment on an individual or group for the purpose of suppressing that person or group

Bill of Rights: the first ten amendments to the Constitution

Bipartisan: politics that emphasizes cooperation between the major parties

Brown vs. Board of Education of Topeka: the Supreme Court declared the doctrine of "separate but equal" unconstitutional

Bureaucrat: an appointed government official who insists on rigid adherence to rules

Capital Punishment: the execution of an individual by the state as punishment for heinous offenses

Capitalism: an economic system in which the means of production are held by an individual for the benefit of that individual

Caucus: a closed meeting of Democratic Party leaders to agree on a legislative program

Checks and Balances: constitutionally distributed power where the powers overlap so that no branch of government may dominate the other

Civil Law: the legal code that regulates the conduct between private parties

Civil Rights Act of 1964: legislative act that removed racial barriers in all places vested with a public interest

Class Action Suit: a lawsuit filed on behalf of a group of persons with a similar legal claim against a party or individual

Cloture: parliamentary procedure for ending debate and calling for an immediate vote on a pending matter

Common Law: a body of judge-made law created as court cases are decided

Concurrent Powers: powers held by both the national and state governments

Concurring Opinion: the opinion of a Supreme Court justice who agrees with the majority ruling, but for different reasons

Confederated System: a system of government created when nation-states agree by compact to create a centralized government with delegated powers, but the nation-states do not give up individual autonomy

Conference: a meeting between committees of the two branches of the legislature to reconcile differences in pending bills

Conglomerate: a corporation that has many businesses in unrelated fields

Consent Decree: an individual or party agrees to modify future behavior or activities along court or regulatory agency guidelines

Constitution: the rules that determine the scope and function of government, as well as how the government is to be run

Constitutional: formal limitations on how political power is granted, dispersed, or used within the framework of a government

Court Packing: the act of placing members of the same political party on the bench so that opinion of the court will be consistent with the political party's (seen most dramatically with Franklin Delano Roosevelt)

Criminal Law: the legal code dealing with the actions of all people

De Facto Segregation: segregation that results from nongovernmental action; i.e., administered by the public

Declaration of Independence: the formal declaration of the United States' secession from England

Defendant: the party in a civil action or criminal action charged with the offense

De Jure Segregation: legally established segregation

Demagogue: a person who gains power through emotional appeals to the people

Democrat: any member of the Democratic Party, one of two major parties in the U.S.; party's lineage traces to Jefferson's Democratic Republican Party (1792)

Deregulation: the act of reducing or eliminating economic controls

Desegregation: the removal of racial barriers either by legislation or judicial action

Dissenting Opinion: disagreement with the majority opinion of the Supreme Court by another Supreme Court justice

Dred Scott vs. Sanford: the Supreme Court upheld the right of a slave owner to reclaim his property after the slave had fled into a free state

Double Jeopardy: the act of being tried for the same crime twice by the same level of government

Eminent Domain: the power of a government to seize private property for public use, usually with compensation to the owner

Equity of Redemption: judicial solution used when suits for money damages do not provide just compensation

Ethnocentrism: a belief that one's ethnic group is superior

Excise Tax: a tax on a specific consumer item such as alcoholic beverages

Executive Agreement: informal agreements made by the executive with a foreign government

Ex Post Facto Laws: laws created to make past actions punishable that were permissible when they occurred

Expressed Powers: powers constitutionally given to one of the branches of the national government

Federal System: governmental system in which power is constitutionally divided between a national government and its component members

Federalist: person who supported the ratification of the Constitution before 1787

Fighting Words: words that inflict injury upon persons

Filibuster: a senator who gains the floor has the right to go on talking until the senator relinquishes the floor to another

Franchise: the right to engage in the electing of public office holders

Gerrymander: redrawing of congressional districts in order to secure as many representative party votes as possible

Gideon vs. Wainwright: case decided by the U.S. Supreme Court in 1963 that established the right to legal representation for all defendants in criminal cases

GOP: the Republican Party

Implied Powers: powers that have been reasonably inferred for the carrying out of expressed powers

Immunity: granted exemption from prosecution

In Forma Pauperis: decision that indigents bringing cases to the Supreme Court do not have to pay regular fees or meet all standard requirements

Inherent Powers: powers exclusively controlled by the national government such as foreign affairs

Interest Group: group of persons who share some common interest and attempt to influence elected members of the government

Iran-Contra: the selling of arms to Iran so that the profits from these sales could be used to fund the *contras* in El Salvador

Jim Crow Laws: laws designed to promote racial segregation

Judicial Activism: using the power of the bench to broaden the interpretation of the Constitution

Judicial Restraint: using the power of the bench to limit the interpretation of the Constitution

Judicial Review: assumed power of the courts to declare an action of the president or Congress unconstitutional

Judiciary Act of 1789: congressional act which set the scope and limits for the federal judiciary system

Jus Sanguinis: citizenship acquired through one's parents

Jus Soli: citizenship established through place of birth

Kennedy, John F.: elected in 1960 as youngest president of the United States; established the Peace Corps in 1961; issued challenge to NASA to land a man on the moon; assassinated in 1963

King, Jr., Martin Luther: civil rights leader who fought for the rights of minorities by the use of peaceful civil disobedience

Lame Duck: a defeated office holder after that person has lost their re-election, but is still in office until the newly elected official is sworn in

Libel: published defamation of another person

Line-Item Veto: the objection by the president to a single item in a piece of legislation; this authority, signed into law by President Clinton in 1996, was unsuccessfully challenged as unconstitutional by six members of Congress, with the U.S. Supreme Court saying the plaintiffs had no legal standing to bring a case

Lobbying: activities aimed at influencing public officials and the policies they enact

Logrolling: mutual aid among politicians to achieve goals in each one's interests

Malcolm X: radical Muslim leader who wanted a total separation of the races

Mapp vs. Ohio: the Supreme Court recognized that evidence seized without a search warrant cannot be used

Marbury vs. Madison: the U.S. Supreme Court, in a landmark decision in 1803, established the concept of judicial review

Maverick: a person who holds no party allegiance and has unorthodox political views

McCarthyism: the act of seeking out subversives without cause or need (seen during the 1950s when Senator Joseph McCarthy stoked fear of Communism)

Military-Industrial Complex: the assumption that there is an alliance between the military and industrial leaders

Miranda vs. Arizona: 1966 case in which the U.S. Supreme Court decided that all persons who are detained or arrested must be informed of their rights

Misdemeanor: offense that is less than a felony with punishment ranging from a fine to a short jail term

National Supremacy Clause: constitutional doctrine that the actions or decisions of the national government take priority over that of the state or local governments

Naturalization: process by which persons acquire citizenship

New Deal: legislation championed by Franklin Delano Roosevelt during the Great Depression that provided a safety net (e.g., Social Security) for all members of society

New Jersey Plan: single-house legislature with equal representation for all states

Nixon, Richard M.: the only president of the United States to resign after being confronted with impeachment because of his alleged actions in the Watergate scandal

Nonproliferation Treaty: an agreement not to distribute nuclear arms to countries that do not have them

Obscenity: any work that taken as a whole appeals to a prurient interest in sex

Oligarchy: government by the few based on wealth or power

Ombudsman: person or office that hears formal complaints against the government

Original Jurisdiction: the authority of a court to hear a case being brought up for the first time

Partisan: political opposition drawn along party lines

Patronage: dispensing government jobs to persons who belong to the winning political party

Personal Property: all property held by an individual excluding real estate

Petit (or Petty) Jury: a trial jury of 12 that sits at civil/criminal cases

Plaintiff: the party who brings a civil action to court for the purpose of seeking a monetary remedy

Plessy vs. Ferguson: the Supreme Court established the rule of "separate but equal" as being constitutional

Police Power: power to regulate persons or property in order to promote health, welfare, and safety

Political Question: constitutional question that judges refuse to answer because to do so would encroach upon the authority of Congress or the president

Poll Tax: the requirement of a person to pay for the right to vote

Precedent: judicial use of prior cases as the test for deciding similar cases

Prior Restraint: censorship enacted before the speech, publication, etc., is released to the general public

Procedural Due Process: constitutional requirement that a government proceed by proper means

Reagan, Ronald W.: two-term president during the 1980s whose economic policies followed supply-side theory

Referendum: the process whereby a legislative proposal is voted upon by popular vote

Remand: to turn over authority of a case

Republic: form of government that derives its powers directly or indirectly from the people, and those who govern are accountable to the governed

Republican: any member of the Republican Party, one of the U.S.'s two major political parties; the GOP came into being 1854-1856, unifying anti-slavery forces

Reserved powers: powers retained by the states

Rebellion: an organized military action designed to replace the existing leaders but maintain its structures

Revolt: a disorganized military action aimed at gaining attention for a specific cause

Revolution: complete change of the form of government and its leaders

Roe vs. Wade: the Supreme Court established a woman's right to an abortion

Roosevelt, Franklin Delano: president of the United States during the Depression and World War II; most noted for his enactment of New Deal programs such as the Social Security Act

Rule of Four: in order for a case to be heard by the Supreme Court, four justices must agree to hear the case

Safe Seat: electoral office, usually in the legislature, for which the party or incumbent is strong enough that reelection is almost taken for granted

Sedition: conduct/language inciting rebellion against authority of the state

Slander: verbal defamation of a person's character

Stare Decisis: a rule of precedent where an established rule of law is considered binding on all judges whenever a similar case is presented

Statism: the rights of the state over those of the citizens

Statutory Law: law enacted by a legislative body

Stay: the temporary delay of punishment, usually in a capital offense case

Substantive Due Process: constitutional requirement that government actions and laws be reasonable

Suspect Classification: racial or national origin classifications created by law and subject to careful judicial scrutiny

Symbolic Speech: nonverbal communication of a political idea

Tariff: any tax levied on imported goods

Trial Court: any court of original jurisdiction that empowers a jury to decide the guilt or liability of an individual

Unicameral Legislature: single-house legislature

Unitary System: a system of government in which power is concentrated in the central government

United States vs. Nixon: the Supreme Court ruled that material vested with a public interest could not be withheld from evidence under the rule of executive privilege

Virginia Plan: strong central government with a bicameral legislature

Watergate: the illegal entry and phone monitoring in 1972 of Democratic headquarters in the Watergate complex in Washington by members of the Republican Party

West Virginia Board of Education vs. Barnette: the Supreme Court decided that compulsory flag salute in schools is unconstitutional

Writ of Appeal: formal request to have a court review the findings of a lower court

Writ of Certiorari: a formal appeal used to bring a case up to the Supreme Court

Writ of Habeas Corpus: court order requiring jailers to explain to a judge why they are holding a prisoner in custody

Writ of Mandamus: court order directing an official to perform a nondiscretionary or ministerial act as required by law

X, Malcolm: see Malcolm X

COMPARATIVE

Anarchy: a state of absence of political authority

Apartheid (South Africa): constitutionally established segregation and disenfranchisement

Aryan (Germany): the idea of racial purity and racial superiority established by the Nazi party

Auschwitz (Germany): one of several Nazi concentration camps built to systematically slaughter Jews and other prisoners

Barrister (Great Britain): trial lawyer

Bicameral: a two-house legislature

Bolshevik Revolution (USSR): the Russian Revolution of 1917 that removed the Czar from power and put in its place a communist system of government

Bonaparte, Napoleon (France): first leader of France following the French Revolution

Bourgeoisie (USSR): the capitalist class that has power over the proletariat

British Constitution (Great Britain): an unwritten collection of customs, conventions, acts of Parliament, and Common Law

Chairman (USSR): leader of the state

Churchill, Winston (Great Britain): prime minister during World War II

Civil Law (France): a codified legal system where the law is uniformly interpreted and is the expressed will of the state

Collectivism: state ownership of both the means of production and distribution of consumer goods

Communism (USSR): any system of government based upon Marxist theory in which state ownership of the means of production is employed for the benefit of all

Communist Manifesto: Karl Marx's plan and explanation of how Communism is to be implemented by the natural economic development of industrialized nations

Confederation: power is concentrated in the component members of a larger system with limited grants of power given to a central government by the component members

Cultural Revolution (China): Mao Zedong's revolution which would purge the elder leaders and put in a younger generation whose zeal would not let the country self-destruct, as Mao felt the Russian Revolution did to the Soviet Union by taking the "Revisionist Road to Capitalist Restoration"

Das Kapital: Karl Marx's work giving his analysis of the economics of capitalism

De Facto: a political entity actually exercising power, but not by right of law

De Gaulle, Charles (France): president of the French Fifth Republic from 1959 to 1969; known as a reformist

De Jure: a political entity exercising power by right of law

Demokratizatsia (USSR): democratization

Deng Xiaoping (China): China's paramount leader from 1982 until his death in 1997.

De Tocqueville, Alexis: French political scientist that discussed dangers of majority rule, influence of the press and parties on the government, and the functioning of democracy (author of *Democracy in America*)

Engels, Friedrich: author of the first socialist theories

Ex Officio: by virtue of office or position

Fascism: a political system based on one-party militarism and nationalism

Federalism: two or more levels of mutually autonomous governments each of which can act directly upon an individual

French Revolution (France): the revolution that removed the aristocracy from France in 1789 and established a weak democracy

Gang of Four (China): four high-ranking officials who were arrested, and two executed for attempting to overthrow the government

Gaullists (France): followers of Charles de Gaulle

General Secretary (USSR): leader of the party

Glasnost (USSR): aspect of Gorbachev's recent reforms for the Soviet Union meaning "openness"

Gorbachev, Mikhail (USSR): former General Secretary of the Soviet Union

Great Britain: area composed of England, Scotland, Wales, and Northern Ireland

Great Leap Forward (China): Mao Zedong's plan to aid the agricultural peasant labor force in a "democratic" method unlike Stalin earlier; it failed miserably because authoritarian methods were used instead of peasant self-management, and led to an utter depletion of the peasant labor force

Hitler, Adolf (Germany): elected leader who established a Fascist form of government in Germany

Hobbes-*Leviathan*: political theory that governments were formed out of man's desire for protection

House of Commons (Great Britain): popularly elected legislative body who control all real power, but are responsible to the public

House of Lords (Great Britain): composed of Heredity Peers of Right, but has no real legislative power

Imperialism: any form of government policy in which territories are conquered or colonized for the benefit of the mother country

KGB (USSR): the ubiquitous terroristic state secret police in charge of internal and external security

Labour Party (Great Britain): party in Great Britain whose views tend to be in opposition of and to the left of the Tory Party

Lenin (USSR): brought Marxist ideology to Russia during World War I

Locke, John: wrote that natural law consists of man's right to life, liberty, and property

Major, John (Great Britain): prime minister of Great Britain; succeeded Margaret Thatcher in 1990 and was re-elected in 1992

Mao Zedong (China): communist leader of China who began the Cultural Revolution in order to create new Chinese values

Marx, Karl: author of the *Communist Manifesto*

Militarism: any system of government in which the military forces have absolute power within the country

Mitterrand, François: president of France during the 1980s and early '90s; died in 1996

Monarchy: a system of government in which all power is vested within a king who is chosen by right of heredity

Mussolini, Benito (Italy): leader of Italy who established a Fascist government in 1922

National Assembly (France): the popularly elected legislative body

National Leader System: legislature is responsible to the executive, and legitimizes the executive's decisions

Oligarchy: all power in the state is vested in the minority ruling class

Parliamentary System: executive is chosen by and is responsible to the legislature

Perestroika (USSR): aspect of Gorbachev's reforms for the Soviet Union meaning "restructuring"

Plato-*Republic:* a dialogue written in Ancient Greece on the evolutionary process of government

Politburo: the chief political and executive committee of the Communist Party

Premier: prime minister of the Communist Party

President (France): the chief of state and the administrator of all the real power in the executive branch

Presidential System: the executive is chosen separately from the legislature and is not responsible to the legislature

Prime Minister (France): head of state responsible for the routine operation of the government

Prime Minister (Great Britain): the head of state and majority party leader elected by the House of Commons

Privy Council (Great Britain): ex officio officers/cabinet members appointed as honor; life membership; no important function except Judicial Committee which acts as Appellate Court

Pro Forma: done or carried out in a routine manner

Proletariat (USSR): the working class, such as laborers and others who are economically disenfranchised

Republic: a political entity in which the supreme power lies with the public who vote for the officers/representatives responsible for them

Rousseau-*Social Contract*: governments are conventions of man established so that man could be free

Senate (France): the upper house in the French legislature; members are elected by an electoral college

Socialism: a system of government in which the state is responsible for the general welfare of its citizens

Socrates: Greek philosopher whose purpose in questioning was to make the other party contemplate ideas they took for granted

Solicitor (Great Britain): a lawyer who is not a member of the bar; heard only in lower courts

Soviet (USSR): a form of government in which the political party, e.g., the Communist Party, is the decision-making branch of the government while the government is reduced to implementing party decisions

Stalin, Joseph (USSR): absolute leader of the Soviet Union who modified communist doctrine into totalitarian doctrine by the suppression of his people

Thatcher, Margaret (Great Britain): prime minister of Great Britain 1979-1990

Totalitarian: form of government in which person/party has absolute power and rival parties are not allowed to exist

Treaty of Versailles: treaty that formally ended World War I

Trotsky, Leon: argued for worldwide revolution and bitterly opposed the leadership of Stalin

Unitary: all power is concentrated in a central government

Voltaire: French theorist whose works urged men to think for themselves, to not accept traditions or the Bible, and prepared the way for the French Revolution (freedom of religion and the press)

Welfare State: government takes responsibility for the personal welfare of its citizens

Whitehall (Great Britain): the civil service branch of the government that is responsible for implementation of the acts of Parliament

Wilson, Woodrow: president who represented the United States at the Treaty of Versailles and implemented the 14 Points

Yeltsin, Boris (USSR): took office in 1991 as president of the Russian Federation; re-elected in 1996

ANSWER SHEETS

AP Government & Politics Practice Test 1

1. Ⓐ Ⓑ Ⓒ Ⓓ Ⓔ
2. Ⓐ Ⓑ Ⓒ Ⓓ Ⓔ
3. Ⓐ Ⓑ Ⓒ Ⓓ Ⓔ
4. Ⓐ Ⓑ Ⓒ Ⓓ Ⓔ
5. Ⓐ Ⓑ Ⓒ Ⓓ Ⓔ
6. Ⓐ Ⓑ Ⓒ Ⓓ Ⓔ
7. Ⓐ Ⓑ Ⓒ Ⓓ Ⓔ
8. Ⓐ Ⓑ Ⓒ Ⓓ Ⓔ
9. Ⓐ Ⓑ Ⓒ Ⓓ Ⓔ
10. Ⓐ Ⓑ Ⓒ Ⓓ Ⓔ
11. Ⓐ Ⓑ Ⓒ Ⓓ Ⓔ
12. Ⓐ Ⓑ Ⓒ Ⓓ Ⓔ
13. Ⓐ Ⓑ Ⓒ Ⓓ Ⓔ
14. Ⓐ Ⓑ Ⓒ Ⓓ Ⓔ
15. Ⓐ Ⓑ Ⓒ Ⓓ Ⓔ
16. Ⓐ Ⓑ Ⓒ Ⓓ Ⓔ
17. Ⓐ Ⓑ Ⓒ Ⓓ Ⓔ
18. Ⓐ Ⓑ Ⓒ Ⓓ Ⓔ
19. Ⓐ Ⓑ Ⓒ Ⓓ Ⓔ
20. Ⓐ Ⓑ Ⓒ Ⓓ Ⓔ

21. Ⓐ Ⓑ Ⓒ Ⓓ Ⓔ
22. Ⓐ Ⓑ Ⓒ Ⓓ Ⓔ
23. Ⓐ Ⓑ Ⓒ Ⓓ Ⓔ
24. Ⓐ Ⓑ Ⓒ Ⓓ Ⓔ
25. Ⓐ Ⓑ Ⓒ Ⓓ Ⓔ
26. Ⓐ Ⓑ Ⓒ Ⓓ Ⓔ
27. Ⓐ Ⓑ Ⓒ Ⓓ Ⓔ
28. Ⓐ Ⓑ Ⓒ Ⓓ Ⓔ
29. Ⓐ Ⓑ Ⓒ Ⓓ Ⓔ
30. Ⓐ Ⓑ Ⓒ Ⓓ Ⓔ
31. Ⓐ Ⓑ Ⓒ Ⓓ Ⓔ
32. Ⓐ Ⓑ Ⓒ Ⓓ Ⓔ
33. Ⓐ Ⓑ Ⓒ Ⓓ Ⓔ
34. Ⓐ Ⓑ Ⓒ Ⓓ Ⓔ
35. Ⓐ Ⓑ Ⓒ Ⓓ Ⓔ
36. Ⓐ Ⓑ Ⓒ Ⓓ Ⓔ
37. Ⓐ Ⓑ Ⓒ Ⓓ Ⓔ
38. Ⓐ Ⓑ Ⓒ Ⓓ Ⓔ
39. Ⓐ Ⓑ Ⓒ Ⓓ Ⓔ
40. Ⓐ Ⓑ Ⓒ Ⓓ Ⓔ

41. Ⓐ Ⓑ Ⓒ Ⓓ Ⓔ
42. Ⓐ Ⓑ Ⓒ Ⓓ Ⓔ
43. Ⓐ Ⓑ Ⓒ Ⓓ Ⓔ
44. Ⓐ Ⓑ Ⓒ Ⓓ Ⓔ
45. Ⓐ Ⓑ Ⓒ Ⓓ Ⓔ
46. Ⓐ Ⓑ Ⓒ Ⓓ Ⓔ
47. Ⓐ Ⓑ Ⓒ Ⓓ Ⓔ
48. Ⓐ Ⓑ Ⓒ Ⓓ Ⓔ
49. Ⓐ Ⓑ Ⓒ Ⓓ Ⓔ
50. Ⓐ Ⓑ Ⓒ Ⓓ Ⓔ
51. Ⓐ Ⓑ Ⓒ Ⓓ Ⓔ
52. Ⓐ Ⓑ Ⓒ Ⓓ Ⓔ
53. Ⓐ Ⓑ Ⓒ Ⓓ Ⓔ
54. Ⓐ Ⓑ Ⓒ Ⓓ Ⓔ
55. Ⓐ Ⓑ Ⓒ Ⓓ Ⓔ
56. Ⓐ Ⓑ Ⓒ Ⓓ Ⓔ
57. Ⓐ Ⓑ Ⓒ Ⓓ Ⓔ
58. Ⓐ Ⓑ Ⓒ Ⓓ Ⓔ
59. Ⓐ Ⓑ Ⓒ Ⓓ Ⓔ
60. Ⓐ Ⓑ Ⓒ Ⓓ Ⓔ

AP Government & Politics Practice Test 2

1. Ⓐ Ⓑ Ⓒ Ⓓ Ⓔ	21. Ⓐ Ⓑ Ⓒ Ⓓ Ⓔ	41. Ⓐ Ⓑ Ⓒ Ⓓ Ⓔ
2. Ⓐ Ⓑ Ⓒ Ⓓ Ⓔ	22. Ⓐ Ⓑ Ⓒ Ⓓ Ⓔ	42. Ⓐ Ⓑ Ⓒ Ⓓ Ⓔ
3. Ⓐ Ⓑ Ⓒ Ⓓ Ⓔ	23. Ⓐ Ⓑ Ⓒ Ⓓ Ⓔ	43. Ⓐ Ⓑ Ⓒ Ⓓ Ⓔ
4. Ⓐ Ⓑ Ⓒ Ⓓ Ⓔ	24. Ⓐ Ⓑ Ⓒ Ⓓ Ⓔ	44. Ⓐ Ⓑ Ⓒ Ⓓ Ⓔ
5. Ⓐ Ⓑ Ⓒ Ⓓ Ⓔ	25. Ⓐ Ⓑ Ⓒ Ⓓ Ⓔ	45. Ⓐ Ⓑ Ⓒ Ⓓ Ⓔ
6. Ⓐ Ⓑ Ⓒ Ⓓ Ⓔ	26. Ⓐ Ⓑ Ⓒ Ⓓ Ⓔ	46. Ⓐ Ⓑ Ⓒ Ⓓ Ⓔ
7. Ⓐ Ⓑ Ⓒ Ⓓ Ⓔ	27. Ⓐ Ⓑ Ⓒ Ⓓ Ⓔ	47. Ⓐ Ⓑ Ⓒ Ⓓ Ⓔ
8. Ⓐ Ⓑ Ⓒ Ⓓ Ⓔ	28. Ⓐ Ⓑ Ⓒ Ⓓ Ⓔ	48. Ⓐ Ⓑ Ⓒ Ⓓ Ⓔ
9. Ⓐ Ⓑ Ⓒ Ⓓ Ⓔ	29. Ⓐ Ⓑ Ⓒ Ⓓ Ⓔ	49. Ⓐ Ⓑ Ⓒ Ⓓ Ⓔ
10. Ⓐ Ⓑ Ⓒ Ⓓ Ⓔ	30. Ⓐ Ⓑ Ⓒ Ⓓ Ⓔ	50. Ⓐ Ⓑ Ⓒ Ⓓ Ⓔ
11. Ⓐ Ⓑ Ⓒ Ⓓ Ⓔ	31. Ⓐ Ⓑ Ⓒ Ⓓ Ⓔ	51. Ⓐ Ⓑ Ⓒ Ⓓ Ⓔ
12. Ⓐ Ⓑ Ⓒ Ⓓ Ⓔ	32. Ⓐ Ⓑ Ⓒ Ⓓ Ⓔ	52. Ⓐ Ⓑ Ⓒ Ⓓ Ⓔ
13. Ⓐ Ⓑ Ⓒ Ⓓ Ⓔ	33. Ⓐ Ⓑ Ⓒ Ⓓ Ⓔ	53. Ⓐ Ⓑ Ⓒ Ⓓ Ⓔ
14. Ⓐ Ⓑ Ⓒ Ⓓ Ⓔ	34. Ⓐ Ⓑ Ⓒ Ⓓ Ⓔ	54. Ⓐ Ⓑ Ⓒ Ⓓ Ⓔ
15. Ⓐ Ⓑ Ⓒ Ⓓ Ⓔ	35. Ⓐ Ⓑ Ⓒ Ⓓ Ⓔ	55. Ⓐ Ⓑ Ⓒ Ⓓ Ⓔ
16. Ⓐ Ⓑ Ⓒ Ⓓ Ⓔ	36. Ⓐ Ⓑ Ⓒ Ⓓ Ⓔ	56. Ⓐ Ⓑ Ⓒ Ⓓ Ⓔ
17. Ⓐ Ⓑ Ⓒ Ⓓ Ⓔ	37. Ⓐ Ⓑ Ⓒ Ⓓ Ⓔ	57. Ⓐ Ⓑ Ⓒ Ⓓ Ⓔ
18. Ⓐ Ⓑ Ⓒ Ⓓ Ⓔ	38. Ⓐ Ⓑ Ⓒ Ⓓ Ⓔ	58. Ⓐ Ⓑ Ⓒ Ⓓ Ⓔ
19. Ⓐ Ⓑ Ⓒ Ⓓ Ⓔ	39. Ⓐ Ⓑ Ⓒ Ⓓ Ⓔ	59. Ⓐ Ⓑ Ⓒ Ⓓ Ⓔ
20. Ⓐ Ⓑ Ⓒ Ⓓ Ⓔ	40. Ⓐ Ⓑ Ⓒ Ⓓ Ⓔ	60. Ⓐ Ⓑ Ⓒ Ⓓ Ⓔ

AP Government & Politics
Practice Test 3

1. Ⓐ Ⓑ Ⓒ Ⓓ Ⓔ	21. Ⓐ Ⓑ Ⓒ Ⓓ Ⓔ	41. Ⓐ Ⓑ Ⓒ Ⓓ Ⓔ
2. Ⓐ Ⓑ Ⓒ Ⓓ Ⓔ	22. Ⓐ Ⓑ Ⓒ Ⓓ Ⓔ	42. Ⓐ Ⓑ Ⓒ Ⓓ Ⓔ
3. Ⓐ Ⓑ Ⓒ Ⓓ Ⓔ	23. Ⓐ Ⓑ Ⓒ Ⓓ Ⓔ	43. Ⓐ Ⓑ Ⓒ Ⓓ Ⓔ
4. Ⓐ Ⓑ Ⓒ Ⓓ Ⓔ	24. Ⓐ Ⓑ Ⓒ Ⓓ Ⓔ	44. Ⓐ Ⓑ Ⓒ Ⓓ Ⓔ
5. Ⓐ Ⓑ Ⓒ Ⓓ Ⓔ	25. Ⓐ Ⓑ Ⓒ Ⓓ Ⓔ	45. Ⓐ Ⓑ Ⓒ Ⓓ Ⓔ
6. Ⓐ Ⓑ Ⓒ Ⓓ Ⓔ	26. Ⓐ Ⓑ Ⓒ Ⓓ Ⓔ	46. Ⓐ Ⓑ Ⓒ Ⓓ Ⓔ
7. Ⓐ Ⓑ Ⓒ Ⓓ Ⓔ	27. Ⓐ Ⓑ Ⓒ Ⓓ Ⓔ	47. Ⓐ Ⓑ Ⓒ Ⓓ Ⓔ
8. Ⓐ Ⓑ Ⓒ Ⓓ Ⓔ	28. Ⓐ Ⓑ Ⓒ Ⓓ Ⓔ	48. Ⓐ Ⓑ Ⓒ Ⓓ Ⓔ
9. Ⓐ Ⓑ Ⓒ Ⓓ Ⓔ	29. Ⓐ Ⓑ Ⓒ Ⓓ Ⓔ	49. Ⓐ Ⓑ Ⓒ Ⓓ Ⓔ
10. Ⓐ Ⓑ Ⓒ Ⓓ Ⓔ	30. Ⓐ Ⓑ Ⓒ Ⓓ Ⓔ	50. Ⓐ Ⓑ Ⓒ Ⓓ Ⓔ
11. Ⓐ Ⓑ Ⓒ Ⓓ Ⓔ	31. Ⓐ Ⓑ Ⓒ Ⓓ Ⓔ	51. Ⓐ Ⓑ Ⓒ Ⓓ Ⓔ
12. Ⓐ Ⓑ Ⓒ Ⓓ Ⓔ	32. Ⓐ Ⓑ Ⓒ Ⓓ Ⓔ	52. Ⓐ Ⓑ Ⓒ Ⓓ Ⓔ
13. Ⓐ Ⓑ Ⓒ Ⓓ Ⓔ	33. Ⓐ Ⓑ Ⓒ Ⓓ Ⓔ	53. Ⓐ Ⓑ Ⓒ Ⓓ Ⓔ
14. Ⓐ Ⓑ Ⓒ Ⓓ Ⓔ	34. Ⓐ Ⓑ Ⓒ Ⓓ Ⓔ	54. Ⓐ Ⓑ Ⓒ Ⓓ Ⓔ
15. Ⓐ Ⓑ Ⓒ Ⓓ Ⓔ	35. Ⓐ Ⓑ Ⓒ Ⓓ Ⓔ	55. Ⓐ Ⓑ Ⓒ Ⓓ Ⓔ
16. Ⓐ Ⓑ Ⓒ Ⓓ Ⓔ	36. Ⓐ Ⓑ Ⓒ Ⓓ Ⓔ	56. Ⓐ Ⓑ Ⓒ Ⓓ Ⓔ
17. Ⓐ Ⓑ Ⓒ Ⓓ Ⓔ	37. Ⓐ Ⓑ Ⓒ Ⓓ Ⓔ	57. Ⓐ Ⓑ Ⓒ Ⓓ Ⓔ
18. Ⓐ Ⓑ Ⓒ Ⓓ Ⓔ	38. Ⓐ Ⓑ Ⓒ Ⓓ Ⓔ	58. Ⓐ Ⓑ Ⓒ Ⓓ Ⓔ
19. Ⓐ Ⓑ Ⓒ Ⓓ Ⓔ	39. Ⓐ Ⓑ Ⓒ Ⓓ Ⓔ	59. Ⓐ Ⓑ Ⓒ Ⓓ Ⓔ
20. Ⓐ Ⓑ Ⓒ Ⓓ Ⓔ	40. Ⓐ Ⓑ Ⓒ Ⓓ Ⓔ	60. Ⓐ Ⓑ Ⓒ Ⓓ Ⓔ